SOLVING T

Every day thousands of s_____ are labeled "dumb" or "lazy," when in fact they may actually suffer from a hidden inner-ear/cerebellar impairment called dyslexia. SMART BUT FEELING DUMB has already helped thousands of dyslexics and their loved ones with vital, "lifesaving" information on this signal-scrambling disorder and Dr. Levinson's own remarkable system of treatment. Complete with the case histories and the research that led to his medical breakthrough, and totally updated, expanded, and revised to include the medical establishment's recognition of Dr. Levinson's theories, this book is the definitive volume on dyslexia and its related attention deficit, phobic, and a host of other differently named disorders—and the book that shows you how to get safe, effective, immediate help for you and your child today.

"A marvelous resource to share with parents of our children with dyslexia . . . a model to all who do research with the hope of making life better for others."
> —Joan M. Smith, Ed.D., licensed speech pathologist and educational psychologist, Melvin-Smith Learning Center, Sacramento, California

"This text is brilliantly written . . . may well prevent the bruising of the self-esteem and egos of young schoolchildren."
> —Leonard S. Girsh, M.D., director, Allergy & Clinical Immunology, Medical College of Pennsylvania, and chairman, Neuro-Allergy Committee, American College of Allergists

"SMART BUT FEELING DUMB for the first time catalogues in an easy-reading manner the various presentations of dyslexia. It brings hope to the many afflicted and will spur relevant research in this area to further improve the concepts and treatment."
> —Kenneth H. Brookler, M.D., M.S., F.R.C.S.C., F.A.C.S., past president, American Neurotology Society, and clinical professor of otolaryngology, New York Medical College

"Magnificent . . . a spectacular breakthrough . . . a monumental step forward in managing learning disabilities and the attending frustrations."
> —Wallace Rubin, M.D., clinical professor of otorhinolaryngology and biocommunication, Louisiana State University of Medicine

"An important contribution, linking years of clinical experience with recent discoveries. This book provides a wealth of clearly presented clinical information. It is appealing to both the parent and the professional."
> —Reuven Kohen-Raz, Ph.D., chairman, Department of Special Education, Hebrew University of Jerusalem, Israel

"A much-needed book for the many thousands of persons with learning disabilities . . . should be most useful to all parents and teachers who wish to help children and adults with inappropriate learning behaviors."
> —Eli Tash, director of research, St. Francis Children's Activity and Achievement Center, Milwaukee, Wisconsin, and former president, Association of Children and Adults with Learning Disabilities

REVISED AND UPDATED

SMART

BUT FEELING

DUMB

The Challenging
New Research on
DYSLEXIA —
and How It
May Help You

Harold N. Levinson, M.D.

WARNER BOOKS

An AOL Time Warner Company

If you purchase this book without a cover you should be aware that this book may have been stolen property and reported as "unsold and destroyed" to the publisher. In such case neither the author nor the publisher has received any payment for this "stripped book."

The 3-D Optical Scanner, the 3-D Auditory Scanner, the 3-D Tactile Scanner, and the 3-D Visual Trainer are patented.

Names have been changed to protect the confidentiality of those concerned.

PUBLISHER'S NOTE: The information herein is not intended to replace the services of trained professionals or be a substitute for medical advice. You are advised to consult with your health care professional with regard to matters relating to your health, and in particular regarding matters that may require diagnosis or medical attention.

Copyright © 1984, 1994, 2003 by Harold N. Levinson
All rights reserved.

Warner Books, Inc., 1271 Avenue of the Americas, New York, NY 10020

Visit our Web site at www.twbookmark.com

 An AOL Time Warner Company

Printed in the United States of America

Originally published in hardcover by Warner Books, Inc.
First Trade Printing, Revised Edition: January 1994
First Trade Printing, Revised and Updated Edition: September 2003
10, 9 8 7 6 5 4 3 2 1

Library of Congress Control Number: 2003049689
ISBN: 0-446-69117-8

Book design by Charles A. Sutherland

About Dr. Levinson, Physician, Researcher, and Author

HAROLD N. LEVINSON, M.D., is a world-renowned psychiatrist and neurologist. He is credited with bringing about a dramatic medical breakthrough in the understanding, diagnosis, and successful treatment of dyslexia and its many related signal-scrambling disturbances of the inner ear and its supercomputer, the cerebellum, the lower brain of humans and the highest brain of most animals.

Dr. Levinson began his dyslexia research thirty-five years ago within the New York City Board of Education. Formerly clinical associate professor of psychiatry at New York University Medical Center, Dr. Levinson is now director of the Medical Dyslexic Treatment Center (also called the Levinson Medical Center for Learning Disabilities) in Great Neck, New York.

The original insights and content within his many books and research papers dealing with the origins, treatment, and interrelationships of dyslexia, learning disabilities, attention deficit, and anxiety or phobic disorders have appeared in scientific and educational journals and have been reviewed by medical/science editors and such popular media as the *New*

York Times, Science, TIME, Smithsonian, etc. After more than three decades of research based on the detailed examination and successful medical treatment of over thirty-five thousand children and adults, Dr. Levinson's pioneering insights and discoveries have recently been independently validated by scientists worldwide and are currently referred to as "groundbreaking," "brilliant," "pioneering," "highly original," and "decades ahead of its time."

As a result of Dr. Levinson's extensive research, there is now renewed hope and often rapid and dramatic help for all children and adults with the above-mentioned signal-scrambling disorders, as well as those patients with related but differently named inner-ear/cerebellar syndromes, i.e., dysgraphia (poor writing), dyscalculia (poor math), dysphasia and dysnomia (poor/impaired speech and word recall), dyspraxia (poor balance/coordination), pervasive developmental delay (severe dyslexia), Asperger syndrome (social dyslexia), psychosomatic disturbances (headaches, dizziness, motion sickness, etc.), and many other previously perplexing disorders included within this work.

For the very first time, there is now medical help for a series of distinct major processing disorders in which Dr. Levinson discovered the often coexisting but hidden "minor" presence of dyslexic or inner-ear/cerebellar-determined signal-scrambling symptoms. These major disorders include mental retardation and Down's syndrome, cerebral palsy, brain injury, and autism.

It is now possible to envision cures, and even prevention, of all the dyslexic-related disorders, as well as significantly enhanced benefits for those with "mixed" or combined major processing and "minor" signal-scrambling disorders.

Dr. Levinson's Other Books

A Solution to the Riddle—Dyslexia, Springer-Verlag, 1980.
Renamed and unedited as *The Discovery of Cerebellar-Vestibular Syndromes & Therapies—A Solution to the Riddle Dyslexia*, Stonebridge Publishing, Ltd., March 2000
Phobia Free, Evans, April–May 1986
Total Concentration, Evans, September 1990
The Upside Down Kids, Evans, June 1991
Turning Around—The Upside Down Kids, Evans, April 1992
A Scientific Watergate—Dyslexia, Stonebridge Publishing, Ltd., September 1994

For more information, contact:

www.dyslexiaonline.com
1-800-334-READ

Prior Support and Recent Validation

Although my "challenging" inner-ear/cerebellar-dyslexia research was previously supported by a Nobel Prize–winning researcher and a significant minority of other outstanding neurophysiologists, clinicians, and educators, only recently have these concepts been independently validated in worldwide studies. As a result, I thought it imperative to provide readers with the above content right up front, rather than limiting it to the appendix and bibliography.

Prior Support—Favorable Comments About Dr. Levinson's Research

"Dr. Levinson . . . your 3-D Optical Scanner for screening dyslexia is fascinating."

—*Sir John Eccles, Nobel laureate, cerebellar research*

"Your emphasis on a cerebellar contribution to learning disabilities and emotional disorders meshes very well with our own overviews."

—*Henrietta and Alan Leiner, neuroscientists*

"Unique and tantalizing. . . . Dr. Levinson's work convincingly describes the discovery and implementation of a nontraditionalist scientific method resulting in a dramatically successful method of medical treatment."

      —Reuven Kohen-Raz, Ph.D., professor emeritus, the
      Hebrew University, Jerusalem, former chairman,
      Department of Special Education

"There is little doubt that Dr. Levinson's multimodal approach to dyslexic patients and various medications can improve reading and writing skills. I recommend this book and believe in the author's approach to these children, many of whom benefit from his diagnostic evaluation, treatment, and management."

      —J. T. Jabour, M.D., Journal of Clinical Psychiatry

"Dr. Levinson has obviously drawn on extensive practical experience and a thorough review of relevant basic science and research data. This book should give hope to parents of children who have experienced phobias, balance disorders, disequilibrium, and learning disabilities."

      —Kenneth M. Grundfast, M.D., chairman, Department of
      Otolaryngology, Children's Hospital, National Medical Center

Recent Independent Validation

The recent understanding of my inner-ear/cerebellar-dyslexia findings and derived concepts triggered a wide range of validating independent studies, albeit decades after the fact. But better late than never! Only a few typical of the many publications are included here for review.

"The Role of the Cerebellum in Cognition and Behavior: A Selective Review," *J Neuropsychiatry Clin Neurosci*, 12, 193–8. Rapoport, M., van Reekum, R. & Mayberg, H. (2000). A study on the role of the cerebellum in cognition and behavior, highlighted cognitive deficitis, and personality changes associated with cerebellar disease.

"Rational Dosages of Nutrients Have a Prolonged Effect on Learning Disabilities," *Altern Ther Health Med*, 6, 85–91. Carlton, R. M., Ente, G., Blum, L., Heyman, N., Davis, W. & Ambrosino, S. (2000). A study on the effects of certain nutrients on children with learning disabilities showed significant academic and behavioral improvements within a few weeks of treatment with nutrient supplements.

"Physiological and Behavioral Effects of an Antivertigo Antihistamine in Adults," *Percept Mot Skills*, 88, 707–32. Lauter, J. L., Lynch, O., Wood, S. B. & Schoeffler, L. (1999). A study found physiological support for the use of an antimotion-sickness antihistamine to improve cognitive-related performance with obvious implications in treating learning-disordered children.

"Association of Abnormal Cerebellar Activation with Motor Learning Difficulties in Dyslexic Adults," *Lancet*, 353, 1662–7. Nicolson, R. I., Fawcett, A. J., Berry, E. L., Jenkins, I. H., Dean, P. & Brooks, D. J. (1999). A study found lower-brain activation in dyslexic adults undertaking tasks known normally to involve cerebellar activation.

"Does the Cerebellum Contribute to Cognitive Aspects of Speech Production? A Functional Magnetic Resonance Imaging (fMRI) Study in Humans," *Neurosci Lett,* 247, 187–90. Ackermann, H., Wildgruber, D., Daum, I. & Grodd, W. (1998). Positron emission tomography studies suggest a contribution of the lateral aspects of the right cerebellar hemisphere to higher level (cognitive) aspects of speech production.

"Metabolic Abnormalities in Developmental Dyslexia Detected by 1H Magnetic Resonance Spectroscopy," *Lancet,* 351, 1849–52. Rae, C., Lee, M. A., Dixon, R. M., Blamire, A. M., Thompson, C. H., Styles, P., Talcott, J., Richardson, A. J. & Stein, J. F. (1998). Using proton magnetic resonance spectroscopy, this study led to the conclusion that the cerebellum is involved in dyslexia.

"Cerebellum in Attention-Deficit Hyperactivity Disorder: A Morphometric MRI Study," *Neurology,* 50, 1087–93. Berquin, P. C., Giedd, J. N., Jacobsen, L. K., Hamburger, S. D., Krain, A. L., Rapoport, J. L. & Castellanos, F. X. (1998). Clinical, neuroanatomic, and functional brain-imaging studies suggest a role for the cerebellum in cognitive functions including attention. It was found that a cerebello-thalamo-prefrontal circuit dysfunction may contribute to deficits encountered in ADHD.

"Cerebellar Size and Cognition: Correlations with IQ, Verbal Memory and Motor Dexterity," *Neuropsychiatry Neuropsychol Behav Neurol,* 10, 1–8. Paradiso, S., Andreasen, N. C., O'Leary, D. S., Arndt, S. & Robinson, R. G. (1997). Results indicate that the cerebellum contributes to cognition and cerebellar volume significantly correlated with the ability to retain already encoded information—verbal and fine motor skills.

"Cerebellum Implicated in Sensory Acquisition and Discrimination Rather than Motor Control," *Science,* 272, 545–7. Gao, J. H., Parsons, L. M., Bower, J. M., Xiong, J., Li, J. & Fox, P. T. (1996). Magnetic resonance imaging suggests that the cerebellum may be active during motor, perceptual, and cognitive performance.

"The Human Cerebro-Cerebellar System: Its Computing, Cognitive, and Language Skills," *Behav Brain Res,* 44, 113–28. Leiner, H. C., Leiner, A. L. & Dow, R. S. (1991). Results of a study suggested that the cerebellum contributes to the learning of cognitive and language skills, as well as its acknowledged traditional role in motor functions.

A 1980s Poem—
Before and After Treatment

A dyslexic girl's simplistically composed poem symbolizes the tragic essence and frustration characterizing this highly misdiagnosed and misunderstood scrambling disorder. And the quality (rather than the quantity) of her writing, spelling, grammatical, and math errors as well as her response to treatment were found helpful in solving the riddles underlying the traditional misconceptions of dyslexia.

Handwritten by Karen Van Ettinger, age twenty-three, just prior to treatment. Notice the poorly formed or coordinated letter and word (graphomotor) formation as well as the tilting, spacing, sequencing, and spelling errors. These errors, as well xiv   SMART BUT FEELING DUMB

as the attempts at correction or compensation, are all indicative of the dyslexia disorder as well as the inner-ear dysfunction that creates the disorder.

I do it
It's done
They're all wrong

I try
I cry
They're all wrong

Whats wrong ?
It s wrong
They're all wrong.

Following successful treatment just prior to college graduation, Karen rewrote her poem as she originally intended it to read—clearly highlighting her new beginning. Notice how inner-ear–enhancing medications can rapidly and effectively improve the underlying graphomotor mechanisms needed for writing, spelling, and even grammatical detail.

Contents

Acknowledgments

The basis and focus of *Smart but Feeling Dumb* is the presentation of real, live, suffering, and successfully treated dyslexics, both children and adults. Inasmuch as most of my patients and their families enthusiastically volunteered not only descriptions of symptoms, treatment responses, and their many frustrations in finding meaningful help, but also the use of their true names and circumstances, I feel compelled to credit them for the creation and essence of this book.

My patients and their families did not donate their time, efforts, and identities merely for the sake of acknowledgment. Rather, they wanted all readers really to know what dyslexia and dyslexics are all about. Most important, they wanted to spare current and future dyslexics the pain, confusion, and frustration that they themselves experienced in attempting to understand and find a solution to this puzzling and confusing disorder.

Smart but Feeling Dumb represents the current scientific reality of dyslexia. If readers—patients, parents, educators, and clinicians—are willing to learn from the insights described within this text, a new era of hope, enlightenment, and success awaits all dyslexics and all those involved with the diagnosis and treatment of the learning-disabled.

Preface and Self-Test

Many experts *erroneously* view dyslexia as merely a *severe* reading disorder often characterized by letter and word reversals. My research—encompassing the treatment of more than thirty-five thousand dyslexics over the past three decades—has clearly shown that dyslexia is a syndrome of many and varied symptoms that coexist in all combinations and severities. In other words, some dyslexics may compensate and even overcompensate for their reading impairment and only manifest problems with typical dyslexic writing, spelling, and math difficulties. And many a dyslexic does not reverse letters and words while reading. However, the vast majority will lose their place if reading symptoms are present. And there are many "normal reading score" dyslexics who experience reading reversals, tracking difficulties, and related reading symptoms such as blurring, word movement, and fatigue. In other words, dyslexics may evidence normal and even superior reading scores despite manifesting underlying difficulties with their reading mechanisms.

Unwittingly, many so-called authorities have traditionally defined dyslexia in a manner similar to the way we must have viewed diabetes many years ago: as a comatose state. Now we all know that the number of mild and compensated diabetics far exceeds those who lapse into coma. And the same holds true for dyslexics. In clinical reality, the number of mild and reading-score–compensated dyslexics far exceeds those traditionally viewed as having the severe or "comatose" disorder characterized by reversals and severely impaired reading abilities and scores.

To familiarize the reader with the many and varied symptoms characterizing dyslexia, as well as to provide crucial diagnostic insights, the following *self-test* is provided.

Does your child, student, or patient have a learning problem? Is he or she smart but feeling dumb? Do you?

If one or more of the following symptoms are evident, dyslexia may be present:

Reading

- Memory instability for letters, words, or numbers
- A tendency to skip over or scramble letters, words, and sentences
- A poor, slow, fatiguing reading ability prone to compensatory head tilting, near-far focusing, and finger pointing
- Reversal of letters such as *b* and *d,* words such as *saw* and *was,* and numbers such as *6* and *9,* or *16* and *61*
- Word blurring or movement or double images
- Headaches, vertigo, or nausea brought on by reading

Writing

- Messy, poorly angulated, or drifting handwriting prone to size, spacing, and letter-sequencing errors similar to those characterizing Karen's poem on page xiii.

Spelling, Math, Memory, and Grammar

- Memory instability for spelling, grammar, math, names, dates, and lists; for sequences such as the alphabet, the days of the week, and the months of the year; and for following directions

Speech

- Speech disorders such as slurring, stuttering, minor articulation errors, poor word recall, and auditory-input and motor-output speech time lags, rendering speech perception and enunciation more slowly than desired; and a tendency to word scrambling, slips of the tongue, or misperception of the ear

Direction

- Right/left and related directional uncertainty, such as difficulty knowing or remembering east or west, north or south

Time

- Delay in learning to tell time, as well as a host of time-related symptoms, including lateness, compulsive scheduling, and even procrastination or difficulty starting things on time

Concentration and Activity (ADD or ADHD)

- Impaired concentration, distractibility, hyperactivity, or overactivity
- Behavior, temper, or impulse disturbances

Balance and Coordination

- Difficulties with balance and coordination functions, e.g., walking, running, skipping, hopping, tying shoelaces, and buttoning buttons; accident proneness

Phobias and Related Mental Disorders

- Fears of the dark, heights, getting lost, going to school
- Fear or the avoidance of various balance, coordination, sports, and motion-related activities
- Mood disturbances
- Obsessions and compulsions

Did you have academic problems or dyslexia as a child? Do you have phobias and related psychological and physical symptoms that have thus far defied a clear understanding and successful treatment?

- Are you frightened by heights, cars, planes, bridges, elevators, subways, tunnels, open spaces, crowds, department stores, getting lost, losing control, and/or going crazy?
- Do irresistible, repetitive thoughts and actions—obses-

sions and compulsions—harass you and rigidify your ability to relax freely?

- Are you compelled to touch and retouch, check and recheck, think and rethink, and forever make lists of what must be done to avoid memory uncertainty and related anxiety?
- Are you prone to indecisiveness and feelings of inferiority, stupidity, ugliness, and clumsiness?
- Have headaches, stomachaches, nausea, excessive fatigue, concentration and memory difficulties, or related "psychosomatic" symptoms sent you from medical pillar to post, to no avail?
- Are you prone to dizziness or motion sickness?

If any of the above symptoms is present, your phobias and related emotional and physical disturbances may be due to the same *inner-ear dysfunction* as that which I have discovered to cause symptoms of dyslexia in children.

As a result of a series of major medical breakthroughs or insights resulting from over three decades of my research, dyslexia and its related neurotic and psychosomatic symptoms may now in most instances be successfully diagnosed and medically treated. And with treatment, the inevitable emotional scarring resulting from the dyslexic disorder and its wide-ranging symptomatic fallout can now be prevented or dramatically lessened. At the very least, complex, lengthy, and frustrating psychiatric, neurological, educational, optometric, auditory, and occupational therapies have been rendered significantly more successful—once a simple and safe medical treatment restores functioning within the inner ear and its supercomputer, the cerebellum, to more normal levels.

Variations of Dyslexia

My research has shown that a dysfunctioning inner-ear/cerebellar system may also result in a wide range of dyslexia-related disorders, albeit called by different names, i.e., LD (poor learning), dysgraphia (poor writing), dyscalculia (poor math), dysphasia (poor speech), ADD or ADHD (poor concentration and attention), dyspraxia (poor coordination), anxiety and mood disorders (phobias, depression), Asperger syndrome (social dyslexia), pervasive developmental delay, and pseudo-autism, as well as pseudomental retardation (severe forms of dyslexic or cerebellar-vestibular dysfunctioning), etc. As will be evident within this book, all these differently named disorders, including cerebellar ataxia, often respond favorably to inner-ear-enhancing medications and nutrients.

Major Neurological Disorders and Dyslexia—Mixed Dyslexia

Even more surprising and important, a group of severe neurological disorders (i.e., mental retardation, Down's syndrome, autism, cerebral palsy, brain injury due to trauma, tumors, surgery, or infections [multiple sclerosis], etc.) resulting from thinking brain and other noncerebellar-vestibular (CV) impairments were discovered in my research to frequently manifest dyslexia-related symptoms and thus CV dysfunctioning. These mixed-neurological cases, as I call them, can and do show improvements with CV-enhancing medical treatment, albeit the major disorder remains unchanged.

A Simple Explanation

The hundreds of diverse symptoms characterizing the dyslexic syndrome result when normal thinking brain and related nervous system processors experience secondary difficulties upon receiving scrambled signals from a dysfunctioning "inner-ear" or CV system. The quality and intensity of the symptoms are determined by (1) the specific CV signals scrambled and the degree of scrambling, (2) the normal brain centers receiving these scrambled signals, and (3) the brain's capacity for descrambling or compensation.

In mixed-neurological disorders, the higher brain and other nervous system processors are primarily impaired and so experience even greater difficulties upon receiving scrambled "dyslexic" signals for interpretation and/or action.

By analogy, medical and even nonmedical conditioning therapies help by decreasing signal-scrambling and increasing processing capacity. With this simple explanation, readers will easily be able to fully comprehend all the symptoms and variations characterizing all dyslexics, as well as their improvements via maturation, medical and nonmedical therapies, and even the medically triggered improvements in mixed dyslexia.

Toward the dissemination of this unique, "therapeutically helpful" information and understanding—and the early implementation of new and invaluable lifesaving medical diagnostic/treatment methods for *all* dyslexics and all their signal-scrambling variations—*Smart but Feeling Dumb* was written.

Harold N. Levinson, M.D.
Director, Medical Dyslexic Treatment Center
Great Neck, New York

A 2003 Dyslexia Update

There is nothing more gratifying for a clinician and medical researcher than to review his scientific and related writings from over two previous decades and find little, if anything, of substance to correct. Even more rewarding is the fact that leading researchers have recently validated most, if not all, of my prior inner-ear/cerebellar dyslexia research efforts and now refer to these concepts as "pioneering," "groundbreaking," and even "decades ahead of its time," rather than "controversial." Because of the amazing therapeutic benefits now available for all dyslexics, young and old, as well as the foreseeable possibility of medical cures and even prevention, this 2003 dyslexia update attempts to present the reader with:

- Additional clinical content and associated insights derived from newly examined and treated patients, including some recently elucidated symptoms and new methods of therapy
- More readable and understandable explanations for each and every symptom that characterizes this disorder

- The way this research has shaped current concepts by refuting and replacing a wide variety of traditionally espoused but erroneous century-old assumptions and convictions, including the nonsensical dyslexia definition requiring that, to be classified as dyslexic, one must be two years or more behind peers or potential in reading scores
- Independent research by outstanding neurophysiologists indicating, and thus corroborating, that the cerebellum or "inner-ear system" plays a vital role in sensory and motor (spatial-temporal) integration as well as in memory, attentional, and speech-language functioning*
- Unique comments and perspectives on the latest independently performed dyslexia research, critical and otherwise
- A more detailed presentation of Appendix D, "Criticism and Its Analysis," including highly distorted—even libelous—content by severely "biased" defensive and even offensive critics.
- The highest form of compliment: a recent turn of events in which some independent validators have attempted to claim originality by omitting vital references.

As previously noted, during most of the past thirty-five years my "challenging" or "breakthrough" research had often been referred to as "controversial"—the latter term clearly implying that the hundred-year-old traditionalist dyslexia assumptions, convictions, and definitions dating back to 1896 were valid. Nothing could be further from the truth. The majority-held scientific views on dyslexia have led absolutely

---

*Refer especially to the research of Leiner, Leiner, and Dow (1991).

nowhere diagnostically and therapeutically! Few if any symptoms were recognized, none were explainable, and just about every new and innovative method of therapy was initially criticized as "impossible" or nonsensical by the traditionalists.

Never did the traditional "experts" ask themselves the following alternative questions:

- If 100-year-old assumptions, definitions, and convictions about dyslexia have led nowhere diagnostically and therapeutically despite escalating research efforts by outstanding scientists, might these prior views be incorrect?

- How can dyslexia be due to a language impairment within the thinking brain, as many traditionalists still maintain, when many dyslexics are linguistically gifted and have no speech-related symptoms (e.g., Winston Churchill as well as actors and actresses such as Tom Cruise, Cher, etc.), and when each and every dyslexic symptom (including speech impediments such as stuttering, stammering, and articulation disorders) can be easily explained on the basis of known, but often denied, inner-ear (or cerebellar-vestibular) functioning and dysfunctioning, and improves with inner-ear–enhancing medications and related therapies?

- If indeed a wide variety of helpful therapies (eye exercises, tinted lenses, occupational and reflex therapy, sensorimotor integration or vestibular exercises, the use of anti–motion-sickness antihistamines and stimulants) do work—albeit to varying extents—then might this evidence not refute the hundred-year-old "accepted" cerebral cortical theories, which are completely incompatible with these helpful therapies?

Simply restated: How can vestibular or inner-ear–related therapies significantly help dyslexics if the latter suffer from a severe impairment within their language-thinking brain processing centers rather than from inner-ear–determined symptoms? They couldn't! But if these therapies do work, then how can one logically still uphold the century-old thinking-brain theories of dyslexia? One can't! But many "experts" still do so! Then why? the reader might ask. Sad to say, the reasons are tragically simple. And anyone capable of reading through *Smart but Feeling Dumb*—and especially the analyses of criticism in this work, in *A Solution to the Riddle Dyslexia,* and in *A Scientific Watergate—Dyslexia*—will readily find the answers for themselves.

In addition, if reported ear infections, whiplash injuries, and a variety of disorders of the inner ear trigger *acquired* "dyslexic" symptoms, including speech-related impairments, how in the world can dyslexia be considered to be of (*prenatal*) "cerebral" or thinking-brain origin—especially if no one to date has demonstrated any such localizing neurological evidence within the cerebral cortex? Indeed, in the above-mentioned "criticism" discussions, two outstanding neurologists from the Neurological Institute, Columbia Presbyterian Hospital, found only localizing (inner-ear) "cerebellar deficits" in a "blindly referred" sample of dyslexic children sent to them by this researcher. These neurologists did not know anything about my research project and thus examined all of the referred cases *as usual.* And guess what they concluded: In the absence of any localizing neurological cerebral (thinking-brain) signs and in the presence of *only inner-ear or "cerebellar" deficits,* they diagnosed their dyslexic patients as suffering from "minimal cerebral dysfunction" or "minimal brain damage." How can that be? Bias!

When patients experiencing and complaining only of dizziness were sent to these neurologists and also were found by them to have "cerebellar deficits," they were diagnosed as having (inner-ear) "vestibular dysfunction." In other words, the neurologists used *only* the presenting complaints (dizziness or learning difficulties) to make a final diagnosis—and *their final reported diagnosis was completely independent of their stated neurological findings.* (So why, one might ask, did they have to examine the patients?) In reality, those examined for learning symptoms and those for vertigo were all dyslexic—and thus were all found to have identical inner-ear or cerebellar-vestibular neurological findings.

And guess what happened later on, as reported in *A Solution to the Riddle Dyslexia* and here in Appendix D, "Criticism and Its Analysis": These very neurologists denied, publicly and to other critics, having found "cerebellar deficits" in these very same patients. Also, at a scientific meeting sponsored by the Orton Dyslexia Society in 1975 and arranged to discuss my reported cerebellar findings in dyslexia, these very same neurologists refused to attend. Instead, they sent a colleague who claimed that they hadn't meant to report "cerebellar deficits" in those cases that had only *mild* and *moderate cerebellar impairments.* Obviously, this makes as little sense as saying that women are pregnant only just prior to delivery—not really during the first and second trimesters and not even during most of the third.

Furthermore, one might ask how repeated rotation or spinning can trigger temporary dyslexic symptoms in normal individuals and intensify these symptoms in dyslexics if dyslexia is not of an inner-ear origin. They couldn't! And how can one explain the temporary onset of "space dyslexia" in cosmonauts under zero gravity using cerebral theories?* One can't! And how can cerebral (thinking-brain) processing theories explain why "space dyslexia" is significantly avoided or minimized by pretreating the cosmonauts with dyslexia-oriented therapies, such as anti–motion-sickness medications as well as vestibular rotation exercises—both of which are known to enhance "inner-ear" functioning? They can't!

In summary, I will merely ask readers to read *Smart but Feeling Dumb* and other works on dyslexia and conclude for themselves which theory—the traditional versus the "inner-ear"—should be considered "controversial": a theory that has led us nowhere but in circles for almost a century? Or one that leads to a comprehensive understanding as well as definitive methods of medical diagnosis and treatment? I will leave you with two equally puzzling questions:

- If dyslexia experts are truly interested in understanding and helping dyslexics, why have they completely avoided contacting any of the many patients and their parents in *Smart but Feeling Dumb* (or within my Medical Dyslexic Treatment Center)? These patients have deliberately volunteered to use their real names and speak up so that others might be helped. Are the "traditionalists" afraid of the truth? Of change? And if so, why?
- Why have these "experts" attempted to delay the diagno-

*The French-Russian cosmonauts were reported to have developed reading reversals at zero gravity (Academia Rodienensis Conference of the Royal Society of Medicine in London, 1986).

sis and medical treatment of so many millions of desperately suffering dyslexics, while offering them only the illusion of so-called tutorial cures instead?

As is customary, I will end this update by presenting the reader with some recent case studies and letters from patients who benefited from my concepts. Many others will follow. Judge these and all other presented cases and their self-reported facts for yourselves! And arrive at your own conclusions—based on reported realities rather than on traditionally supported misassumptions and biased fiction. *I challenge all remaining critics and skeptics to do the same!* Had the traditionalists listened to patients, such as those that follow, rather than prior experts, they would have solved all the many riddles of dyslexia over a century ago. They would have realized, as I did, that only dyslexics—not experts—can accurately define dyslexia.

Meredith Smith Lewis*

This letter was received from Meredith Smith Lewis, a forty-two-year-old woman I treated:

> It is so perfect that the last question in every section of your Progress Report [which patients must compile while on medication] is about anything else being easier. My life is easier!
> Ask anyone who has ever known me and they would say I had the total package to be or do anything I wanted.

*The following four cases were taken from *A Scientific Watergate—Dyslexia*, Levinson, H., Stonebridge Publishing, Ltd., 1994.

Looking from their shoes it did appear to be so. So, why wasn't I? I finally summed it up to my therapist (approximately six months before I came to see you) that my life is so hard—everything is so hard for me! I realize now how there would be no way for her to *begin* to understand the complexities behind those words, and even less of a chance for her to help. I just told myself what I had always, "Just get on with it, Meredith, it's just something you'll have to live with."

I felt helpless, disheartened, misunderstood, insecure, and angry, while I continued to chip away at the process of building a life. But, something would not let me give up in spite of the pain. Finally, after years of searching for the answer to that ultimate question, "What is wrong with me?"; after therapists, counselors, groups, EST, Transactional Analysis, Yoga, and a fortune in books, I found *Smart but Feeling Dumb*. And what I found that day was a miracle.

I knew when I read your book that you were talking to me. Every doubt, every hurt, every symptom and emotion was as if I had written the words I was reading! I realized how my affliction was not so severe as to hold me back totally, but severe enough to keep me crippled both mentally and emotionally beneath a veneer of a "well" person. Every action and reaction of my 39 years found explanation, and I knew my healing had begun.

Upon my return from your New York office, I was ecstatic! I felt I had been given the key to my prison cell and was freed—finally. I rushed to get my medicine. Within days I could sense a difference in myself. It was so subtle, just gently washing over me. When I first started noticing that I was happy without a reason to be I was certain I knew what Heaven was going to be like. I was still forgetting things and running into frustrating situations, but I **was coping!** I began handling more on my agenda, not becoming overwhelmed by the planning, doing, and follow-up.

At this same time, my husband's rejection and hostility toward me could previously have sent me into a severe depression. Instead, every day I was less triggered by him. I seemed able to fuel my heartache and anger into school, the club, and my volunteer activities. When he started getting really ugly, I was able to maintain my studies and work-out schedule while preparing a detailed, organized, and explosive war chest for my attorneys. Whatever the final outcome, I feel 100 percent confident with my efforts toward providing for my future, and will be able to move ahead with my life in spite of more disappointment or cash flow interruption, based on his irresponsibility and shabby treatment.

My school work takes one millionth of the time it used to. I find that I can breeze through a chapter, my notes and handouts, and go in and get an "A" on a test. **And, I received an "A" in math!** In fact, I was tutoring other students in the class! I could sit for hours doing my homework, not getting restless, bored, or frustrated, rather working straight through from the first problem to the last. And, what's more, I liked it! Of course it helped that we had an excellent professor. However, I am not diminishing my being able to sail through!

Dr. Levinson, I used to feel like a vulnerable little chick who clung to the nest. All the other birds said there was no reason why the chick shouldn't be flying with the rest of them, that it *looked* like it was ready! But the little chick knew he "wasn't done" and couldn't explain why it was taking so long. I was like that little chick. Now, I'm complete and flying and soaring with the others, and people say, "See, Meredith, we always knew you were ready," and I think how they never knew, but it's okay now because I'm finally "done." And not only can I fly, but I know I'll trip and stumble, but that I can pick myself right back up again. Now, looking from the shoes of another at the person they see, I know that I am that person on the inside too. And everywhere I look I see a reflection of confidence, talent, strength, and beauty.

Dr. Levinson, you have given me the gift I have searched for all of my life! You have given me happiness where depression used to brood, self-esteem where doubt and shame once prevailed, and courage where fear dominated. You have replaced my anger and frustration with humor, while redirecting it to create purpose in my life. And thank you, because of you I can focus with intent on that purpose.

Ann Dixon

The following letter was received from Ruth Dixon, Ann's mother. To those who view dyslexia as *merely* a reading disorder, review Ann's experiences carefully and then ask: Are not the reading and academic-related symptoms merely the recognized tip of the dyslexic iceberg?

How do I begin to thank you, Dr. Levinson—that one visit to your office last year changed our sixteen-year-old daughter's life. I came looking for help with school-related problems, e.g., reading, omitted words, careless errors, concentration, etc. The medication has helped a great deal in those areas, but to my surprise and joy we now have a daughter who is much happier, feels much better about herself and is far more confident.

The strongest single memory I have of Ann during the last twelve months is about ten days after she began the medication. I looked at her as she walked towards me. She was no longer the girl who slouched, head down, but a person who walked straight, tall, looking more confident. When she reached me, I asked her if she thought the medication was helping. Her reply was: "Something is happening to me." It was and is as if she has found a lower center of gravity. Now, whether Ann is running, playing basketball, RollerBlading, or biking we no longer hold our breath fearing that she will fall.

I have also noticed that during the last twelve months many of Ann's fears have faded. She's gone on several school trips and has had no fear of riding in a bus, going on elevators, and even sliding on her belly in a deep dark cave. Ann is the first to say that life is just more enjoyable. I can't tell you how happy that makes me feel!

I have also seen tremendous improvements in her schoolwork. Ann still works as hard as she always has, but thanks to the medication her hard work now pays off.

Before starting on medication Ann always had trouble reading and understanding what she had read. No matter how much I tried to help things seem[ed] to get worse. It wasn't until after we were riding home from our first visit to your office that she told me that "the words change places when I read." I asked her why she hadn't told me, and she replied "because you would never have believed me." In a sense I was shocked to hear that, but also felt relief because now I believed we were getting some help for her. Even though our daughter has attended a private day school for the past six years where classes are small, a learning disorder was never suggested to us. Last year I was simply told that Ann had an emotional problem and needed psychiatric care. Except for you, no one understood or took the time to find out what was wrong—what a terrible burden Ann had to labor under.

Last year in her ninth grade English course Ann's teacher wrote this comment at the end of one of her papers.

> You make some excellent points, and you give good details, but you need to read this aloud so it will make sense—it sounds almost illiterate as I read it— there are omitted words, incorrect spellings, and odd choices of words. This really needs work! Conclusion is really quite good. Also—remember to avoid "you." *D+*

After Ann had been on medication almost a year the above comments may be contrasted with the comments made by Ann's tenth grade English teacher at the end of the term.

> Her writing has been consistently good, and her *Macbeth* paper (*B+*) was a particularly well-written and nicely argued piece of analysis.

> Again, in math class the symptoms were there for them to see—time and time again she was told that she made careless errors, had difficulty putting concepts together and lacked self-confidence.

This year these comments have ceased. Ann (who had to struggle last year to get a *C–*) this year in Algebra IIA received a B first semester, *A–* second semester, *A–* third semester and *B+* for the fourth semester.

It has been a good year for Ann. It is as if you unlocked the door to the world for Ann. She has changed from a shy, unhappy, insecure, girl to a much more self-assured sixteen-year-old.

I would like to quote once more, this time from her advisor's comments at the end of this school year. Please bear in mind Dr. Levinson, that the school is unaware of your diagnosis or medication—that is the way Ann wants it.

Ann finished with a very strong academic record . . . Ann seems to have had a much better year than last. She seems happy, more self-confident, and carries a wonderful smile and friendly greeting wherever she goes. I look forward to having her again next year. It should be even better!

(Ann's academic record this year was: English B, European History *A–*, Spanish 1 *A–*, Algebra IIA *B+*, Chemistry *B+*)

Thank you again, Dr. Levinson, for your research, for the books you have written (because without them I wouldn't have learned about you), and for helping so many children, including Ann.

Debbie Iberger

This letter came to me from Debbie Iberger, forty years old, a patient of mine:

> I could never thank you enough for "giving me back my brain." I am now in control of my life (and on top of all my husband's business paperwork!)—days don't pass by "dizzyingly"; I'm out of a heavy, dense fog.
>
> I've read much of the non-technical literature about dyslexia in the last four months. I find it amazing that you've stuck to your beliefs and research despite the verbal lashings (poundings?) you've taken from America's "esteemed" dyslexic community.
>
> I'm waiting for the day, and I know it will come, when the "obstructionists" will be unable to refute your work.
>
> P.S. If you need a guinea pig for any experiments on dyslexia, I'm available, (and only 1 hour away).

Tom Henderson

Tom is an eleven-year-old dyslexic who has responded very well to nine weeks of treatment. His parents reported the following content:

> We have started to see a calmness in Tommy that has never been there before. His self-image has gotten so much better. He is so much more organized. His school work seems to be getting easier for him to do.
>
> Tommy also seems to be making friends with more kids in school, and around the neighborhood.

When he gets mad, he will catch himself and say "I'm sorry," whereas before he would just stay mad.

Tommy seems to be sleeping better at night. He is not having as many bad dreams. He seems more rested.

In reviewing specific areas, Tom's parents noted definite improvements as follows:

Reading: easier, more spontaneous, smoother; less word and sentence skipping errors; words are clearer, less jumping around, double vision is gone, fewer reading headaches, less head tilting; greater visual span, better reading memory and concentration

Writing: better, more spontaneous, smoother and easier to read, straighter on lined paper with better spacing, faster, more detailed

Spelling: better orally and written, easier visualization

Math: easier addition, subtraction, multiplication, division, fractions, less reversals, neater columns, and less careless errors

Memory: significantly improved short-term

Time: sense is better

Direction: sense is better; is distinguishing right/left, north/south, east/west

Speech: increased spontaneous expression and speed in saying what he wants, improved clarity and sequencing for speech heard

Grammar: better understood and memory for details, fewer errors

Concentration/distractibility/overactivity: all improved, more alert, less impulsive

Mood: steadier, less depressed and happier

Frustration tolerance: better, temper controlled

Self-image/body image: feels smarter, more confident, more together—mentally and physically

Socialization: better

Psychosomatic symptoms: fewer headaches, stomachaches; dizzy spells and motion sickness gone

Balance/coordination: better, steadier, less accident-prone, better sports ability

Organization/planning: improved for writing, drawing, thinking—even his room is much neater

Fears/phobias: less repetitive thoughts and decreased need to check things; fear persists (e.g., needles)

This brief letter is from Tom himself:

Thank you for finding out what was wrong with me. I am feeling much better in what I am doing. I have only felt one side effect I think . . . and that is crankyness. Tomorrow I have to get a blood test! (OUCH!) Dad is going to give blood first! (Good) Ha! Ha!

II

Introduction and Overview

Dyslexia is commonly recognized as a learning disorder characterized by reading, writing, and spelling reversals. Despite the growing attention this elusive disorder has received since it was first recognized in 1896–97 by two English physicians, W. P. Morgan and J. Kerr, dyslexia has remained a scientific enigma, defying most attempts at medical understanding, diagnosis, prediction, treatment, and prevention.

Researchers and clinicians were unable to comprehend and define the dyslexic disorder—unable to understand its wide range of fluctuating educational, medical, mental, and emotional symptoms as briefly summarized in the Preface and Self-Test.

Clinicians and educators were incapable of simply explaining to patients and their families the various underlying mechanisms affecting reading, writing, spelling, math, memory, speech, direction, grammar, concentration, behavior, balance, and coordination. Few, if any, recognized fully the depths to which this disorder penetrated the very souls of its victims.

...xia was naively viewed as if it were merely a severe reading disorder characterized by a fascinating array of reversals.

- Not recognized was the agony, suffering, humiliation, and despair experienced by patients and their families.
- Not recognized was the fact that dyslexics frequently compensate, thus becoming normal or superior readers, and that a variety of educational, psychological, and IQ test scores could not diagnose or rule out this disorder.
- Not recognized was the fact that dyslexia could be a consequence of ear infections, mononucleosis, post-concussion syndromes, or multiple sclerosis.
- Not recognized was the fact that dyslexia may be associated with a wide range of more serious surface disorders, such as mental retardation, cerebral palsy, and deafness.
- Not recognized was the fact that the hidden dyslexic component of the above disorders could be effectively treated medically for the first time, resulting in an overall improvement in both the hidden and surface disorders.
- Not recognized was the fact that almost all the previously existing assumptions and convictions pertaining to this disorder were found to be in error.
- Not recognized was the fact that most phobias and many so-called mental, emotional, and psychosomatic disturbances were caused by the same physical disturbance underlying and causing dyslexia.
- Not recognized was the fact that many so-called Freudian slips of the tongue, pen, hand, mind . . . were really dyslexic slips.
- Not recognized was the fact that no traditionally accepted

theories and concepts of dyslexia had ever been scientifically validated.

- Not recognized was the fact that no theory could explain and encompass the improvements resulting from all other theoretical approaches: optometric, occupational, educational, psychological, chiropractic, and temporomandibular-joint (TMJ), allergic, and nutrition therapies.

In my medical text *A Solution to the Riddle Dyslexia,* I provided the scientific basis needed to comprehend fully and explain the mechanisms and symptoms characterizing this disorder. Moreover, I provided the insights leading to the first medical means of diagnosis, treatment, and prevention, as well as medically determined educational techniques. However, that book was highly technical, and only the most determined readers worked their way through it. Yet, its complexity did not stop many readers; it merely slowed them down. In fact, the difficulty readers experienced with that reading process may be compared to that of dyslexics attempting to read ordinary material: The resulting frustration stops some but not all. For many, the difficulty of *A Solution* merely served to steel their determination to succeed. And a surprising number completed the book from cover to cover—with dictionaries in hand. Many dyslexics and their family members fully digested that technical treatise with a voracity and interest, shaming many an expert. However, a simplified version of that text was needed. Crucial insights and medical-educational breakthroughs had to be shared with those afflicted and those interested in helping the afflicted.

With that aim in mind, I undertook the writing of a new book. However, I wanted this new book to contain additional case material and concepts. Accordingly, *all new case material* has been carefully selected and presented, with the exception of one case that was published earlier, in order to link the old book symbolically with the new.

In *Smart but Feeling Dumb,* I felt the need to highlight the multidimensional nature and complexity of the dyslexic disorder. The common misconception that dyslexia is merely a severe reading or learning disorder characterized by reversals had to be exposed. Clinicians and educators had to be informed that this disorder was as serious and as traumatizing as diabetes, hypertension, and heart disease—and that, like diabetes, this disorder occurs in many and varied shapes and intensities. In retrospect, the traditional "wisdom" of equating dyslexia with *only* severe degrees of *only* one of its many symptoms (severe reading-score impairment) makes as much sense as defining diabetes as *only* a comatose state.

Many educators and clinicians often overlooked or denied the disorder's presence—especially of reading-score–compensated cases—and would use such poorly understood diagnostic labels as *stupid, lazy, spoiled, immature, undisciplined, bad,* and even *retarded.* The use of these terms emphasized the underlying presence of "professional" frustration and ignorance. And the use of such treatment techniques as scolding, name-calling, and "conditioning" merely added insult to injury. Having no scientific alternative, and out of desperation, well-intentioned educators and clinicians often encouraged their patients to exercise increased amounts of willpower and determination—as if dyslexics were not already using these functions to capacity—generally with little success.

To highlight and symbolize the emotional and mental depth as well as the scope of the dyslexic disorder, I chose to use a title that emphasized the feelings underlying and characterizing dyslexia. I hope the title and content of this book will trigger the understanding and empathy needed to inspire the interested parent, dyslexic, and professional to seek and implement early diagnosis and treatment.

Thirty-five years of research into the nature of dyslexia, and the analysis of over thirty-five thousand cases, have led me to conclude that most dyslexics feel dumb despite being smart; hence the title *Smart but Feeling Dumb*. Most often a dyslexic's compulsion to succeed is motivated by an overwhelming desire to prove to herself and others that she is not really as stupid as she feels. Accordingly, the dyslexic disorder frequently serves as a potent stimulus to achieve, reflecting a desperate attempt to reverse the humiliating feelings of inferiority that are invariably present.

Unfortunately, tangible success and peer recognition—even adulation—do not neutralize or eliminate a dyslexic's feeling dumb. All too often, accomplished, even famous dyslexics merely feel that they have succeeded in fooling everyone around them, and that others are not truly aware of how inept they really are. They attribute their successes to chance, a lucky break, a fluke of nature. Bright dyslexic children who feel dumb invariably become bright adult dyslexics who continue to feel the very same way. Pretty girls feel ugly, and handsome boys feel clumsy and klutzy. And many feel like impostors, acting smart on the outside while feeling inwardly dumb.

Contrary to the opinion of many authorities, dyslexia does not disappear with age. It is not outgrown. It merely is partially compensated for, which often results in severe emotional scarring. As a result, most dyslexics do not succeed. They do not become famous. They do not overcome. What becomes of them?

Some withdraw or exhibit other antisocial behavior. Most are forced to settle for mediocrity and an inner sense of isolation. Their hopes and aspirations are desperately suppressed, often beyond recovery. Frustration and anger become all-consuming. Many are motivated to direct outward their deeply felt feelings of inferiority, inflicting and infecting those about them. And without proper understanding and treatment, the lives of millions of dyslexics are doomed to a continuous stream of failures.

My research has led me to recognize the existence of an unfortunate psychological equation that links dyslexia with feelings of stupidity, ugliness, and klutziness or lack of coordination—feelings of inadequacy often resulting in social withdrawal, shyness, depression, alcoholism, drug addiction, criminal acts, and years of fruitless psychotherapy. This psychological equation was found to be an intrinsic aspect of the dyslexic disorder in which:

- Feelings of klutziness and clumsiness are derived from the dyscoordination resulting from an underlying inner-ear dysfunction
- Feelings of ugliness are derived from a dyscoordinated, scrambled sensorimotor scheme, resulting in a distorted, "ugly" sense of self, or poor body image
- The disturbances affecting reading, writing, spelling, math, memory, speech, direction, and a host of other related functions result in feelings of stupidity

The task of writing this book for the layperson has not been easy for a medical clinician and researcher. However, an intense need to share my vast clinical experience and success with a greater audience of interested readers has motivated me to compensate for my rather limited writing skills. I hope the content will more than compensate for my rather unconventional organization and style.

This book is as simply written as I was able to do. But it is not simplistic or pedantic. It is intended to be thought-provoking rather than condescendingly simple. The reader should find it *natural*. By natural I mean that the conclusions will smoothly follow from the case material presented. Complex statistics and scientific design will be avoided, as the scientific background for this book has already been established in *A Solution to the Riddle Dyslexia* and in a series of research papers.

Most individuals will read this book in order to learn:

- What the symptoms of dyslexia are all about
- What positive results can be expected from medical and nonmedical treatment
- How best to diagnose and treat this disorder early and thereby minimize emotional scarring while maximizing compensation

Thus, I decided to write this book in a dyslexialike fashion— by presenting the end before the beginning.

Inasmuch as most individuals interested in my research are eager to learn about the patients' symptoms, which define the essence of this disorder, and their responses to my treatment, I decided to present a variety of short case histories right up front. These case histories highlight the disorder and its symptomatic variations at first glance. A sample of individual patient improvements follows, so that the reader may quickly learn the multitude of fascinating responses medications may have.

In viewing the varied case histories as well as the responses to medication, the reader will naturally and intuitively develop a feel for the nature and symptoms underlying and characterizing dyslexia. The many diverse case histories presented will provide the reader with the clinical background needed to judge my research findings independently. Also, by exposing readers to a large clinical sample, it is anticipated that their understanding will develop as mine did—directly from the patients themselves.

In treating dyslexics both psychiatrically and neurologically over many years, I have come to learn that the only way to neutralize and dissolve their feeling stupid and ugly is to explain to them in honest, straightforward terms exactly what their problems are. They must come to recognize that they have only one relatively simple problem that radiates in a thousand directions, often causing them to feel they have a thousand different disorders and therefore must be crazy and hopeless. In order to feel differently about themselves—to change—they must develop a meaningful insight into the true nature of their problem. They must have a realistic alternative to feeling dumb, ugly, and hopeless.

They must know why they have reading, writing, and spelling difficulties. They must know why and how their reversals and directional disturbances occur, disappear, and even reoccur with fatigue and other conditions. They must truly understand how and why their memory and concentration vary. Dyslexics must fully comprehend why they do poorly in some subjects and well in others. Simply stated, they must understand the essence of their varied dyslexic symptoms to the point of feeling them—a point at which intellectual understanding is transformed into a feeling of conviction, or true insight.

With insight, new avenues of approach and compensation will invariably materialize. As a result, dyslexics will develop new ways and means of getting around their problems or working their way through them to a resolution. However, there is one drawback: Someone who thoroughly comprehends the full significance and range of dyslexia must impart this knowledge to the patient and his family.

Inasmuch as I have specifically and thoroughly explained the panoramic nature and cause of dyslexia to thousands of patients and family members, I feel especially qualified to explain this disorder to the reader. I hope you will develop the same understanding as have my many patients and their families.

Patients and their families come into my consultation and diagnostic rooms after an unfortunately long wait. They listen to me, and other patients and are amazed at how similar the symptoms of others are to their own despite the many differences and variations that exist among dyslexics. They experience what in psychiatry is called a catharsis. Some are on the verge of tears. They are able to voice their inner emotions and frustrations for the very first time, simply because they have shared them with others with similar backgrounds. Many adults tell me, "You know, I don't really feel *as* stupid or *as* isolated as I did before. I never really told anybody in my whole life how I felt or exactly what symptoms I had."

Following examination of their children, parents are relieved to hear my diagnosis. They have often been previously traumatized with devastating and inappropriate clinical terms such as *minimal brain damage, minimal cerebral dysfunction,* and *mental retardation*—and even *inept parenting.* And patients are similarly relieved to find out that they are not just "lazy" or "stupid." Several children have spontaneously asked, "You mean I really have a brain?" Others ask hopefully, "Can I really be helped?" and "Will I be able to play kickball with the other kids?"

In writing *Smart but Feeling Dumb*, I have kept in mind what patients and their families have told me, and I would like to share that information with you. Perhaps you will empathize or identify with their experiences. Accordingly, the book contains many variations of case histories, from short vignettes to deep and extensive revelations. You will hear patients convey their agony in dealing with the dyslexic symptoms. You will hear the frustrations and pain of family members, as well as their added suffering when periodically dealing with clinically inexperienced, defensive, sometimes offensive professionals.

The sample case variations have been chosen to facilitate the reader's finding himself in the situations presented, just as my patients and their parents do while they patiently and hopefully chat and listen to others in my waiting room. After assimilating the case histories and the patient responses to the medication, I feel the reader will be ready to grasp naturally both the history and significance of my research efforts—efforts that have led me to resolve the medical diagnostic and therapeutic void in dealing with dyslexia. Thus, for example, a typical treatment response as observed by a patient's mother highlights the meaning and significance conveyed by this introduction and overview—indeed, this book:

Words cannot express the new Karen you have given us! There is a lot of work to be done to help her compensate for the basics she lacks, but with her newfound abilities, we are all optimistic! I feel that you have, indeed, changed our lives to the good! Thanks to you and your staff.

No doubt this favorable ending presented up front will catalyze your interest in the details that follow:

Karen

Karen Torgenson is an attractive, extremely articulate, and socially mature fifteen-year-old. She is also very gifted musically and artistically. However, as the Torgensons relate, it was as though Karen were two girls rather than one. One girl was charming and attractive, with a prodigious capacity for self-discipline in art and music and admired in both areas by her peers and by adults.

The other girl was seething with anger, resentment, and frustration with her academic subjects and her teachers. She seemed to have a total block to learning subjects that required reading, math, memory, concentration, and organization. She lacked interest and self-discipline with her homework and school projects other than those pertaining to art and music. This Karen either lashed out bitterly and unreasonably at her family or retreated behind the closed door of her room.

It was very difficult for her parents and others who knew and loved Karen to reconcile these two completely different halves of her character.

All of her life Karen talked in her sleep and sleepwalked three or four nights a week. During these episodes she appeared very pensive, worried, and anxious either to rearrange items in her room or leave the house, mumbling in an agitated fashion about needing to "fix things" or about some impending crisis. For her parents, both of whom are teachers, the situation was particularly painful. They gave Karen loving support and assistance in studying and completing assignments. Karen's father, who teaches at her school, tried to keep open the lines of communication and understanding between his daughter and her teachers while simultaneously attempting to both encourage and inspire Karen. Needless to say, this task was most difficult and emotionally draining for all. It was often like walking a tightrope—high up in the sky.

Karen's Favorable Response to Treatment

Eight weeks after Karen's diagnosis and treatment at my Medical Dyslexic Treatment Center, Mrs. Torgenson wrote: "Karen surprisingly stated, 'I don't feel mad anymore!'" Moreover, Karen felt less tension and irritability, and her sleepwalking stopped the very first day she was given medication. "I can see an inner composure and tranquility not previously present," Mrs. Torgenson observed. "She is able to concentrate, to follow through on homework, and to learn new information."

Karen was now accepting and responding to hugs and expressions of love from members of her family. "It had gotten to the point that she would hardly acknowledge a kiss on the cheek," Karen's mother continued. "However, since I think hugs and kisses are indispensable to children of all ages, I continued to seek her out, even though she felt unlovable. Some days it was the only way I could tell her that we loved her in spite of her problems. It is a joy to have her come up and hug me now!

"At home, she is reasonable and more controlled. There are far fewer outbursts of frustration. I sense in Karen a feeling that she is able to take control of her life. She has pride in getting her homework done on her own. She has even seen the English teacher, for example, about how to improve her basic skills, and she is keeping a check, on her own, of all her grades."

Karen's father remarked that one year earlier, Karen's grades had been D's and F's, even in below-average-track classes. She had skipped some classes and done her homework only under duress. After treatment, Karen's grades were C's and C-pluses in regular classes. She no longer skipped classes, and on her own initiative she completed her homework on time. "There is still much work to be done—gaps to be filled in . . . but giant steps have been taken toward achieving these goals," Mr. Torgenson said.

Karen's mother related several additional instances that showed clearly the remarkable changes in her daughter's attitude and personality.

The first occurred about six weeks after medication had begun. Karen sat down at the piano to sight-read a song. Previously this was a very frustrating task for her, one accompanied by tenseness in posture, scowls, and many mistakes of which she would not normally be cognizant unless pointed out. On this day, however, she sat down at the piano and approached her task with composure and logic. When she made a mistake, she immediately picked up on it and corrected it on her own. Since I am a piano teacher, I was nothing less than thunderstruck at the improvement that occurred in her.

A second incident occurred a few months later. Karen was working with her sister on a very difficult saxophone solo. Since it was a Saturday, she was off her medication.* She approached the practice irritably and somewhat negatively. As they progressed she became increasingly frustrated and angry with herself because she could not execute the notes as she knew they should have been played. Pretty soon she was stomping her foot and berating herself quite vocally for her "stupidity." I told the girls to take a break and gave Karen her medication. Forty-five minutes later she returned to practice, calm and with no signs of irritability. Karen was amenable to suggestions, concentrating, and working through her difficulties.

Later her sister commented to me about the difference the medication made in Karen's attitude and behavior. The two girls had worked intensively for two hours, and Karen had handled it quite well. Both girls accomplished much during this time.

A third incident occurred one month later. Karen and I were playing tennis. Nothing seemed to go right for her: Either she missed balls or the balls went into the net. She became angry and disgusted with herself. She took her medication, and after a half hour's respite she resumed playing.

---

*I often instructed patients not to take medications on weekends and holidays and over vacations, if possible. Initially, I thought this procedure minimized the chances of becoming "immune" to the medications while it increased the chances for maximum compensation. However, clinical experience over many years led me to an alternative treatment plan. For more on treatment and how dyslexics compensate for their symptoms, see Chapter X, "The Symptoms and Mechanisms Defining Dyslexia," p. 204 (*Author's note*).

Karen performed normally and with composure. She occasionally hit a crazy ball, as everyone does, but her feelings and behavior were more appropriate to the situation.

The dichotomy in Karen's personality and performance has become more and more a thing of the past. The Karen whom friends, parents, and teachers now see and deal with is an integrated person who reflects a happier, more self-assured, more enthusiastic personality and who eagerly anticipates each day. She has learned to care for and respect herself and, in doing so, has become able to express love and admiration for those closest to her.

No Longer Feeling Stupid

Of no small significance is the fact that Karen's feelings of stupidity and inferiority rapidly dissolved as soon as there appeared a positive inner change secondary to the medication. Thus, she could accept her mother's affection and even return it. She no longer felt ugly, stupid, hopeless, and "unlovable."

Additional Insights

By reading similar positive case responses in chapters to follow, you will develop a feel for the many symptoms and their variations characterizing dyslexia. Clearly, for every improvement there preexisted a dyslexia-related symptom. And by listening to and recording spontaneously reported improvements, you will eventually discover the previously hidden hologram or portrait of dyslexia—just as I initially did, repeatedly stumbling onto new and fascinating unexpected dyslexic symptoms.

Here I have attempted to report Karen's dyslexic portrait, including her sleepwalking symptom. By realizing that sleepwalking stopped on medication, it became obvious that yet another symptom could be added to the evolving list of dyslexic characteristics. In a similar fashion, a whole series of unexpected findings were recognized when patients and/or their parents spontaneously reported favorable changes triggered by the medications—findings highlighted in the Preface and Self-Test.

For example, I discovered that many dreams of falling and flying, and even dizzy dreams, are shaped by dyslexic mechanisms. In fact, the rapid eye movements (REMs) used to track dream content are identical to the eye movements and mechanisms utilized by nondyslexics and dyslexics to track letters, words, and numbers. And both inner dream tracking mechanisms and outer word tracking mechanisms may be similarly disordered in dyslexics.

Levels of sleep may be altered by the dyslexic process and the response to medications. Thus, insomnia and sleepwalking may be reversed by restoring the patient to normal levels of alertness and sleep states. Individuals who thought they never dreamed will suddenly dream—and remember their dreams. And the dream content may even change or become more colorful.

Analyze my patients' responses very carefully. I hope you will find them helpful. Reason out your own inferences and conclusions, and match them to mine. Do not be misled by theories and theorists unless what is said corresponds to the clinical responses reported by dyslexic patients. *Remember:*

Dyslexic patients, not experts, ultimately define the dyslexic disorder. To date, most experts have mistakenly attempted to fit patients into preconceived theoretical molds, often with confusing and illogical results. Thus, for example, bright and articulate patients such as Karen were said to suffer from a primary language disorder stemming from an assumed dysfunction within their thinking-speaking brains:

- despite the fact that Karen had no language disorder; and
- despite the fact that her thinking-speaking brain was intact, and that neurological findings indicated only a dysfunction within her inner-ear system and its supercomputer, the cerebellum.

In retrospect, most of what I have read about dyslexia seems to be completely or significantly wrong. And the reason for this is tragically simple: Too much written and published information by traditionalists appeared to be based on biased and erroneous convictions that remained independent of clinical experience and validation.

By the end of the book I hope sufficient content will have been presented to enable you to clearly discern dyslexic fact from fiction. Also, any correct theory or explanation of dyslexia must explain each and every symptom characterizing all dyslexics—certainly all those presented within this and all other related books. To date, all prior theories have been what I call "part theories"—capable of explaining only very tiny "bites" or parts of the whole disorder.

III

Understanding Dyslexics

The only way really to understand dyslexia is to understand dyslexics. Reading, writing, spelling, and math scores do not really tell you what dyslexia or dyslexics are all about. In fact, these scores are often confusing to readers, parents, and patients—and especially testers. Although some scores are truly needed for educators to begin responsible remediation, I doubt that all the reported scores and numbers are helpful to anyone except the computer and test salesperson.

Clinicians, parents, and dyslexics all want to know the same things:

- What symptoms characterize the dyslexic disorder?
- What distinguishes these symptoms and this disorder from other types of learning-related disabilities?
- How can the symptoms and the disorder be most effectively, expeditiously, and accurately diagnosed and treated medically, educationally, psychologically, optometrically, and so on?

All of these questions will be answered by the time you finish this book. However, this chapter is primarily devoted to answering only the first question: *What symptoms characterize the dyslexic disorder?* By reading the case histories, you will develop a feel for the *quality* of the dyslexic disorder and its diffuse and varied symptomatic fallout. This *quality* has never before been clearly recognized and appropriately described. The reason for this failure is tragically simple.

Dyslexics cannot answer questions they have never been asked! They do not specifically and spontaneously relate and describe their many symptoms and feelings to testers only interested in obtaining numbers and scores. And sad to say, quantities and numbers—and the statistical analysis of these numbers—often fail to elucidate the quality and essence of the disorder tested. Indeed, the seemingly infinite variety of tests and scores (what I call the "test-and-number compulsion") actually masks and further complicates the recognition and definition of the disorder under investigation.

Numbers and scores most certainly have their place in science and research. They are most effective in biological research, especially where the subject tested cannot or does not verbally respond, as in the cases of apes, dogs, unconscious patients, and in chemical assays. But as scientists we should not rely *entirely* on numbers when attempting to understand the symptoms experienced by human beings who are desperately attempting to verbalize and clarify them.

Why not ask these patients what is wrong with them or how they feel? Let them tell you! Record the details in the same meticulous manner you would record their test scores. And when a pattern of symptoms emerges, ask more specific questions in order further to pin down and define this pattern. And behold: Much of the dyslexic disorder will develop and materialize before your eyes!

In other words, where possible, first learn the *quality* and essence of the disorder. Develop a feel for the scope of its symptomatic and variable fallout. Then obtain the needed scores and statistics to highlight and determine more closely the disorder's dimensions.

The numbers that have been used until now to characterize and define what has been commonly referred to as learning disabilities, dyslexia, attention deficit disorder (ADD), attention deficit–hyperactivity disorder (ADHD), and developmental delay have not been able to separate one disorder from another or one symptom from another. Indeed, these numbers have led to a dyslexialike scramble, serving no one except perhaps those attempting to deny their own scientific confusion and frustration.

Utilizing recorded cases and symptoms, I will sketch a simple nonnumerical concept of the dyslexic disorder that can explain and encompass every known symptom and mode of therapy characterizing dyslexia and its related overlapping disorders to date. Just remember: All prior theories of dyslexia were able to explain only severe degrees of only their reading disorder—and absolutely nothing else that was part and parcel of the dyslexic syndrome.

Stated another way, prior traditionalist theories defined dyslexia as a severe reading disorder due to a primary cerebral processing impairment in which one had to be two or more years behind one's peers or potential. And by mistakenly ignoring all reading-compensated dyslexics as well as excluding all other vital nonreading dyslexic symptoms (e.g., writing, spelling, math, memory, and so on) from their overly simplistic quantitative concept, by analogy the traditionalists unwittingly equated the incredible complexity of a human being with merely the size of the tip of one's nose. Amazing, but true!

I hope the following content will enable all readers to grasp the true depth and scope of the dyslexic panorama.

Katie

Katie, you are just too slow! You make the same stupid errors over and over again. Can't you remember the difference between a *b* and a *d* and the words *was* and *saw*?

And you still can't add or subtract correctly without using your fingers. You're not a baby: Don't act like one!

Katie's teacher yelled at her thoughtlessly. A dozen years later, a troubled teenager was brought to my office for psychiatric treatment. She could not think or talk about that day without crying.

Not much had changed for Katie over the years. She continued to feel stupid and ugly, despite a superior IQ and a very attractive appearance. She cried, "How smart can I be? I still can't tell my right from my left. I really must be a moron!" Unfortunately, she had overheard a noted colleague of mine diagnose her as having "minimal brain damage." "Not only am I stupid, but I am brain-damaged as well. How do you expect a moron to feel?"

Reported symptoms:

- directional difficulties, difficulty visually distinguishing letters

- memory instability recalling math facts
- difficulty knowing right and left
- smart but feeling dumb and ugly

The same colleague reported that Katie was clearly malingering—just wanting attention. Thus he wrote in his report: "When she mixed up *b* for *d*, I scolded her. She then quickly gave me the correct answer." Amazing, isn't it? Even Katie realized that the letter she saw was either a *b* or *d*. If it wasn't *b*, it had to be *d*.*

Jimmy

- Jimmy couldn't ride a bike, participate in sports, climb a fence, or climb a tree.
- He held a pencil tightly and awkwardly, as though he were holding on for dear life.
- He often lost his balance and fell. He frequently walked into walls and doors or tripped over his feet. "Klutzy" and "Clumsy" were his nicknames.
- Reading triggered headaches, dizziness, nausea, and stomachaches.
- Finger counting enabled him to add and subtract. When

*When I was in a psychiatric/psychoanalytic practice years ago, I would often receive referrals from clinicians who didn't believe in psychiatry. Invariably, I asked myself: Why are they referring this case to me? The answer was simple. They could not find a clear-cut medical explanation for the patient's symptoms. Accordingly, these physicians assumed the problem was not medical and so it had to be mental. So a complex and/or frustrating riddle was disposed of by *referral* to me.
- Invariably, I would reexamine every one of these patients medically and neurologically.
- Invariably, I found hidden medical determinants to the patients' so-called mental symptoms.

older, he would forget the multiplication tables as rapidly as he learned them.

- Jimmy avoided heights and sports. Elevators and escalators panicked him. Amusement rides and flying in planes led to disorientation. New and unfamiliar places made him clinging and fearful of becoming lost.
- Anxiety appeared to trigger bed-wetting.

When Jimmy turned fifteen, he was referred to me for psychiatric treatment because of depressive feelings and suicidal thoughts. When I first asked him what was wrong with him, he stated: "I'm just stupid and klutzy. The school says I have to accept these facts. And one of my teachers even thinks I am retarded. . . . So do I."

Reported symptoms:

- balance/coordination/rhythmic difficulties, including bed-wetting, and associated phobias
- motion and spatial/direction triggered fears
- psychosomatic symptoms
- depression due to the above and other factors

Karl

Karl cried continually from the day he was born. He was restless, colicky, and unable to sleep. Repeated examinations found him to be a "normal" infant. When he was six weeks old, his ears were found to be badly infected and his eardrums bulging, ready to burst. Surgery relieved this pressure. Suddenly gone were his crying, restlessness, and colicky symptoms. He slept peacefully. However, he remained hyperactive.

- Although Karl ran and climbed early, his speech developed very slowly.
- His words and sentences were poorly articulated and organized, rendering his speech difficult to understand.
- Although he was sharp and alert, his attention span was short and he was easily distracted.
- Despite normal hearing tests, statements and directions had to be continually repeated, slowly and one at a time.

Kindergarten and first grade intensified Karl's hyperactivity and distractibility. Teachers frequently complained that he didn't listen and that he left his seat and roamed around the room. He was forever squirming in his seat or moving about restlessly. At first Karl was ignored. Then he was teased, which provoked him to lose his temper and overturn chairs, desks, or anything else in his way.

Karl could not express or verbalize his feelings and thoughts. He preferred action to speech. Accordingly, his acting-out behavior was not really purposely antisocial; it merely reflected an emergency discharge of frustration by a child who could not verbalize what was really bothering and frustrating him.

By first grade Karl refused to attend school. He found it too confusing, frustrating, and humiliating. Psychologists believed him to be suffering from a school phobia and advised his parents that Karl's fear of leaving them was due to their overconcern and overpampering.

- Ignored by clinicians was the fact that Karl did not fear leaving his house.
- Ignored was the fact that Karl did not fear leaving his par-

ents. He merely feared the frustration and confusion triggered by the school situation.

- Overlooked by the school personnel was the fact that Karl could not handle reading, writing, spelling, drawing, and the many distractions of a classroom full of other children.
- Overlooked was the fact that Karl was not truly antisocial. He liked individuals but could only handle one at a time. He was not truly aggressive; he just had difficulty acknowledging and verbalizing his many frustrations.
- Overlooked was Karl's sensitivity to fluorescent lights. They confused and disoriented him while triggering severe degrees of anxiety and hyperactivity.

School phobia was the first of many diagnostic terms used by subsequent clinicians. Karl's diagnoses encompassed everything from school phobia and behavior disorder to minimal brain damage and even congenital aphasia.*

- No one recognized that Karl was dyslexic.
- No one realized that his behavior disturbances were merely part of the hyperactivity and distractibility or ADHD characterizing the dyslexic syndrome.
- No one knew that the speech disorder he suffered from was a consequence of his dyslexia. It was not an expression of a dysfunction in the thinking brain. It was certainly not aphasia. Rather, his scrambled auditory input interfered with his normal thinking-brain's processing capability. It was like trying to understand distorted radio or TV signals.

---

*Aphasia is a severe speech disorder in which disturbances of the thinking brain result in difficulty understanding the meaning of what is heard and/or difficulty formulating the meaning of words and thoughts one wishes to express.

- No one appeared to understand that underlying Karl's apparent bravado and "delinquentlike" acts were feelings of intense stupidity.

- No one suspected that these hidden but devastating feelings existed until they suddenly and dramatically materialized during psychiatric treatment.

- No one appeared to acknowledge that early diagnosis and treatment would have saved Karl and his parents a great deal of tragic suffering.

- No one had yet realized that ADD and dyslexia were overlapping syndromes, stemming from one and the same common denominator.* (See my book *Total Concentration* for more information.)

Laura

Laura was a gifted child. She spoke when she was six months old and conversed with adults when she was a year old. She knew her basic skills from watching *Sesame Street*. As a result, she skipped kindergarten, breezed through the first and second grades, and captivated everyone with bright and delightful ways. In the third grade, however, something happened: Laura seemed bored. And during the fourth grade her joy in school seemed to have vanished. She tried to avoid reading and writing assignments and showed no interest in classwork. Psychiatrist friends told her parents that Laura was spoiled, overpampered, overloved, and not sufficiently disciplined.

---

*My research had clearly indicated that over 90 percent of patients diagnosed as dyslexic have ADD or ADHD, and the reverse. This finding clearly suggests that these so-called separately defined and named disorders, dyslexia and ADD, are *one*.

Laura was diagnosed by me to be dyslexic. Fortunately, she responded successfully to medication. Laura regained her curiosity, confidence, and interest in school.

Laura was not the only one to benefit. Her parents, who were very much affected by their daughter's suffering, could never have held together as a happy, loving, caring family without a thorough understanding of Laura's symptoms and a way to treat them.

My insight into Laura's condition developed as I considered her symptoms and realized that she:

- Avoided reading because she skipped or reversed letters and words
- Perceived sentences to be slanted and, in order to compensate, used angulated reading postures that are generally considered to be careless or sloppy
- Could not keep her handwriting from drifting off the page, because the physical act of writing was dyscoordinated for her
- Frequently tripped and fell
- Turned in "sloppy" homework and kept her bedroom "messy" due to the same factors that resulted in her scrawled handwriting, awkward walking, and propensity for accidents
- Knew right from left only because she had learned at a very young age that she wrote with her right hand and wore her baby ring and watch on her left
- Feared leaving home and going to camp—fears related to her directional uncertainties, the same compass disturbance that earlier had her clinging to her parents and home
- Was susceptible to motion sickness, which in turn resulted in motion-related fears of elevators, escalators, planes, and so on
- Suffered from so-called psychosomatic headaches, dizziness,

and abdominal pains—symptoms triggered by motion-sickness mechanisms

- Was very hesitant and reserved with strangers because of her secret feelings of being overwhelmed, uncoordinated, or "klutzy"—that is, different!

To summarize, all of Laura's symptoms were intimately related to, and primarily determined by, her dyslexic disorder.

I arrived at my diagnosis of Laura when I discovered that *a youngster could begin school as a good reader yet still be dyslexic.* In other words a dyslexic need not be word-blind and often is not. The reading symptoms in dyslexics often reveal themselves only when there is an increase in the quantity of material to be read and when the print is smaller and closer together than usual, requiring an increase in reading speed and targeting accuracy, all of which happens in third grade.

Laura taught me that the reading process could be impaired in dyslexics who obtained normal or superior reading scores on tests. Although Laura reversed letters (such as *b* and *d*) and words (such as *was* and *saw*), and her reading tracking for sequential words was impaired, she somehow learned to rapidly skim and process the scattered visual targets she saw. In other words, she intuitively grasped the essence of what she skimmed; and she rapidly found answers to the test questions she initially read.*

---

*An article in the *New England Journal of Medicine* in January 1992, by S. E. Shaywitz and coauthors, confirmed that dyslexics improved their reading scores over time. Unfortunately, these researchers mistakenly concluded that dyslexia may not exist as "a discrete diagnostic entity." In other words, they mistakenly equated the total syndrome of symptoms called *dyslexia* with *only severe degrees of only one* of its highly variable and overdetermined parameters: severe reading-score impairment, also referred to as "dyslexia." And so, when they found that the reading-score symptom ("dyslexia") decreased or disappeared with time, they erroneously concluded that the disorder—dyslexia—also disappeared and thus was not a "discrete diagnostic entity." (See discussion in Appendix E, "Letters to the Editor.")

When an accurate diagnosis led the way to Laura's treatment, I felt that all my prior efforts, determination, and years of research had rewarded me in full with the recovery of this one special patient. Laura's case was not the initial impetus for my original studies, but she has been a most important patient, and one of many to benefit from my research. Laura is my daughter. And she is now a pediatrician helping other children as she was helped, and as she wanted to be helped by others.

Joy

Joy mastered the first few years of school effortlessly. But suddenly, she developed a paralysis of her limbs due to infectious mononucleosis. She became dizzy. Her concentration became foggy. Fortunately, her paralysis was overcome, but her immunity system had been impaired. This resulted in repeated viral and strep ear and throat infections, which further lessened Joy's ability to concentrate and tolerate frustration. At the same time, her sensations of dizziness and motion sickness intensified. She began to reverse and misplace letters and words when she read, spelled, or wrote—thus becoming disinterested in studying and schoolwork. She recalled being extremely dizzy and nauseated while taking achievement and IQ tests; nevertheless, she scored in the ninety-ninth percentile.

Joy's parents were advised by physician friends and teachers that Joy was overloved and indulged as well as manipulative. Whether this was true was beside the point. How could parental concern and love create word reversals and other symptoms of dyslexia?

They cannot, of course. The fact that dyslexic symptoms are found to be present in pampered, neglected, and even abused children leads to the important conclusion that the presence of dyslexic symptoms is independent of child-rearing patterns. In fact, I discovered this disorder to be dependent upon hidden physical factors that lie in the inner-ear system and its super-computer, the cerebellum—the lower brain of humans and the highest brain in animals.

Understandably, Joy's parents were very concerned. They knew that their daughter's problems were caused not by their concern and love but by repeated ear infections. Joy's difficulties—her impaired concentration, her word reversals—all sprang from middle-ear inflammations or infections that affected her inner-ear system, the system responsible for the fine tuning and coordination of all sensory input patterns and all body movements.

I placed Joy on medication, which initially led to an improvement in her *acquired* dyslexic symptoms. Also, I suggested that she have her tonsils and adenoids removed and that draining tubes be placed in her ears, a procedure used to eliminate and prevent fluid accumulation. Happily, these surgical procedures successfully eliminated her repeated ear and throat infections.

Joy, too, is my daughter. She is now obtaining a doctorate in psychology, again attempting to help others as she was helped.

Studies I conducted over the past few years clearly indicated that well over 95 percent of similar cases responded to these surgical procedures as well as my daughter did. Unfortunately, many physicians were previously unwilling to perform these simple surgical procedures, preferring to wait until children "outgrow" their susceptibility to ear infections and tonsilitis. However, too many cases do not outgrow this tendency, just as they do not outgrow their dyslexic tendencies.

What happens while we wait? Children remain vulnerable to repeated and chronic ear and throat infections. They miss school and fall behind in their subjects. They are unable to socialize or participate in sports. Their immune systems become increasingly impaired. They develop allergic reactions to antibiotics and other medications. And they are predisposed to permanent hearing loss and/or inner-ear disorders resulting in dizziness, motion sickness, and a host of dyslexic symptoms.

It appears that medical opinions often swing from one extreme to another. When I was a child, all one had to do was open one's mouth for tonsils and adenoids to be removed. Until recently, one practically has to be on one's deathbed before they are taken out. Needless to say, these extremes make no sense.

To return to Joy's case: After her surgery she felt stronger, but this did not last long. Her dizziness returned, as did some of her previous symptoms. In addition, she developed severe, chronic headaches—at times migraines. The medications no longer seemed effective. At first I thought her body had developed an immunity to them, but something else was wrong.

Joy walked in a slumped fashion and appeared depressed. She could not overcome her feeling of fatigue. Her concentration and memory functions dwindled significantly, from superior to frighteningly poor. She developed facial, neck, back, and leg muscle spasms.

She experienced pain in her ears, which persisted even after the draining tubes were removed. We returned to the ear, nose, and throat doctor, who claimed that the procedures he had performed were successful. Nothing appeared to be wrong with her ears.

Then, one summer, Joy's mysterious symptoms were accidentally diagnosed while she was a junior counselor at camp. She noticed that one of the other counselors missed camp periodically and that this counselor's personality varied from time to time, just as her own did. At times the counselor was "sweet as sugar," and at other times she was irritable.

Joy discovered that the counselor had severe migraines, which were responsible for the fluctuations in her mood and behavior. Upon talking to her, Joy learned that the counselor had temporomandibular joint syndrome (TMJ). Further questioning revealed that the counselor had symptoms identical to her own. Joy's diagnosis with TMJ was later confirmed by radiological tests.

In retrospect I realized that Joy's TMJ syndrome was caused, or significantly intensified, by the clamps that had kept her jaws widely separated during her tonsil and adenoid surgery. It seemed ironic that the surgery needed to save her ears and health had inadvertently resulted in a disorder with symptoms similar to the ones it was intended to alleviate.

In addition, the dentist treating her TMJ and I independently but simultaneously realized that Joy also had symptoms suggesting the presence of an underactive thyroid, or hypothyroid, condition. She also required treatment to correct and compensate for both her TMJ syndrome and thyroid disorder. As a result, the majority of her symptoms were alleviated by means of this multidimensional therapeutic approach.

Joy's case clearly highlights the fact that dyslexia may be *acquired or intensified* by mononucleosis or ear infections. Moreover, dyslexia, a highly misunderstood and oversimplified disorder, may be complicated by other hidden coexisting disturbances such as TMJ, thyroid disease, diabetes, and hypoglycemia. And all disorders must be recognized and treated for best results. Clearly, my daughters, Joy and Laura, did not need tutoring.

An Important Lesson in Simple Reasoning

Bonnie: A Previously Overlooked Dyslexic in Psychotherapy

Bonnie was twenty-nine years old when she initially consulted me for severe depressive feelings and phobias—a fear of becoming ill and dying as her mother did, a fear of traveling and new places, and a fear of heights. Also, she had "heard voices" intermittently during her entire life. This symptom had led psychiatrists to misdiagnose her as a schizophrenic, although I recognized her to have hysteria.*

Bonnie has two children. Following each childbirth her symptoms had intensified so much that she required hospitalization.

I came to realize that Bonnie's depressions, fears of illness and dying, and even her voices were all related to her mother's having died immediately following Bonnie's birth.

Bonnie felt extremely guilty about her mother's death. Had she not been born, she believed her mother still would have been alive. Her "voices" were found, upon analysis, to be related to her mother's absence. She had always thought about her mother and conversed with her while daydreaming, forever imagining what her mother would say in this situation or that. She could actually hear these daydreams—just as people with eidetic imaging can see things within their minds in photo graphic detail: Bonnie's "voices" reflected her need to regain

*Hysteria is a relatively mild and psychoanalytically treatable emotional disorder in which the symptoms are determined by unconscious needs and wishes. By comparison, schizophrenia is a severe emotional disorder of unknown origin and uncertain prognosis ("Auditory Hallucinations in a Case of Hysteria," by Levinson. *British Journal of Psychiatry*, vol. 112, no. 482, January 1966, pp. 19–26).

and maintain contact with her beloved but lost mother. Thus, her symptom reflected an unconscious attempt at neurotic compensation rather than a dysfunction reflecting a psychosis.

Following the birth of each of her children, Bonnie became increasingly depressed, anxious, and fearful. Her conscience became increasingly harsh and intense during these episodes. Clearly, Bonnie was suffering from hysteria, not schizophrenia.

Upon careful questioning I found Bonnie had been a poor student as a child, had had difficulty reading, writing, and spelling, and had been a stutterer. She also admitted to always having felt stupid and unattractive. The stuttering still persisted, as did her feelings of inferiority. I initially assumed that all of Bonnie's symptoms were emotionally determined, and treated them all psychotherapeutically. Her treatment was successful. She eventually raised three children, survived two surgical procedures without emotional relapses, returned to college, and earned master's and doctorate degrees. And she no longer felt stupid and ugly.

Only in retrospect did I recognize that Bonnie's early academic and speech difficulties, as well as her fears of heights, elevators, needles, illnesses, new places, and driving, were manifestations of a physically determined inner-ear disorder—dyslexia. I came to realize that her feeling stupid and ugly were as much determined by her dyslexic disorder as by her hysterical disorder. Even her "voices" appeared to have a physical codetermination. Dyslexic children occasionally compensate for their memory disorder by developing eidetic* imagery. Bonnie's voices had had a compensatory eidetic quality. In fact, many a dyslexic can actually hear the sound of the words they are reading—otherwise the meaning

---

*Eidetic pertains to the faculty of clearly visualizing objects and events that one has actually seen or heard or has thought up.

doesn't sink in. They use a compensatory form of auditory imagery to compensate for impaired or delayed visual processing.

When I first began treating Bonnie psychotherapeutically, I had not yet recognized the physical basis of her many symptoms. I had been treating her *only* psychiatrically, not physically or holistically. I did not yet appreciate the full significance and wisdom of Sigmund Freud's remark that underlying and codetermining all emotional symptoms is a physical basis. This basis he called "somatic compliance"—meaning that the quality or shape of symptoms is significantly determined by the body's physical compliance to mental or emotional conflicts. Unfortunately, many less gifted and less experienced clinicians have failed to recognize and implement the true genius underlying Freud's remarks.

Randy

Randy, married and the mother of two children, is a thirty-four-year-old homemaker. She came to see me for psychiatric help because she was subject to mounting fears and anxieties.

Randy was literally becoming unable to function. She described how, in a grocery store or supermarket, she would suddenly experience severe anxiety, dizziness, a pounding heart, and waves of nausea as she walked up and down the aisles. Cans, cartons, and even people would merge crazily, spinning and blurring into space. It was like a nightmare. If shopping alone, she would race out of the store.

Soon, Randy became fearful of driving her car, especially when she was alone. Other fears appeared and mushroomed— fears of heights, escalators, water, and trains. As a child, she had suffered from motion sickness; suddenly that reappeared.

In the course of her psychoanalysis I learned that, as a child,

Randy had been a slow learner and unable to read until the fourth grade, and had therefore felt stupid and inept. After high school she attended college because her mother had pushed her to do so, but she had been a mediocre student. It was in graduate school that she bloomed academically, achieving a 4.0 average. She was a very late, late bloomer.

Randy confided to me that she really understood math for the first time only when she began to teach her first-grade class. She also realized that her desire to teach children mirrored her own desire to be taught how to read, write, spell, and do math.

Randy's anxieties and phobias were eventually discovered to be caused by a fascinating array and interplay of physical and emotional forces. Her agoraphobia* was due in part to her fear of becoming dizzy and losing her balance with nothing or no one to hold on to, and partly to her inward desire to leave a husband she did not love. Her other phobias were found to be caused by inner-ear mechanisms required to process motion- and visual-related sensory signals. Her inner-ear–related dyslexic symptoms caused her to feel dumb and inept despite her academic degrees.

In a sense, even Randy's marriage was determined by her dyslexic disorder and the resulting emotional scarring. She had married a man she did not love, simply because he felt her to be smart and tolerated her "crazy" and "stupid" fears.

---

*Agoraphobia is a fear of walking across large, open spaces. Since recognizing the crucial relationship between phobias or anxiety disorders and the inner ear, I have written several research papers on the subject, as well as a book called *Phobia Free*. Inasmuch as hidden forms of dyslexia and related inner-ear symptoms predispose individuals to anxiety, mood, behavior, psychosomatic-like and body-image symptoms, it stands to reason that a majority of patients seeking psychological help should be medically tested for this hidden inner-ear disorder.

IV

A Simple but Comprehensive Concept of Dyslexia and Its Treatments

I will now sketch a commonsense—and proven—concept of the mechanisms characterizing and defining dyslexia. This concept will easily and naturally account for all the symptoms voiced by my patients, past and present. Moreover, it will prove immeasurably helpful in accounting for all the symptomatic improvements resulting from medications as well as other therapies. By carefully reading the various mental, educational, emotional, behavioral, and physical characteristics responding to medication (Chapter V), you will easily see and understand the many different mechanisms responsible for and determining the complex, multidimensional disorder called dyslexia.

This conceptual sketch of dyslexia is the latest that I developed, and is the one I currently use successfully with my patients. I hope you, too, will benefit from it. As you will soon realize, this unique concept has led for the very first time to new and successful methods of diagnosis, treatment, and prevention—and will eventually lead to a cure.

Four Major Inner-Ear Functions

Dyslexia, as defined by the various symptoms highlighted in this book, is due to an inner-ear dysfunction. Simply stated, the inner ear and its supercomputer—the cerebellum—serves several crucial functions, including these four:

1. The Guided-Missile Function

It acts as a guided-missile computer system, guiding our eyes, hands, feet, and various mental and physical functions in time and space. Thus, a disorder within this system may deflect our eyes while they reflexively and automatically fixate and sequentially track letters, words, and sentences while we read. The dyslexic's reading process is characterized by letter, word, and sentence fixation and tracking difficulties, requiring compensatory slow reading, finger pointing, the use of cards, etc. Moreover, the resulting visual scrambling will trigger the insertion and omission of words, the illusion of new words formed from word parts separated by unseen distances, and so on. Frequently words will be experienced as blurred or in movement, requiring compensatory blinking and squinting in order to restabilize the drifting input.

Inasmuch as the tracking is coarse and jerky, the reading process becomes tiring and unpleasant. Often these dyscoordinated or clumsy eye movements, mistakenly referred to as apractic, keep retargeting the same words in a sentence over and over again—a process clinically labeled *ocular perseveration.*

If the hand holding a pen is misguided in space, our writing will look "discombobulated" or "dysgraphic." Most often the writing will drift off the horizontal when utilizing unlined paper and if concentration and effort are not used to extraordinary degrees.

If our hands, our feet, or our speech mechanisms are not accurately guided in space and time, a wide range of dyscoordinated, clumsy acts or "Freudian slips" will occur ("dyslexic slips"). And if our speech mechanisms become stuck on a word and unable to let go, stuttering may occur.

2. The Sensorimotor Fine-Tuning Function

The inner-ear system also acts like the vertical and horizontal knobs on a television set. It fine-tunes all motor (voluntary and involuntary) responses leaving the brain and all sensory responses coming into the brain.

If voluntary motor responses leaving the brain are improperly fine-tuned, one's motor acts become dyscoordinated and imbalanced, resulting in delayed speech; impaired ability to walk; difficulty tying shoelaces, buttoning buttons, zippering zippers, and holding and using writing implements; and speech disturbances, such as slurring and stuttering.

If involuntary motor responses leaving the brain are improperly fine-tuned, then toilet-training delays may arise, as well as such symptoms as bed-wetting and -soiling. When reflexes are impaired, difficulties with sleeping, sucking, swallowing, breathing, and even blowing one's nose may occur. Indeed, even chemical and postural reflexes may be disturbed, resulting in tendencies toward hypoglycemia and orthostatic hypotension (low blood pressure upon sitting up or standing), of previously unexplained origin.

If the sensory input to the brain is improperly fine-tuned,

then this input will drift or scramble. The thinking brain, however bright, receiving drifting, scrambled inputs will have difficulty with interpretation, memory, and concentration. If the drift is 180 degrees, then reversals occur, both for incoming and outgoing signals.

Even a genius watching or listening to a drifting input (or a drifting TV channel) will have great difficulty remembering and concentrating on the picture seen and heard. Variations in the drifting will account for variations in the degree of clarity. Some segments will be seen and heard clearly while others will be only partially seen and heard, and others will be completely blurred out, resulting in compensatory guessing and even illusions.

If this very same genius is asked about the content of what she observed on the TV show, she will not be able to answer too many questions. And if this genius is unaware that her difficulties are due to the drifting of the TV's image, then she will instinctively feel stupid, regardless of her IQ. *In fact, the smarter she is, the more frustrated she will become and the dumber she will feel.*

Most of the time, compliments make bright dyslexic kids feel worse. These kids know they are not able to grasp, remember, and reproduce information as well as their classmates or as well as their instincts and feelings tell them that they should. Reassuring these children that they are smart when they instinctively feel frustrated and stupid often makes them feel worse. They feel they are being lied to in order to make them feel better, to make them feel less stupid. Thus, they conclude that they really *are* dumb; otherwise, the compliments and reassurances would not be necessary.

In other words, bright dyslexics are instinctively aware of the many difficulties they have, and therefore react with feelings of stupidity. *Although reassurance does not reverse feeling stupid—and, in fact, may seem to heighten it—it is nevertheless crucial because it keeps dyslexics going and striving until compensation occurs—if it occurs.**

Criticism, on the other hand, is felt very deeply, for it reinforces their gut feelings of stupidity, resulting in a deeper sense of inadequacy.

How can a teacher help but view these children as "stupid," "indifferent," and "defiant," especially if the teacher is viewing and judging them as if from the back side of the TV set? If, by analogy, the teacher does not see or hear the drift, he or she will naturally assume that the child is watching and listening to a simple, clear TV picture. Thus, the teacher cannot comprehend the resulting errors and learning disabilities. Moreover, the child watching and listening to the drifting TV channel will lose her concentration and become distracted and restless. She'll want to get away from this frustrating input and change TV channels—to those coming in clearly.

By analogy this experience is very similar to how one reacts to motion sickness. Instinctively one wants to eliminate the input, either by fight or flight.

---

*The only way to really enable stupid-feeling but bright dyslexics to feel as smart as they are is to offer them a clear and comprehensive scientific explanation for their many and varied symptoms. If they can truly comprehend the physiological link between the inner ear and the dyslexic syndrome, they won't feel as guilty as before. They won't have to blame themselves, their parents, teachers, sibling, peers, or others.

To facilitate this explanation, I cowrote *The Upside-Down Kids* and *Turning Around—The Upside-Down Kids*. Adult dyslexics unable to read *Smart but Feeling Dumb*, as well as kids, can now listen to or read the novelistic dialogue in the above books and *naturally grasp* the mechanisms responsible for each and every symptom characterizing the dyslexic syndrome. This insight is absolutely vital in any attempt to psychologically reverse the deadly feelings of guilt and shame that characterize most bright dyslexics. Only the exceptional dyslexic is able to escape these tragic feelings without extra help.

If a child can't play hooky or change the channel in school by means of distracting mechanisms, he'll fight. If his anger and fight are inwardly directed, he'll become depressed and give up. If his anger is acted out, he'll be viewed as a behavior problem with disruptive tendencies. Children will sometimes unconsciously behave in a manner that provokes authorities to suspend or expel them from school, thus attempting to get out of a most frustrating and humiliating situation. At other times, underlying guilt associated with feeling stupid and inadequate will trigger mechanisms that invite punishment and consequently alleviate guilt—a most unfortunate cycle. If, on the other hand, a child tries to avoid the frustrating drifting channel altogether, he'll be labeled as a "school phobic."

In order to understand all the variations and complexities of the dyslexic disorder, one has to carry the TV analogy a few steps further.

Picture the brain as a giant TV set with millions and millions of specific channels. Imagine each separate event as being independently processed on its own wavelength or TV channel. Thus, one channel may drift while another remains fine-tuned. One channel may drift mildly while another is completely blurred out. One channel may drift vertically while another drifts horizontally. One channel may drift from right to left while another drifts from left to right. On and on the possibilities go, accounting for the diverse combinations of symptoms seen from patient to patient and from sample to sample.

Furthermore, the fine-tuners may vary in function from moment to moment, depending on a series of known and unknown variables and circumstances. Spontaneous variations in the fine-tuning mechanisms may result in corresponding variations in symptoms from time to time, most often beyond the individual's control. Allergies, seasonal influences, foods, sugars, dyes, even changes in humidity, altitude, and barometric pressure may trigger signal-drifting, accounting for regression and symptomatic changes.

3. The Compass Function

The inner ear is also a compass system. It reflexively tells us spatial relationships such as right and left, up and down, front and back, east and west, and north and south. If this compass system isn't working efficiently, one must use one's brain to devise such consciously directed compensatory methods as wearing a ring or a watch on one hand, or recalling which hand has a scar or was broken or was used to pledge allegiance.

The inner-ear/cerebellum tells us where all our body parts are in space and time as well as integrating all these signals into a hologram called "body image." Needless to say, disturbances in this scheme result in body- and self-image distortions or negative illusions, explaining the reason this impairment often triggers feeling dumb, ugly, and so on, regardless of normal or above-average IQ and outer physical appearance.

This compass system directs all body functions: sensory, motor, speech, thought—even biophysical patterns. Moreover, one sequence may be misdirected or scrambled while another remains unaffected or compensated for and is seemingly unaffected.

4. The Timing and Rhythmic Function

The inner ear also acts as a timing mechanism, setting rhythms to motor tasks. A disturbance within this system may result in difficulty in learning to tell time and in sensing time. Frequently, dyslexic children do not know *before* from *after* and can't sense whether a minute, an hour, or several hours have gone by. Accordingly, dyslexic individuals may become "compulsively" late or early. Speech timing may be off, resulting in slow or rapid talkers and even dysrhythmic talkers, or stutterers.

The inner-ear system—better yet, the cerebellum, or brain of animals—enables us to *rapidly* process and maintain the sequence of all sensorimotor signals by adaptively slowing down or inhibiting the rate of transmission speeds. A failure in this and related functioning will result in, and thus readily explain, the series of typically reported speed and motion illusions. Thus, for example, dyslexics typically report seeing cars moving *too* fast, hearing speech *too* rapidly to interpret normally without extra time or repetition, experiencing themselves and other stationary objects in motion or vibrating (oscillopsia), and so on. A similar failure to regulate the speed and order of motor signals will often result in difficulties with rapid or reflex balance and coordination tasks, speech and writing included.

In many ways, these timing or temporal disturbances are analogous to the spatial illusions in which dyslexics report seeing objects smaller or larger or reversed—symptoms called *micropsia, macropsia,* and *reversals,* respectively. Accordingly, *I came to view dyslexia as an inner-ear/cerebellar-determined spatial-temporal and sensorimotor dysfunction in equilibrium with compensatory vectors.*

Any combination of these inner-ear functions may be impaired. Similarly, any mechanism may be compensated for, or even overcompensated for. By recognizing that the impaired mechanisms underlying dyslexic symptoms are in a dynamic equilibrium with compensatory factors, a concept of symptom formation evolves in which each symptom is viewed as a resultant of opposing forces, dysfunctioning versus compensatory. If gifted functions are also taken into consideration, as are self-corrective versus regressive forces, then we have truly arrived at the concepts needed to understand dyslexics and their fascinating disorder.

The above-described inner-ear mechanisms and concepts have resulted in the first comprehensive explanation of *why* and *how* the various theories about dyslexia and their corresponding therapies, including my own, work or do not work.

Medical Treatment

In discovering that dyslexia is due to a dysfunction of the inner-ear system, and realizing that anti–motion sickness medications helped strengthen the inner ear's capacity to handle motion input and balance/coordination output (thus alleviating the various sensorimotor symptoms characterizing motion sickness), I reasoned that these very same medications may indeed improve the ability of the inner-ear system to fine-tune and process the *total* sensory input as it does the motion input, and the *total* motor output as it processes the balance and coordination difficulties noted in motion sickness. Indeed, this reasoning was clearly and decisively validated when dyslexics were successfully treated with a variety of anti–motion sickness and related medications, and their favorable responses were carefully recorded. A series of typical medication responses will be presented in the following chapter, and the varied sensori-motor improvements will be noted.

The wide range of expected and unexpected improvements due to my medical treatment more than justifies my theory of the inner-ear system as the fine-tuner for the brain's entire sensory input and motor output.

Now that you better understand why and how various medications I use help dyslexics, you must be curious about the mechanism underlying the favorable responses reported by allergists and nutritionists, occupational therapists, optometrists, psychologists and psychiatrists, chiropractors, dentists, and educators. Until now, most theories unwittingly confused and reversed hidden dyslexic causes with the resulting symptomatic effects. For example, the emotional symptoms and poor self-image triggered by or resulting from the previously hidden dyslexic process were mistakenly assumed to be the cause of dyslexia. And the resulting reading and speech symptoms triggered by the underlying inner-ear dysfunctioning in dyslexia were mistakenly thought to be part of a primary language disorder of cerebral-cortical or thinking-linguistic origin.

Clearly, an understanding of why various therapies work or do not work will significantly contribute to every professional's ultimate aim: a meaningful, multidisciplinary, and interdisciplinary cooperative approach. It is anticipated that this understanding will lead to new and better ways of helping dyslexics, regardless of the professional's title or the name of the therapy.

Nutritional Treatment

Inasmuch as dyslexia was found to be caused by an inner-ear disturbance, and in view of the fact that niacin, related B vitamins, and minerals were reported to sometimes improve inner-ear–related symptoms, the findings of nutritionists in dyslexia became readily understandable.

Nutritionists have published reports of improvement in dyslexic symptoms when vitamins and minerals are appropriately used. Other researchers have found that niacin, related B vitamins, and minerals may improve vertigo or dizziness resulting from certain inner-ear disorders, especially Ménière's disease. Ben F. Feingold, a noted allergist, recognized that sugars, dyes, and various other allergenic substances *may* aggravate such dyslexic symptoms as hyperactivity and distractibility. Accordingly, the elimination of these substances leads to a corresponding improvement in symptoms. In my experience, allergies merely magnify or intensify dyslexic symptoms. They typically do not cause dyslexia—unless the allergic attack is of a severe enough magnitude to damage inner-ear mechanisms and structures.

Generally speaking, any harmful process or substance, whether stress-related, allergic, metabolic, infectious, or toxic in nature, may impair or disrupt inner-ear functioning, aggravating a dyslexic disorder.

Occupational and Optometric Treatment

Occupational therapists and optometrists have reported academic as well as coordination improvements when dyslexics perform various motion-related and/or eye-training exercises.

And other therapists have noted that conditioned inhibition of old or primitive reflexes, and the facilitation of adaptive reflexes, result in enhanced inner-ear/cerebellar functioning. Since the inner-ear system controls all body and eye movements as well as all reflexes and motion-related activities, and in view of the fact that practice leads to improvement in the specific motor task practiced, it seems reasonable to assume that practicing motor and reflex activities could result in an improvement in the underlying inner-ear/cerebellar mechanisms governing them. However, one must still account for the reported academic improvements when only motor exercises are performed. In other words, how and why will a child read, write, and concentrate better if she is given eye exercises or asked to participate in various balance and coordination or reflex tasks? The answer is not very difficult to figure out if one goes back to my previously described concept of dyslexic mechanisms and functioning.

Transfer of Function: Specific Versus Generalized Improvement

If, indeed, repetitive motor tasks improve underlying inner-ear coordination mechanisms, and if we assume that this improvement extends to or is transferred to neighboring inner-ear–modulating sensory and related concentration, cognitive, and language-related circuits or channels, then we can readily explain the generalized improvements that sometimes occur when specific "TV" circuits are strengthened by repetition, practice, or conditioning.

Athletics Improve Concentration and Cognition

Fortunately, transfer of functional improvements to neighboring circuits does occur, at least in certain contexts. In my practice I've repeatedly noted the existence of an initially puzzling and strange phenomenon: Dyslexic athletes often do best academically when in training, despite the short study time they have. Upon termination of their sports activities, due to either a changing season or an injury, a significant number of athletes report a corresponding decrease in their concentration, memory, and overall academic functioning. On the other hand, clinical observations suggest that visual stimulation may generalize and improve auditory, concentration, and even motor functioning. And the same transfer of improvement may occur when either auditory or concentration or motor channels are enhanced via conditioning therapies.

At first glance, one might mistake this correlation as an excuse conjured up by athletes to justify their training time. However, this was not the case, for most often it was their parents who reported this fascinating but puzzling correlation. It therefore appeared that sports activities and exercises resulted in a transfer of function to neighboring underlying inner-ear circuits, which in turn resulted in an academic improvement. Cessation of practice led to a regression in underlying inner-ear/cerebellar-determined functioning, and the transfer of function was in turn eliminated or wiped out. The unexpected observation that physical exercise in dyslexics may result in increased mental capacity is in accord with the adages "Practice makes perfect" and "Sound body, sound mind."

Conditioning experiments in humans and animals follow a

very similar pattern. If not continuously reinforced, conditioned functions and improvements disappear with time.

Over my long research career, I have repeatedly tried to understand and explain seemingly paradoxical data. I have learned that confusing events—or events occurring contrary to my expectations—invariably have a significant and important explanation if enough time is spent looking for this explanation. Most often the resulting solution to apparently contradictory or puzzling data provides us with general insights that would not emerge if confusing or contradictory data are denied or swept under the scientific "rug." As a result of this observation, I have disciplined myself to record and explain contradictions or criticism. When criticism is valid and constructive, surmounting it carries research a significant step forward. When criticism is destructive, it points out hidden flaws in the critic—flaws of which the critic and his audience are most often unaware, once again highlighting areas requiring additional attention and explanation.

The analysis of flaws, in oneself or in one's critics, has provided me with answers crucial to solving the riddle of dyslexia and dyslexic research. As a result, I have devoted Chapter 13 in *A Solution to the Riddle Dyslexia* to the investigation and analysis of this phenomena, and I have completed a book on the same subject: *A Scientific Watergate—Dyslexia* (1994).

Chiropractic and Dental Treatment (TMJ)

Patients have occasionally reported to me some symptomatic improvements arising from chiropractic manipulation and/or dental corrections of their temporomandibular joint (TMJ) syndrome. Needless to say, these observations are as valid as any other type and must be accounted for rather than "criticized" away. It is well known that many a dyslexic will tilt his head, neck, and body in order to read, write, and concentrate better. The neck is an important integration point for the inner-ear circuitry. Perhaps the chiropractic adjustment of these and other positions serves a similar purpose to that performed instinctively and reflexively by dyslexics from within.

Dental problems affecting the temporomandibular joint may often lead to headaches, dizziness, impaired concentration, and dyslexialike functioning. To explain these symptoms, I have assumed that an inflammation or misalignment of the temporomandibular joint may be transferred to the neighboring inner-ear system, thus either mimicking or aggravating dyslexic symptoms.

Educational Therapy: How It Works and Fails

Educational therapy is as complex as it is crucial. Specific memory functions are characteristically impaired in dyslexia. Thus, repetition of specific inputs is crucial if any improvement is to result. As stated earlier, specific channels of information invariably drift in dyslexics, leaving their victims relatively "blind," "deaf," and/or unable to "feel" certain inputs.

Thus, the task of educators is to find and utilize clear, open channels, as well as channels that drift very mildly, so that they may be used to impart crucial information. This teaching-learning process is very similar to what we do for the blind and deaf. However, in view of the fact that the majority of dyslexics are neither deaf nor blind, it is vitally important to improve the drifting channels via repetition or conditioning while simultaneously utilizing and stimulating open and especially "gifted" channels.

If a given sensory input drifts, its corresponding message to the thinking brain is received in a blurred, reversed, or scrambled fashion, rendering it difficult to remember and/or understand. Moreover, these drifting or blurred imprints are frequently wiped out or erased, as they are perceived as faulty. Repetition and conditioning frequently force an adaptation in which these drifting inputs are somehow finally "imprinted" or accepted for storage and memory retention. In other words, the underlying inner-ear–related mechanisms processing sensory inputs have been triggered to compensate in a manner similar to the way repetitive motor tasks force an underlying improvement in the specific circuits that process these tasks.

Just as repetitive motor tasks lead to an improvement in the underlying controlling mechanisms, as well as a possible transfer of function to neighboring circuits, the repetition and stimulation used in teaching with a multisensory approach (visual, auditory, tactile, proprioceptive) may also lead to both underlying and transferred functional improvements.

Tinted Lenses

Recently, the use of tinted lenses was recognized to be helpful in minimizing or compensating for the various reading symptoms characterizing dyslexia. Since inner-ear–dysfunctioning subjects may be *light-sensitive* or *photophobic* due to impaired light-wave–specific filtering, then it appears reasonable that tinted lenses may be as helpful for some dyslexics as is increasing the print size for others. Both color and increased target size enable the eye, as an inner-ear–directed missile, to hit its target better.*

Although many dyslexics benefit from magnified, darker, and colored print, some dyslexics find smaller print with shorter spacing better. This seemingly paradoxical observation led to the insights that the "dyslexic" eye may not be able to accurately and efficiently let go of big, dark, or colored targets and normally traverse larger spaces in order to fixate the next letter or word in a reading sequence.

Until my research, each therapeutic approach had its own corresponding theory. However, I have tried to harmonize and integrate the successes and failures of all treatment techniques with those of my own, so that patients and professionals will have a choice of which combination of therapies may best suit specific needs. And I have saved the complex medical (neurologic *and* psychiatric) theories and treatment approaches for last.

Psychotherapy

Until very recently, psychoanalysts, psychiatrists, and related professionals believed child-rearing and emotional disturbances were responsible for the many learning, emotional, and behavioral symptoms characterizing dyslexics. Consequently, a host of very specific subtheories and psychological mechanisms were formulated in order to account for each of the many

---

*I might add that I was one of the first and only doctors to initially recognize the benefit of this method. It fit perfectly with my inner-ear research and significantly tended to refute the language theory and origin of dyslexia. In other words, if dyslexia were due to a language disorder, then how could tinted lenses help? They couldn't! So the "traditionalists" solved their theoretical dilemma by refuting the benefit of the lenses.

dyslexic symptoms. Invariably, psychotherapy was advised in an effort to cure and/or alleviate the emotional factors deemed responsible for the dyslexic symptoms.

The fact that psychotherapy often alleviates a dyslexic's symptoms does not prove that psychological factors caused the disturbance. Indeed, psychotherapy merely alleviates the stress and the secondary feelings of stupidity, frustration, and helplessness—factors that further complicate and destabilize an already impaired fine-tuning system. My research has clearly indicated that the psychological symptomatic fallout of dyslexia is caused by a primary physiological disturbance within the inner-ear system. In other words, the surface psychological and behavioral symptoms are a reaction to dyslexic's physiological inability to function and compete normally.*

The traditional neurological approach to dyslexia was significantly guided by the mistaken belief that the disorder was due to a dysfunction within the cerebral cortex—the thinking, speaking brain, the seat of IQ. This "cortical theory" has led its clinicians to misdiagnose dyslexics as having minimal brain damage, minimal cerebral dysfunction, static encephalopathy, or cerebral developmental delay, despite the *complete absence* of tangible neurological findings supporting a diagnosis of cerebral dysfunction. Clinicians still clinging to this outmoded point of view openly admit that they can neither diagnose this disorder properly nor treat it medically.

Following a rather stereotyped but traumatizing diagnosis of cerebral dysfunction, the neurologic treatment most fre-

---

*I leave you, however, with an interesting preview. The inner-ear theory of dyslexia was further corroborated by the fact that the French-Russian cosmonauts became temporarily dyslexic at zero gravity—despite their use of inner-ear–enhancing treatment and conditioning techniques, which enabled the majority of astronauts to remain symptom- or dyslexia-free.

quently consists of *referrals*. Thus, patients are sent to any one or combination of therapists, often in a biased, helter-skelter fashion.

Indeed, the cortex, or thinking brain, *is* impaired in dyslexics. However, it is *only secondarily* impaired. For example, if our thinking brain, however bright and intact, receives a drifting, blurred, scrambled, or reversed input, it cannot deal effectively or efficiently with the content it receives, regardless of how capable it is under normal circumstances. Thus, even the cortical dysfunction theory of dyslexia is consistent with my conviction that dyslexia is due to an impaired inner-ear system. The "cortical" theorists merely confused the *primary* (inner-ear/cerebellar) *site* and cause with its *secondary* effects on cortical dysfunction.*

In retrospect, psychiatrists and neurologists were similarly misled. They confused the secondary fallout of the dyslexic disorder with its primary underlying cause in the inner ear. Psychiatrists mistakenly assumed the presence of a primary

---

*Indeed, this mistaken cortical theory has led most researchers and clinicians to erroneously define dyslexics as those two years or more below their peers or potential in reading scores. Not 1.9, or 1.8, or 1.6, or 1.3. As a result, the vast majority of dyslexics with mild, moderate, and even compensated or overcompensated reading scores are overlooked or misdiagnosed as lazy, indifferent, or neurotic, or are called by different names, depending on the severity of the leading symptoms recognized by teachers, psychologists, psychiatrists, or neurologists. Thus, it is commonplace for many a reading-compensated dyslexic with typical writing, spelling, math, memory, directional, speech, or other problems identical to those of reading-score–impaired dyslexics to be termed as having *dysgraphia* (poor writing), *dyscalculia* (poor math), *dyspraxia* (poor balance and coordination), *dysnomia and disarticulation* disturbances (speech and word-finding, including stuttering and stammering), or *attention deficit disorder with and without hyperactivity* (impaired concentration and high distractibility and activity levels). As previously reported, the traditional inability to recognize dyslexics with compensated reading scores also misled a group of outstanding Yale researchers to conclude erroneously (January 1992) that dyslexia may not exist "as a discrete diagnostic entity." This mistake is one of many that I've been attempting to correct for over twenty years (Refer to Appendix D).

psychological or mental dysfunction to explain the emotional and behavioral symptoms of dyslexia. And neurologists mistakenly assumed the presence of a primary cortical dysfunction to explain the presence of intellectual and speech symptoms in dyslexia. Each and every specialty unwittingly held on to its assumptions tenaciously.

Invariably, misdiagnosed patients are returned to educators with either no helpful information or misinformation. Thus, educators have been given a near-impossible task, one that requires Herculean effort, patience, and intuition. In the final analysis, educators were ultimately responsible for the education and treatment of the children and adults before them. They were forced to assume the total burden of the psychiatric, neurologic, pediatric, and optometric specialties, without the benefit of any meaningful medical understanding. They were forced to help, or attempt to help, millions and millions of dyslexics in the dark. Many accomplished wonders under the circumstances. Some were not equal to the task—leaving patients and their loved ones desperate for help and often despondent.

In retrospect, I realized that the frustration and despair I initially encouraged in my attempt to understand and help dyslexics led and even drove me to solve the many riddles characterizing dyslexia.

V

Responses to Medication

My aim in this chapter is to explain how and why medications and nutrients work to compensate for dyslexic symptoms. I encourage you to read through a series of progress reports containing the observations of parents, patients, and associated clinicians and educators. They detail and highlight the many varied responses of dyslexic patients and their symptoms to medications I recommend.

Favorable responses such as these occur approximately 75 to 80 percent of the time with the treatment program currently in use. Several years ago, when fewer medications and chemical compounds were known to me, the favorable response rate was closer to 50 percent. I hope this success rate will be closer to 100 percent several years from now, when newer inner-ear–enhancing medications are designed and used.

Factors That Determine Responses

To date, my studies clearly indicate that the yield of favorable responses to medication is completely *independent* of the severity of the dyslexic disorder. Over the past thirty-five years I have treated many thousands of dyslexic children and adults with medications. As a result, I have come to recognize the importance of *two* crucial factors determining favorable responses:

1. The pattern of signs and symptoms defining this disorder for any given patient
2. The success or failure of the body's immune system in filtering out or neutralizing the favorable effects of medicines

Patterns of Signs and Symptoms

There exists a complex series of clinically determined correlations suggesting that specific patterns of dyslexic signs and symptoms will best respond to correspondingly specific combinations of medications. These correlations were initially highlighted by trial-and-error investigations. In other words, large numbers of dyslexic patients were treated first with one type of medication, then another, then yet another, and finally with combinations of medications. The results of these studies were carefully recorded and analyzed. Eventually, correlations were established between patterns of dyslexic signs and symptoms and the medications to which these patterns responded most favorably. It is hoped that ongoing computer studies will help further define these therapeutic correlations, so that specific patterns of dyslexic functioning may be more predictably and therefore more efficiently treated.

Immune Response to Medication

There also exists a currently undefinable and unpredictable complex interaction between medicines and the specific ways the body's immune system reacts to them. Were all currently utilized medicines "accepted" by the body's immune system, the current response rate by dyslexics to medication would be closer to 100 percent than to 80 percent. Unfortunately, the body's defense mechanisms cannot always distinguish good from bad foreign substances and chemicals. As a result of this relatively "blind" filtering system, many potentially beneficial medicines are rejected and thus have no chance to help. On the other hand, medicines that do penetrate our defensive barriers may result in significant improvements.

Not infrequently, medications will work wonders initially. Then their therapeutic effect appears to decrease with time or when use is interrupted. It is as if the body develops a tolerance or resistance to the medications, rendering them ineffective. This observation is noted with many medications, not just the ones I use for the treatment of dyslexia. Often, changing the medication restarts the favorable response, clearly indicating the highly specific nature of the immune system and its associated rejection and filtering mechanisms.

The specificity of the immunity and filtering mechanisms is most apparent when observing how one medication will result in a favorable response while a host of very similar chemical structures will either have no effect or result in side effects ranging from irritability, tiredness, and moodiness to an intensification of the very dyslexic symptoms which the medication was intended to correct.

Not all responses to treatment are black-and-white or all-or-nothing. Most often there are gradations of responses. To explain these variable responses to medications, I was forced to assume that the degree of the favorable response is significantly dependent upon the degree to which the body's chemical defenses reject or accept the medication. Total rejection results either in no response or in side effects. Partial rejection results in partial improvement. Minimal or no rejection (i.e., acceptance) results in dramatic improvement.

Inasmuch as my success rate has greatly depended upon my becoming increasingly experienced with larger numbers of medications in more varied doses and combinations, it appears safe to assume that in the future there may be a 100-percent response rate. There is only one variable crucial to this prediction: Researchers must supply us with greater numbers of safe medications whose chemical structures are capable of improving the inner-ear dysfunction that has been demonstrated to be responsible for the dyslexic syndrome. The greater the number of medicines available, the greater the probability of finding one that will prove effective for any given patient.

What Medications Are Helpful in Treating Dyslexics?

Anti–Motion Sickness Substances

To date, I have found a wide-ranging series of chemical structures helpful, including anti–motion sickness medications, antihistamines, stimulants, antidepressants, antipanic drugs, and vitamins.* All these various chemical groupings were found to improve inner-ear functioning, albeit in different ways. I have come to view them all as "chemical fine-tuners" of the inner-ear system. Moreover, each chemical structure was found to fine-

---

*These specific chemical substances are listed in Appendix A.

tune a specific pattern of sensorimotor channels, suggesting that combinations of chemicals would result in the best possible response. Indeed, clinical studies have confirmed this prediction.

Readers are reminded that no medicine—even if it is available over the counter—should be taken without a doctor's advice. Side effects from the wrong medicine or dosage include irritability, tiredness, moodiness, and even intensification of dyslexic symptoms. Although some medications I use are sold over the counter, I advise parents not to treat children or themselves without the approval and supervision of an experienced physician. All medicines, however "simple," may have side effects—sometimes serious—particularly when taken in improper doses or at the same time as other medications. In fact, I do not know why some of these medications are even sold over the counter, inasmuch as they affect a significant number of wide-ranging brain functions. Such medicines should be prescribed and supervised by knowledgeable physicians. Antihistamines and seasickness medications have infinitely greater potency and effects than their names may imply. Their purchase and use should not be taken lightly! Furthermore, potentially effective medications may intensify dyslexic symptoms if the dose is too high for any given patient. Thus, vertigo, nausea, motion sickness, headaches, balance and coordination difficulties, moodiness, phobias, and bad temper may all intensify unless therapeutic doses are carefully controlled and monitored.

How Do I Determine the Best Doses?

Contrary to what may be written in medical journals, *The Physicians' Desk Reference,* and pharmaceutical books, my clinical experience in treating dyslexic children with antihista-

mines and seasickness medications clearly indicates that therapeutic doses are significantly independent of such factors as
age and weight. Each patient has his or her own specific sensitivity and reactivity to medications—*his or her own personal
threshold.* As a result, a sensitive adult may need only one-
eighth of the recommended dose, whereas a child may benefit
from twice the average dose.

Traditionally recommended doses are most often too high
for half the patients and not high enough for the other half.
For this reason I start all patients on approximately one-quarter
of the average therapeutic dose. Their responses are observed,
and the medication is either lowered or increased, depending
on the results.

How Do These Medications Work?

No one really knows the way or ways these medications work
in treating dyslexia. The simplest and probably the most accurate explanation is based upon the analogies I have used to
explain the dyslexic symptoms resulting from an inner-
ear/cerebellar dysfunction:

- If, indeed, the vertical and horizontal fine-tuners are malfunctioning in dyslexia, and
- Inasmuch as the medications result in significant improvements in dyslexic symptoms,
- It is reasonable to assume that the medications result in
  improved functioning of the inner-ear's "TV fine-tuners."

In other words the medications are assumed to help regulate and
fine-tune the "TV knobs" so that the motor output and sensory

input are better tuned, sequenced, and coordinated, leading to symptomatic improvement and eventual compensation.

I have repeatedly noted that each medication will result in a unique spectrum of symptomatic improvements for any given patient. The various dysfunctioning "TV channels" in dyslexia will be more receptive and responsive to some chemical adjusters than to others. This fascinating insight has led me to use combinations of medication in the treatment of dyslexia. By combining several different medications, one can obtain a greater degree of symptomatic improvement.

The medications used to treat reading, writing, spelling, and other symptoms in dyslexics were also found to improve the compass and timing mechanisms of the inner-ear system, thus accounting for the frequently observable improvement in direction, timing, and the ability to learn to tell time.

Since many of the medications often work rapidly and dramatically, and since Computerized Tomography (CT) scans and NMR's (Nuclear Magnetic Resonance) of dyslexic patients tend to show normal inner-ear structures, one might assume that the vast majority of dyslexics suffer from a neurotransmitter impairment rather than a structural defect.

Recent validating studies have noted cerebellar differences in dyslexics versus nondyslexics. However, some of these differences in my opinion may be secondary or compensating in nature vs. dysfunctioning—and so require more intensive investigation.

How Long Do Patients Have to Remain on Medication?

Most patients need to remain on medication somewhere between one and four years. Some patients require shorter periods of treatment, while others require longer periods. After one to four years of treatment, 80 percent of my successfully treated dyslexics will continue to do as well off the medication as they did on medication. In other words, their medical treatment clinically continues to facilitate compensation even when medication is stopped.

To explain these observations, I have assumed that chemical readjustment of the fine-tuning inner-ear mechanisms may become relatively stable or permanent when used for long enough periods of time. These chemical stabilizers do not cure the disorder; rather, it is as though they teach the body how to compensate for the underlying disturbance.

Similar observations are noted in all phases of medicine. For example, high–blood-pressure medication may sometimes lead to a continued correction of this symptom despite discontinued use of the medication. Dysrhythmias of the heart and brain are often compensated for by using medications for relatively short periods of time. Stopping the medication does not frequently lead to recurrence of the symptoms, even though a cure has not been effected.

Thus, childhood epileptics, for example, are helped by pharmaceutical treatment. We often stop treatment at a given age and point, without recurrence. Have we cured the underlying disorder, or has this disorder merely been compensated for?

For a medical concept to have the ring of truth and the weight of conviction, it should correspond and be compatible with other, similar observations. My observations regarding the medical treatment of dyslexic symptoms are in perfect harmony with the responses noted when other medical disorders are similarly treated with medication.

Should Medications Be Stopped on Weekends and Holidays?

Many clinicians treating children with attention deficit disorder (ADD) or attention deficit hyperactivity disorder (ADHD) advise that parents stop administering medications on weekends and holidays. This advice is predicated on the assumptions:

- That continued and uninterrupted use of the stimulants will invariably lead to a need for increased doses over time; and
- That continued use of these medications will result in an enhanced rate of medication rejection (i.e., the medications will stop working).

Since these assumptions were often given the weight of conviction by most researchers, I, too, began treating patients in a similar fashion. However, since the stimulants used for ADD or ADHD are anti–motion sickness medications and are also used by the astronauts before space flights, I've experimented and found that combinations of antihistamines and stimulants—provided they enhance inner-ear functioning—should be used in all patients where possible and where the combined effect is significantly greater than the use of one medication alone.

Over the past thirty-five years, I've gleaned an enormous amount of insight regarding the above use of interrupted treatment:

- Although some patients do require increased doses of stimulants or antihistamines over time, the vast majority of patients do not. Should we discontinue medications in

all patients, or just in those in whom the need for increased doses appears to be a problem?

- Although repeated interruption of dosages on weekends
  and holidays may reduce development of medication rejection mechanisms for some patients, my experience has
  shown that there is a higher frequency of rejection for
  those who frequently stop and then restart the medications. All too often, patients report losing all or some
  treatment benefits upon restarting dosages after an interruption following Christmas, Easter, or summer vacations. Indeed, this has been shown to be true for many
  who develop sensitivity reactions to drugs after repeatedly
  restarting them, especially with antibiotics and antidepressants.

These observations must be included in any treatment plan
so as to reduce the overall frequency of drug-resistant responses. Also, many patients do poorly while off medications
on weekends and holidays and suffer tremendously with the
return of all their symptoms. Accordingly, I have revised my
initial instruction to patients. I tell them to continue medications on weekends and holidays or to merely reduce the
dosages, unless there are reasons to do otherwise.

Do Patients No Longer Need
Medications at or After Puberty?

Parents or adult patients have often read or been told that
stimulant medications no longer work at or after puberty.
Nonsense!

Just ask or listen to some of what my dyslexic adults report.

Since I've always attempted to figure out what logical basis there might be to even the most inaccurate statements, I began to wonder if there was not a grain of truth to the above fiction. And as usual, I did come up with a theory that might explain the basis of the above-mentioned error: Since many of the medications useful for ADD might have been started when patients were six to eight years old, and many patients no longer need medication after four years of treatment, then these twelve-year-olds, or pubescents, would no longer need so-called "ineffective" medications.

Are There Dangerous, Long-Lasting Side Effects?

To date, the medications I have used to treat dyslexia for the past thirty-five years have been around for many, many years. They have been used safely for other conditions without any observable or recorded irreversible side effects. Remember that the wrong dosage or treatment without a doctor's care can result in moodiness, tiredness, irritability, and even intensification of dyslexia's symptoms. Also, as I explained earlier in this chapter, longtime (uninterrupted) use often leads to immunity. As noted, if low doses are administered by a doctor, if patients are treated sensibly and carefully observed—if doses are appropriately lowered rather than interrupted over weekends, vacations, and summers—both short- and long-term side effects can be minimized and avoided.

Special Side Effects to Look Out For

Tics and/or Tourette's Syndrome

Studies have indicated that patients with tics or Tourette's syndrome, or a family history of these disorders, may develop these symptoms on stimulant medications. As a result, one must be very cautious with this group of patients. Surprisingly, an occasional but rare patient may even develop these particular symptoms on antihistamines. This observation indicates that antihistamines must be used with similar caution as stimulants, and also suggests that they may have similar mechanisms of action. Paradoxically, there are patients whose tics disappear on antihistamine and stimulant therapy. As a result, all these observations must be factored into any treatment plan. Recently, studies have shown that stimulants do not significantly trigger tics and Tourette's and so may be used in these individuals with ADHD. However, caution is crucial!

Abnormal Liver Function Tests and Cylert

Since Cylert or pemoline may cause a rise in abnormal liver function tests, it is imperative that all treated patients receive a SMAC, or liver function study, every three to six months throughout therapy. In my experience, elevations in these enzymes are completely reversible once dosages are stopped.

However, recent evidence indicates that this medication can cause a higher incidence of liver failure than expected—and so more frequent blood tests are advised when and if this medication is needed (i.e., after other stimulants fail).

What Are the Short-Term Side Effects?

The most common short-term side effects of the medications used to treat dyslexia are fatigue, irritability, moodiness, and intensification of symptoms. All these side effects are readily reversed by either reducing or discontinuing the doses. *No side effects should be tolerated.* They all indicate that the dose is too high or that the medication is inappropriate for the patient. All medications can and should be changed when side effects are noted. As a result, careful monitoring of patients is crucial if improvements are to be maximized and side effects avoided.

Are the Stimulant Medications Useful for ADD Also Helpful in Improving the Typical Dyslexic Symptoms?

Stimulant medications, such as Ritalin (methylphenidate), Dexedrine (dextroamphetamine), and Cylert (pemoline), have been used effectively for concentration, distractibility, impulsivity, and activity symptoms characterizing syndromes currently labeled ADD and ADHD. More recently, a variety of so-called antidepressants and B-blockers (Inderal) were also noted to help these symptoms.

Since these stimulants and related medications, especially when used in high doses for hyperactivity, were infrequently noted to improve the typical reading, writing, spelling, speech, and other symptoms of dyslexia, their use in dyslexia was ignored. My findings and reasoning were completely different: Any improvement is better than none! And most important, enhanced concentration can significantly improve academic and all other symptoms characterizing dyslexia.

Although *all* research authorities currently distinguish between dyslexia and ADD or ADHD, my research clearly indicates that:

- 90 percent of all referred dyslexics have typical ADD-related symptoms; and
- 90 percent of all referred ADD-related subjects have some typical dyslexic symptoms.

Accordingly, I reasoned that both separately named disorders must have a common origin. As a result, I successfully treated all attention deficit and hyperactivity symptoms in dyslexics with low doses of stimulants and/or antidepressants as well as antihistamines, depending on circumstances. And guess what happened? The combined use of anti–motion sickness antihistamines with *low* doses of stimulants gave the best overall results. Moreover, recent research has clearly shown that all anti–motion sickness antihistamines, stimulants, and most antidepressants or antipanic drugs have one common denominator: They all improve inner-ear functioning and thus minimize or eliminate motion sickness. Accordingly, astronauts were treated with combinations of anti–motion sickness antihistamines and stimulants before space flights. Also, low doses of stimulants appear to be significantly more beneficial for memory and related dyslexic symptoms than do higher doses. Indeed, I recently discovered that the drug Piracetam, now used in Europe for improving reading, memory, and speech functioning in dyslexics, is also an inner-ear–enhancing medication, and thus has been shown to benefit patients with dizziness.

Recent studies tend to validate my clinical observations that dyslexia, ADD, and LD are all interrelated and stem from a common source—most likely the inner ear and cerebellum.

What About the Stimulant Ritalin?

Just about every parent whose child might benefit from Ritalin becomes petrified at the mere use of the name. They've all read such terrible things about this medication in newspapers, magazines, and other sources. They've been told that it makes kids sleepy and groggy, that you can become addicted to it, that it stunts growth and inhibits compensation.

I tell parents that when properly utilized in small enough doses, this is one of the safest medications around—that all the negatives they have heard about this drug have to do more with the way it has been given than with the drug itself. Were aspirin given in doses far higher than needed, there would be more side effects. In my experience, for concentration enhancement most patients need only 5–10 mg of Ritalin or less, three times a day—especially when combined with the anti–motion sickness antihistamines. Higher doses usually are counterproductive. For severely hyperactive, impulsive, destructive kids, higher doses are usually necessary. Now there are once-a-day Ritalin and Dexedrine doses that provide steadier and more consistent benefits while avoiding the negatives sometimes experienced when therapeutic levels become ineffective or produce side effects.

I also convey to parents that I treat Ritalin like any other medication, including those given over the counter. All medications are potentially useful. And many can be dangerous if improperly administered and supervised. The key is to gauge each patient's tolerance and response carefully.

What Do I Tell My Patients Before They Start Medical Treatment?

Medications may cause side effects and therefore incur risks, however small. All untreated symptoms cause damage or pain, emotional and/or physical. Unfortunately, nothing in life is without cost or risk. No patient or parent should agree to treatment before weighing the alternatives. No one should be *told* what to do. The possible advantages of treatment must be carefully considered by the patient *and* the doctor before a decision is made.

I present the facts of treatment to my patients and/or their parents. I may even tell them what I would do and have done in treating my own children. But I tell them to think things out for themselves and do whatever they feel is correct. After all, *clinicians and experts are only professionally responsible for the well-being of their patients. Parents are totally responsible for their children.* They must be aware of the pain and consequences of "professional errors and unknowns."

Indeed, I respect patients and parents who raise questions and express different opinions. And I work with them to the extent that I can, in the manner in which I would like my colleagues to work with my decisions regarding my children's treatment.

Many anxious parents prefer trying helpful nonmedical therapies first before considering my medical treatment. Initially, my new patients and/or their parents sought medical help only after all prior nonmedical therapies failed. Now, many come to me first—so that the anticipated medical improvements might enable more "normal" responses to educational and other nonmedical methods.

Improvements Noted with Medications

For the sake of clarity and economy, only a handful of progress reports have been selected out of thousands for presentation. The criteria for selection were as follows: They had to be typical, instructive, natural, and clear.

Analyze the recorded improvements carefully. These responses not only highlight the first and only medical treatment of dyslexia but also specifically *magnify* and thus *reveal* the complex nature and symptomatic array defining the essence and core of dyslexia. Needless to say, improvements do not occur unless an underlying corresponding dysfunction or symptom already exists.

All too often, patients do not even recognize that many of their difficulties, quirks, and idiosyncrasies are part and parcel of their dyslexic disorder. Many patients react to improvement with astonishment, often stating: "You know, I was so used to doing things this way, I thought it was normal."

Children have even more difficulty spontaneously revealing their symptoms than adults. They have no way of knowing what is normal and what is not, or how other children function. As a result, they may not reveal that they get dizzy and headachy when reading, that words get blurry and seem to bounce around, that they keep losing their place over and over again and have to use their finger or a marker, that their reading concentration and memory are poor, that letters and words appear to reverse, that they are sensitive to fluorescent lights or light in general (photophobia), and that they must hear in their mind what they are reading in order to understand.

Denial of symptoms is a commonplace and universal reaction of dyslexic patients. Consequently, all scientific attempts at elucidating the various symptoms defining this riddle-packed disorder were most difficult and painstakingly slow. Were it not for the dramatic and rapid highlighting of dyslexic symptoms via their improvements on medications, my ability to map out and detail the symptoms defining dyslexia would still be in its infancy.

Few researchers develop an early and rapid grasp of the totality of the disorder they are investigating. Years of extensive effort are required to recognize even small parts of the unseen and unknown whole. Most often there initially exist significant degrees of unconscious bias and tunnel vision. One sees and recognizes only a few apparently disjointed bits of data at any given time. To succeed, this bias and resulting tunnel vision that limits our ability to see and hear what is obviously present must be resolved and replaced by the realities of the clinical situation.

Unfortunately, bias is not easy to resolve. Often one doesn't even realize it is there. We deny its existence in a manner identical to the way patients deny their symptoms. Yet, bias actively distorts what we see, what we hear, and how we reason.

When I first began treating dyslexic patients with medications, I looked only for improvements in reading, writing, and spelling. At the time that was what I naively thought dyslexia was all about. I hadn't the foggiest idea that a whole range of inner-ear–determined dyslexic symptoms would improve as well: math, grammar, speech, direction, memory, time, balance, coordination, concentration, behavior, phobias, body image, and so on.

Despite my initially naive and biased concept of dyslexia, I questioned my patients in a careful, open-minded fashion. Intuitively or by accident, I did not in any way restrict or direct their responses. In fact, I utilized a "free-association" or "free-flow" approach in which patients were merely told to tell me whatever they noticed *on* the medications and *off* the medications, good, bad, or indifferent. As a result of the carefully recorded and collected responses of large numbers of treated dyslexics, I was able to piece together a picture of the dyslexic disorder and its response to medications never before contemplated.

Read the medical responses reported by patients as I did. Draw your own conclusions. Make your own lists and charts. I hope your studies will both confirm and extend my own.

Criticism and My Response

Before presenting the responses of dyslexic patients to my medical treatment, I think it wise to present the reader with some negative, critical points of view.

Some critics have attempted to deny entirely the obvious results of my treatment. Others have termed the undeniable positive responses to treatment merely imaginary, or wish-fulfilling placebo effects. In other words, they felt that sugar pills would have had the same effect.

I pose the following questions to my critics:

- Why did other wish-fulfilling methods of treatment not work before? Surely these patients were desperate and had wanted help previously.
- Why did they respond to one medication and not to a series of others, independent of the color or the taste of the pill?
- Why did parents recognize academic improvements *before* knowing or seeing me, when their children were taking antihistamines for colds and allergies?

Criticism is certainly easier than going to my office, speaking to my patients, observing them, and duplicating my results. To date, no critic has ever *disproved* any of my reported results.* Indeed, many a skeptic has been scientifically converted once he witnessed my diagnostic-treatment results.

I have also been criticized for not performing "double-blind" studies—studies in which some patients are given placebos, such as sugar pills, and others "real" medications, while both examiner and patient remain "blind" to who gets what. There is some merit to this criticism.

However, I have thus far successfully managed to help over 75 percent of my patients improve while simultaneously sketching a portrait of dyslexia never before seen or imagined. All this was done without the help of double-blind studies. The results of my treatment are most clear and dramatic. In fact, the vast majority of reported symptomatic improvements were completely unanticipated and thus free from bias.

Had I *restricted* myself or my patients to viewing only reading scores, or writing scores, or spelling scores, as prescribed by

---

*See Appendix D. Despite reporting improved balance and improved ocular tracking in patients given meclizine, Fagan et al. (December 1988) paradoxically concluded that anti–motion sickness medications do not work in dyslexia. Among the many fallacious assumptions and errors in the study's design, they inadvertently equated reading scores with dyslexia and did not measure or inquire about improvements in the many and varied dyslexic symptoms characterizing Appendix B, "Responses to Medication"; nor did they count any of the reported reading fixation, tracking, and balance improvements noted as important. Moreover, most researchers recognize that to obtain reliable improvements in reading scores, one must wait at least six months on medications. These researchers only waited three months. Also, they followed *only a few* dyslexics given *only one dose* of *only one drug*, meclizine—failing to recognize that this dose gave *toxic* results in several of their dyslexic patients. For a more detailed critique of their flawed study, refer to my research paper (1991) entitled "Dramatic Favorable Responses of Children with Learning Disabilities or Dyslexia and Attention Deficit Disorder to Antimotion-Sickness Medications: Four Case Reports."

the traditional double-blind method, I would have lost the forest for the trees. I would have inadvertently recorded only reading, writing, or spelling scores, since patients would not have been asked and encouraged to report freely *whatever* they noted, in as unbiased a fashion as possible.

I have no regrets. Quite the contrary! I was forced to realize that traditional methods of research, however neatly and carefully reported and charted, often resulted in nothing more than a mass of data. Were this not true, dyslexia would not have remained scientifically scrambled and fragmented for over one hundred years—a perplexing riddle requiring a solution.

Double-blind and placebo studies have their place in research. In fact, I truly believe these studies will be immeasurably more helpful now inasmuch as they can measure single variables in the context of a theme and an understood whole rather than in the preexisting scientific scramble.

I realize now why some critics are driven to *demand* double-blind studies: Underlying this need is no doubt a feeling of uncertainty as to the reality, objectivity, and honesty of their own observations.

Typical Responses of Dyslexic Patients to Medication

I will now present you with my dyslexic patients' responses to the medication I currently use. The careful study of their symptoms and responses will indeed reward you with a picture of the depth and scope of dyslexia, which cannot be appreciated or learned in any better way.

For the sake of completion, I will note that there have been double-blind drug studies with dyslexics. Thus, for example,

Piracetam was shown by a number of researchers to improve the reading and related symptoms of dyslexics. And only in retrospect did I find this medication to have inner-ear–improving or antivertigo functions. And recently a group of scientists confirmed that meclizine or Antivert improved cognition—validating my use of this and related medications in dyslexia of LD.

In the back of the book, I have summarized in Appendix B most of the collective responses reported to date. However, new, unexpected responses appear to surface with each additional sample of dyslexics treated.

Appendix B was quite small many years ago. I hope that the use of new and varied combinations of medications will lead to the expansion of the improvements noted, as well as higher yields of additional significant treatment responses.

(To meaningfully understand the syndrome called dyslexia, I encourage the reader to underline or highlight each and every symptom reported by patients and/or relatives and improved by the medication in the various cases presented. You will rapidly see how ridiculous it is to equate the entire dyslexia syndrome with *only one* of its highly variable symptoms, e,g., a severe reading-score impairment.)

After thirty-five years, many dyslexia experts are beginning to follow my lead and recognize dyslexia as a syndrome of many and varied symptoms, rather than just a severe reading impairment.

Fred and Mike Carter

This letter was received from Catherine Carter, the mother of two dyslexic boys:

Fred was examined a year ago and received prescri[
and vitamins, which he took as instructed. His behavior, at-
titudes, personality, etc., *all* went very smoothly for the first
time in his life. His teacher sent home a note after the first
three days back at school in January: "I don't know what
you are doing differently, but please keep it up!"

The improvement was dramatic and came about quickly.
Fred's homework is no longer a five-hour chore; it takes only
a few minutes most of the time now, because he doesn't have
half of his classwork to do too! He finishes his classwork on
time at school and sometimes so early that he gets his home-
work done there as well. The difference this has made in our
household is absolutely amazing. Every morning used to be
dominated by Fred's tantrums over going to school in the
first place, over homework in the afternoons and evenings,
until his bedtime. His teachers have nothing but praise for
the progress he has made on his treatment program.

Fred's progress after taking vitamins and medication has
been much more dramatic and far-reaching than anything
previously done for him. He had tried the prescription drugs
Cylert and Ritalin, the Feingold diet, an allergy diet, and vi-
sual training. The visual training helped a small amount, in
very specific ways with coordination, but didn't carry over in
a general way to all of his school and play activities or help
the frustration levels. The inner-ear treatment you have
given him has helped in a general manner with all types of
coordination—running, hitting a baseball, catching a ball,
handwriting, tying his shoes, etc. When I asked him if he
could notice any changes in how he felt or how things were
going with schoolwork, he said that the words no longer

jumped around on the pages when he was trying to read—for the first time in his life that he could remember!

Fred remains on a closely monitored diet for food allergies; however, these seem to be going away to some degree. His allergist is the one who sent us to you in the first place, hoping to get some of the stress resolved so his system could settle down. Maybe this treatment has helped his system cope with allergies better; we really think so but certainly can't prove it. Chemicals in food still affect his behavior and performance drastically and have to be avoided.*

Fred's optometrist performed a one-year follow-up developmental exam in August to evaluate improvement since the visual-training program's completion. The optometrist could see a big improvement.

We have tried taking Fred off the medication on weekends and holidays, with mixed results. Sometimes he will do fine and other times he will become cross and difficult until we resume administering at least some medication; the improvement shows inside of an hour.

Fred's brother, Mike, also showed great improvement:

We began the treatment [the day after Mike was examined by you] and it calmed him a great deal. . . . The new medications were tolerated very well.

No improvements in schoolwork were noted at home or at school until [he began taking] the prescription drug

---

*Although recent double-blind studies have tended to reject the influences of dyes and chemicals on behavior, my own personal clinical experience indicates that in 5 to 10 percent of hyperactive and distractible patients, dyes and chemicals have anywhere from a mild to severe effect. So much for these studies?

Marezine. . . . Improvement has not been as quick as with his brother but has been steady.

The temper tantrums about school and schoolwork, which began after a severe illness and ear infection, have stopped. His grades have now returned to the A's that he used to get before the disaster struck. His attitude toward others and behavior have improved to the levels we had come to expect from him before his illness happened.

Mike's teachers are very pleased with the improvement he has shown in his schoolwork and handwriting. Math facts and times tables have become a lot easier to remember too. He is once again a cheerful little boy!

The eye squinting in the classroom that had his optometrist perplexed and [prompted him to lend Mike] a pair of glasses for reading and board work "to see if they helped, though his vision didn't really seem to warrant such a step," has now stopped. He is finishing his board work quickly and with fewer errors. All of the "dyslexic" errors are not gone, but the majority are. The frustration that he was showing is gone now. . . .

Mike's allergies have improved since the inner-ear treatment, as have Fred's, possibly due to the reduced stress of life. His allergist has been very pleased with the progress. . . .

Fred and Mike's father and I, their teachers, and their pediatrician are all extremely pleased with the boys' improvement.*

---

*Note how an ear infection was observed to create or intensify Fred's dyslexic symptoms.

Laura Hagan

This letter from twelve-year-old Laura Hagan's mother was sent to me three months after Laura began taking medication:

Laura has made excellent progress in all areas!

Her balance has improved tremendously. She could never ride a bike steadily before she was placed on medication. Now her riding is perfect, even with "no hands."

She complained of frequent headaches before, which she no longer has.

Previously, Laura would never read a book solely for pleasure, but now there have been quite a few times when she has actually turned the TV off to read!

Laura's concentration was poor and her attention span short. She was easily bored. Now she shows more interest in what she is doing and is doing it longer!

Her spelling is also better. No matter how much help or coaching she received in the past, she constantly failed and felt discouraged. Now she is achieving marks that range from 80 to 100 percent.

Laura's reading is tremendously better—she is reading at the appropriate seventh-grade level now, and her greatest advance is in reading comprehension.

Her memory or recall for math facts and concepts has also improved. She is finally making good strides in memorizing her multiplication tables and retaining them.

Laura shows more patience with herself and with others. No doubt this patience and interest is a result of the excellent progress she has made and is continuing to make, particularly with her reading ability and reading comprehension. . . . Thank you!

Sam Bowles

Nine-year-old Sam Bowles's mother sent the following letter after Sam was on medication for one week. Although it is unusual for treatment to be effective this quickly, it does happen often enough to warrant this report's inclusion here.

> I had to write and share our exciting news with you. Sam never, under any circumstances, read aloud.
>
> As you recall, prior to leaving your offices in New York, you gave Sam medication. We immediately left for Kennedy Airport and were caught in a terrible traffic jam, arriving at the airport with only two minutes to spare. We flew from the cab into the airport, frantically searching for directions to our gate. Suddenly, Sam began to read the instructions written on the signs and the overhead, guiding us correctly to our plane. The full impact of what he had done—read the signs and overhead—did not hit me until we had boarded the plane and were safely on our way home.
>
> Shocked, I looked at Sam—the sparkle in his eyes and his broad grin mirrored my own as he said: "I really did it, didn't I?"

Julie Carol Ellis

Julie Ellis is fourteen years old. Her mother writes:

> Julie has developed a keen interest in reading and has completed four books this past summer. In the past she could not read well, rarely completing more than one book in a summer.

She has improved in her coordination and balance. She is able to throw and hit a ball far better than previously, and she is now able to ride her bicycle and engage in other sports.

Julie reports that she doesn't feel as dizzy as she did before. Her ability to ride elevators, amusement rides, autos, trains, etc., is much improved. Julie doesn't suffer from motion sickness and phobias anymore.

Happily, her speech is better, with increased vocabulary and more verbal content.

Julie is able to concentrate for longer periods of time and can deal better with frustration because it happens less and less.

She is more assertive at home, and at the same time her attitude is better. All in all, Julie shows a much more positive self-image.

T. J. Lage and Steven Junge

Lois Hanusa, a second-grade teacher in Emmanuel Lutheran School in Nebraska, wrote to me as follows:

This past school year, I taught two of your patients: T. J. Lage and Steven Junge. At school's end, May 26, I was absolutely sure the boys should be retained; but now with their improvement, I am considering promoting both of them.

During this summer, for eighteen days, for a half hour each day, I tutored the boys. They had seen you in April and I could see changes for the better in both of them.

I am very pleased with the boys' reactions to your medication treatment. Your solution to the problem of dyslexia seems so logical and "on target," although at first it seemed just too good to be true. I was somewhat skeptical, but am convinced now and very glad I had this opportunity to work with both T. J. and Steve and observe the effects of your treatment firsthand.

Frank P. Watson

Eight-year-old Frank Watson is a dyslexic child who showed remarkable progress after placement on medication. Frank went from being in a learning-disability program to being considered for his school's gifted program—in only five months.

Within two months after he was placed on medication, Frank's LD (learning-disabled) teacher reported that his concentration and attention span had improved considerably and that his reading and general schoolwork reflected that improvement. Mrs. Watson happily added that "Frank is calmer, less irritable, and getting along well with most of his classmates. He realizes . . . that he is able to remember facts and sequential information (days of the week, months of the year, etc.) better since he has been on medication."

Two months later my office received the following enthusiastic letter from Mrs. Watson:

I simply must share with you the most wonderful news about our son Frank. After the end of the first grading period (third grade), Frank was awarded the Eager Beaver Award for Scholastic Achievement, and a few weeks later he was presented with the Citizenship Award—all firsts for our boy.

At the same time, Frank's LD teacher called us for permission to have him retested and reevaluated because of the great strides he had made in reading and other academic areas and behaviorally as well. I gave permission.

I was then called by the school and requested to attend a conference about this new evaluation. His LD teacher enthusiastically reported that she could see *no signs* of any learning disability! I was also asked to give my permission to have Frank tested for the gifted program. I was so shocked and happy I almost fainted. I quickly signed my consent.

This does not mean that Frank will be accepted into the program, but it is quite an honor even to be considered for such a placement! The more so for Frank, who had been in the LD program for three years!

With each day, we see a happier, calmer, more well-adjusted boy developing—one who eagerly anticipates going to school to learn and to be with his friends. It isn't only Frank who has profited from seeing [you] but our entire family as well. Daily, we thank God; you, Dr. Levinson; and Frank's strong determination to do well in school.

Ted and Rita Powers

Ted and Rita Powers are a ten- and fourteen-year-old brother and sister. This letter came to me from their father:

Watching a rerun of *Donahue* my eyes filled with tears of joy and gratitude. (And tears come rarely to a forty-one-year-old soldier who has seen a great deal of life.) You see, it was on that show that we first saw and heard you speak.

[My wife's and my whole lives] and those of our children were turned around as a result.

As I am writing this letter to you, my son Ted is playing soccer, a game that previously filled him with fear. This season he joined the team and is having the time of his life. He has also begun to play football with the boys in the neighborhood. It is such a joy to us to see him happy and having fun with boys his own age.

Ted is also doing much better academically. His problems with letter and word reversals and right/left confusion don't bother him anymore. He even does his reading and math homework without being pushed and without trying to extract the answers from his mother or me.

Our daughter Rita, who suffered from recurring nightmares and fears and anxieties, also appears to be better since medication. She is calmer and more relaxed. Throughout the summer I noticed she was reading much more than she ever had.

The new semester grades have just been announced and she told us she received a 99 percent in her accounting course and an 85 percent on an assignment having to do with business accounting terminology. I hope this is a portent of the future, because last year her overall average was a *D*.

Mindi Knowles

Fifteen-year-old Mindi Knowles's mother wrote the following letter one year after her visit:

All the scholastic help we provided for Mindi didn't help her one bit until you placed her on medication. We see improvement in her schoolwork, grades, and sociability.

Mindi is able to write compositions now and receive good grades. Her ability to spell has improved tremendously. Mindi said to us one day, "I sure wouldn't want to be in high school the way I was—ugh! All *F*s!" We didn't realize how handicapped she was until we saw the real child emerge from the fog, the daze of dyslexia.

Mindi is able to focus her attention and concentrate on a particular subject and is more alert to her surroundings. She is even able to deal with a very aggressive fourteen-year-old sister. Again, this is something she was not able to do successfully before.

Socially, Mindi isn't on the outside anymore. She no longer looks or acts as if she is spaced out or daydreaming. To see Mindi function as she now is is truly a joy.

I received a letter from Dr. Stibel of the Great Falls, Montana, Optometric Group, in which he informed me that he had examined Mindi prior to treatment and found her to be lacking in the areas of eye tracking, figure-ground discrimination, short-term visual memory, and phonetic word-analysis skills. He also stated that he examined Mindi after she had been placed on medication: "[Mindi's] eye-tracking, figure-ground discrimination, and phonetic word analysis skills were all significantly improved."

Jan Hatch

Another parent wrote about her fourteen-year-old son, Jan Hatch:

> We are extremely pleased with the results of your treatment of Jan. He is particularly gifted in mathematics and computer science, and it is gratifying to know that his problems no longer stand in the way of a good education in this field. Thanks to you.
>
> Jan has shown significant improvement in several important areas:
>
> *Memory:* He remembers to write down homework assignments, to do the homework once he gets home, and to take the homework back to school.
>
> *Balance/coordination:* Jan doesn't trip or seem as clumsy as before. He received an A in gym, a first for him because he never performed well athletically. He even qualified to test for a black belt in a martial art. His movements in general are quicker and smoother. He doesn't move back and forth when he is speaking, something he's done since he was a small boy.
>
> *Concentration:* Jan says that he thinks more clearly now and he is able to concentrate much better.
>
> The most notable difference since medication treatment is in Jan's grades. He has gone from a *D* or *C* student, with an occasional *A* or *B,* to an *A* or *B+* student. He received five *A*'s and two *B*'s this last quarter, qualifying him for Honor Roll!

Everyone has noticed the differences in Jan, and he is particularly heartened by all of this.

Ronald Webb

This report on Ronald Webb, seventeen years old, arrived two months after he began medication:

> Ron's reading is easier, fluent, and faster, and his reading level has improved with tutoring. Although his spelling memory is not much improved, he does not reverse letters anymore.
>
> Ron has noticed a big difference in his balance and space orientation. He bike rides and skates better. In school he does not experience the occasional confusion and disorientation he was sometimes prone to. Also, he does not bump into school walls and doors as he did before. He does not fall or trip as he used to, either.
>
> All of Ron's teachers have noticed some changes. In fact, his art teacher remarked about it before she knew he was on medication.
>
> Ron is a lot happier with himself. He notices things he never did before, such as the texture of walls and fabrics, the designs in rugs, the texture of different wood grains, etc.
>
> His grades have always been good, but he had to work very hard to achieve them. Now it all seems easier for him. Thank you!

Steven Brown

Steve, seventeen years old, exhibited marked improvement in school and life situations. Specifically, his mother stated:

> Steve's mood is also more optimistic: Two and a half years ago he painted his room a dark green color; six months ago, he painted it white. He never cared much about keeping his room neat and attractive, but now he does.
>
> I can't help but believe that the colors reflect Steve's feelings about himself and the world around him.
>
> Even school has become less of a tense situation for him. His untimed SAT scores showed a marked improvement of about 80 points!
>
> We are all so pleased.

Gale Martin

For much of her life, forty-two-year-old Gale Martin was plagued with hyperactivity. She also manifested a host of dyslexic symptoms related to reading, writing, memory, poor attention span, and concentration, as well as fears of heights and confined places. When she was placed on medication, she experienced the following significant improvements:

> I can now paint in my studio for long periods of time, something I had been unable to do before.
>
> I am much better about heights and confined places; they don't seem to bother me as much as they did.
>
> My writing, reading, concentration, and memory seem better too.

John Frank

John, six and a half years old, was referred to me because of academic difficulties. He had the third highest IQ for his grade, the 96th percentile nationally for second graders. According to teachers, he was an "underachiever."

John's difficulties included:

- Reading on a lower grade level than his comprehension ability indicated
- Memory instability for letters and words
- Letter and word reversals in reading and writing
- Tracking problems that were responsible for his slow reading
- Poor handwriting—angulation and reversals

On medication John has shown steadily increasing progress in the following areas:

- Basic reading skills
- Reading and math skills (he is now on grade level); marked handwriting improvement
- Concentration and attention span, as verified by his parents and his violin teacher

A detailed report outlining John's difficulties and the basis for the difficulties—dyslexia—as well as recommendations for the teachers, was mailed to his school. However, the report was ignored and John continued to be termed an underachiever or a victim of "maturation lag." It almost appeared as if the child

were being punished for having a high IQ while simultaneously experiencing academic problems in school.

John's parents, both professionals, arranged to meet with
the principal of the school, a reading specialist, the school psychologist, and his teacher. They brought a copy of my medical
text *A Solution to the Riddle Dyslexia* to the conference. Mrs.
Frank wrote to me regarding this meeting:

> The faculty had seen copies of your book review outlining
> its main concepts. They came to the conference and admit-
> ted that they couldn't understand the book review, let alone
> the book. We explained the book, at their request. They
> were attentive. But at the end of the conference they all
> agreed that our son's problem was a maturational one, not
> dyslexia.
>
> Our son is the only child in our town to have dyslexia,
> according to our school officials. But right across the river,
> in the next town, the school district has special classes for
> dyslexics.

Obviously, not all school systems are characterized by such
stereotyped, biased thinking, and many reflect a more objective, rational approach, appreciating the importance of recep-
tivity to new scientific and clinical theories to promote the
physical, emotional, and educational welfare of our young people. But as the reader can see, many professionals still believe
that dyslexics can't read, and thus, that anyone who can read is
not dyslexic. And although dyslexics are typically defined as
having normal or above-normal IQs, many an expert has reasoned and stated as follows: "Your son can't be dyslexic. He's
too bright."

David Greenfield

David Greenfield's parents wrote the following about their thirteen-year-old son:

> Within the two-month period that David began taking his medication, his reading level improved from grade 4.5 to 7.1 and the intelligence tests given to him by the school psychologist indicated that he qualified for placement in a program for mentally gifted children.
>
> In other areas, we see a marked change in David's behavior. He is calmer and less hyperactive. His frustration tolerance has improved, but he still flies off the handle from time to time. His concentration, memory, and auditory perception have also improved greatly. In school he is well liked by most of his teachers, but he still has retained some of his overtalkativeness, which tends to annoy some others.
>
> David has not received any grade lower than a 94 percent on any paper he has done this year. He is doing especially well in math, social studies, and, believe it or not, English. He is also enjoying art, music, and sewing. Also, he has completed a very successful year in religious studies and Hebrew. Since he had never been able to learn any Hebrew before, he had to start from the beginning. But he has caught up satisfactorily with his classmates.
>
> Recently, David's application to the William Penn Charter School was accepted. (This is the oldest private school in the country and maintains extremely high standards.) David's sense of accomplishment and self-confidence has been greatly boosted. He feels a lot better about himself, and he has quite a bit of insight into his own behavior.

None of this could have happened without your treatment. David takes his medication regularly, none on the weekends. Sometimes he misses the evening dose, and we can both tell the difference on those days! See you on our revisit.

Mark Yilmaz and Scott Rothstein

This report is from the director of the Long Island School for the Gifted and concerns two students, Mark Yilmaz, six years old, and Scott Rothstein, nine:

Mark couldn't sit still long enough to learn anything and he could not learn to read. His intelligence revealed itself in his ability to solve mathematical problems. When math concepts were introduced to him orally, he was able to complete tasks in this area comparable to an eight-year-old.

Although his mother tried all programs suggested for dyslexic children, his reading ability did not improve and his visual skills and auditory integration continued to be weak.

After Mark saw Dr. Levinson and was placed on medication, the results were remarkable. When he was given standardized reading and math tests, seven months later, his scores placed him in the highest percentiles.

Scott has an IQ of 180. He was a hyperactive child who kept everyone on the go.

He learned very quickly and was at least four grade levels above the norm in all disciplines, but he couldn't express himself on paper. He was also very disorganized. There was some attempt to give him help via the learning disability specialist. . . . Little was accomplished through this method.

In other words, his teacher couldn't reconcile the fact that many dyslexics have superior IQ's, despite the often repeated facts that Einstein, Da Vinci, etc. were dyslexic.

The director went on to say, "Scott was taken to Dr. Levinson and placed on medication and vitamins. His behavior improved dramatically and we are working on his writing problem."

Although Scott was initially referred to me by a teacher who stated that he was gifted, she later said, "He's either dyslexic or gifted. Since he's dyslexic, we'll have to retest his IQ. The first IQ score must have been an error."

Chris Johnston

Chris Johnston is twelve years old and in fifth grade. His mother wrote:

> Your book finally reached Boise! Thank you for writing *A Solution to the Riddle Dyslexia* and enabling us to understand our son's reading problem.
>
> He was diagnosed in the second grade as having a reading problem by the University Reading Center in Boise. But Chris was never diagnosed as dyslexic. He was in a special reading class for four years and is presently in Reading Disabilities, in connection with the fifth grade.
>
> After reading your book, I became convinced Chris was dyslexic.
>
> After he was placed on medication, we noticed immedi-

ate improvement in his reading and writing skills, in his balance and coordination, and in his ability to deal with frustration. His teachers noticed too.

After a year on medication, Chris is like a new child! His math is on grade level and his reading has gone up a whole grade level!

Words cannot say enough to thank you for helping us by ending our years of frustration.

Esther Porter

Esther Porter's parents report on their eighteen-year-old daughter:

Esther's improvement is just fantastic—almost a miracle to us. Her grades are now A's and B's and she will graduate from high school one semester early.

She is continually reading and writing, now that she has experienced this success. She is even talking about becoming a writer and has written a few short stories and plays. She seems able to communicate her thoughts so much better—verbally and in written form. This her tutor has told us, confirming our own observations.

Also, Esther's psychologist sees improvements in her behavior. She is calmer and her rashes are clearing up; the night activity that upset her no longer does. If you recall, she felt as though the stars in the sky and high bridges were falling as she looked at them in the evening. And most wonderful—she is finally coming out of her shell. Esther got herself a job, selling three hours a day in a department store. We are finally succeeding!

Cherie Otto

A patient named Cherie Otto, twenty-three years old, wrote the following report:

> My spelling and writing have improved, primarily because I can pick out my own mistakes. I never was able to do that before.
>
> My balance and coordination, eye coordination, and memory for things in a series have also improved. I am able to remember multi-stepped commands or instructions because my auditory retention is much improved.
>
> I find I can concentrate better and my attention span is longer. Therefore, my organizational skills are also better and I have more patience with myself. I don't lose things as frequently as I did.
>
> If for some reason I forget to take my medication, my close friends remind me. They can tell from my behavior.
>
> I finally passed my chemistry test after five failures!
>
> Both my schoolwork and my personal life have improved greatly since last year.

Kimberly Price

Kimberly Price's mother wrote about her eight-year-old:

> I have been very happy and impressed with Kimberly's improvement on medication. I don't think I can ever express my gratitude to you for the help that you have given to my daughter. The following are the changes that we have noticed:

Handwriting: Kimberly's writing has improved dramatically. The letters have gone from a large scrawling to being better formed and of uniform size. There are also fewer letter reversals.

Math: She is experiencing less difficulty in math computation and appears to be grasping concepts with more ease. Her number formations are also better.

Fine motor skills: Kimberly is doing [jigsaw] puzzles for the first time in her life. She is now able to construct puzzles of 60 to 100 pieces with relative ease.

Balance and coordination: She is now walking in a totally upright position. She no longer needs to walk slightly bent forward in order to maintain her balance.

Todd A. Brake

Todd Brake's parents report the following:

We have seen a number of dramatic improvements in Todd's overall ability to perform during the year he has been on medication. We have seen progress in his comprehension of math/arithmetic, very significant improvements in his verbal skills, and development of a better attitude and high morale.

Todd was transferred from a small private school to a public high school. And he has made the transition quite well, enjoying rather than fearing the new challenges. He is doing particularly well in sports, especially with wrestling. His eye-hand coordination has improved. But tennis is somewhat difficult for him, although he is practicing hard.

Summary

Having read summaries of a mere handful of favorable therapeutic responses made by dyslexic children and adults to inner-ear–improving medications and nutrients, I truly believe that readers will have grasped two major points:

- That dyslexia is not just a severe reading disorder, but a complex, multidimensional syndrome affecting most areas of an individual's life and, especially, self-image
- That this treatment method is capable of rapidly and often dramatically helping the vast majority of dyslexics

However, I hope that the following presentations detailed within the next three chapters will more thoroughly enhance your understanding and conviction concerning the inner-ear/cerebellar origins and successful treatment of the dyslexic syndrome.

VI

"Trust Me, Sunshine, I'll Find You Help!"

Sometimes the hardest part of dealing with a complex, multifaceted disorder is learning that it has a specific name, and finding a professional who really understands how to treat it. This mother's ordeal is typical of the frustration many parents experience in attempting to find help for the many varied symptoms characterizing dyslexic children. Mrs. S. describes her loving and desperate attempt to help her daughter Jennifer as follows: "Jennifer never liked to go to sleep at night, especially without a light of some kind. One evening when she was particularly anxious, she asked to sleep with me. She feared and thus hated to sleep by herself. I told her that as a single parent, I had to sleep alone too. To reassure her, I said, 'You have your teddy bear and all these stuffed animals to sleep with.' Because her teddy bear had been a friend of long standing, and a good one at that, she finally consented to go to sleep alone. Later that evening when I went up to bed, I found her teddy bear on the pillow of my bed.

"The sight of the bear on my pillow brought tears to my eyes again. Just three hours earlier Jennifer, the sunshine of my life, and I had reached a new level of frustration and anxiety.

"I had known Jennifer had a problem since she was seven months old. Most children sit up and play at that age. Jennifer sat up and fell over on her side. Some forty-four sleepless nights and four pediatricians later, we discovered severe ear infections. (Even though I had suspected such, the first three pediatricians insisted she was teething.) In a matter of days, with the proper medication and care, she was well. But her ears had been scarred to the point where they now look as though they had had draining tubes in them.

"To help her overcome her lack of coordination, I enrolled Jennifer in a ballet class when she was three. Several months later I discovered she still didn't know her right from her left. By putting a round blue sticker on her left ballet shoe, she learned to determine the difference most of the time. Her coordination and balance were not good, however, and her ability to follow a sequence of directions was poor. Jennifer also needed an outlet for a great deal of hostility. As a result, I enrolled her in a karate class when she was five. She enjoyed karate, and it has provided opportunities for her to experience a number of successes.

"Starting school was exciting for Jennifer, and she looked forward to each day throughout kindergarten. She worked well in groups and learned a great deal. Of course, there were days when she forgot her sweater or coat or lunch box or book bag, but in general she did well and loved school. (She and her friends even 'played' school.) Therefore, her first formal academic experience was a positive one.

"Jennifer frequently complained of stomachaches and

headaches that seemed to be nonexistent. She had nightmares often. It was difficult to bring her out of the dream and back to reality. I had no answers and neither did her doctors.

"About halfway through the first grade, more serious problems started. At that point she was learning to read and write. She would finish some assignments but not others. There were some that she didn't even attempt. Her teacher and I were puzzled. We made games out of learning; that proved successful on several occasions, and the learning-resource teachers worked on various ideas. Some helped for a little while; others didn't work at all.

"Learning to read was difficult because Jennifer had to reread passages constantly in order to comprehend them.

"Second grade started out the same way that first grade had ended: Jennifer finished some projects and not others, and a number of assignments were never started. She seemed to lack the ability to concentrate when reading, although she could concentrate if a subject interested her. I requested that the school test her, and she tested quite well. Jennifer was not distractible in a one-on-one situation; she finished everything she was asked to do. It took some time but she did finish. She was judged to be more than one year beyond her grade level in reading and mathematics. Hence the school system suggested only psychological help. We made an appointment and spent an afternoon with a group of psychologists. They recommended that she *not* work with them; there was no evidence of any need for counseling.

"Even though she continued to have the same problems in school, Jennifer finished second grade and went on to the third. She still used her finger to point when reading or writing and had trouble remembering words she had studied an hour earlier. She had difficulty with basic math facts, such as adding and subtracting simple numbers. I bought games designed to help with mathematics, including flash cards and a math kit that consisted of plastic blocks. We worked through that kit—three times. I learned a lot of mathematics; Jennifer did too. But the next day her knowledge was gone.

"When Jennifer entered the fourth grade, she encountered the same problems. Her teachers were concerned and very helpful in that they understood what I faced each evening; in turn, I knew what they had to contend with daily. At least I had Jennifer by herself. Had I to cope with another twenty-seven students in the same room, I'm sure I would have been a wreck.

"Fourth grade brought further insight, as the multiplication tables are taught that year. What a fiasco that was! We would go over and over the multiplication tables, but she would remember only some of them. She worked very hard, because she wanted to do well, but without success. One night we *sang* them together and laughed. (She had a terrific, totally uninhibited laugh.) But I sang too fast for her. She would tell me it was all right, that she was just dumb. I tried to convince her she was not dumb, that she was indeed a very smart little lady. I could hear her cry herself to sleep that night.

"Jennifer was described by some as hyperactive. We tried the Feingold diet, which prohibits preservatives and artificial ingredients, but the diet made no difference in her progress at school or her behavior.

"Jennifer still complained of headaches. She also mentioned problems reading the chalkboard, so I took her to an optometrist. She got glasses, but the same behavior and learning problems persisted. The glasses only proved to be something else to lose.

"Jennifer's handwriting was extremely messy and the letters crudely formed. I noticed letters that were backward, mirrored. She had brought home instructions that she should practice her handwriting. So practice she did, but to no avail. I began to notice that she would capitalize words in mid-sentence. When I asked her about that, she had no answer.

"Having taught for nearly fourteen years, I felt I should know the solution to my daughter's problem. After all, there I was, with two degrees in education and nearly half the course work for a doctorate. Yet, I was unfamiliar with these kinds of problems or what to do about them. I had taught special-education classes, but I felt helpless.

"I started reading everything I could get my hands on and consulted a medical dictionary often. I realized that Jennifer had all the symptoms—not just some but *all* the symptoms—of dyslexia. I called the school and requested that she be tested again, specifically for dyslexia.

"Two weeks later I was told that my daughter's IQ was above average. Her work, they said, *when she did it,* was all above average. Therefore there was no problem. But I knew there *was* a problem. If they would just listen . . . !

"I was beside myself. The same problem that had first surfaced in first grade continued. Why couldn't we get any help? I began to search for help outside the school.

"We went to audiologists, optometrists, and pediatricians. We visited medical school teams (who are teaching *tomorrow's* doctors!). Most of them tested her. All of their cash registers jingled. None of them helped. Audiologists and optometrists suggested we see ear, nose, and throat specialists. We saw them

all; *no one had the answers*. Not only was I filled with frustration, I was throwing away good money after bad. No one
helped. I sobbed uncontrollably for hours.

"My patience had long since worn thin, as had Jennifer's.
Her problems made her feel like a failure. I've always felt that
the best thing parents can do for their child is to give him or
her a positive self-image. I was a practicing positive parent; I
still am. But my child had the poorest self-image! Because Jennifer sings well, I enrolled her in voice lessons so she could experience positive feelings about herself. Although she did quite
well, her negative self-image remained unchanged.

"Jennifer continued to spend three hours doing homework
that should have taken fifteen minutes. We argued; we got
frustrated. We both lost our patience. We would end up sob-
bing. We would hug each other and apologize for 'losing it.' I
could see that she was trying so hard. Helping Jennifer do her
homework was like being a referee for an elementary school
basketball game: If you call all the fouls, you have nothing but
foul shots and the kids don't learn to play the game. If I called
all the fouls with Jennifer, we had absolutely no positive time
together. I refused to do that.

"The school situation continued to get worse. Jennifer not
only refused to turn in her homework (she was afraid it was
not right, even though I checked it every night); also she did
not do her classwork. She would get frustrated and throw a
temper tantrum. She would make ugly remarks to her classmates and her teachers. I would get phone calls from the
teacher, who told me Jennifer wasn't developing meaningful relationships with other children, that Jennifer was bossy and
childish.

"I knew my daughter was crying out for help. I just didn't

know *how* to help. I began to call doctors again. This time I decided they had to prove to me over the phone that they knew what I meant when I said, 'Jennifer doesn't receive and process information like the rest of us.' Some of them wouldn't talk to me unless I came in for an appointment; others indicated that they didn't know what I meant. One of the doctors who seemed to understand was an ear, nose, and throat specialist. He even knew that the condition has been likened to motion sickness and was being treated with motion-sickness medication and antihistamines. I was elated. We made an appointment.

"The doctor's first comment was 'How long ago did you first notice a hearing loss?'

"I told him, 'Jennifer doesn't have a hearing loss; in fact, she hears better than most.'

"'We'll see,' he said, patronizingly. He brought in an audiologist, who led Jennifer away for testing. Ten minutes later, they returned. The audiologist gave the doctor a form that had been dutifully filled out. The doctor said, 'This child doesn't have a hearing problem; in fact, she hears better than most!' I thought for a moment there was an echo in his office.

"He continued to examine Jennifer. He blew air into her ears. He looked inside her ears. 'Let's face it, Mrs. Scharle,' he said to me, 'maybe she just doesn't like it.'

"'Like what?' I said.

"'School,' he replied.

"'Are you telling me a child who doesn't like school comes home and plays school?' I asked him.

"'Perhaps you should see a psychologist,' he said.

"I thanked him and took Jennifer's folder to the front desk. After writing a check, we left. I was appalled. This man had convinced me he knew what he was talking about! How could I have been so dumb? Another $89 down the drain. (Outpatient testing is rarely covered by group health insurance.) What were we going to do?

"Everyone referred us to someone else. I watched Jennifer become more and more frustrated and hostile. She saw me subtract more and more from my checkbook. Family and friends recommended one counseling service after another. (It seems that a child whose parents are divorced is supposed to be emotionally imbalanced and a behavior problem. I knew better. I knew that Jennifer was a warm, loving, sensitive child with a learning problem and no self-image to speak of. She just didn't receive and process information like the rest of us.)

"Jennifer became convinced that no one understood. She spent hours trying to help me, trying to make my life easier. By folding clothes and vacuuming, setting the table and clearing it, feeding the dog and letting him out, she sought my approval because she believed she couldn't get it otherwise. She felt like a failure.

"I continued to work with her on homework assignments, but we both frequently lost our patience. I couldn't come up with a successful learning approach. Nothing we tried worked. We cried, hugged each other, rocked each other, and patted each other's back. 'We'll find an answer,' I told her. 'Your mother will find a way to help you if it kills her.' She insisted she was just dumb.

"In despair I tried to scare Jennifer into working better, a conditioning technique I had read about. I told her perhaps I was in the way. I was going to let her be responsible for her own homework. She was on her own. Remember, I said, if you are in the fourth grade again next year, the kids will be teasing *you,* not *me,* at the bus stop. And I left her to do her homework. She worked and cried and worked and cried. It still took her three hours to do fifteen minutes of work.

"Jennifer developed frustration problems at school: One day her frustration exceeded even her norm.

"Jennifer had been assigned to do a work sheet. She couldn't do it, or so she thought. When her teacher questioned her, her frustration reached its peak and she threw her notebook against the wall. Just then the school secretary called over the intercom that Jennifer's father was there to pick her up, which he did every Tuesday and Thursday. Her teacher asked another teacher to keep an eye on her class and went out to speak with Jennifer's father.

"While she was telling him that she had taken as much as she could from Jennifer, Jennifer became convinced that the other teacher (someone she didn't know) was not going to allow her to go to her father. When Jennifer insisted that the lady let her go, and the other teacher insisted that Jennifer was to stay there where she was, Jennifer got frustrated again and threw her lunch box against the wall.

"By the time I was informed of the situation, Jennifer's father had had enough too.

"What could I say? He didn't spend every evening doing fifteen minutes' worth of homework for three hours. He didn't see the daily frustration she experienced.

"Jennifer's father may have known how difficult it was for her to tell time; he may have known that she had a special system for remembering the days of the week. But he didn't know that she had a list in her book bag that said, 'book bag, lunch box, sweater or coat, homework books, assignment pad, and *you!*' (Not only had she forgotten one or more of these items many, many times, but once she caught the wrong bus and didn't come home!) Sometimes she even forgot to check the list.

"Jennifer got in my car and started crying. She was expecting a reprimand from me, a reinforcement of her negative self-image. She sobbed—as I did—all the way home. 'Why do I have to be different? Why can't I just be like everyone else?' she asked. I cried harder. My poor little girl—no one understood. The whole situation tore at my heart. We went inside and sat down. I promised her once again, 'I'll find you help. Trust me, Sunshine, I'll find a way to help you.'

"I had no idea how I was going to accomplish that miracle. I couldn't eat; sleep didn't come easily.

"One day a friend of mine noted my mood and asked if he could help. I told him how I wished he could, and gave a brief description of the problem. Surprisingly, he proceeded to tell me how he had been illiterate when he graduated from high school. I listened in disbelief. The man owned his own company and was doing extremely well. Beyond that, he had graduated from college with second- and third-grade reading and writing skills. No public school system had ever helped him. It was not until he was twenty-eight and wanted to learn something on his own that a tutor pointed out what his problem was and whom he should see about it.

"My response was frantic: 'Who?'

"He gave me the doctor's name and phone number. I had a million questions. Did it work? What did he do? How did the doctor help him? What kind of doctor was he?

"The doctor was a local optometrist. After extensive testing he had given my friend eye exercises that had to be done regularly for some six months. Yes, it had worked. He might have the answer for Jennifer; then again, he might not. It was worth a try, surely.

"First thing Monday morning I called and made an appointment. I sent my chronicle of Jennifer's development and samples of her handwriting, plus a multitude of other reports, before we arrived at his office.

"The nurse came into the waiting room and asked if I would see the doctor alone for a few minutes. Jennifer agreed to wait in the lobby. And then the warmest voice said, 'I feel like I already know you.' Somehow I knew Dr. Howard Kahn would help.

"He was pleased with the paperwork I had sent ahead. He had read it with 'incredible interest,' he said, and realized the frustration Jennifer and I had been through. I couldn't help but believe that this man would provide the assistance we needed.

"He called Jennifer in and tested her eyes. (A young boy down the street had destroyed her glasses two days earlier, so the eye test came first. This is not his normal procedure.) The rest of the tests would follow.

"I stayed in the room while he tested Jennifer, and I noticed that his bookshelves were loaded with books about learning disabilities. I would have killed to get my hands on that literature just one week before!

"The eye tests provided tremendous insight into Jennifer's problem. At least some of it was due to the eyes—they weren't fixating and tracking properly.

"The relief I felt from having found a doctor who not only understood the problem but thought he could help is nearly impossible to describe. The knots in my stomach disappeared. My headache and furrowed brow left me on the way home. I took a deep breath and looked at Jennifer. She was singing a song with the radio. She felt the relief too.

"She now had two people to help her—her mother and her new eye doctor. She admitted to being a bit leery on the way to his office, but now it was okay. She trusted him, she said.

"I didn't tell her that the doctor had said the worst was yet to come, because I couldn't believe that myself. Not knowing what to expect was the scary thing. Jennifer and I could do anything. After all, we had made it that far.

"That night, as I kissed Jennifer good night, she hugged me a little tighter and longer than usual. 'Mom,' she said, 'you're the best mother in the whole wide world. I'm really lucky I have you.'

"'Thank you, Sunshine,' I said. 'You're the best daughter in the whole world too.'

"I wondered what would have happened if I had had no background in the field of education. I wondered what would have happened if I were a high school dropout on welfare and food stamps and with four or five kids. What do the children do under those circumstances?

"The photographer Susan Jacobs, herself the parent of a learning-disabled child, has said, 'I feel very strongly that a parent must trust himself and the desire to help his child. He must not let himself be intimidated by people who are critical of him and think because he's concerned and worried about his child, he is an "overprotective parent." . . . As a parent, you know your child better than anyone else, and you must trust your knowledge and feelings to find the best support for your child in enabling him to feel better about himself.'

"The Foundation for Children with Learning Disabilities says, 'Let no child be demeaned, nor have his wonder diminished, because of our ignorance or inactivity. Let no child be deprived of discovery because we lack the resources to discover his problem. Let no child—ever—doubt himself or his mind because we are unsure of our commitment.'

"There are many such children. It is estimated that 25 to 30 percent of the school-age population in this country has a learning disability. It's an invisible handicap. These children have diverse sets of characteristics that affect their development and achievement. There is no physical disability or visual characteristic to guide us in distinguishing learning-disabled children.

"This is simply the story of one child's fight for the right to learn and be just like everyone else. This story is written in the hope that no other child will have to fight as Jennifer has. I hope that no other parent has to go through the same frustration of not knowing what to do.

"Now we're on our way to success. We've found an eye doctor who knows what to do. Less than a week after our first appointment with him, a directory arrived from the Foundation for Children with Learning Disabilities. It's published by Academic Therapy Publications, Novato, California, and it lists facilities and services for the learning-disabled all over the country. These people know how to test and what one should learn in order to cope with the disability.

"Early in Jennifer's fourth-grade year, I made an appointment for her with a neurologist-psychiatrist in Great Neck, New York—Dr. Harold N. Levinson. The earliest appointment we could arrange was for May 25 of the following year, but the wait was worth it. Jennifer spent some three hours being tested and interviewed and I was interviewed as well. Technologists administered some of the tests and Dr. Levinson conducted others.

"Jennifer knew that the doctor understood. As we flew back home she quietly wrote me a note that said, 'Thanks, Mom, you're the greatest.' She knew he was going to help because he understood all the problems she'd been having. Those symptoms and quirks that made her 'different,' those that she had questioned so many times, were soon going to be corrected, and she knew it.

"Jennifer started the fifth grade as she had no other in her academic history. After a month and a half she has yet to fight with homework. She has yet to go without finishing her work in school. We have not had one cross word; we have not spent one frustrating evening together, although she still has to work harder than most of the students simply to catch up on things such as basic math facts.

"In addition to taking medication, Jennifer is currently studying with a tutor who is also a diagnostician and counselor. She has spent a number of hours working with Jennifer and her assistance has proved successful. Jennifer will begin eye exercises, too, in the next few months. Dr. Levinson has prescribed vitamins, lecithin, motion-sickness medication, and an over-the-counter cold remedy.* The difference in the child is phenomenal. She is indeed the child I raised her to be.

---

*This combination was right for Jennifer. It is *not* necessarily appropriate for anyone else. After one year of treatment, Mrs. S. called me, very upset. All of Jennifer's symptoms were returning. The medication she had been taking was apparently no longer working. So we changed the medications and tried several new ones. Nothing seemed to work. She appeared to be heading back to square one. I thought that she had developed an "immunity" or rejection reaction to the various medications and that nothing further might help.

Mrs. S. called me back one day with excitement in her voice. She had solved Jennifer's medication problem. By accident, she had discovered significant amounts of medications in the drawer of Jennifer's night table. Upon questioning, she discovered that Jennifer no longer wanted to feel different—needing medications. So she had stopped taking them, even giving some to her dog. And upon resuming the drugs, Jennifer's symptoms once again completely disappeared. Jokingly I asked Mrs. S., "How did the dog do on reading tests while taking the medications?"

"I'm not a scientist; I'm an educator. But first and foremost I'm a parent who loves her daughter more than words can tell. It's been a long, hard battle, but we have gotten this far and we'll go farther. Sheer determination on Jennifer's part and mine has provided a great deal of insight and progress. Luck has been on our side as well.

"Above and beyond all else, I can say this: Jennifer has taught me commitment. She has taught me patience and compassion. Most important, she has taught me to love. We are closer because of this. We love more deeply because of this. No one can possibly understand without having lived through such an ordeal. Jennifer fought for me as I fought for her and her rights. You will find no greater love than that of someone who has made the commitment to fight for you. Nor will you find greater love than that of someone who puts you before herself."

VII

Determination

The Stones were determined to see their son Rob succeed despite the ignorance and defensive malice of the "experts."

Usually, youngsters of preschool age eagerly anticipate the beginning of the school year. They can't wait to learn reading, writing, spelling, and math, to mix with other children and enthusiastic teachers. Very few of us aren't touched by sparkling faces, shiny eyes, and small fingers tightly clutching prized notebooks and pencil cases. How sad, though, when the light and joy go out of a youngster's eyes, and instead of eager anticipation of school, there is only anxiety and even dread.

Such was the case of Robert Stone.

Shortly after starting kindergarten, Rob's mother, Jean, received a call from his teacher. Rob was observed to be hyperactive and distractible in the classroom. Moreover, he was unwilling or unable to follow instructions, and the teacher suspected the presence of perceptual motor difficulties.

Despite the Stones' attempts to remedy the classroom situation, the situation deteriorated. The school psychologist met with Rob's teacher and parents, reviewed *all* the findings, and strongly intimated that emotional conflicts within the Stone household were no doubt responsible for Rob's problems in school.

Strangely enough, the psychologist's findings were in stark contrast to what the Stones and Rob's teacher thought. In fact, Rob's teacher recognized the boy's restlessness to be a hyperactive rather than an anxiety or attention-seeking symptom. In addition, she observed his clumsiness and accident-proneness and called those factors to the attention of the clinical personnel. Rob had difficulty walking through a hallway with a sloped floor without tripping or bumping into walls or other children. In the classroom he frequently dropped things and would even fall from his seat periodically. Rob's teacher advised the Stones to have Rob start perceptual motor training rather than the psychotherapy advised by the school psychologist.

The Stones' and the teacher's opinion was negated by the school's clinical team. After all, the team consisted of "experts" in child development and psychoeducational techniques. What did Rob's teacher and parents really know about him? Nothing! They were condescendingly viewed as uninformed, biased onlookers.

Had Mrs. Stone not been a teacher herself for a number of years, she might have been confused and intimidated. As it was, she followed the kindergarten teacher's suggestions that Rob be tutored and trained in perceptual and motor coordination tasks during the summer in preparation for the upcoming school year. These techniques seemed to work.

Unfortunately, Rob began first grade under fairly distracting circumstances—an added handicap for him. Four first- and second-grade classes were grouped together in one large room, separated only by shelves that were three feet high. Almost immediately Rob's inattentiveness and hyperactivity escalated. He began to wander around the classroom and even hid in the coatroom, instinctively attempting to avoid sensory overloading.

Rob's teacher was unable to control him and had to drag him out of the closet. Frustrated and in despair, she spanked him several times in front of the class. Obviously, that was no solution; he just could not be controlled. As a result, Rob was placed in the library with an aide as his teacher. This situation greatly disturbed his parents.

Again meetings were called. The school clinical team's evaluation had not changed too much. Rob's problems were diagnosed as emotionally based. In addition, the team decided that there must also be some kind of brain damage present. Therefore, they advised that he be placed in a hospital for a week of testing, and they recommended placement in a special school for brain-damaged children.

Understandably, these proposals thoroughly surprised and shook Rob's parents. They totally rejected this whole line of "reasoning." They firmly believed their son was not brain-damaged. He was bright, responsible, and sweet, and he had never exhibited at home the behavioral problems he exhibited in school. Moreover, his vocabulary and verbal skills were exceptional. Obviously, something was wrong, but the Stones intuitively knew that the school clinical team's solution was out in left field. After much deliberation and in despair, they decided to send Rob to live with his maternal grandparents in a nearby state. There was no alternative; they could not afford private schooling, and they obviously had to get him out of the school district he was in.

Despite their anguish and guilt, Rob's move to a new school proved to be a good one initially. He learned to read and write better in the stricter, more structured and demanding environment. However, the problems did not disappear; they were just less intense and dramatic.

Although he received additional help in reading, Rob remained six months behind his peers. And although his behavior was less of a problem, he continued to be disorganized, restless, and inattentive and still experienced coordination problems in gym. Rob's separation from his parents also created new problems. His mother worried about him continuously and couldn't tolerate the separation. Rob's maternal and paternal grandparents—good friends for many years—suddenly began to fight among themselves over his rearing and education. Guilt and recriminations ran rampant. Rob sensed he was the cause of it all.

In an attempt to resolve the escalating concerns, antagonism, and conflicts, the Stones decided to relocate to the grandparents' town. Mr. Stone would stay behind until he completed his doctorate, while Mrs. Stone would move back to her hometown, rent a house, and rejoin her son. "Although we made this decision with such care, concern, and even sacrifice for Rob's welfare, in hindsight it all seems to have been a bad move."

Rob regressed emotionally despite his concerned mother's presence. Once a sweet, lovable child, he became morose, stubborn, defiant, even hostile. One evening he was overheard saying his prayers, "Please, God, please give me a brain!" His mother was filled with indescribable sadness, frustration, and hopelessness.

Rob felt stupid because he continued to lag behind his peers in reading, even with tutoring and continued reassurance by his mother. Yet, the Stones knew their son was bright. At times he even seemed gifted. But they couldn't explain his learning and coordination difficulties. Although Rob's six-month lag in reading didn't bother the school much, it frustrated and devastated Rob and his parents. The Stones asked the school to test him for a learning disability.

Upon testing, his IQ was found to be at least 117 in spite of his concentration difficulties and restlessness. The clinical team leader, Mrs. Harris, realized Rob was easily distracted, and so she decided not to remove him from his regular classroom. Had she placed him with other distractible children, his behavior no doubt would have worsened. This decision drew a sigh of relief from Rob's entire family.

Although Rob remained in his regular classroom setting and received help from a gifted and dedicated, supportive reading teacher, Mrs. Wright, he was removed from his regular gym class. The new gym class had only one other student, a child whose legs had been amputated from the knees down. As Mrs. Stone stated, "Rob could see the obvious physical disability the child had, but he must have asked himself what his disability was. He already felt stupid. He continually called himself klutzy. What else did he think was wrong with him now?"

From this point on, Jean Stone will tell her story in her own words:

"Rob was devastated at being removed from his friends; he also felt humiliated to be placed with only one other physically handicapped child.

"We all, including his friends, tried very hard to make him feel loved and wanted. We were determined to help Rob retain his sense of worth and to keep intact one very special and lovable boy.

"Rob began the new school year in the third grade, but soon there began a repetition of the past. We had to meet with the school clinical team several times. My friend and ally, Team Leader Harris, was replaced by a Mr. Smith, who accepted the recommendation of the school psychologist and Rob's teacher without evaluating things for himself. That meeting was a nightmare! The psychologist and the teacher insisted that the child was incapable of handling third-grade material and was emotionally disturbed. The only person to object to this evaluation was Mrs. Wright, his reading teacher. She voiced her opinion that 'he was one of the most intellectually curious and sweet children that she had worked with in fourteen years.'

"This meeting and the others that followed convinced me that there was a lack of compassion or caring for Rob. These people seemed to be condescending in tone and manner, hoping to intimidate and confuse me, to manipulate me to accept their conclusions. But I would not!

"I was an educator myself for many years, and familiar with the jargon of the profession—familiar also with the methods. I was therefore able to deal with these people on their own level and with their own terminology. I frequently asked myself what other parents did in similar circumstances. Do they fight against the 'experts' edicts, as we did, or do they cower and capitulate, assuming that the 'experts' know best?

"Whichever position they take, there is heartache for the child who is the object of the controversy. However, for us there was no choice. We were determined to do what was best for our son, regardless of the consequences. Time and time again, after each painful session, I wondered where the clinical team's sense of compassion lay—that quality so essential for every good educator. Certainly this school's clinical team lacked empathy. In addition, the team was very annoyed with me because I was able to question their advice. I needed to have answers that would help my son, and I was not going to be put off or intimidated by anyone.

"Fabrications about my son's academic performance were told—that he was unable to remember math facts when math was his best subject. The psychologist insisted that Rob's stomach upsets were avoidance tactics. I told them that he had always had such upsets—not only when he had classwork to do, but also after the bus ride to school and again when he came home, after gym, or after any hectic activity. The true significance of these stomach upsets was not pieced together until our visit to you, Dr. Levinson.

"Teachers sympathetic to Rob and to us were subtly and overtly told to present a united front at the meetings and to allow the clinical team leader to speak for the team as a whole. Mrs. Wright became the butt of gossip that was spread by members of the team. It was difficult to comprehend that this slander was intended to vindicate the team's position.

"Mrs. Wright informed me that Rob had the highest IQ (by 50 points) in the private-instruction class. She knew all the children in the class, and she strongly felt that Rob did not belong with them.

"I pleaded with Mr. Smith not to place my son in the class, but he refused to listen.

"At midyear, Rob was placed in a special-education, self-contained class, the PI [private instruction] class. Our little boy was devastated. In all schools these segregated classes have stigmas attached to them, and Rob felt demoralized to be placed in such a class after our long, hard battle. Our hearts ached for him.

"We did our best to comfort him and stem the flood of tears, but by the second week of placement, Rob had undergone a transformation for the worse. He cried at the drop of a hat. He was mean to his sister, to his brother, and to us, his parents. He spent most of his school day in the principal's office because of bad behavior. He brought no work home from school. In general, his behavior was obnoxious, uncontrolled, and impulsive.

"One day I received a call from the music teacher, informing me that Rob was lying on the floor, rolling around. I was horrified and decided to see for myself.

"I went to school, spoke to his teacher, and asked to see Rob's schoolwork. The only work he had produced in a two-week period was an incomplete work sheet—at kindergarten level—with black scribbling. The teacher said she could neither reach nor control him. When I looked at that page of scribbling, I almost crumbled. Two short weeks earlier he was only six months behind third-grade level! Tears, then anger, took over—searing, hot, red anger. How dare they do this to my son?

"I removed Rob from school and informed the school clinical team, especially the psychologist, that Rob would not return to school until he was reinstated in his regular third-grade class. In the meantime I would teach him myself at home.

"In spite of threats and nasty phone calls, I stood firm in my resolve to teach our son. All I had to do was look at my son's face and I knew I had done the right thing: He was happier, performing beautifully, and soon approaching grade level! After six weeks I received a phone call from the team leader: I was told that Rob could attend his regular third-grade class. However, first a meeting between us and the team members had to be held.

"In spite of the failure of the PI class, attitudes were unchanged. The school psychologist, the school system's head of psychology, and the other team members still felt that Rob needed to be in a special class. In fact, the team leader commented, 'It's a shame Rob is so bright. . . . What good is a high IQ if you can't use it?' My mother-in-law was with me and I had to restrain her at that point.

"Once again the reading teacher, Mrs. Wright—who had taught Rob the longest and who knew him better than any other teacher—was ignored and made to feel that she had nothing valid or important to contribute to the proceedings.

"We felt extremely frustrated by the narrow-minded attitudes we encountered, but we never wavered in our resolve to have Rob placed in a normal classroom setting. We were bolstered in our purpose by our intimate knowledge of our son and the dedicated, unswerving support of the reading and music teachers.

"Rob spent the last month of school in a regular class, elated to be with his friends, but under pressure with the understanding that he must perform or be returned to the commotion, confusion, and stigma of the PI class. The balance of the year went fairly well.

"The end of the school year brought us a shocker. The school team announced that Rob should not go on to the fourth grade because his behavior was inappropriate and distracting to other students. Also, since he had not done well in the school's PI class, he should be placed in another school district's special-education program.

"Despite all our efforts, the team clung stubbornly to its position, completely ignoring the fact that their insistence on placing Rob in the PI class nearly destroyed him. The team would not acknowledge its failure, adhering to the psychology report findings that stated that Rob was emotionally disturbed, with a minimal learning disability, and therefore should be placed in an open, nonstructured classroom. We, his parents, and Mrs. Wright disagreed, contending that retention in the third grade with additional help in reading was the best way to meet Rob's needs. The illogical stance of the school's clinical team's argument was apparent to everyone but the members of the team.

"They censured Rob for his distractibility and at the same time insisted that he be placed in an extremely distractible environment. The team—almost vindictively, it seemed to us— insisted that they knew better how to meet Rob's needs.

"We consulted with a friend who was involved with the state education board. He advised us to have Rob retested by another clinical team located elsewhere, independently and at our own expense. We did so.

"This new evaluation, the support of Mrs. Wright, and the illogical stance of the school team's proposal forced the district superintendent to override his team's recommendation. Rob would be retained in the third grade with a teacher who was reputed to maintain a strict, structured classroom. We were elated over this decision.

"However, in the same breath that the superintendent announced his decision to override the proposal, he peremptorily said, 'What will you do when this fails? I know your son will become a drifter throughout school and eventually a nobody. The monkey is on your back now.'

"It was at this time that we saw Dr. Levinson on the *Phil Donahue Show.* For the first time my husband, our parents, and I were truly able to understand what Rob had been dealing with. No longer could we blame Rob or ourselves—no longer could we even think to ourselves that Rob was 'slow' or 'not quite right.' Not that we ever consciously verbalized these thoughts, but they nevertheless were there, and perhaps, unbeknownst to us, they were conveyed to Rob.

"Suddenly, Rob's inability to traverse certain school halls without falling, tripping, or bumping into other children became plausible in the light of his inner-ear dysfunction. Suddenly it was as though our characterization of Rob as a perfectly lovable and intelligent human being was validated.

"Most important, I could explain to Rob what he had. He quietly listened while I showed him pictures and sample writings of other dyslexics from your book. He looked into my eyes and was totally attentive. Finally, he asked, 'Is that why I always get sick on a swing?' I never knew that that had happened. All the pieces began to fit together—the stomachaches, the sensory overloading and upset when too much was happening too fast, the inability to sit still for more than a few seconds, etc.

"I called and made an appointment with Dr. Levinson. He examined Rob and determined that he was dyslexic.

"We began to have good results almost immediately. Rob was able to negotiate the halls, doorways, and steps without holding on to the walls. After only the third day of medication the reading teacher observed that Rob was reading faster than her fingers could track the lines. Rob's spelling and punctuation also showed improvement and have continued to do so.

"When Rob wrote compositions, he used only words that he knew how to spell, but between memory and spelling improvement and the teacher's encouragement and understanding, his creativity in writing has amazed us.

"For the first time Rob has been able to attend services in the old log-cabin Protestant church to which the entire family belongs. He had never been able to attend services because the white masonry and dark cedar logs horizontally laid made him nauseous. Now Rob not only attends services but also sings in the choir. His position is in the middle of the line, on the middle step; he stands straight and does not weave, stumble, or fall—another fantastic first!

"Due to motor coordination/balance improvement, Rob was once again placed in a regular gym class. His medication, plus his tremendous drive to perform well, have produced amazing results. Within a few months of the change, he became captain of the hockey team and an effective player—truly amazing when you consider that he had been unable to run twenty feet without falling down!

"Rob experienced two other successes that were a great source of pleasure to him and that emphasized how far he had come. He entered a roller-skating race with his classmates. The race took place in a large indoor rink—and he won second place! He also competed in a footrace held in the school gym and handled himself creditably, not coming in first but ahead of two of his friends. The gym teacher kidded him and asked Rob if he had eaten frogs' legs for breakfast.

"I could go on forever discussing Rob's improvements and successes, both big and small. I must also add that when he is off his medication on weekends, his old problems and difficulties return in full force. By Sunday evening his coordination and disorganization are very bad: He falls against the furniture and bumps into walls. In fact, one Saturday night Rob got out of bed and fell against the bedpost and broke his nose. Whenever the medication is changed or accidentally forgotten, I receive a call from the teacher along the lines of 'Rob had a bad day; it was difficult to get him to settle down and do his work. He was disorganized' or 'He kept bumping into the other children.'*

"At the end of the first semester, our son's report card reflected improved grades in all subjects. Three of his teachers wrote him letters in which they congratulated him upon his newfound success in speech, in reading, and in the classroom! In fact, Rob's remarkable progress has become the source of much discussion among parents and teachers. We've received many inquiries about Dr. Levinson and his diagnostic and treatment techniques.

"Four months after treatment had begun, we all experienced a new 'high,' especially Rob. He had just completed his first novel of 125 pages—in only two days! Rob was so excited about his accomplishment that he promised to read a book each week, circumstances permitting (no vacations or family holiday outings). He has stuck to his word.

"Also, he no longer needs to track with a finger while he reads.

"Other positive developments we noticed were:

- Rob's penmanship has gotten better. Originally he drew his letters, but now he uses cursive script, and his lettering is both even and fluent.
- Rob is in the school band, playing sax. At one time his participation would have been unthinkable!
- His schoolwork and reports showed steady, consistent im-

*For patients such as Rob, it is very important that they remain on medication seven days a week, with perhaps reduced doses on weekends.

provement. His classroom teacher said that at the beginning of the school year she was very satisfied with good effort and a few good papers a week. For Rob to complete his work at all was truly an accomplishment. However, in May, the end of the school year, Rob's teacher reported that she never received less than *A-* or *B*-quality material from him—quite astounding, not only to his teacher but to us as well! We are so proud of him that there are no words that can possibly convey our feelings.

- Rob shows a real flair for arts and crafts, the discovery of which was an unexpected bonus. Several of his creations were chosen to go on display in the school showcase. On the strength of his contributions, he was chosen to participate in the Gifted Art Program offered by the school for the next year.

"Rob still tires easily upon occasion, but he does not get wiped out the way he did before treatment. Also, he experiences reversals, but these occur *less and less frequently.* School days that are particularly hectic with extra activities are difficult for him—the less confusion, the better. He is also able to function well in small groups. Before, he could only do so on a one-to-one basis. Family gatherings on holidays were never really enjoyable for any of us because Rob would become physically ill from the confusion, noise, and distraction. Today we all enjoy them, particularly Rob!

"Our entire family circle was dominated by the problem of having to deal with the many personnel in the educational system. We worried that Rob would be unjustly classified as retarded or pushed into delinquency by complete frustration. We all benefited from having Rob see Dr. Levinson. We were lucky that the medication brought about such good changes for our son—in the nick of time. But even more important, in understanding the root of Rob's learning disabilities, all our lives have been turned around.

"Last, but by no means least, has been the great improvement in his feelings about himself. I have tried to deal only with absolutes in listing Rob's triumphs and accomplishments. There have been many other positive, noticeable, more subtle changes that relate to Rob's attitudes, self-esteem, and sense of well-being that I have not included but are very much a part of this year's success story."

In a progress report one year after treatment began, Mrs. Stone glowingly wrote about Rob's year in the fourth grade, a school year characterized by the same wonderful and positive results in his academic and behavior performances:

> Dr. Levinson's program of treatment and follow-up, good teacher support, Rob's self-determination, and the guidance of a loving reading teacher contributed to the transformation of a floundering, unhappy young child to a much talked about, successful, happy youngster.

The early years of life are the most formative, shaping the personality, behavior, and values of young people. The influence of the school upon the child, like that of the family, is immeasurable. That influence has the potential for both good and bad, depending upon the individuals in the educational structure, their qualifications, and their predilections to be fair, open-minded, and responsive to the needs of children. Educators and counselors with whom a child is in daily contact, and the positive and negative experiences in the school and class-room, determine, in large measure, how the child views him-self and how he views others—his parents, siblings, teachers, and peers. This, in turn, influences his behavior and attitudes, facilitating or hindering a successful and happy adjustment to his world scholastically, personally, and socially.

The two school systems depicted in the story of Rob Stone and his family thought they were caring and responsive. One was just beginning to deal with children who have learning disorders. However, it was antiquated and not sufficiently knowledgeable in its approach. Had the Stones followed its proposal, their son would have been placed in a school for brain-damaged children, probably resulting in emotional scar-ring.

Upon returning to visit friends in the community in which they had lived, the Stones learned that four families had re-moved their children from the same school for reasons similar to theirs. The school did not have the program or facilities to deal effectively with children who had learning disabilities. Their staff was limited in its thinking and lacked the open-mindedness and flexibility needed to explore different con-cepts and theories. Fortunately, the Stones and the other four families recognized the deficits in the school before emotional fallout and other consequences permanently damaged their children. Unfortunately, there were other families who did fol-low the recommendations of the school.

On the other hand, the second school system, which was similar in size and population, did have a program for learn-ing-disabled children and had qualified personnel to execute it. However, their personnel's knowledge and diagnostic tech-niques were incomplete and, in some instances, biased. They were victims, in a way, of their own "dyslexia"—blind to the problems of those children who did not fit the "pattern," who did not conform to their psychoeducational theories.

Just as this chapter was being completed, in walked Dr. Larry A. Sternson, Professor of Pharmaceutical Chemistry at the University of Kansas's College of Pharmacy, with his son, Tom. They had come for a revisit. He expressed his delight with Tom's progress and discussed some of the problems he experienced with members of the educational system. With his permission I am including some important comments:

> Some educators are reluctant to learn, to read, and to change their opinions as to how children with dyslexia should be treated. It is easier to blame parents, environmental situations, and other factors, and to conclude with the statement that "if the little guy would just buckle down, we know that he would succeed." They seem unable to grasp that the inability to buckle down is a direct manifestation of the disorder and is not controllable. . . .

Inasmuch as some critics have attributed the favorable responses of my patients to "the placebo effect," at the end of our clinical visit I jokingly asked Professor Sternson what he thought of his son's remarkable response to the "placebo" treatment I had prescribed. He replied:

> There is no way in the world a placebo effect could produce such dramatic and long-lasting effects in a child, especially a child unfamiliar with the effects of medication. No other therapy I have ever offered to Tom has had a placebo effect. He

has been to optometrists, occupational therapists, and special educators, and he has never had an effect like this before. Surely his mother, he, and I all wanted the same response effect from the beginning. Moreover he responded better to certain medications than to others, and not at all to one.

And when we took him off the medication on weekends, his symptoms came back again after two days and lasted until Tuesday or Wednesday of the following week. We had to rearrange the manner in which we took him off the medication to avoid this effect.

How is my son to psychologically know when the medication effect wears off and then begins again?

It is very obviously a medication effect—a true medication effect.

Although many educators and school psychologists believe only *they* have the understanding and the knowledge of the dynamics of child development and the educational process, this is not true. More and more parents are knowledgeable, aware, and anxious to participate in this process. The children can only benefit if these two most important and powerful forces combine their strengths to achieve their common goal: helping each child fulfill her or his own potential to become all she or he has the capacity to be.

Obviously, not all school systems are like the two depicted in the story of the Stone family. There are others whose professionalism, objectivity, and open-mindedness about new ideas and proven concepts are supportive to both the dyslexic child and his family. I hope this chapter serves to enlighten further and to enlarge the numbers of such school systems.

VIII

A Deaf Girl Can Hear
More Clearly

One of the most remarkable cases I have thus far treated is that of Consuelo Brody, a pretty, insightful, and highly intelligent seventeen-year-old who either was born deaf or became deaf shortly thereafter. Amazingly, her auditory discrimination improved when treated with the very same medications I use with dyslexics. And because Consuelo's word discrimination became so much better, she was able to attend a college for "normal" persons.

The background surrounding this truly remarkable story might be the subject of a program such as *That's Incredible.* It illustrates how a mother's determination led to the unexpected relationship between inner-ear–determined deafness and dyslexia, and highlights the important therapeutic ramifications of this correlation.

It was Consuelo's childhood deafness that motivated her mother to delve into the study of hearing loss. She was determined to do all she could to help her daughter overcome this handicap. Accordingly, Mrs. Brody became a speech and hearing specialist.

Consuelo's deafness was not typical: Her mother noticed two episodes in which her daughter appeared to hear despite having been diagnosed as severely hearing-impaired.

The first incident occurred at the time Consuelo was two years old. Mrs. Brody related the following:

I put the new baby's bottle to my mouth and said "Bottle, bottle." Consuelo looked at me and put her finger into her ear, pulled it out, and said "Bott." She repeated it. I couldn't believe it! Consuelo had never repeated a word in her life up to that point.

A couple of years later the second incident occurred. Consuelo was in the bathtub. Outside the bathroom her sister Denise was playing the harmonica. Suddenly, Consuelo put her finger in her ear, smiled, and uttered the sound "Ahh!" She had obviously heard the sound and she was not wearing her hearing aid. I asked Denise to continue to play so that I could observe Consuelo's reactions. Every time Denise began to play, Consuelo would put her finger into her ear and smile. She had heard! I was so excited!

Consuelo knew about twenty-five words. I covered my mouth and repeated these words. She then repeated them, getting every word right! I was stunned! An hour later I said the words once again in a similar manner, but this time Consuelo did not hear anything. I could not understand how this occurred. I had to find out what was wrong!

Mrs. Brody read through book after book in order to understand how her deaf child could episodically hear. She stumbled upon a disorder called Ménière's disease, one that causes an adult to lose hearing acuity and impairs the balance and coordination system, i.e., the inner-ear system.

Mrs. Brody wondered: "Could my daughter have had Ménière's disease since birth? Could that explain why her hearing appeared to deteriorate with age, and account for the episodes in which her hearing came and went?"

While taking speech and hearing classes, Mrs. Brody consulted many teachers. Some were sympathetic, but they all said the same thing: "How could a child have Ménière's disease?"

Two additional unexplained but related episodes helped convince Mrs. Brody that her daughter indeed had Ménière's disease. One morning, when Consuelo was six years old, she was standing perfectly still and suddenly fell forward. Consuelo had apparently momentarily lost all balance control.

When seven and a half years of age, Consuelo was seated in the living room and suddenly, very calmly, drew a circular motion with her hand and repeatedly said "Round." Following this motion, she stood up and appeared to stagger across the room, unable to climb the stairs. A few minutes after this episode, she was back to normal.

These two episodes of imbalance and dizziness convinced Mrs. Brody that her intuition and theory regarding her daughter were accurate. She consulted a famous ear, nose, and throat specialist. The following are excerpts from his consultation report, supporting Mrs. Brody's conclusion:

There are a number of factors that make it a most unusual case. . . . I do not believe that Connie's hearing loss is of a congenital nature but due to some abnormality in the inner ear. This may explain the occasional return of good hearing, the tinnitus ringing and recurrent vertigo and imbalance.

This is a most unusual situation and I feel that every effort should be made to improve her hearing on a conservative basis.

She also consulted a neurologist. However, this specialist was skeptical of Mrs. Brody's observations, due to the fact that she was both a mother and a specialist in hearing and speech. Thus, he states, "This has raised a suspicion of overenthusiasm concerning the reported signs and symptoms. . . . If, indeed, Consuelo has had dizzy episodes and remarkable spontaneous episodes of improved hearing, then an end-organ (ear) disease causing profound deafness should be seriously suspected. However, one must be very cautious. . . ."

All too often biased convictions lead professionals to minimize and even discard vital observations and insights, in this case those made by a loving mother who also happened to be a specialist in the very audiological area she was personally involved with. As a result, the burden of determining a valid diagnosis was dumped back on the parent—rather than investigated by the consulted expert.

Fortunately, Mrs. Brody made the correct decision. She took her daughter to see a famous neuro-otologist—a surgeon specializing in correcting deficits within the ear and the inner-ear system. He confirmed Mrs. Brody's suspicions and operated on Consuelo.

This surgery appeared successful in arresting further hearing deterioration. "But," wondered Mrs. Brody, "what would have happened if I had taken Connie to this doctor when she was an infant? Had he operated on her at that time, could this surgery have kept her hearing from getting so much worse?"

Following Mrs. Brody's visit to the specialist and prior to Connie's surgery, a trial of an antihistamine was advised. Mrs. Brody noted an improvement in her daughter's hearing discrimination. However, upon retesting her audiologically, the doctor did not find any change.

Only in retrospect did Mrs. Brody stumble upon the reason for the discrepancy in her observation and the doctor's testing. In reality, both pieces of paradoxical observations were correct.

The doctor had tested Connie with individual "beep" tones, a test to evaluate auditory acuity. Mrs. Brody, on the other hand, observed an improvement in Connie's ability to discriminate spoken sounds. Her testing revealed an improvement in her auditory discrimination.

Indeed, Connie's hearing acuity had not improved on the antihistamine. Thus, her scores when tested with "beeps" did not change while using the medication. However, Mrs. Brody's testing was also correct. Her daughter's auditory discrimination had significantly improved, and the reasons for this discrepancy will be described shortly.

Connie also exhibited another interesting and seemingly paradoxical symptom: Her ability to read lips was significantly worse when wearing her hearing aid. This observation was corroborated by all. Mrs. Brody stated, "I noticed that when her hearing aid was on, she would say, 'What? What?' Then, when the hearing aid was turned off, she understood me. Needless to say, this is a most unusual reaction. Generally, when one wears a hearing aid and does lipreading, one's comprehension is much better. Lipreading and use of a hearing aid tend to complement one another. But with Consuelo the opposite was true. She became more confused."

Although Consuelo's hearing had stopped deteriorating as a result of the surgery, the picture she presented to her parents was not only confusing but bleak. While vacationing, Mrs. Brody happened to be watching a *Donahue* rerun. She reports: "I almost fell out of my seat because Dr. Levinson began to talk about the prescription drug meclizine (Antivert) and its importance in treating people with dyslexia, describing how it improved their reading and how the inner-ear system and its computer, the cerebellum, act as a mediator between the senses and the higher centers in the brain."

Mrs. Brody ran to the library and read *A Solution to the Riddle Dyslexia* from cover to cover. She suddenly understood all the paradoxical observations made of her daughter. She suddenly understood why her daughter's hearing acuity had not improved with the medication, whereas her auditory discrimination had: "Suddenly, I began to see it all very clearly. It was almost like a revelation. A revolutionary discovery had been made within the speech and audiology fields."

Connie's auditory acuity did not really improve on the medication. That's all the "beeps" tested for. However, she did improve in her ability to discriminate *sounds* and sound sequences in sentences. In other words, the medicine helped her inner-ear system better fine-tune the sound sequences coming into the brain. Accordingly, she could better discriminate them, despite the fact that her hearing acuity did not change. That is to say, Connie had two problems: an auditory acuity problem that did not respond to medication, and a dyslexic disorder secondary to a dysfunction within her inner-ear system. Stated another way, her total hearing was a result of two factors: hearing acuity and the ability to distinguish sound sequences. Treating the latter factor improved Connie's overall ability to hear words and sentences more clearly.

If the auditory input is not properly fine-tuned, it is received by the thinking brain as blurry and scrambled, just as visual signals are in those reporting word-blurring, double images, and moving words, or oscillopsia. The medication tends to fine-tune the auditory input, thus helping spoken words become increasingly clear and comprehensible.

After Mrs. Brody brought Connie to my office and following appropriate testing, I noted that Connie indeed had dyslexia. This diagnosis also cleared up the last remaining confusing observation: why Connie couldn't read lips and use a hearing aid at the same time. Dyslexics frequently have difficulty coordinating two or more functions simultaneously.

Connie was placed on the prescription drug meclizine as well as a series of other vitamins and medications shortly thereafter. She improved remarkably. Her auditory discrimination has dramatically increased from about 15 percent to about 65 to 70 percent using a hearing aid. This means that she can function in a world of normal hearing.

Connie's response to medication has also helped solve another very difficult problem associated with Ménière's disease: *recruitment.* Recruitment is a phenomenon that occurs when the volume or amplitude of the hearing aid is turned up. Suddenly, there is the mushrooming surge of sounds that fuzzes and confuses the incoming signals, rendering discrimination difficult, even impossible.

With the medication, however, Consuelo can now increase the amplitude of her hearing aid without the occurrence of high-frequency distortion or screeching. The medication enabled her to filter out selectively or inhibit background and even mushrooming noises, thus greatly improving her ability to use a hearing aid effectively. These observations and discoveries have added a whole new dimension to the treatment of Ménière's disease and related hearing losses in which there exists a hidden disturbance within the inner-ear system.

For many years Consuelo had been having her hearing tested by audiologist Dr. Harvey J. Gardner, the director of the Huntington Hearing and Speech Center and former director of audiology at the Manhattan Eye, Ear and Throat Hospital. One year her test on July 27 showed an auditory discrimination (clarity of heard words) score of 16 percent in her better ear. While she was on medication Dr. Gardner conducted a series of retests until, on October 19, her score jumped to 52 percent—a fantastic improvement. Even more important, on March 14, just six months later, her binaural score climbed to 60 percent, up from 12 percent in earlier testing. Now she could integrate information heard in both ears! Mrs. Brody also took her daughter to visit the surgeon who had operated on her in 1977. His testing further substantiated that of the new doctor. A fantastic improvement was noted: Her auditory discrimination jumped from 0 to 32 percent. The second score was slightly less than the first only because the second doctor used recordings that tend to distort the sound slightly, whereas the first doctor's testing was with the live voice. However, both groups of tests showed the same results: a 32 percent differential and improvement without the use of a hearing aid.

For the very first time a deaf patient with Ménière's disease could discriminate between voices better with a hearing aid as a result of simple antihistaminic treatment, which improved inner-ear functioning.

Consuelo is now a much happier, more confident, more outgoing young lady. On the Stamford Reading Achievement Test, her scores indicated that she had jumped five years in one—a jump never seen before at her school. Consuelo's visual and auditory senses are now in harmony, complementing and catalyzing each other. Moreover, her improvement extends to other areas: math, biology—indeed, all her other subjects. She is now scoring at the top of her class in almost all subjects. And she is able to understand and enjoy watching TV. For the first time in her life she will go to stores alone and shop. Consuelo's success story is remarkable, not only from the medical-scientific point of view but also from her own inner "feeling" point of view. Entirely new vistas inevitably opened up to a previously word-deaf child, enabling her to explore and appreciate *all* the beauty and wonder that is a part of life for a normal, healthy youngster. Her life and feelings have been rekindled and further awakened.

Mrs. Brody found an answer as a result of her determination, dedication, and prayers.

Connie's life is now open-ended for the first time ever. She is no longer restricted and confined by her severe hearing and dyslexic disability. She can become anything she desires.

However, there is more to this story. As a result of Consuelo's significant improvement, her brother Fred, at age sixteen, and sister Marie, at age fifteen, were also brought to me for examination and treatment. Both Marie and Fred had attended the Learning Disability Unit of Adelphi University for five years, but their progress was minimal. Both had superior IQs but were having trouble in school. Both had difficulties with reading, spelling, and concentration. And both had experienced visual-word inputs as blurry. By contrast, Consuelo had experienced sounds as blurry. Inasmuch as Marie's blurred vision bothered her significantly, she was examined by an optometrist who found her eyes to be within normal limits. Unfortunately, glasses did not help.

Of the two children, Fred seemed to have the more severe problem. Although he had a high IQ and an inquisitive mind, Fred was unable to sit still or concentrate on anything for more than a few moments. His grades were not good and he hardly spoke, appearing to be very much an introvert. He was neither verbally dull nor schizoid. He just found it very difficult to verbalize his thoughts, even with his family. Consequently, he withdrew, finding it much easier to listen than to speak.

Both Fred and Marie were diagnosed as dyslexic. And after treatment, both children showed marked improvement.

Despite extra help, Marie had been a C student. After treatment she began to earn grades in the nineties in math, social studies, and biology. During tests, her teachers sat her at the back of the room to be sure no one copied from her. Eventually, Marie successfully completed medical school.

Fred was able to get A's in math and chemistry and B's in his other subjects. His reading, grammar, spelling, and sentence structure so improved that his already amazed family felt even more amazed. His writing now appears normal; he is more verbal and is now an active participant rather than a silent, introverted observer. Fred is able to practice law.

This family of dyslexic individuals highlights the already known fact that dyslexia can be inherited. (Mr. Brody is dyslexic, as well.) But although multiple family members may have the very same underlying disorder, both the intensity and combination of symptoms may vary significantly from one family member to another. Thus, family members who are normal readers but have only mild writing, spelling, mathematical, or directional disturbances most often do not realize they have dyslexia. Researchers who do not detect dyslexic family members with normal reading problems often make a similar mistake. As a result, most statistics having to do with genetic dyslexia have been subject to significant degrees of errors.

In Summary

Impaired auditory acuity due to damage within the hearing apparatus and a silent but coexisting impairment of the inner ear with auditory discrimination difficulties may lead to a *mixture of symptoms* that must be clearly distinguished from one another. Researchers have continually reported a relationship between repeated middle-ear infections, fluid, and a higher than expected incidence in resulting speech, concentration, and learning disorders. Until now, the latter were blamed on the ear infections and the middle ear. Should not the inner ear be further explored? Might not inner-ear improvement result in improved verbal discrimination in those previously thought to have *only* hearing acuity loss? And might a host of other inner-ear–determined dyslexic symptoms coexist and be medically treatable?

IX

Solving the Dyslexia Riddle—
A Historical Perspective

After having been exposed to a rather large sample of dyslexic patients, to their symptoms, experiences, and responses to treatment, as well as to my latest concept of the dyslexic disorder, the reader may find this belated presentation of history after the fact, out of joint—indeed, reversed in time and space or position.

Do not be thrown by this reversal. Indeed, dyslexics frequently use their unstable directional and reversal mechanisms to significant advantage. And I have attempted to learn from them what I can. By shifting the history of my research effort from the beginning to the middle of this book, I have given the reader time, experience, and perspective. I hope this dyslexia-like organizational device will prove immensely helpful.

The ability to reverse flexibly, backtrack, and change directions in time and place has indeed been immeasurably helpful to me in guiding my research effort to a sound conclusion.

Most often, research does not proceed along a straight line. Clues suddenly appear and disappear and even twist into elusive arcs. Researchers must be able to adapt to these rapidly shifting and directed flashes.

In many ways I felt my research techniques oscillating between the typical behavior of Oscar and Felix in TV's famed *Odd Couple*. Interestingly, both Oscar and Felix reflect the extreme variations characterizing the dyslexic disorder. For example, Oscar's disorganization highlights the underlying dyscoordination, whereas Felix represents its overcompensatory extreme, reflecting a rigid need to control one's underlying chaos by developing rigid personality controls. Although the discipline symbolized by Felix is crucial to any research endeavor, this discipline must become an aid rather than the burden of compulsive rigidity hampering Felix. Therefore, I have attempted to escape the restrictions imposed by a Felix-like mental and scientific rigor mortis by choosing a flexible, "dyslexialike" (as opposed to "normal") sequential writing style.

Having completed this introductory apology, I will now relate to you the path leading me to resolve the riddle characterizing dyslexia and my dyslexic research.

My "dyslexic" career began entirely by chance some thirty-five years ago. I had just completed my psychiatric residency and sought an interesting position that might help support me economically while I began a private practice in psychiatry. A new position suddenly opened at the Bureau of Child Guidance (BCG), New York City Board of Education. Psychiatrists were needed to treat the many children experiencing learning, emotional, and behavioral difficulties within the New York City educational system.

By chance I was assigned to a tiny bureau within this giant educational complex, the Bureau of Special Reading Services (SRS). Children within this special reading tutorial service were accepted only if (1) they were two or more years behind their peers in reading, (2) they had a normal or above-normal IQ, (3) they were not disruptive or behavior problems, and (4) they had no evidence of brain damage or any type of sensory defect. Only later did I realize that the acceptance criteria of the SRS were by chance identical to the criteria utilized by most experts to define dyslexics.

In any event, the prevailing opinion within this clinically oriented tutorial service was that reading disabilities were caused by psychological factors. Accordingly, the clinical team examining children consisted of a specially trained reading teacher, a social worker, a psychologist, and a psychiatrist.

Every child within the SRS received two hours of tutoring a week in very small groups. And each child received a complete social work and psychological workup. Only those children failing to benefit significantly from the tutoring were seen and treated psychiatrically.

Having been trained psychiatrically, and initially having had little experience with the reading-disabled, I had no question or quarrel with the psychological point of view of the SRS. Indeed, I read through all the available psychiatric and psychoanalytical theories linking reading disorders with such emotional causes as sibling rivalry, competitive difficulties, fear of success, child-rearing difficulties (abuses and/or pampering and overpampering), sexual and/or aggressive fantasies having to do with looking or the eye, Oedipal conflicts, classroom abuse, and so on.

Thus, over a period of many years, I came to examine psychiatrically and later neurologically over one thousand reading-disabled children from all socioeconomic and cultural areas of New York City. Diligently I attempted to apply all existing psychological and analytical theories and principles when analyzing and treating the reading-disabled children psychotherapeutically. After a number of years of painstaking effort, I reluctantly concluded that a vast majority of psychological theories attempting to explain the causes and symptoms of reading disabilities had little to do with the cases I saw. The many symptoms characterizing the reading-disabled and the psychological theories attempting to explain them just did not correlate despite all my determined attempts to link them together. Reluctantly I was eventually forced to wonder:

- Was I personally inadequate in applying psychological theories espoused by respected analysts to the reading disorders I examined, or
- Was it possible that my respected teachers and researchers were inadequately espousing theories that had little or nothing to do with clinical reality?

Although personally I felt inclined to blame myself, and repeatedly did so, I eventually came to recognize that the vast majority of reading-disabled children and their families just did not fit into the psychologically accepted molds. Existing psychological theories could neither explain the cause of reading disorders for the vast majority of children I examined nor explain the typical reading and related symptoms characterizing the learning-disabled.

It is easy to understand how researchers originally formed the conviction that the reading and academic disturbances in dyslexia were of a primarily psychological origin. Do not dyslexics and the learning-disabled feel dumb, ugly, and hopeless? Are these not psychological symptoms? Are not dyslexic individuals prone to emotional and behavioral disorders, as well as a series of phobias, obsessions and compulsions, mood disturbances, and even psychosomatic symptoms such as bedwetting, muscle tics and tumors, headaches, dizziness, nausea, vomiting, and abdominal pain? Are not these symptoms typically those that fall within the psychiatric and psychological realms and spheres of influence?

However, my past mathematical training and intuition taught me that if the theory does not clinically and statistically fit the facts, the theory must be in error. It sounds simple to say this now, but it was not easy to detach myself from theories and convictions I'd lived with for years. Old, established scientific theories seldom fade away. They are clung to like religious symbols, even when they defy all new scientific realities.

Scientific frustration and clinical despair can be handled in two ways. You can either start all over scientifically or sidestep the whole conflict by initially denying the existence of fallacious theories based on created or fantasized data.

Starting over scientifically appears easy and exciting only in hindsight. In the beginning it is a lonely, time-consuming, frustrating experience. And only those with an intense curiosity and/or a low frustration tolerance are appropriately motivated to leap into new and unsanctioned scientific spheres.

Dyslexic patients and their teachers needed help. And I needed a scientific theory and concept I could live with and hang my hat on. I needed a way of helping my patients and their families, a way to justify my many years of training.

I began to search out other nonpsychological theories in my

attempt to explain the causes and symptoms of learning disabilities and dyslexia. Because of my medical background, it seemed only reasonable for me to assume that dyslexia had to be of a neurological origin if it was not psychologically based.

The prevailing neurological theory at the time was that dyslexia and its related symptoms were due to a disturbance within the thinking, speaking, IQ brain—the cerebral cortex. Ever since Kerr and Morgan* first recognized and described "word blindness" in 1896, it was assumed and believed that this disorder was due to a structural defect within the dominant half of the thinking brain—the side of the brain responsible for recognizing written symbols and seen objects, the side of the brain responsible for and determining meaningful speech functioning and handedness.

In the vast majority of right-handed individuals, the left side of the thinking brain is crucial or dominant in determining perceptual and speech functioning. Thus, the conviction developed that an impairment of the left side of the thinking brain was responsible for dyslexia. This conviction was based upon the following assumption: *If, indeed, damage to the dominant half of the thinking brain is proven responsible for the loss of reading and speech ability in previously normal adults via autopsy studies—resulting in alexia and aphasia—then children failing to acquire normal reading and/or speech functioning (dyslexia and dysphasia) must have an impairment in this very same area of the brain.* In other words, it was assumed that alexia was equal to dyslexia, and aphasia was equal to dysphasia.

The basis of this scientifically irresistible neurological theory is still widely held in high esteem, albeit in slightly modi-

*See p. 17.

fied forms. However, there was an obvious flaw in this theory. Inasmuch as there currently exists no clinical evidence of cerebral damage in dyslexia, and in view of the fact that many *bright*, even gifted children and adults had and have dyslexia, it seemed reasonable to assume that there was really nothing structurally wrong with the thinking brain. As a result, many neurologists assumed that the dominant brain was intact, but that its development was *delayed*.

This watered-down version of cerebral damage and dysfunction was more in harmony with the facts, although it still did not explain *all* or even a fragment of the data. And most unfortunately, it could not be proven. This theory *had* to be accepted as is, without validation. Clinicians were taught and expected to dance to the traditional scientific tune. And resistance to any challenge and change was—and still is—intense.

Interestingly, an alternative hypothesis was denied: If, indeed, a cerebral developmental lag or delay was present, and if, in addition, there was no clear-cut clinical evidence of any cerebral dysfunction, might not the searched-for disturbance be caused by a dysfunction in a noncortical area of the brain—a dysfunction secondarily causing this cerebral lag or delay? No cortically based investigator attempted to search for the root of dyslexia in noncerebral-cortical areas of the brain.

Some neurologists believe that dyslexia is due to a *lack* of dominance of one half of the thinking brain versus its other mirrored half. This theory is based on the reasoning and findings of a gifted psychiatrist-neurologist, Samuel Orton. Orton correlated dyslexia with speech disorders and a high incidence of left-handedness, and renamed the disorder *strephosymbolia*, meaning twisted symbols. He based his cerebral dominance theory and conviction on the following reasoning:

- If, indeed, the dominant half of the cerebral cortex, or thinking brain, controls reading and speech functions as well as right-handedness, and
- If cases with reading disorders have a higher incidence of speech disorders and left-handedness than they should have when compared with normal individuals,
- Then there must be a *lack* of dominance or control of the left-thinking brain.
- Moreover, this lack of left-sided dominance results in a *dominance conflict,* or dyscoordination, between the two halves of the cerebral cortex, resulting in reversals.

Although this dominance theory was interesting, it had many drawbacks. The most crucial drawback was one that Orton himself later recognized—that one of his basic assumptions was wrong: Dyslexia does *not* occur more often in left-handed individuals.

In addition, the speech disturbances noted in dyslexia are of a type found only in disorders of balance and coordination, i.e., inner-ear–related disorders. They are not of cerebral origin (the aphasic type)—speech disturbances in which individuals have difficulty understanding the meaning of what is said and/or difficulty in formulating the meaning of what they wish to say. Thus, I concluded, Orton's second assumption was also wrong: The speech disorders in dyslexia are not of a type due to a dysfunction within the thinking brain. And many a dyslexic with severe reading, spelling, math, and other difficulties has gifted speech functioning—

a finding highly incompatible with a primary aphasic or language disorder!

In addition, the cerebral-dominance theory of dyslexia suffers from the same drawbacks that negate the cerebral-lag theory of dyslexia:

- There is no way to prove or disprove the dominance theory of dyslexia.
- Its basic assumptions were found to be in error.
- It cannot explain the vast majority of symptoms in dyslexia.
- It cannot explain the absence of *language* symptoms in many dyslexics as well as the presence of *gifted linguistic* functioning in others.
- It has led nowhere diagnostically, therapeutically, or medically.
- An alternative explanation was never considered: that if indeed there were dyscoordinated and conflicting dominance of the two hemispheres, this difficulty might be caused by a primary disturbance elsewhere, namely the inner-ear system.

Despite all the above drawbacks, the dominance theory of dyslexia still has its believers and followers.

To date, the cortical theorists of dyslexia view the findings and results of optometrists, occupational therapists, etc., with suspicion. They reason as follows: If, indeed, dyslexia is a disturbance of the thinking, speaking, IQ part of the brain, how in the world can eye exercises, physical exercises, vitamins, diet, and medication improve the functioning of the thinking brain?

Once again, these cortical theorists have failed to view an alternative viewpoint: If eye therapy, occupational and reflex therapy, vitamins, diet, and medication as well as colored lenses improve the functioning of dyslexics, and if these therapies do not primarily improve the functioning of the thinking brain, then might not dyslexia be caused by a disturbance in a noncortical area of the brain? A finding in the late 1970s by Albert Galaburda and Thomas Kemper at Harvard has created ecstasy among "cerebral cortical" followers. Autopsy studies on one assumed "dyslexic" brain revealed the presence of abnormal cells in the dominant, thinking brain. Unfortunately, similar studies were not done on the noncerebral parts of that brain—certainly not the inner-ear system and the cerebellum. Why not? Might not a primary disturbance within the inner-ear system and cerebellum result in secondary disturbances within the cerebral cortex or thinking brain? Might not this secondary disturbance result in impaired cellular function and an ensuing cerebral lag? If this consideration was valid, then these alleged "cellular abnormalities" would have to occur many years after birth—and thus, they *couldn't* be of embryonic origin as these theorists suggest.

Perhaps another example would help the reader more fully understand the difference between a primary site of dysfunction and a secondary reaction to it. Consider a plant and a primary disturbance within its root system. Would not this root disturbance affect the coloring and the microscopic picture of the leaves? Most certainly! After carefully examining the leaves, should we conclude that the disturbance in the leaf is responsible for the disturbance of the plant—especially if its roots are never looked at?

Should we not weight the available data appropriately? If at that time I found well over 96 percent of more than a thousand dyslexic cases to have evidence of an inner-ear dysfunction—and if this theory led me to new methods of diagnosis, treatment, and a comprehensive explanation of all the symptoms characterizing this disorder—why should one case in which there allegedly exists prenatal cellular abnormalities within the cerebral cortex result in overenthusiasm, especially if the cortical theories led nowhere scientifically for almost a century?

In an attempt to harmonize this apparent "cortical" exception with my inner-ear dyslexic rule, I wondered if the first reported dyslexic patient whose brain was studied was not a *mixed dyslexic*—a dyslexic having inner-ear dysfunction mixed in with other evidence of brain dysfunction. If my assumption was correct, it would explain both the exception and the rule.

I then reviewed the findings of Drs. Albert Galaburda and Thomas Kemper reported in *Annals of Neurology* 6:94–100 (1979), entitled "Cytoarchitectonic Abnormalities in Developmental Dyslexia: A Case Study." Interestingly this patient was reported to have developed "nocturnal seizures at 16 years," a symptom unrelated to dyslexia and frequently highlighting an underlying *cerebral* dysfunction. As the authors state in this article: *"It is not possible to tell from a single case whether or not the anatomical findings have any causative relationship to the clinical findings, much less whether the malformation is responsible for the seizure disorder, the learning disability, both, or neither."* Interestingly, cortical theorists continued to use this single case study to "prove" their unprovable theories, in spite of the overwhelming evidence I have amassed. Moreover, this *single* case of unproven dyslexia has been reported in the media by cortical theorists *as if the cause and site of dyslexia may have been found.**

Instead of attempting to understand and explain this *single* case study in its proper scientific perspective, an unwarranted and overenthusiastic response was both promoted and publicized.

I always find psychological overreactions suspicious.

More recently, Galaburda and others have found these prenatal or fetal cellular abnormalities all over the cerebral cortex—not just in the reading-language center. And in an apparent theoretical reversal in which visual processing rather than language is considered to be the cause of dyslexia, Livingstone and coworkers as well as Galaburda (1992) now report cellular abnormalities in the "magnocellular visual subsystem," which processes rapid signals.

Since these so-called cellular abnormalities appear according to theoretical expectations, I strongly suspect their true and meaningful significance. And since dyslexia involves not only visual but auditory, tactile, motor, and other processing, it

---

*The following is an excerpt from an article entitled "Wen Smart Kids Cant Learn" by Nancy Rubin, and appeared in the February 1984 issue of *Ladies' Home Journal*:

> Other scientists are looking for answers in the cellular structure of the brain. Recently, neurology professor Albert Galaburda of Harvard Medical School and Dr. Thomas Kemper of Boston City Hospital conducted landmark research on the brain of a dyslexic man who died in an accident. While the brain appeared perfectly normal to the naked eye, microscopic examination of thin slices of the brain revealed a general immaturity in the structure of the left side of the brain as well as in the cells of its language centers. The doctors found gray-matter cells in parts of the brain usually containing white matter, as well as a disordered arrangement of nerve cells in the cortex, or brain covering.
>
> As a result of such findings, Drs. Galaburda and Kemper have concluded that profound differences may exist in the brains of dyslexics, which may be the result of some chemical abnormality during an early stage of fetal development. Such chemical aberrations, says Dr. Galaburda, may have a genetic component, which would explain why dyslexia tends to run in families.

would seem that cellular abnormalities will be found all over the brain.

But how can bright and gifted dyslexics—Einstein, Edison, Leonardo da Vinci, Nelson Rockefeller, Presidents Ford and Bush, Olympic stars Bruce Jenner and Greg Louganis—have such abnormal brains? They can't! And what happens to all those "found" and predicted abnormalities when dyslexics respond favorably and rapidly to treatment? Do these abnormalities, stated to be present in adult brains since embryonic development, suddenly dissolve or disappear? Obviously not!

In other words, these alleged cellular abnormalities seem completely inconsistent with what we know about the dysfunction and compensation in dyslexia—and thus with the vast majority of the content within this book.

To summarize: Picture each and every sign and symptom characterizing the many dyslexics in this and my related books and papers. And consider how bright and gifted so many of these dyslexics are. Consider that they often respond dramatically to maturation (the brain physiologically develops and compensates on its own), colored lenses, tutoring, occupational, reflex, and optometric therapy . . . as well as the anti–motion sickness medications. Then ask yourself again: Are these cellular abnormalities and resulting cerebral embryonic dyslexia theories "real"? Or are they incompatible with the dyslexia database presented within this and my other text?

My thoughts are: No one who really understands dyslexia and dyslexics could scientifically accept their reality and validity until they are proven.

Over a period of many years I became as disillusioned with the prevailing neurological theories of dyslexia as I had with the psychiatric ones. Upon analysis, I concluded that both psychiatric and neurological theories, and the alleged "evidence" used to support them, were a mixture of fact, fantasy, and fiction, with less fact than fiction. I came to view the dyslexic disorder and its research as a riddle defying all attempts at meaningful understanding, explanation, diagnosis, treatment, and prevention. This riddle, however, was scientifically solved and its existence explained in *A Solution to the Riddle Dyslexia,* and again in *A Scientific Watergate—Dyslexia.* For ease of presentation I will quickly summarize the steps leading to this solution.

Having been reluctantly forced to abandon the prevailing psychiatric and neurological theories, and finding all other co-existing theories limited in their explanatory scope and diagnostic-therapeutic efficacy, I sought to find the elusive cause of dyslexia and its symptomatic array.

I carefully reevaluated and analyzed all the available data, objectively searching for the hidden clues. I reviewed my own data very carefully in 1970, and to my dismay, I realized that 750 out of 1,000 consecutively examined dyslexic cases showed distinct evidence of some difficulty with balance and coordination. Only 1 percent of the cases exhibited evidence suggesting a possible cortical dysfunction.

In other words, my case histories indicated that the vast majority of dyslexic children demonstrated one or more of the following:

- Delayed ability to sit, crawl, walk, and/or talk
- Difficulty skipping, hopping, running, and/or participating in sports
- Fine motor coordination disturbances, such as difficulty tying shoelaces, buttoning buttons, zippering, holding a

pencil, using crayons, and coloring within guidelines, and/or awkward use of a knife and fork

- Dyscoordinated speech functioning, e.g., slurring, articulation impairments, stuttering or stammering
- Difficulty with balance and coordination, evidenced by delays in learning to ride a bike or walk a balance beam
- Accident proneness: frequent tripping, falling, bumping, and dropping things

Moreover, neurological examination revealed a series of clear-cut balance, coordination, and rhythmic signs consistent with the above difficulties and diagnostic of an inner-ear–system dysfunction.

As stated earlier, only 1 percent of cases showed evidence of a dysfunction within the thinking brain, e.g., low IQ, difficulty with comprehending and formulating meaningful speech, or left- or right-sided weakness indicative of an earlier paralysis, epilepsy, and so on.

Inasmuch as the vast majority of dyslexics revealed hard and fast evidence of dysfunctions within their inner-ear systems, despite my primary search for signs of dysfunction of the thinking brain I was logically forced to conclude that dyslexia correlated only with inner-ear/cerebellar signs and not with any cortical signs.

Circular Logic—and Traditional Theories

Even researchers and clinicians believing that dyslexia was of a cerebral-cortical origin found only balance and coordination (inner-ear) signs in the cases they examined. They concluded, however, that the presence of noncortical balance and coordination signs indicated that there must be something wrong with the brain. And since there were reading difficulties present, then there *had to be* a disturbance within the thinking brain, despite the complete statistical absence of cortical signs.

In other words, the cortical theorists, in order to prove their theory, reasoned in circles. Their circular reasoning may be summarized as follows:

- They naturally assumed that dyslexia was of cerebral-cortical origin.
- Since only inner-ear signs could be found, they termed these signs "soft" in a perhaps unconscious effort to minimize their significance.
- They further assumed that there must exist "hard" signs of cerebral dysfunction in view of the fact that "soft" signs were found, the latter (so they said) clearly suggesting the presence of a disturbance within the central nervous system.
- They concluded that dyslexia was of cerebral-cortical origin and were completely satisfied that they had proved their assumption.

These cortical theorists began with an assumption that the reading disturbance in dyslexia was of cerebral-cortical origin, and utilized the presence of inner-ear signs to justify the conclusion that there was a cortical dysfunction despite the fact that there were no cortical signs to be found. They then utilized the *assumption* that the reading disorder in dyslexia was of cerebral origin to conclude or prove their assumption correct.

I, too, had initially assumed that dyslexia was of cerebral-cortical origin and sought to find corroborating evidence of a cerebral dysfunction. But as I found only balance and coordination difficulties—difficulties that pointed to an inner-ear/cerebellar dysfunction—I was forced to conclude that dyslexia is obviously not of a cerebral-cortical origin and that this disorder may well be due to a dysfunction within the inner-ear system. I then conducted further clinical studies of dyslexic cases, attempting to better clarify the signs and symptoms present. These studies clearly revealed the presence of inner-ear/cerebellar–related disturbances 96 percent of the time. However, in these studies I was specifically looking for signs characterizing an inner-ear/cerebellar dysfunction. In the previous study I had been searching mainly for cortical signs, so I had found that only 75 percent of the cases had evidence of an inner-ear dysfunction.

Independent Scientific Corroboration: The Neurological Study

To corroborate independently my clinical findings, I sent significant samples of dyslexic cases to be examined neurologically at a major metropolitan hospital. These neurological studies also revealed that 96 percent of the cases showed signs of inner-ear dysfunction. Despite the presence of only inner-ear or cerebellar signs, these cases were frequently labeled as having minimal cerebral dysfunction or cerebral damage. Interestingly, the same hospital's neurologists invariably would label almost identical cases as having inner-ear dysfunction if the parents or children presented them with complaints of dizziness or vertigo. In other words, *the neurologists frequently diagnosed their cases independently of their own clinical findings.* Restated:

- If a child complained of learning difficulties, the case was diagnosed as having "minimal cerebral dysfunction"—despite the reported presence of only inner-ear or cerebellar signs.
- If a very similar child with identical clinical findings complained of dizziness, he or she would be diagnosed as having an "inner-ear dysfunction."

These studies clearly revealed the correlation between dyslexia and inner-ear/cerebellar dysfunction. At the same time, an analysis of these reported data in dyslexia exposed the bias characterizing the interpretation of neurological data.

Special Inner-Ear Corroborating Studies

In addition, a rather large group of dyslexics was sent to a series of hospitals for special physiological inner-ear testing called electronystagmography (ENG). According to testing performed at New York University Medical Center, Lenox Hill Hospital, Manhattan Eye, Ear, and Throat Hospital, and Mount Sinai Hospital, 90 percent of the cases were found to show definite evidence of an inner-ear dysfunction, further confirming my own findings and even those of the Columbia Presbyterian Hospital group of neurologists.

Having thus proved neurologically and physiologically that dyslexia definitely correlated with an inner-ear dysfunction, I attempted to explain how this dyslexic disorder—this sensory-input disturbance with resultant academic and intellectual dysfunctioning—can be explained on the basis of an inner-ear–related balance and coordination disturbance. Initially, I reasoned as follows:

- Most dyslexics examined display eye-tracking difficulties when reading. For example, almost all dyslexic children lose their places when reading. Their eyes seem to jump wildly from letter to letter, word to word, and line to line, resulting in letter, word, and line scrambling as well as a compensatory need to guide one's eyes with a finger or card.
- The inner-ear system has been proven to direct and guide our eyes and tracking responses automatically during the reading process.
- Thus, a dysfunction of the inner ear could explain the tracking difficulties in dyslexia, and the resulting visual scrambling could explain the secondary memory, comprehension, and concentration difficulties resulting when the thinking brain receives messages that are out of sequence and/or blurry.

3-Diagnostic Instruments
(Visual, Auditory, and Tactile)

To prove that there truly existed tracking difficulties in dyslexics, I devised an instrument called a 3-D Optical Scanner. This instrument is capable of accurately and rapidly measuring the fixation and tracking capacity of the eye during a readinglike process.

The 3-D Optical Scanner projects a moving series of elephants (or any target), which the eyes of the tested individual are reflexively forced to follow. As the speed of the moving elephants is increased, the speed at which the eye is forced to track these accelerated elephants must correspondingly increase. Ultimately, the speed of the moving elephants exceeds the ability of the eye to follow them. Blurring is then experienced; the point at which this happens is called the blurring speed.

Further testing revealed that the average dyslexic had one-half the blurring speed or tracking capacity of nondyslexic individuals, proving that there existed an eye-tracking defect in dyslexics.

Individuals were also asked to look at a stationary sequence of elephants while a series of moving lines resembling a picket fence moved across them. Only dyslexics experienced the elephants as blurred or in movement. Nondyslexic individuals were able to fixate clearly on the stationary elephants despite the moving, overlapping background. Dyslexics' eyes would repeatedly wander off target, from foreground to background, without stability or constancy, and foreground and background were mixed and scrambled or reversed with each other.

Inasmuch as the 3-D Optical Scanner was capable of rapidly and accurately measuring eye-tracking defects, I realized it could be used as a very useful diagnostic screening instrument to detect dyslexics. Refinements in the procedure now render it more than 95 percent accurate in predicting dyslexia and thus the presence of an underlying inner-ear dysfunction. For the very first time a medical means of detecting dyslexia had been found—an instrument independent of IQ, prior learning experiences, socioeconomic factors, language barriers, and pencil-and-paper reading-and-writing tests.

Because this test was medically based and independent of reading scores, it proved highly useful in screening kindergarten children with dyslexia. Utilizing the 3-D Optical Scanner, I screened an entire kindergarten population in District 26, Queens, New York City—1,500 children. My findings revealed that approximately 20 percent of this middle-class population had dyslexia or a related underlying inner-ear dysfunction. I also demonstrated that the blurring speeds of males versus females and left-handed versus right-handed individuals were identical.

These and other data of mine suggested that handedness and gender played no significant primary role in dyslexia—refuting the views of Orton and other traditionalists such as Geschwind (1982). Interestingly, a recent Yale study by Shaywitz et al. (1992) confirmed my views in this regard: that handedness, sex, and dyslexia are unrelated (see Appendix D).

In proving that dyslexia is due to an inner-ear dysfunction, I searched for a medical means to treat this disorder. By viewing the dyslexic tracking impairment as similar to that experienced by normal individuals when reading in a car moving along a bumpy road, or while in a boat tossed by waves, or after spinning, I realized that dyslexia may also be viewed as similar to a form of motion sickness, although it is not necessarily accompanied by the nausea and vomiting that characterizes motion sickness. I therefore attempted to treat dyslexics with anti–motion sickness medications and related pharmaceutical agents.* I reasoned that if such medications helped the inner ear handle the motion input in motion sickness, thus alleviating the motion-sickness symptoms, then these very same medications might similarly help the dyslexic reading process resulting from a dysfunctioning inner-ear system.

Fortunately, testing proved the above assumptions to be correct in most cases, as noted in Chapter V. Initially, I ex-

*Reminder: Because of possible side effects, people should never attempt to treat themselves without a doctor's supervision.

pected only the reading symptoms in dyslexia to improve with medication. To my delight and surprise a whole series of sensorimotor symptoms improved, including hearing (auditory) and touch (tactile) sequencing functions.* Accordingly, I designed two new additional instruments capable of measuring *auditory blurring* and *tactile blurring* in a manner similar to the way my 3-D Optical Scanner measured visual blurring.

To measure auditory blurring, I devised an instrument capable of speeding up a series of clear sounds until they could no longer be distinguished, with and without an interfering background, thus establishing the auditory blurring speed. In a similar fashion I designed another instrument capable of tapping out touch patterns on one's arm or hand. As the pattern speed intensified, one could no longer distinguish or feel the pattern, at which time tactile blurring would result. Further experiments clearly highlighted the fact that auditory blurring and tactile blurring speeds are often different for dyslexics versus unimpaired individuals—compensatory exceptions aside—just as the visual blurring speeds are lower for dyslexics. By obtaining visual, auditory, and tactile blurring speeds, the observer can better diagnose the underlying inner-ear/cerebellar dysfunctioning and delineate the corresponding sensory-processing defects.

---

*Many a dyslexic would hear a tune, or sound sequence as blurry or partially blurry, mirroring the way in which they experienced letters and words as visibly blurred, scrambled, reversed, or moving. The same was found true for the perception of accelerated sequences of touch sensations.

A Panoramic Concept of Dyslexia

The collection and analysis of the dyslexic treatment responses to the anti–motion sickness medications led me to an entirely new concept of dyslexia, a concept far wider in scope and depth than my original, rather simplistic tracking hypothesis.

I realized that the dyslexic disorder reached into and affected most areas of one's waking and sleeping lives. Hence, I came to view the inner-ear system as a fine-tuner for the entire sensory-input and motor-output system. Interestingly, I later found the above observations to be in perfect harmony with a series of animal experiments conducted by an outstanding group of neurophysiologists: R. S. Snider, A. Stowell, R. S. Dow, R. Anderson, and E. D. Adrian—one of them, Adrian, a Nobel Prize winner.

Perhaps a quote from Ray Snider's magnificent *Scientific American* article "The Cerebellum" will highlight this "fine-tuner" theory:

In the back of our skulls, perched upon the brain stem under the overarching mantle of the great hemispheres of the cerebrum, is a baseball-sized, bean-shaped lump of gray and white brain tissue. This is the cerebellum, the "lesser brain." In contrast to the cerebrum, where men have sought and found the centers of so many vital mental activities, the cerebellum remains a region of subtle and tantalizing mystery, its function hidden from investigators. . . . Its elusive signals have begun to tell us that, while the cerebellum itself directs no body functions, it operates as monitor and coordinator of the brain's other centers and as mediator between them and the body. . . . As in the cerebrum, the various functions of the cerebellum are localized in distinctly defined areas of its cortex. Detection and plotting of the electrical activity of the cortex has made it possible to map these areas. The control of the body's equilibrium, for example, is localized in the extreme front and rear surfaces of the cerebellum. . . .

For a long time it was thought that . . . the cerebellum was restricted to the management of the body's equilibrium and muscular activity. However, at the Johns Hopkins University in 1942 Averill Stowell and I undertook an investigation which has established that the cerebellum is equally involved in the coordination of the sensations of touch, hearing and sight. . . .

Our investigation showed also that the tactile, visual and auditory centers of the cerebellum are linked to the corresponding centers in the cerebral cortex. . . .

. . . In sum, the cerebellar circuitry is an accessory control system imposed upon the basic ascending (sensory) and descending (motor) circuits of the nervous system. . . . One is tempted to see the cerebellum as the great "modulator" of nervous function. . . . In the meantime we may have to contend with the possibility that the cerebellum is involved in still more diverse aspects of the nervous system. It becomes increasingly evident that if "integration" is a major function of this organ, trips into the realm of mental disease may cross its boundaries more frequently than the guards in sanitariums suspect.*

*R. Snider, "The Cerebellum," *Scientific American,* vol. 174 (1958), pp. 84–90.

Recent Scientific Corroboration of the Cerebellar-Vestibular Role in Dyslexia

Over the past number of years, several very prominent neuro-physiologists have agreed with my research and the role of the cerebellum in dyslexia and related symptoms:

- Sir John Eccles claimed that the cerebellum, not the cerebral cortex, is responsible for dyslexia, before the Rodin Dyslexia Society (1986) at the Royal Academy of Medicine, London, and in personal correspondence with me in 1987.

- In a brilliantly written paper entitled "The Human Cerebro-Cerebellar System: Its Computing, Cognitive, and Language Skills" (*Behavioral Brain Research* 44 [1991] pp. 113–28), Leiner, Leiner, and Dow state:

> The role of the cerebellum in these [cognitive and language] functions has tended to be obscured by the traditional preoccupation with the motor functions of the cerebellum. . . . In the human brain, some phylogenetically new parts evolved and enlarged in the cerebellum, concomitantly with the enlargement of the association areas in the cerebral cortex. Anatomical evidence, and behavioral evidence, combine to suggest that this enlarged cerebellum not only contributes to motor function, but also to some sensory, cognitive, linguistic and emotional aspects of behavior.

And in a written correspondence to me (6/3/1991), Alan and Henrietta Leiner state:

> Your emphasis on a cerebellar contribution to learning disabilities and emotional disorders meshes very well with our

own views, as you will see from the enclosed manuscript. . . . we wish we had included your data [in our work].

Sincerely,
Alan and Henrietta Leiner

• In a personal discussion (1989), Rodolfo Llinas of the New York University Medical Center wholeheartedly agreed with my view that dyslexia represents a spatial-temporal sensonimotor dysfunction of cerebellar origin. His research also clearly indicated the role of timing within the cerebellum. This content was the focus of his presentation before the Rodin Remediation Academy and the New York Academy of Sciences at New York City, on September 15, 1992, entitled "Cerebellar Involvement in Temporal Sensory-Motor Processing: Relevance for Speech, Reading, and Writing."

Finally:

• At this same Rodin Remediation conference, Paula Tallal of Rutgers University indicated that dyslexics experienced difficulties processing rapid visual, auditory, and tactile as well as motor signals—but she attributed this impairment to a *primary* cerebral deficit.

My research has also found these sensorimotor difficulties in rapid processing. As a result, I developed and patented the 3-D Optical, Auditory, and Tactile Scanners to measure these impairments. However, I found that the cerebellar-vestibular or inner-ear system was primarily impaired—failing to slow down or properly inhibit transmission speeds to the cerebral cortex— thus resulting in detectable secondary rapid-processing impairments unless compensation occurs and masks the problem.

• Over the past few years, utilizing sophisticated magnetic and related imaging studies, a wide range of scientists have belatedly but conclusively validated my thirty-five-year-old cerebellar-dyslexia research effort, as detailed in this work.

Analysis of the symptoms of thousands of dyslexics, and the study of their treatment responses to medications, eventually led me to the insight that a vast number of phobias, mood and behavior disorders, "psychosomatic" symptoms, and so on, are part and parcel of the dyslexic disorder. While still in psychiatric practice, I examined all my psychiatric patients for dyslexia, utilizing my 3-D Optical Scanner. Surprisingly, *all* my phobic patients were found to be dyslexic. Thus, I was forced to revamp completely the psychiatric theory of phobias and related disorders, just as I had been forced to revamp the psychiatric and neurological theories of dyslexia. Many theories, which perpetuated myths about dyslexia, corresponded to what the renowned philosopher and writer Arthur Koestler refers to as a "closed system" of scientific thought.* Inasmuch as a significant number of traditionally accepted neurological and psychiatric assumptions were found to be either incorrect or inadequate, and in view of the fact that these previously unquestioned and unchallenged assumptions originally guided my research's directions, it is no wonder that my efforts frequently went astray. Backtracking and beginning anew became

---

*A closed system is a cognitive structure . . . where parallels intersect and straight lines form loops. Its canon is based on a central axiom, postulate or dogma, to which the subject is emotionally committed, and from which the rules of processing reality are derived. The amount of distortion involved in the processing is a matter of degrees, and an important criterion of the value of the system. It ranges from the scientist's involuntary inclination to juggle with data as a mild form of self-deception, motivated by his commitment to a theory, to the delusional belief-systems of clinical paranoia. [Arthur Koestler, *The Ghost in the Machine* (New York: Macmillan, 1968), p. 264.]

commonplace techniques for me. However, with determination and more than thirty-five years of effort, each and every apparent dead end and paradox has been resolved. And following each resolution, I stumbled upon unexpected and undreamed-of insights—and the opening up of entirely new research vistas.

As stated in Chapter II, dyslexia was traditionally viewed as merely a severe reading disorder. In fact, many experts even demanded that dyslexics must be two or more years behind their peers in order to qualify for this diagnosis. In attempting to perfect my 3-D Optical Scanner, I tested dyslexics with severe reading disorders, as well as normal individuals. These studies clearly revealed that the blurring speeds of dyslexics were half that of nondyslexics.

So far, so good.

But when a research team attempted to duplicate and extend my studies, they ran into a number of serious problems that could not be explained until several years later. This team could not clearly distinguish a foolproof correlation between severe reading disorders and low blurring speeds. In other words, they found significant numbers of children with mild and even normal reading scores to have low blurring speeds. And the reverse was true as well. Not all children with low blurring speeds had severe reading disorders. In fact, some were good readers. These findings seemed impossible to me, and I was emotionally devastated and bewildered. These findings were far from predictable.

Only after several additional years of frustrating research did a simple answer materialize: *My instrument was right. The existing concept of dyslexia was wrong.*

Eventually, I found dyslexia to be significantly independent of reading scores—a far cry from the definition according to which dyslexics had to be two or more years behind their peers in reading tests. Several reasons were found to explain the traditional correlation between dyslexia and severe reading impairment. "Experts" saw only the severely disturbed readers, for only the most impaired were referred for expert examination. Consequently, it was assumed that dyslexia occurred only in the form of a severe reading impairment.

There was another good reason for confusing and even equating dyslexics with severely impaired readers. In 1896, when dyslexia was first recognized, clinicians assumed that this disorder was similar to alexia, a total inability of previously normal adults to recognize the meaning of written symbols. Alexia occurred in normal-reading adults only following a stroke or lesion of one specific area of the dominant half of the thinking brain. The clinicians therefore mistakenly assumed that the failure of dyslexic children to acquire normal reading ability resulted from a disturbance within the cerebral cortex, identical to that causing normal reading adults to lose completely their recognition of written symbols.

As natural as this assumption was, it turned out to be completely wrong. No one had properly analyzed the *quality* of the reading disturbances in alexic adults and compared it with the *quality* of the reading disturbances in dyslexic children. Although alexic and dyslexic individuals both have reading difficulties, the quality of the reading disturbances in the two disorders is as different as night and day.* (Perhaps an example

---

*Some alexic individuals appear to display a secondary release and destabilization of interconnecting inner-ear (cerebellar) circuits, which results in a combined cortical–inner-ear symptomatic mix. Accordingly, these cases are now under investigation.

might be helpful. Just because two children have high temperatures does not mean that they both have infections. There are many causes for high temperatures. Similarly there are multiple origins for reading difficulties.)

All dyslexics know the meanings of written symbols; it is just that they have difficulty remembering them. For example, all dyslexics know that the letter *b* is a letter, but sometimes they confuse its directional orientation. Hence, they may guess and call a *b* a *d,* or a *p* a *q.* They know the word *was* is either *was* or *saw,* again highlighting a directional uncertainty, not a conceptual or symbolic disturbance.

Alexic adults look at the letter *b* and the word *saw* and haven't the foggiest idea of their respective meanings. If they guess, a *b* may be called *3,* and *was* may be called *elephant.* Inasmuch as alexic adults have difficulty recognizing the meaning of the written symbols they see, their reading disorders are invariably severe.

Dyslexics, on the other hand, can and do learn to read. They merely have difficulty doing so. Their reading difficulties are characterized by memory and directional uncertainty, dysfunctions that may be significantly compensated for. Thus, many dyslexics have compensated and overcome almost all of their symptoms: There are dyslexic doctors, dentists, lawyers, engineers, architects, scientists, politicians, and generals.

How could these successful dyslexic adults have become successful if they were still reading two or more years behind their peers? How could they have succeeded if they failed to understand the meaning of letters and words?

What do we call dyslexics who have compensated for their reading deficiencies and now read normally or even above normal levels? Are they suddenly not dyslexic once their reading scores cross the "magic" two-year limit? If, indeed, their reading scores worsen again and their scores fall two grades below those of their peers, do they suddenly become dyslexic again?

Of course not! The whole concept of diagnosing dyslexia on the basis of reading scores is completely nonsensical. And yet, many experts fervently believe in this nonsense.*

Unfortunately, I did, too. However, scientific reality eventually prevailed, and I came to recognize that some dyslexics read better than they spell, write, or recall math and directional sequences. Others spell better than they read, while still others can do math better than they read, spell, or write. In short, the symptoms in dyslexia vary in intensity from one dyslexic to another. And the combinations of symptoms may vary significantly from one dyslexic to the next, too.

From this insight I recognized that my daughters Laura and Joy were dyslexic despite their normal and even superior reading abilities. As a result, I was fortunately able to treat them effectively. I also came to recognize that dyslexics need not have normal or superior IQs to be dyslexic, and that IQ and dyslexia have nothing to do with each other, contrary to another misconception held by many dyslexia experts.

Moreover, I eventually realized that dyslexia need not occur in "pure" form. I discovered that mentally retarded, cerebral-palsied, and deaf patients may also be dyslexic. In such *mixed* cases the retardation, cerebral palsy, or deafness is due to damage to one part of the brain or nervous system while the dyslexia is due to damage or dysfunction of the inner-ear system.

In a similar fashion I discovered that dyslexia need not occur before or during birth. It may be *acquired* as a result of infectious,

*Refer to Shaywitz et al. (1992).

toxic, metabolic, traumatic, or degenerative processes impairing inner-ear functioning. I realized that ear infections, allergies, toxins, chemicals, head traumas, and whiplash injuries, as well as multiple sclerosis, may impair inner-ear functioning and result in *acquired* dyslexialike functioning. Inasmuch as the medications I used to treat "pure" dyslexics improved inner-ear dysfunction, I came to realize that these very same medications also improve the same symptoms in *mixed* and *acquired* dyslexic disorders. In recognizing that most mentally retarded individuals also have a hidden impairment of the inner-ear system (cerebellum), treating their dyslexia has resulted in the first significant improvement in the overall functioning of the retarded.

Dyslexia "experts" have always thought in terms of black and white. You were either cerebral-palsied or dyslexic; you were either deaf or dyslexic. Not true! Many individuals are deaf because of impairment or injury to the nerve that conducts sound impulses to the brain. However, the inner-ear or vestibular nerve runs alongside this hearing or eighth acoustic nerve. And, not infrequently, damage to the acoustic nerve results in an overlooked damage to the inner-ear nerve, which runs adjacent to it into the brain.

Invariably all the learning difficulties of the deaf have been arbitrarily attributed to either the deafness or the emotional disturbances resulting from the deafness. No one thought that the learning difficulties in deafness may also be due to the presence of a coexisting but hidden inner-ear dysfunction and the resulting dyslexia. On the basis of this knowledge I have been able to help a number of deaf individuals with their academic difficulties. Moreover, the same medication that helps their academic symptoms often minimizes some of the deafness by improving their auditory sequencing abilities. Even "pure" dyslexics with auditory sequencing difficulties experience a significant improvement in their hearing or auditory memory for phonics and related patterns once they respond favorably to medication.

Without exception, all the learning and motor difficulties in the retarded have been blamed on the impairment resulting in the retardation despite the obvious presence of dyslexic symptoms. And on and on these oversights go. I thought the same way until my patients, their symptoms, and my desire to help them forced me to change my mind.

Most clinicians see four times as many male dyslexics as female dyslexics. Naturally, it was assumed that dyslexia is a sex-linked hereditary disorder occurring four times more frequently in males. Wrong again! As stated earlier, I personally screened over 1,500 kindergarten children at a Queens, New York, school district, utilizing my 3-D Optical Scanner. The results of this study indicate that the incidence of male dyslexics equals that of female dyslexics. Male dyslexics are merely referred to clinicians four times more often than female dyslexics. And experts confused the male-female *referral* ratio with the true male-female *incidence* ratio. This is because boys with dyslexia become more frustrated, feel dumber, and act out their frustrations more than girls: hence, they are referred to experts four times more frequently.*

---

*In a personal communication and a research paper, Kohen-Raz noted the following seemingly paradoxical findings:

- Normal-reading young girls demonstrate significantly better balance functions than corresponding boys.
- Poor-reading girls demonstrate significantly poorer balance functions than corresponding boys.

To explain this data, I reasoned as follows:

- Inasmuch as normal-reading girls have better balance and, thus, inner-ear functioning, they may be expected to better compensate physiologically for any given dyslexic disorder—thus contributing to the 4:1 male/female referral ratio.

Many an expert still believe that left-handedness and dyslexia are somehow related. Indeed, Norman Geschwind and colleagues at Harvard went so far as to state that the incidence of dyslexia in left-handed males was ten to one—greater than chance alone. And by postulating a sex hormone–embryonic theory, Geschwind and associates attempted to account for their reported higher frequencies in dyslexia of (1) left-handed *males,* and (2) autoimmune (allergic) disorders as well as the alleged cerebral cellular abnormalities noted by Galaburda.

In my experiences with thousands of dyslexics:

- Handedness and gender have little to do with dyslexia— also confirmed recently by Shaywitz et al. at Yale (1991).
- There is no higher incidence of severe autoimmune disorders, allergies aside, in dyslexics versus nondyslexics.
- Allergic phenomena, if increased among dyslexics, are most probably (a) triggering and/or enhancing more recognizable inner-ear–determined dyslexic symptoms, and (b) secondary expressions of increased stress levels among failing and frustrated dyslexics, and the resulting effect on the immune system.

- Inasmuch as young normal girls have better developed inner-ear functioning relative to boys, girls may require greater degrees of inner-ear impairment in order to result in impaired reading scores—thus accounting for the presence of poorer balance functioning in reading-score–deficient girls versus boys.

[Reuven Kohen-Raz, Ph.D., "Developmental Patterns of Static Balance Ability and Their Relation to Cognitive School Readiness," *Pediatrics,* vol. 46, no. 2 (August 1970), pp. 276–84.]

Professor Kohen-Raz and I have since developed reliable balance parameters for diagnosing the inner-ear dysfunction underlying dyslexia, as well as measuring rapid balance responses to meclizine. Moreover, Fawcett and Nicolson (1992) confirmed the presence of a balance impairment in dyslexics and suggested an "automatization deficit" identical to that proposed by me.

Moreover, for reasons previously discussed, I believe the abnormal cerebral cell theory is as completely incompatible with the clinical realities of dyslexia and dyslexics as is the above proposed hormone-embryonic theory.

Before completing this highly condensed summary of my research efforts and their outcome, I would like to mention how one of my initial oversights led to a new means of helping dyslexics physiologically while simultaneously enabling me to improve significantly the reliability of my blurring-speed instrument.

After years of using my 3-D Optical Scanner, and after obtaining significant numbers of atypical and paradoxical correlations of poor reading ability and high blurring speeds, I one day discovered that dyslexics have more than one blurring speed. They have the same blurring speed as nondyslexics do— a *sequential blurring speed,* in which a whole sequence is seen as a panorama and the whole blurs out at once. However, they also have another blurring speed, which I called the *single-targeting* blurring speed. This second tracking mechanism is a compensatory one and takes over when the first—the reflexive, sequential-tracking mechanism—is impaired.

For years I assumed, and even demonstrated, that dyslexics can compensate for their blurring speeds independently of their reading scores. Thus, for example, eye-training exercises performed by optometrists and by me frequently resulted in increased tracking capacity and blurring speeds, with and without a corresponding improvement in reading and related functioning. I knew that compensatory tracking mechanisms were responsible for the atypical and confusing data I obtained, as well as the fact that the blurring-speed methodology was only 80 to 85 percent effective diagnostically rather than 100 percent effective. However, I could not specifically identify or understand the quality of the elusive compensatory tracking mechanism responsible for the seemingly impossible data I had frequently obtained.

This elusive tracking mechanism called single-targeting evaded my grasp for years until I discovered it by accident one day when an adult dyslexic patient suddenly asked me, "Which blurring speed do you want?" Needless to say, I was waiting for several years for someone to give me a clue as to the tracking mechanism responsible for explaining a host of atypical and seemingly paradoxical findings. Upon detailed questioning, this patient told me that she could either follow all the elephants and see them at once until they blurred out, or she could just follow one or two at a time until they blurred out. The first blurring speed was her *sequential* blurring speed. The second blurring speed was her compensatory *single-targeting* blurring speed.

The single-targeting mechanism explained why approximately 15 to 20 percent of dyslexics appeared to have normal blurring speeds and why a few dyslexics even reported above-normal blurring speeds. These dyslexics obviously had developed a compensatory tracking mechanism, but the mechanism remained unclear until it was explained to me in great detail by this adult patient.

The concept of a single-targeting tracking mechanism also explained another puzzling finding. I had always assumed that the blurring speed would equal the recognition speed. Let me explain what I mean. If a moving visual sequence is speeded up to the blurring speed, one cannot identify the moving sequence—it looks like a blurred streak. If this blurred streak is slowed ever so slightly, it can then be identified or recognized. This I called the *recognition speed*. Thus, during testing, one can speed targets up to the blurring speed, down to the recognition speed, and back up again. This procedure can clearly define the blurring speed with a significant degree of accuracy.

Repeated studies demonstrated that there was no significant difference between the blurring-speed and recognition-speed end points.

I had always thought that the recognition speed would be easier to use to test very young children. One could thus avoid explaining to them exactly what blurring is and means. All I had to ask a young child was, "Tell me what you see as soon as you see it." However, upon further study I came to realize that the blurring speed did *not* always equal the recognition speed as I had predicted. Thus, for example, the research group who attempted to duplicate my blurring-speed findings could not find a correlation between blurring speeds and reading scores. In retrospect, the difficulties were easy to explain: They apparently used recognition speed rather than blurring speed as the end point.

At the time, however, it made perfect theoretical sense to do so, although the results they obtained were most confusing and defied any sensible explanation for many years. They found too many severely impaired readers reporting normal and even above-normal blurring speeds. And the overall dyslexic blurring speeds they obtained were significantly higher than those I obtained myself.

Only later was it easy to understand and explain the research group's findings. In the beginning it was pure torture and frustration. I was extremely disappointed and dejected. I knew my blurring-speed method had to work, for I had been using it for several years. How were the contradictory results to be explained?

Single-targeting, of course, explained it all. If one asks a dyslexic individual, or even a normal individual, to recognize whatever they are seeing, they can identify a single-targeted elephant as easily as they can identify a sequentially targeted elephant sequence. Initially, they were not asked to distinguish between the two. All they were asked was, "Tell me what you see as soon as you see it." And indeed they did. They reported seeing elephants. I naturally assumed that dyslexics and nondyslexics saw the elephants in exactly the same way.

They did not!

Dyslexics most frequently were viewing only one elephant at a time, whereas normals were viewing a sequence of eight elephants. Who could have predicted that dyslexics had more than one blurring speed, and as a result of a hidden procedural inconsistency, that dyslexic blurring speeds going up did not equal their recognition or blurring speeds going down? Who could have foreseen that this procedural error inadvertently resulted in our measuring sequential blurring speeds going up, and compensatory single-targeting or recognition speeds coming down?

Thus, for example, when *I* tested dyslexics for blurring speeds, I asked them, "Tell me as soon as the elephants initially begin to blur." I then obtained a majority of sequential blurring speeds interspersed with some single-targeting blurring speeds, the latter accounting for the unusual and seemingly paradoxical blurring-speed data previously defying explanation.

When another research group tested dyslexics, they asked, "Tell me as soon as you can see or recognize the elephants." In other words, they began testing children who were watching a complete blur and then slowed down the speed of the moving targets until something could be identified. This research team obtained a vast majority of single-targeting blurring or recognition speeds with only a taint of sequential blurring or recognition speeds.

Inasmuch as there exists a 2:1 to 4:1 difference between dyslexic single-targeting blurring speeds and sequential blurring speeds, and in view of the fact that a majority of dyslexics learn to single-target, almost all of the confusing and contradictory results obtained between my data and the independently obtained data were suddenly explained. By recognizing the distinction between the diagnostic sequential-target blurring speed and the much higher compensatory single-target speed, and by correcting the procedural errors in the blurring-speed techniques, the 3-D Optical Scanner jumped from 80 percent effective to over 95 percent effective in diagnostic accuracy. Also, the gap between dyslexics' sequential blurring speeds and normal blurring speeds often widened from 2:1 to 4:1, making it significantly easier to separate dyslexic from nondyslexic groupings.* In addition, the realization that dyslexics may have poor, normal, or superior reading scores helped explain the remaining inconsistencies in attempting to correlate blurring speeds with low reading scores.

Needless to say, if the reading scores of dyslexics varied from one extreme to another, then there could not be a significant correlation between low blurring speeds and low reading scores. After all, my instrument was designed to diagnose inner-ear dysfunctioning and dyslexia, not reading scores.

---

*Some dyslexics with high blurring speeds were found to have significantly compensated eidetic imagery, often *recalling* rather than *seeing* a clear image at the blurring speed. Additionally, others developed compensatory rapid visual processing mechanisms, enabling them to see more clearly despite impaired tracking mechanisms. Recently, I carried out a study that revealed a correlation between severely impaired balance and increased blurring speeds among some dyslexics, further indicating a compensatory relationship between the two.

By analogy, the surprising finding that dyslexic blurring speeds going up did not equal dyslexic blurring (recognition) speeds coming down mirrored the fallacy of the assumption that the process whereby cortically impaired adults lost their reading ability equaled the process in which dyslexic children failed to acquire normal reading ability. Having recognized that single-targeting was a compensatory tracking mechanism that may be improved by tracking exercises, I came to realize that the dyslexic who follows one elephant at a time is merely emulating what most dyslexics do when they initially begin reading: They use their finger for a pointer to track one word at a time. In other words, single-targeting is a learned mechanism by which the brain develops a "mental finger" that guides the eye in time and space so that it can follow a target that is rapidly moving across one's visual field. Without this "mental finger" as a guide, dyslexics' eyes would be lost in space, and so would the visual targets.

The discovery of the single-targeting mechanism not only explained a whole series of facts and dramatically improved the diagnostic and screening accuracy of the blurring-speed method and instrument, it underscored a very, very important fact in science: You can spend a tremendous amount of time with data and come to know that something is missing without being able to find it. In such a case, statistical results may appear to invalidate your findings. However, if one really understands the subject matter and the data qualitatively, then one knows better how to evaluate and interpret the significance of the statistics. Negative statistics, of course, are important. But simply because they appear to negate one's perceptions does not necessarily mean that these observations are incorrect. It may mean that there is a procedural error somewhere that has thus far been unidentified.

Fortunately, I had been working and living with dyslexics for years and years, and I felt I understood their clinical symptoms. I had seen their improvements. I *knew* they had a tracking defect. Just read through the majority of my case histories: All of them, or almost all of them, reported tracking difficulties. Thus, I knew that somehow, somewhere, I would find the missing tracking mechanism needed to explain *all* the findings—the majority as well as the minority, the typical as well as the atypical, the expected as well as the unexpected. I was waiting several years for a clue I could recognize, and consequently was already attuned to my patient's question, "Which blurring speed do you want?" when it was finally asked.

We naturally assume that everyone sees the same way. This is most certainly not true. Single-targeting dyslexics cannot believe that nondyslexics see a whole elephant sequence in an effortless panorama. Parents are astonished, even horrified, when they witness their children reporting seeing only one out of eight elephants.

My 3-D Optical Scanner is a very simple test. But the variations it uncovers could not have been detected had I not performed over 50,000 tests myself. The detection of each and every individual tracking variation and compensation led to ever-expanding insights into inner-ear dysfunctions, dyslexia, and the fascinating ways the brain adapts.

Moreover, the blurring-speed tests revealed a number of findings that were helpful in developing new and useful educational procedures. For example, the blurring speeds of big, black, and colored words or designs were significantly higher than the corresponding blurring speeds for small, light gray, uncolored print spaced closer together. Put another way, reflex eye mechanisms were better able to fixate on, track, and process big, dark, or brightly colored, more widely spaced print, suggesting that printed material and books be appropriately designed for dyslexics, especially those whose tracking mechanisms remain significantly deficient.

As a result of this realization, as well as the photophobia (light sensitivity) characterizing some inner-ear–dysfunctioning dyslexics, it made perfect sense that tinted lenses may help some with dyslexia to better fixate, track, and process visual information. Also, the tracking impairment among dyslexics led me to redesign the print size and spacing in my books *The Upside-Down Kids* and *Turning Around the Upside-Down Kids,* making it easier for the eye to fixate, track, and thus see. Obviously, it's easier for a defective missile to hit a big, fat, dark target than a skinny, faint, small one.

By recognizing that young dyslexics have significant tracking difficulties even though their eyesight or visual acuity is often within normal limits, I developed an instrument capable of projecting letters and words on a single spot so that the need for eye tracking was minimized. Hence, if the letters and words in a sentence are projected one at a time on a given spot, word recognition and reading can be taught with minimal visual scrambling. Of course, this "reading" process should be carried out simultaneously with attempts to improve the eye-tracking mechanisms via repetition and video games.

In addition, the ability to measure auditory and tactile sequencing by means of the 3-D Auditory and Tactile Scanners has led to insights into how "open" these respective channels are for teaching purposes. Moreover, it is anticipated that auditory and tactile conditioning or training will enable these channels to function better, just as visual tracking exercises result in increased visual tracking capacity and blurring speeds. Indeed, treatment groups have been independently using auditory training techniques for dyslexics and autistic individuals and reporting favorable results. However, because the above-mentioned results contradict the traditional language theory of dyslexia, these findings are considered controversial, and thus have been denied significant access within the scientific literature until recently.

Also, the use of my 3D Optical and Auditory Scanners has clearly demonstrated another important group of therapeutic insights: A conditioned improvement in a specific sensory function may often result in a transfer of this improvement to many other sensory, motor, and related mechanisms. Quite clearly, the above insights highlight how interrelated all sensory and motor mechanisms are, and show the importance of clinical observations as a tool in determining neurophysiological functioning—a tool often superior to sophisticated instruments and complex experiments performed in the "dark."

I hope this brief history of my research efforts will enable you to develop a better perspective on the methods and means leading me to solve many of the dyslexia riddles. This solution would never have occurred had I overlooked or denied the significance of data I initially could not account for or explain.

The Symptoms and Mechanisms Defining Dyslexia

Introduction

In many ways this chapter is the most important and insightful one in the book, albeit the most detailed and complex. However, I feel reading its content is well worth your effort. The following truly describes and represents the dyslexic symptomatic core and span, as well as the variations typifying this scientifically misunderstood and elusive disorder.

The analysis of more than 35,000 dyslexia cases during the past thirty-five years has led me to view this fascinating yet devastating condition as an inner-ear/cerebellar dysfunction affecting any or all of fifteen major categories of functioning:

1. Reading
2. Writing
3. Spelling
4. Mathematics

5. Memory
6. Direction
7. Time
8. Speech
9. Grammar '
10. Hyperactivity, overactivity, and impulsiveness
11. Concentration and distractibility
12. Attention Deficit Disorder or Attention Deficit Hyperactivity Disorder
13. Phobias and related mental and behavioral disorders
14. Balance and coordination
15. Psychosomatic symptoms, including impaired self-esteem and body image

In this chapter I describe in great detail the various inner-ear–related dysfunctioning versus compensatory mechanisms and symptoms characteristic of a sample of more than 35,000 dyslexics. This is the largest such sample ever recorded and analyzed. And the recorded symptoms and mechanisms did not readily materialize or fall into place easily. Quite the contrary:

- Every symptom was painstakingly collected and studied for years before its true meaning and significance were recognized.
- Every symptom was analyzed to determine the underlying mechanisms responsible for its occurrence.
- Every symptom was eventually statistically analyzed so that its relative incidence and frequency were determined in large dyslexic samples.
- Every exceptional, atypical, and unexpected finding was studied and analyzed with even more interest and det

mination than was given to the symptoms occurring most typically and frequently.

• Every symptom was used to upgrade and enrich the ensuing concept of dyslexia.

Oddly enough, reading, writing, spelling, and other scores were not at all helpful in correlating and defining the nature and symptoms characterizing the dyslexic panorama. Indeed, the numbers and scores typifying the traditional dyslexic and learning-disability research approaches were most often confusing and misleading. Thus, for example, prior to my research dyslexia was most commonly viewed and defined as a *severe* reading disorder in which an otherwise completely "normal" individual must be two or more years behind equally matched peers, i.e., equally matched for IQ, socioeconomic, psychological, and educational factors. Is this matching process really possible? (And, as repeatedly stated within this text, can the syndrome of symptoms called dyslexia really be equated with *only one* of its many highly variable and overdetermined parameters, e.g., severely lower reading scores? Obviously not! It makes as little sense as equating diabetes with *only* its comatose state!)

This definition was eventually discovered by me to be completely wrong, even foolish. Bright, exceptionally gifted children were found to have normal reading scores but poor, "typically" dyslexic writing and spelling patterns. According to lefinition of dyslexia, these children were cered as dyslexic. Instead, they were mistakenly only average intelligence. And these gifted, hildren were frequently termed "lazy" and/or different."

Quite a distortion! But how else are traditionally biased experts expected to think? We are unwittingly taught or expected to reason as follows: If the clinical facts do not fit the theory, then the facts are wrong!

To make matters worse, most frequently the gifted dyslexic children who managed to compensate and read on or close to grade level are refused help. Once again the traditionally molded experts reasoned: Why do they need help? Are they not reading on grade level, and sometimes even above? None of the educational or psychological testers asked these children the questions necessary to determine whether they were experiencing difficulties within their reading processes; difficulties such as memory instability for letters, words, sentences, and paragraphs; reversals; and tracking problems. In other words experts invariably equated normal reading scores with normal reading processes. Unfortunately, this equation was incomplete and often completely wrong.

Why didn't these experts reason as follows: If a gifted, hardworking child has only a normal reading score, what dysfunctioning mechanisms are preventing his scores from becoming as superior as his IQ and effort? Why is this gifted child writing and spelling as if he is dyslexic?

All too often, if the clinical reality did not fit the ingrained theory, then the clinical reality was unwittingly denied as follows:

- The child's IQ was not really high but merely average.
- The child was not really as hardworking as her family believed.
- Either the child was not asked the specific questions needed to elicit the typical dyslexic reading symptoms, or

these obvious or readily apparent symptoms were denied and were attributed to allegedly nondyslexic factors, such as developmental lag and immaturity.

- The typical dyslexic writing, spelling, and other qualities were denied their proper significance and accordingly sidestepped.

Before continuing, I would like to present you with a typical dyslexic case examined by me. The patient's mother writes:

> I had been to the public schools many times to seek help for David's reading and spelling problems, but to no avail. All his teachers, along with the reading teacher, told me was that he was just "an average kid who was reading on grade level" and why was I pushing him so hard? They said I would only frustrate David if I pushed too hard. I knew David was bright. They didn't. My "average kid" turned out to have an IQ of over 130 with a learning disability. He's now in a school for gifted children, is being helped by a [learning-disabilities] teacher, and is finally feeling good about himself.

Cases similar to this one—similar to those of my daughters Laura and Joy—eventually forced me to abandon completely the traditional views and definitions of dyslexia.

Dyslexia is not just a severe reading disorder with characteristics of reversals. In fact, the reading scores of dyslexics may be normal and even superior, and reversals may or may not be present. I came to realize that dyslexics frequently compensate for a symptom's quantity typically revealed by traditional testing scores but are nonetheless still dyslexic. Thus, they may compensate for some reading mechanisms and scores and not others, while the writing and spelling symptoms may remain, appearing as bad as ever. I also came to realize that although most dyslexics are referred to clinicians for severe reading difficulties, there are many dyslexics who compensate for their reading scores. However, they may experience great frustration with their writing, spelling, math, or concentration.

After years of painstaking clinical and theoretical effort, I reached the simple understanding that *dyslexics, not experts, truly define the dyslexic disorder.* In other words, the patients and the quality of their revealed symptoms are diagnostically correct: If their facts do not fit our established and ingrained theories, then our theories are wrong and must be changed. As a result of major theoretical changes, I arrived at the rather simple, obvious conclusion that any given dyslexic may experience the most frustration with *any one* or *any combination* of categories (1) to (15) listed on pages 204–205.

What happens when a common virus affects five members of a family? Do all members exhibit the same symptoms with uniform intensity? Obviously not! Most frequently, each member will evidence some symptoms of the virus, but the leading symptom may be different and the symptom's relative intensity may vary from one extreme to another. In fact, one member of such a family may even feel "almost" well and thus escape clinical detection altogether. The same is true for many a dyslexic.

I will now present you with the major categories and symptoms categorizing and defining dyslexia.

The Dyslexic Syndrome

Reading

The vast majority of young dyslexics referred for clinical evaluation demonstrate a visual and/or phonetic memory instability for letters and words; hence they repeatedly attempt to recall the shapes and sounds of letter and word configurations only to forget them rapidly. To compensate, many youngsters will initially resort to guessing and even recalling stories by sheer rote, so that often their reading difficulty is not diagnosed until several years later.

Directional disturbances are also frequently present, compounding memory instability by triggering the confusion of such letters and words as *b* with *d*, *was* with *saw*, *on* with *no*, and *god* with *dog*.

Fixation and eye-tracking difficulties are invariably present during the dyslexic reading process, and the eye loses its place as it scans letters, words, and sentences. Accordingly, letters, words, and sentences are skipped over, resulting in poor concentration and comprehension difficulties. Thus, a child cannot understand what he is reading, as the sequence of what his eyes are looking at is significantly scrambled.

As a result of this inner-ear–related tracking difficulty, small words are frequently skipped over completely, resulting in the seemingly paradoxical situation in which small words are harder to recognize than larger words. (Larger words are easier to target and thus recall.) Moreover, letters, syllables, and word parts are frequently skipped over, resulting in the mistaking of *p* for *o* or *l*, *t* for *i*, *read* for *red*, *us* for *bus*, and so on. At times, segments of one word are inadvertently carried by the eye to more distant word segments, resulting in fusion or condensation errors; the dyslexic may see *the* cat or *good* boy and read *that* and *go by.* By reviewing the possible errors and mechanisms resulting when a dyslexic reads the sentence *The cat jumped over the moon,* you will get a clear understanding of how to analyze the mistakes and better understand the mechanisms responsible for these mistakes. Similar auditory or phonetic dyslexic errors occur and must be factored into the final understanding characterizing the reading process in dyslexia.

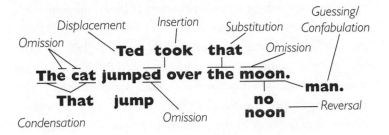

The "typical" dyslexic errors and mechanisms triggered when a reading-disabled sample attempts to read the sentence The cat jumped over the moon. *By means of an error analysis and diagram, the mechanisms underlying the dyslexic reading performance are reconstructed: omissions, insertions, displacements, condensations, rotations/reversals/scrambling, substitutions, and guessing/confabulation.*

The sequential scrambling or tracking dysfunction characterizing the dyslexic reading process results in the omission or disappearance of letters, words, and even sentences from their proper positions. Often these very segments are *displaced* or carried over to new positions, giving rise to the formation of new letters, words, and sentences. Thus, the original visual text or sequence becomes significantly distorted by the underlying scrambling processes.

If, in addition, there exists a similar phonetic or sound-sequencing disturbance that parallels the visual one, then there will be utter chaos and frustration, regardless of the individual's IQ. Phonetic or auditory input blurring, distortions, and reversals characterize the dyslexic reading process as frequently as do the visual symptoms.

Because of the visual and auditory temporal-spatial defects in dyslexics, words or sounds may appear blurry or muddled. At times the eye or ear appears stuck or fixed to a word, finding it difficult to let go and proceed, or uncontrollably returning to the same word over and over again in an obsessive-compulsive-like fashion, called perseveration. If the same symptom or mechanism affects mental or thought processing, it may result in the inability to free one's mind from a thought, concern, or tune; this is referred to in psychiatric terms as an emotionally determined obsessive disorder. If the same symptom leads to a compelling need to repeat the same motor task over and over again, then compulsions occur.

Underlying many so-called mental symptoms are physically based dyslexialike mechanisms. (Even dreams are characterized by the same fusion and displacement mechanisms characterizing the dyslexic reading processes.) Inasmuch as the eyes' "guided-missile system" is impaired, it is reasonable to expect it to more easily hit big, dark, colored targets rather than small, light, almost invisible ones. For this very reason magnification of letters and words by lenses often results in reading improvement in dyslexics despite the absence of visual acuity problems.

There are, however, interesting exceptions to this rule. For example, if eye perseveration is significantly present, and thus the eye cannot free itself from a given target or word, then the smaller the perseveration target, the more readily the eye will escape it, freeing itself to move on to the task at hand. And, also paradoxically, because of ocular accommodation and related visual difficulties, some dyslexics experience dizziness and headaches when attempting to read with glasses that magnify the print. As a result, this technique makes them worse, not better.

Frequently, the tracking defect in dyslexia does not become obvious until a child gets into the upper grades, where the reading rate must increase in order to accommodate the greater reading volume, and where the print size correspondingly shrinks to accommodate this larger volume. To compensate for the tracking defect, the reading process must be slowed down, and often a marker is needed to direct the eye's movement in space. In this case, one's finger or marker acts as a pacemaker, slowing down the eye's movement while simultaneously serving as a reference point for the zigzagging eye, thus stabilizing and guiding its ability to fixate and sequentially track the words and sentences in their appropriate places.

If, however, eye perseveration is present, then even a finger or a marker as a compensatory device may fail. The eye will then often fixate on the finger or marker and will not let go. Letters, words, and sentences will then appear blurry and scrambled and thus difficult to read, To compensate, the *mind* develops a *mental finger* and slowly guides the eye from letter to letter and from word to word, adaptively blocking out all adjacent or peripheral distracting impressions. This process is analogous to a compensatory type of tunnel vision. It was this mechanism that I later termed *single-targeting*.

Compensatory single-targeting mechanisms are forced to

develop when teachers and peers ridicule children who use a finger to read or when the finger cannot be used. Similar compensatory mechanisms were later found to occur during the processing of sequential sounds, touch sensations, and related sensorimotor tasks. Indeed, many a dyslexic develops the compensatory ability to "mentally hear" what the eye sees during the reading process, thus facilitating comprehension when the visual-input channel is impaired or blocked.

Difficulties with concentration and distractibility also complicate the dyslexic reading process. Obviously, poor concentration results in rapid fatigue and boredom, rendering distracting background noises and events "louder." As a result, impaired memory and directional and tracking mechanisms are secondarily intensified, further complicating an already complicated process. Although often overlooked, it is important to note that dyslexics frequently manifest a lag in the visual processing of read material—the latter further complicated by anxiety and impaired concentration and distractibility mechanisms. If severe, this visual input lag may be confused with a primary comprehension difficulty akin to that in alexia.

Often dyslexics will belatedly develop evidence of a reading difficulty upon entering high school or college, where the rate, volume, and quantity of facts to be recalled are significantly intensified. Prior compensatory mechanisms or skills may be insufficient at this point, and it suddenly appears as if a new problem has arisen. Most frequently, it is not a new problem; it is merely the surfacing of an old, hidden, partially compensated-for dyslexic variation.

High school and college problems are most often viewed as emotional in origin, and the affected individuals are frequently termed lazy or disinterested. Few educators and clinicians have the experience and good fortune to recognize fully the scope and variations of the reading process in compensated or partially compensating dyslexics. Thus, they cannot distinguish the quality of the dyslexic reading process from nondyslexic disturbances. And all too often, erroneous assumptions and diagnoses are made, resulting in mistreatment.

Low reading scores alone cannot distinguish the origin of the poor reading performance. Poor reading ability may result from improper teaching, psychological factors, true disinterest, nondyslexic medical and neurological difficulties, or dyslexia. Fortunately, the quality of the dyslexic reading disturbance clearly separates this disorder from all the others, as detected with my 3-D Optical Scanner.*

Dyslexics frequently complain of a host of what appear to be *psychosomatic symptoms* during reading: headaches, dizziness, nausea, double vision, blurred vision, word and sentence movement, changes in word size, colored or black background streaking, and so on.

Significant variations in reading memory characterize the dyslexic reading process. For example, some dyslexics read and recall scientific material more readily than that in novels. For others the reverse is true. Analysis of countless adult dyslexics has revealed the unexpected fact that the compensatory ease

---

*Frequently, reading and related dyslexic symptoms are *overdetermined*, that is, they have multiple primary and/or secondarily determined origins. Consequently, the best therapeutic results are obtained when the multidimensional and interrelated origins of the symtoms are recognized—so that each determinant may be specifically treated. All too often, it appears as if "traditionalists" erroneously view the reading-score impairment in dyslexia as if it were *the disorder itself.* By analogy, high blood sugars are not equivalent to the diabetic disorder; they are mere resultants. And for best results, one must aim treatment efforts both at the multiple pancreatic-related origins of diabetes and their symptomatic fallout.

and facility they develop in processing and remembering reading information frequently determines interest, rather than the reverse. It is a given fact for *all* individuals that interest results in or stimulates improved concentration, memory, and thus reading success. This is even more so for dyslexics. Poor memory processing also slows down the reading speed, to allow for compensation. However, at times the speed is so slow that the memory and concentration functioning for what is read becomes further destabilized—in a vicious cycle.

Upon further exploration, an additional array of dyslexic reading symptoms materialized: head tilting; reading up close instead of far away, or shifting from close to far; blinking; sensitivity to fluorescent and/or natural light; and postural reading preferences, e.g., sitting up, lying down, or tilted. The attempt to understand and explain every single symptomatic variation has resulted in a concept of dyslexia that encompasses all the symptoms found, the typical as well as the atypical.

The analysis of the above symptoms led to the insight that some symptoms reflect the presence of disturbed mechanisms, while others indicate the presence of compensatory mechanisms. Therefore, headaches, dizziness, nausea, motion sickness, blurred and double vision, and word movement reflect disturbances resulting from impaired focusing, tracking, orientation, and memory mechanisms. On the other hand, blinking, finger pointing, and head tilting are adaptive attempts at compensation. Blinking, refocusing, and positional shifting as well as head tilting all attempt to correct for the blurred, double, moving, and changing visual images. The body's inner "gyroscope" is tilted and out of position, and the above maneuvers reflect adaptive attempts to stabilize and realign this "gyroscope."

Many dyslexics will develop rapid scanning devices whereby their eyes "intuitively" pick up key words and phrases; often they are assumed to be superior readers. In fact, my daughter Laura read this way. As a child she was often retested, for teachers could not believe her reading speed. When I eventually retested Laura and others like her, I realized that the rapid scanning was not often in sequence and that she had an uncanny ability to decipher the whole context of a passage from sequentially scattered and incomplete clues. However, she could not read word by word without using her finger; and small print tended to blur out quite rapidly for her.

Another patient of mine read from right to left and from the bottom up. His mind then appropriately reversed and translated the stored content and made sense out of it. He could not track in what we consider the normal left-to-right and top-to-bottom directions. Indeed, many dyslexics can mirror-read and comprehend reversed images better than they can read normally.

With time and effort, many of these dyslexic symptoms and mechanisms may be compensated for, resulting in improved functioning. Most often, improvement is frustratingly slow and requires significant degrees of effort. At other times improvement appears sudden and dramatic. When the improvement is slow, the dyslexic is often mistakenly called a "slow learner"; when fast, he is termed a "late bloomer." My studies, however, have clearly shown that "late blooming" may occur early, perhaps prior to kindergarten or in first grade. And late blooming may even occur as late as junior high school, high school, college, or even graduate school.

A host of descriptive terms have been misused, as if they described different diagnostic categories. In fact, a slew of terms merely described different speeds and styles of compensation for one and the same underlying disorder. No wonder experts were unable to distinguish clearly the slow learner from the dyslexic! Most often there was no basic distinction other than the speed at which the dyslexic compensated for the intensity of symptoms defining his or her particular type of dyslexia.

The dyslexic reading process is far from stable. It may, and does, regress. Thus, fatigue, dyes, allergies, toxins, metabolic and chemical disorders, mononucleosis, Lyme disease, ear infections, and whiplash or concussions may destabillize a preexisting condition and result in variations that are most often misunderstood and, again, misdiagnosed.

Before completing this lengthy but highly condensed description of the symptoms and mechanisms characterizing the dyslexic reading process, I would like to add a few more *exceptional* reading styles.

Although most dyslexics dread reading aloud, for it highlights their slow, poor reading capacity while distracting and disorganizing their already stressed compensatory mechanisms, other dyslexics can remember or know what they visually see only if they feel or hear themselves say it.

The most fascinating style of all is one told to me by several dyslexic artists. They cannot decipher the meaning of a word by viewing the individual letters. Instead, they learn the word's meaning by recalling the shape of the overall configuration, that is, the highs and lows of the letters constituting the words. This interesting mechanism appears to be similar to a mechanism reported to me by other dyslexics whereby they recognize the meaning of a word only after their eyes traverse the word's outline—a reading form I chose to call ocular [eye] braille. By now the reader must surely know that dyslexia—its mechanisms, its symptoms, and its compensatory style—is far from a simple disorder. Certainly, it is too complex a disorder to be defined by reading scores, and too complex a disorder to be understood by the rapid examination of relatively small samples. There are also dyslexic difficulties in reading facial expressions and body language, a disorder best called "social dyslexia." And since cases with Asperger's Syndrome are invariably dyslexic and ADD, it appears reasonable to assume that this syndrome may reflect a severe form of social dyslexia.

Every symptom and compensatory mechanism of dyslexia was slowly and painstakingly discovered over a thirty-five-year period of questioning and requestioning thousands of dyslexics. Slowly but surely, every symptomatic exception and compensatory style received as much attention as the symptoms recurring most frequently.

If a theory is correct, it must be wide and dynamic enough to explain *all* the symptoms and variations. To date:

- No other theory of dyslexia comes close to explaining the vast majority of symptoms and mechanisms described in this book.
- No other research effort has come close to finding the various characteristics that constitute the dyslexic reading process and dyslexia.
- No other theory has described and explained the various specific compensatory mechanisms that tend to diminish and mask the symptoms' intensity, leading some experts to think that dyslexia is merely an outgrown or overcome developmental lag.
- No other theory has led to a medical means of diagnosis

and successful treatment, even offering the possibility of prevention.

Despite significant masking of its surface symptoms, the core of dyslexia remains for life.

Writing

The writing ability of dyslexics is frequently delayed and appears to be dyscoordinated, reflecting the difficulty they have recalling and utilizing learned motor patterns. The shape, spacing, and direction of the written content frequently has a sloppy, "discombobulated," uneven quality; the words tend to drift in space. Concentration and effort are often needed to compensate, whereupon fatigue invariably leads to a reappearance of the same old pattern.

For some dyslexics printing is easier than writing script, whereas the reverse is true for others. Interestingly, the artistically gifted can "draw" the writing in a calligraphic style while remaining unable to write normally in a rapid or reflex coordinated fashion. Accordingly, many a dyslexic will learn to write slowly and deliberately via a drawing mechanism, so that it may appear normal and even supernormal. And eventually, its speed and quality may correspondingly improve as well, via conditioning, and thus truly resemble normal reflex writing instead of calligraphy.

Analysis of the writing errors in dyslexics revealed that when printing was easier, there existed an ability to harness and compensate by writing one letter at a time, thereby sidestepping the continuous rhythmic flow and stream required to produce script. For those dyslexics who had an easier time with script, the timing and flow utilized for cursive writing was helpful. Put another way, the rhythm required to complete script was found to be as helpful to some dyslexics when handwriting as it is to stutterers when singing (stuttering frequently disappears when singing and reappears when talking).

During the process of writing, letters and words are frequently omitted or displaced to more distant parts of the written passage, a condition that resembles the fusion and displacement errors characterizing the dyslexic reading process. At times letters are inadvertently repeated, again highlighting the repetitive or perseverative tendency attending writing as well as reading.

Despite the existence of dyslexic artists, drawing was found to be difficult for the majority of dyslexics. Drawings of human figures were not infrequently tilted and off balance, and arms appeared disjointed; fingers were impossible to draw for the vast majority, and were avoided by drawing gloves, hiding hands behind torsos, or resorting to stick figures (mistakenly interpreted as a symptom of masturbatory or castration anxiety by psychiatrists and psychologists). The various psychological interpretations used to explain dyslexic drawings were found to be as erroneous as those used to explain all dyslexic symptoms.

The dyscoordinated and imbalanced drawings of dyslexics reflect the inner chaos they experience in integrating sensorimotor signals. When attempting to copy a series of designs (Bender Gestalt figures), dyslexics commonly shifted the paper or their bodies in attempts to find compensatory stable reference points. Copied designs were frequently rotated and angled off their intended spatial positions. Moreover, angles and curves were poorly formed and shaped.

In general, the writing and drawing errors of dyslexics are easily explainable if one refers to my "guided missile" concept. Just picture the computer within our inner-ear (cerebellar) system guiding our hands and fingers in space. Any dysfunction within this computer will result in our hands and pens being poorly directed, thereby accounting for the misdirected and dyscoordinated quality of the errors that characterize the dyslexic writing and drawing processes, exceptions aside.

However, the exceptions must and can be accounted for. Not every motor function and reflex is misguided in dyslexia. The writing function is spared for some dyslexics, whereas only one of several writing functions is spared for others, clearly indicating that each specific motor function or task has its own specific wavelength or circuit on or by which it is processed. This is true of sensory functioning as well. Each piece of information entering the brain is processed on its own specific wavelength. Thus, some input functions may be impaired while others function well and still others are viewed as gifted.

Mirror-writing is not unusual for some dyslexics. One of my left-handed patients wrote only in reverse. As a result of the fracturing of his left hand he was forced to write with his right hand. Lo and behold, he wrote normally.

Leonardo da Vinci frequently mirror-wrote. Historians claim he did so to disguise his thoughts. However, he may have been dyslexic; and his mirror-writing capacity may have been carried into adulthood, just as many reading-score–compensated dyslexics retain the ability to mirror-read.

Spelling

Although some dyslexics are excellent spellers (one patient I examined was a proofreader), the spelling function in dyslexia is characterized by a significant memory instability, visual and/or phonetic. The letter sequences of words are frequently forgotten as rapidly as they are learned. At times visual recall is better than phonetic, whereas some dyslexics spell entirely via phonetics, with minimal or no visual recall.

Not infrequently, parents will claim a child spells well simply because he receives 100's on tests. Further exploration may reveal that many of these so-called good spellers forget the words shortly after the exam is over and that their practical or spontaneous spelling ability is poor. Many dyslexics forget what they learned prior to taking tests, and thus obtain poor spelling grades. In both types of dyslexics, there is a short-term memory defect in spelling; it is just shorter for failing spellers than for passing spellers. There are other variations as well. For example, many a dyslexic will have great difficulty remembering or imprinting anything at first. But once learned, it's never forgotten. This compensatory learning style applies not only to spelling but also to reading, writing, math, and other functioning.

Directional and sequential disturbances frequently complicate the spelling process. Letters and syllables are often reversed. Some dyslexics spell orally better than they do when writing, and the determining mechanism was investigated. In dyslexics with poor writing or graphic ability, written spelling is further impaired by a host of dyscoordinating and scrambling writing mechanisms. If, on the other hand, speech functioning is intact, oral spelling scores may better reveal the degree of spelling dysfunctioning.

Spelling can be compensated for by many dyslexics, but certainly not by all. Indeed, there are many dyslexics who find it much easier to spell difficult words than simple words. Upon exploration, a number of mechanisms were found to be responsible for, and thus to explain, this seemingly paradoxical situation. Most commonly, the spelling ability of dyslexics improves with age. And so by the time they graduate from high school or enter college, they have no difficulty learning new, large, complicated professional words accurately—or "normally." But they still retain or remember three or four ways to misspell simple words that they mislearned earlier. As a result, simple words often trigger "spelling doubts": Is it spelled this way, or that way, or another way? Also, these incorrect impressions "stick" via perseverative-like memory mechanisms, and they "stick" more in younger versus older dyslexics.

Mathematics

Mathematical dysfunctioning in dyslexia is initially experienced as an uncertain memory for addition and subtraction facts, requiring compensatory finger or mental counting. Later on, difficulties arise when learning the multiplication tables. The multiplication facts are learned and then rapidly forgotten unless reinforced by almost continuous repetition. It is interesting that some dyslexics experience more disability with certain of the multiplication tables than others. For example, some dyslexics will have difficulty with the 7's table while with others it may be the 8's.

For the majority of dyslexics, learning the multiplication tables is more difficult than acquiring addition and subtraction facts. However, this is not always true: Surprisingly, some dyslexics learn the multiplication tables with normal or almost normal rapidity while still using their fingers to do simple addition and subtraction.

These variations in learning addition, subtraction, and multiplication once again highlight the fact that each specific math function and even subfunction is processed by way of its own corresponding circuit; thus, simple circuits may be impaired while more complicated processing occurs with natural ease.

Reversal and scrambling errors result in dyslexics misreading, miswriting, and misremembering number- and task-related sequences. Accordingly, there results a host of dyslexic slips previously considered psychologically motivated and thus called Freudian slips.

The process of writing numbers in columns and then adding or subtracting them results in characteristic errors. The number columns are frequently crooked. Numbers in column one are inadvertently added to numbers in column two and even three as a result of the same eye-tracking difficulty triggering letter-, word-, and sentence-skipping when reading.

By encouraging young dyslexics to utilize graph paper, I have shown them how to write their numbers in aligned spaces, which in turn enables them to add columns more accurately by utilizing the guidelines provided by the paper.

Not infrequently, dyslexics will reverse directions when performing arithmetical functions. Thus, for example, they will add columns from left to right rather than the reverse, further complicating their difficulties. Even +, −, ×, and ÷ signs are occasionally reversed or confused with one another. For instance, instead of adding two numbers, dyslexics will occasionally subtract them or will divide instead of multiply.

Many high school and college dyslexics encounter difficulties with algebra, geometry, trigonometry, and calculus. Often they fully comprehend the concepts; they just have trouble remembering the equations and theorems needed for problem solving. On the other hand, many a dyslexic finds concept retention more difficult than factual retention. Many cannot connect, coordinate, or integrate sequences rapidly enough for the thinking brain to make sense out of the task before forgetting individual steps or links. Others experience difficulty with both memory and concepts. Fortunately, some dyslexics are gifted in higher mathematics despite earlier memory difficulties with simple arithmetic. Many patients have told and shown me how they can "intuitively" and rapidly come up with a correct answer to even complex math problems, without knowing how they did it. Needless to say, this "savantlike" subconscious mental functioning on tests leaves these pupils open to allegations of cheating, especially when they cannot perform this task in written form.

Some dyslexics have great difficulty visualizing the dimensions and angles in geometry, while others function remarkably well with spatial relationships, even better than nondyslexics.

In many cases, compensated dyslexics have little difficulty with math until high school. Unexpectedly, they become frustrated with algebra, geometry, trig, or calculus. Such cases are invariably misdiagnosed and termed lazy or indifferent, as are dyslexic high school students who suddenly experience similar frustration at having to read greater volumes faster than ever, or at having to recall and process escalating numbers of facts with less time to study than they had before.

Some bright adult dyslexics were noted still to have difficulty counting change. Apparently, their calculation channels were initially "blurred out" severely, and later anxiety resulted in their phobically avoiding situations that would have led to compensation. As a result of this insight, I realized that some dyslexics blurred out the *ability to remember* concepts, just as others readily blur out the ability to remember nonconceptual details. In other words, dyslexic individuals know the meaning of money; they just cannot easily recall the significant operational steps required to use it or to make change. The resulting anxiety and embarrassment lead to secondary conceptual difficulties as an outgrowth of a money phobia.

Many dyslexic teachers learned the basics of simple arithmetic only when forced to teach their first-, second-, and third-grade students. It appears that their initial mathematical difficulties were complicated by severe anxiety factors. And, when forced to teach, the anxiety factors were bypassed. Dyslexics start out being physiologically inefficient at performing certain tasks. Anxiety factors complicate these processes despite the fact that the individuals may eventually learn to compensate physiologically. Thus, a physiologically caused disorder may continue as a result of secondary anxiety factors, even though the initial disturbance was compensated for.

Memory*

Specific patterns and types of memory instability play a vital role in reading, writing, spelling, and mathematical delays.

The analysis of dyslexic functions has clearly revealed that memory is not an all-or-nothing function. One can have a poor memory for visual letter and word recall while having a

---

*Problems with memory, balance, coordination, and speech functioning may intensify with age in dyslexics. Patients and their clinicians frequently fear they are developing the onset of Alzheimer's disease, multiple sclerosis, or even brain tumors.

great memory for phonetics. And one can easily learn addition and subtraction facts while experiencing extreme frustration when attempting to learn and retain the multiplication tables.

Based on this insight, I was forced to recognize that every piece of information is processed, stored, and retrieved independently of other memory functions. Each dyslexic will therefore be characterized by a unique quality and pattern of memory functioning versus dysfunctioning or instability.

Upon analyzing the memory functions of large samples of dyslexics, certain characteristics occurred and reoccurred. The following *specific* memory functions were typically delayed or impaired: learning or retaining the names of colors, shapes, people's names and/or faces, important dates, and even daily events. In addition, sequential memory functioning frequently appeared to be delayed among many dyslexics. Thus young dyslexics will initially experience difficulty recalling their addresses, their telephone numbers, the days of the week, the months of the year, and the seasons in order, until compensation sets in with age. Although many of these memory problems are matters of storage, there are retrieval problems as well. For example, the majority of dyslexics experience subtle difficulties recalling words they know and wish to use in ordinary speech. Known proper names frequently remain "on the tip of one's tongue" rather than in one's conscious memory bank. Occasionally, a successfully treated adult dyslexic with severe reading and spelling difficulties will suddenly read and spell well without further tutoring. This observation indicates the presence of a memory retrieval problem rather than a storage problem. Needless to say, both types of memory problems may coexist, albeit in varying proportions.

At times remembered facts cannot be appropriately erased. Parents frequently tell me: "My child has a fantastic memory. Once he learns something, even if it is wrong, he won't be able to forget and correct it." If a spelling or number sequence is learned improperly, the same error will be made throughout the individual's life. New and correct memory impressions do not lead to the erasing or correcting of facts incorrectly recorded. Instead, retained misimpressions continue to conflict with newly acquired accurate impressions, resulting in doubt and uncertainty. Dyslexic physicians frequently display the ability to spell recently learned medical terms accurately, whereas their spelling of simple words remains poor. The same phenomenon can be observed with dyslexic lawyers, scientists, and even linguists.

In many ways a physiological failure to erase memory impressions appears to be similar to the perseveration mechanisms by which the eye becomes stuck to a word, the pen to a letter, the mind to a thought or an action. Even need and desire may be insufficient to neutralize these perseverative mechanisms affecting the eye, mind, memory functions, and motor tasks. This perseverative-like memory process appears to be on the opposite end of a memory continuum beginning with the pathologically rapid erasure of facts and sequences.

Specific patterns of memory function and dysfunction vary not only from dyslexic to dyslexic but from time to time, depending upon a host of compensatory and decompensatory circumstances, such as fatigue; stress; infection; trauma; and metabolic changes such as those occurring in pregnancy, menopause, or thyroid disease.

Direction

Orientation and directional or spatial difficulties characterize dyslexic functioning, resulting in reversal and scrambling errors affecting reading, writing, spelling, math, memory, and speech. Underlying the directional disturbances is an impairment of the inner ear's compass. Thus, dyslexics have difficulty instinctively knowing right and left and, at times, front and back, up and down, east and west, north and south, and so on. With time and learning, this disturbance may be compensated for. Dyslexics often utilize their thinking brains to reason out right and left. For example, a child will know that he writes with his right hand. As a result, when asked to turn right, he'll squeeze his writing hand, recall that his writing hand is his right hand, and in that way know which direction is right.

One of my patients had a wart on his left hand and used it as a means of determining which direction was left. Following the surgical removal of this wart, he once again became bewildered about directions and required another compensatory device. Some dyslexics become easily confused about where they're going and how to get there, even if they have repeated the sequence a number of times before. Occasionally, bright adult dyslexics will tell me that they get lost each time they go home. In fact, some patients refuse to move once they have learned to travel to and from their homes. Moreover, they will not venture to or from home via a new route.

By contrast, other dyslexics will overcompensate and develop especially keen directional skills. They just seem to know where they are going, even in new places. Ironically, some of these "intuitive navigators" remain uncertain about right and left.

The analysis of countless errors and disturbances eventually led me to recognize that many fears of getting lost or going to new places reflect disturbances in directional rather than psychological functioning. In time I realized that many children who frequently get lost, and those who fear to stray and wander, have one and the same difficulty—an inner-ear compass dysfunction.*

Time

The inner ear is a pacemaker imparting timing and rhythm to various motor skills such as running, skipping, hopping, climbing, sports, reading, writing, and even speaking. Accordingly, a dysfunctioning inner-ear system may result in difficulty or delay not only in the above functions but also in sensing time, as well as difficulty in learning to tell time.

Compensatory and overcompensatory processing may result in "gifted" timing mechanisms whereby dyslexics are able intuitively to measure time spans down to split seconds. Still, they may have difficulties reading an ordinary watch. Although digital watches have been lifesavers for many dyslexics, they have presented difficulties for some. Thus, 7:15 may easily be misread as 7:51 or any reversal combination thereof.

The difficulties in reading time are manifold:

*One expert, Professor J. Money of Johns Hopkins University, even developed and marketed a visual maze test for detecting dyslexia. The only problem with it was that it didn't work. Dyslexics have little difficulty getting out of a maze in which they can see and reason their way through exits. They often experience difficulty sensing and thus knowing right from left, north from south, and east from west—directions that cannot be seen. And the latter directions were not tested for by Money's maze test. In other words, traditional theory—and the implication that this directional difficulty was of a conceptual versus a compass origin—was once again shown to be in error when applied to clinical reality. By contrast, all the concepts within *Smart but Feeling Dumb* were derived from dyslexic patients, not from other theorists. Accordingly, they are based in reality!

- Difficulty recalling and processing number representation and terms, such as quarter to or quarter after
- Difficulty recalling hand representation, that is, which hand tells minutes and which tells hours
- Directional disturbances such as clockwise and counterclockwise, before and after
- Difficulty seeing the numbers clearly, i.e., blurred vision
- Eye-tracking disturbances resulting in skipping and misreading the clock's numbers
- Difficulty in rapidly processing and translating dots and Roman numerals instead of Arabic numerals on a watch face

Even procrastination may represent a time-related symptom for some individuals, resulting in lateness. Difficulties in reading or judging time invariably result either in chronic lateness or in overcompensatory earliness.

Speech

Speech disturbances of varying intensity and quality characterize a majority of dyslexics. While some speech difficulties are readily apparent, the vast majority are subtle and are elicited only upon careful questioning.

Many a future dyslexic will have been a late talker, while others will exhibit a variety of articulation or slurring speech errors requiring speech therapy.

Episodic stuttering was found to taint dyslexic samples periodically, suggesting that there is a relationship between stuttering, dyslexia, and inner-ear dysfunction. Later studies of mine clearly verified this relationship.

As stated earlier, the inner ear imparts timing and rhythm to motor tasks, speech included. As a result of a disturbance in rhythmic activity, speech functions may become dysrhythmic, resulting in starting, stopping, and sequential rhythmic errors.

The concept that rhythm is impaired in stuttering is supported by an interesting observation: Stuttering frequently disappears when individuals sing. Some researchers even notice improvement in stuttering when a metronome is placed next to the ear; the former acts as a rhythmic pacemaker. If rhythmic activity helps compensate for stuttering, then might we not further assume that a disturbance in rhythm underlies stuttering?

Starting and stopping speech activity in stuttering was found to be complicated by another factor already described—perseveration. In other words, a motor speech pattern becomes stuck and interferes with the normal speech flow. Not infrequently stuttering may also be triggered by difficulty pronouncing or recalling a word or thought. The resulting hesitation will invariably affect speech rhythms, especially if preexisting disturbances are already present.

The most common and subtle disturbances found among dyslexics, often leading many to become shy and avoid unnecessary speaking, are input and output speech lags. In the presence of a drifting sound input, many dyslexics will hear the sound and not know its meaning until several seconds or even several minutes later. If the sound sequence coming into the brain drifts, it will take the thinking brain several seconds or several minutes to compensate for the processing disturbance, and the patient will frequently ask, "What?" This reflex response allows the patient time to compensate for the drifting input and eventually know what was said. Not infrequently, dyslexics will speak loudly, perhaps to compensate unknowingly for auditory processing difficulties.

If the motor speech responses drift, or if there are impaired word memory or concentration mechanisms, then there will be a lag between the intention to say something and the actual motor speech response. Memory disturbances for word and thought recall may so complicate the spontaneous speech flow that many dyslexics develop "loose," rambling, and disjointed speaking styles and are naturally viewed as scatterbrained. Some dyslexics often talk rapidly and even interrupt others before forgetting their thoughts. This "dyslexic speech style" must be clinically differentiated, by a clinician, from more serious neurological and psychological disturbances affecting the speech process, such as those that underlie the loose and rambling speech of psychotic or aphasic patients. Not infrequently, dyslexics report a dyscoordination between the speed of their thought process and the speed with which their motor speech mechanisms are capable of working, often resulting in symptoms such as stuttering, word hesitation, and word or thought forgetting—resulting in speech or social phobias. (Similar mechanisms result in writing symptoms.)

Directional disturbances frequently affect speech processing and result in word and even thought reversals. For this reason dyslexics are prone to slips of the tongue, saying words out of sequence, or reversal of directions such as up and down.

Concentration and distractibility disturbances may further complicate all of the above speech disturbances and give the mistaken impression of a hearing loss. Hearing tests are recommended in these circumstances.

The inability to inhibit or block out extraneous background noises or speech patterns while listening to someone nearby or in the foreground may result in severe confusion for some dyslexics. The background contaminates and scrambles the foreground sound sequence and results in an overall sound blurring. This type of situation is frequently present in crowds and restaurants and was found to result in crowd and restaurant phobias.

Grammar

Many dyslexics experience great difficulty in understanding and/or utilizing simple grammatical forms. This disturbance affects written expression much more commonly than verbal expression. When grammatical dysfunction is present, writing and/or speech becomes rambling and run-on in quality and form.

Complex grammar is also affected by the dyslexic disorder. However, this disturbance is more difficult to analyze, for the teaching and learning of grammar varies significantly with educational instruction.

By contrast, every eight-, nine-, ten-year-old child should know simple rules of grammar, as well as when to capitalize letters and how to use periods, regardless of prior teaching methods.

Hyperactivity, Overactivity, and Impulsiveness

The body's motor and energy levels are frequently improperly fine-tuned by the inner ear in dyslexia. The result is hyperactive, overactive—or even hypoactive or decreased—activity levels, as well as fluctuations between these different states.

Dyslexic children may initially show abnormal activity levat an early age, even from birth. Some mothers have even reported feeling hyperactive fetal activity, clearly suggesting that hyperactive or motor racing states may occur prior to birth.

Hyperactivity is frequently distinguished by its onset. When this symptom occurs in the young or during the preschool years, it is frequently referred to as *develomental* in origin. If this hyperactive, overactive, or restless abnormal motor activity first appears in conjunction with school activity, it may be referred to as *acquired*.

Developmental activity forms are frequently viewed as being of physiological origin, whereas the acquired forms are thought to be of psychological origin. However, my studies clearly show that the developmental and acquired forms may both be of physiological origin, although the acquired form is frequently milder in nature and thus requires the frustration and anxiety of school to trigger it so that it becomes belatedly recognizable. Moreover, the analysis of the so-called developmental and acquired activity states reveals the presence of still another hidden dyslexic mechanism: the inability of an impaired inner-ear system to control, regulate, or dampen anxiety buildup. Hence, a dysfunction within this anxiety-regulation mechanism may result in greater degrees of frustration in so-called developmental than in acquired activity states. Thus, abnormal activity levels become more apparent earlier in the developmental state than in the acquired state.

My studies further demonstrate that severe hyperactivity is relatively uncommon in dyslexia. These wild states of "runaway" activity or perpetual-motion activity are most commonly observed in brain-injured children and adults. In contrast, mild degrees of hyperactivity and still milder forms of restless, fidgety, overenergetic activity, all of which I call *over-activity*, are most frequently observed in dyslexics.

High-activity motor levels or energy levels are frequently associated with a poor or low frustration tolerance and result in impulsive, poorly thought-out behavioral and verbal discharges, such as cursing, temper outbursts, stealing, and truancy. And the need to discharge frustration and anxiety rapidly frequently leads to such negative defensive or maladaptive activities as alcoholism, drug abuse, and a series of avoidance or phobic mechanisms: cutting school, avoiding work, and so on.

Overactivity is frequently associated with the increased stress and frustration of school activities, and was termed *acquired* to describe this correlation. My research indicates that the added pressure of school does not invariably cause the abnormal regulation of activity (overactivity); it merely triggers and brings to the surface a previously hidden and compensated-for activity disorder. I therefore came to view "mild" hyperactivity, overactivity, and hypoactivity as mere variations on a common theme. As stated earlier, most often the reported distinction between developmental and acquired activity dysfunctions was found by me to be inaccurate—more apparent than real—and denoted the *degree* of disturbance rather than reflecting a separate causative origin.

There are several reasons justifying my view of hyperactivity, overactivity, and hypoactivity as merely degrees of the same disturbance:

- Frequently, one state spontaneously slides into another and even back again.
- Medications helpful for hyperactive states similarly benefit overactive and even hypoactive states.

- These very same medications are helpful regardless of whether the abnormal activity is labeled developmental or acquired.
- All three states appear to be similarly compensated for with time.

One will often read that hyperactivity or overactivity disappears by puberty and that medications are no longer needed or helpful afterward. Although this assumption is true for some dyslexic individuals, it is by no means valid for all. Many hyperactive dyslexic children will act out their frustrations and develop into explosive, impulsive, drifting, antisocial, driven young and older adults. They still require active medical and psychological treatment, even as adults.

Concentration and Distractibility

Disturbances of concentration and distractibility are frequently associated with hyperactive and overactive states. The racing motor commonly interferes with normally sustained concentration levels. However, concentration may also be secondarily disturbed, or fragmented, by the drifting sensory input characterizing the dyslexic disorder. In addition, concentration mechanisms are similarly fine-tuned by the inner-ear system, as are motor mechanisms and the sensory channels. Consequently, a fine-tuning disturbance will result in drifting concentration levels, or a true short attention span, distractibility, daydreaming, and so on.

In other words, many dyslexics who appear to have short attention spans do not. Often the opposite is true. In order to compensate for their drifting sensory input and motor output channels, dyslexics are forced to expend large amounts of concentration and effort over relatively short periods of time. As a result, they "burn out" and create the illusion of having ADD.

Normally functioning individuals frequently rest their concentration mechanisms while adequately performing many tasks on a "reflex" level. Dyslexics cannot relax or rest their concentration mechanisms without immediately paying the price: a host of typical dyslexic sensorimotor and related cognitive and speech slips and errors. Dyslexics require sustained concentration mechanisms functioning in high gear to control and compensate for their underlying chaotic sensorimotor channels. *There is no rest for the weary dyslexic. She must forever be on guard and remain in an overcontrolled state of high alert.*

As a result, some dyslexics compensate and develop super-concentration mechanisms and abilities that resist normal degrees of fatigue and diversion. However, the vast majority are not so fortunate. They are forced to struggle constantly to keep their concentration mechanisms going. Many fail in this attempt and forever complain of feeling sleepy, tired, foggy, in a trance, or blocked.

The relationship between concentration mechanisms and disturbances of inner-ear functioning is significant and fascinating. Not only do concentration efforts and mechanisms help compensate for the typical sensorimotor dyslexic symptoms, these same mechanisms play a major role in minimizing inner-ear–determined motion sickness and related dysfunctions.

Perhaps a few clinical examples will prove helpful here. During special inner-ear testing (electronystagmography, or ENG), the inner ear is stimulated using warm and cool water as well as rotation. These stimuli frequently trigger dizziness, nausea, even vomiting, as well as a reflex pattern of rapid eye movements called nystagmus, especially if individuals are tested with their eyes closed. The above symptoms can be rapidly reversed if:

1. The subjects are asked to open their eyes
2. The subjects are asked to calculate or perform tasks requiring concentration
3. The subjects are asked to fixate and concentrate upon a specific object. This task best and most rapidly serves to eliminate the induced symptoms

These observations led me to recognize that eye fixation and/or concentration mechanisms inhibit or dampen motion-sickness responses. Similar observations were spontaneously made by dyslexics with motion-sickness tendencies when riding in a car. They are most prone to car sickness when seated in the back: If they sit next to the driver and look out the front window, their car sickness decreases or disappears. Without question they feel best when they are driving, an activity requiring maximum concentration and fixation efforts; and many individuals with motion sickness tendencies refuse to ride in a car unless they drive.*

Psychologists have assumed that individuals who must drive have a need to control others or to avoid being controlled by

---

*There are, however, exceptions to this "driving" rule: Should the visual filter of dyslexics become overloaded by watching moving cars or scenery coming and going, or alternating lights and shadows at night, then they avoid driving or sitting up front. Flicker and sunlight may have a similar destabilizing effect, and thus sunglasses are often helpful. Similarly, rapid visual overloading during the reading process may be compensated for by using tinted lenses or developing overcompensatory concentration and visual processing mechanisms—the latter serving also to inhibit abnormal inner-ear responses.

others. Not so! They merely wish to avoid motion sickness. They wish to control only their own inner-ear systems!

Upon analysis it became apparent that concentration and eye-fixation mechanisms tend to improve inner-ear functioning and thus result in a decrease in corresponding symptoms. A series of animal experiments demonstrated that visual stimulation results in decreased inner-ear reactivity or sensitivity, corroborating the findings I observed while studying dyslexics.

Repeated observations demonstrated that improved concentration results in a corresponding improvement in sensorimotor functioning. As a result, I began treating dyslexics with concentration-stimulating medications while simultaneously utilizing anti–motion sickness agents. Accordingly, there resulted higher yields and degrees of improvement among my dyslexic patients than when they were treated with only antihistamines. No doubt for similar reasons, astronauts were treated with a combination of anti-motion sickness and concentration-improving medications. And no doubt the failure of these medications in some astronauts helps explain their developing what I call "space dyslexia."

Distractibility is frequently reported by dyslexics with concentration difficulties, despite the fact that this symptom may occur in the presence of intact concentration mechanisms. My research has shown that the inner-ear system acts as a filter separating unwanted background stimuli or noise from important foreground events.

A dysfunctioning inner ear frequently results in impaired filter functioning. In this case visual and/or auditory overloading may occur and give rise to such symptoms as light sensitivity or sound sensitivity. Moreover, the visual and/or auditory input may be scrambled by the incompletely separated background and foreground inputs, resulting in variations of visual and/or auditory blurring.

Dyslexics with a dysfunctioning filter will often become fearful of crowds, or demophobic. The crowd represents a situation in which there is either too much visual and/or too much auditory stimulation. The overloading triggers anxiety responses, and the latter in turn trigger avoidance or phobic mechanisms.

Fortunately, the same medications that improve concentration mechanisms also result in improvement of the inner ear's filter functioning, thus minimizing or eliminating distractibility. Improvement in concentration by any means will frequently diminish the distractibility resulting from impaired inner-ear functioning.* Interesting material presented to dyslexics in a manner that stimulates their concentration invariably results in decreased distractibility and increased inner-ear functioning.

All too often *interest* and its beneficial effects on learning have been viewed only in psychological or educational terms. My concepts have added a fascinating physiological dimension to the various psychological explanations of motivational learning. More specifically, by stimulating one's adrenaline, interest neurochemically enhances concentration and cognitive functioning while inhibiting distractibility, dizziness, and related inner-ear symptoms—as do the stimulant medications. Moreover, the use of medications and various physiological conditioning techniques has provided a new medical dimension to the learning-teaching experience.

---

*Exceptions to this general rule invariably materialize. There are patients with good concentration who are highly distractible and hyper, and all combinations thereof—suggesting that these functions are both separate and interrelated. For more detailed information, the reader is referred to my book *Total Concentration* (1990).

Before concluding this topic, I would like to leave the reader with a question to ponder: Is it not possible that a series of *sleep* disturbances, such as insomnia, nightmares, and the inability to wake up in the morning; states of fluctuating consciousness, such as dream states, split personality, etc.; and mood disturbances previously thought to be of psychological origin may be in fact also physiologically determined by mechanisms affecting concentration or alterness?

Attention Deficit Disorder (ADD) or Attention Deficit Hyperactivity Disorder (ADHD)

Since attention deficit disorder (ADD) and attention deficit hyperactivity disorder (ADHD) have recently come into the forefront in diagnostic circles, it seems that a word of explanation is indeed warranted.

In studies I've conducted over the past twenty years, just about 90 percent of the children diagnosed as dyslexic have had related ADHD symptoms. Ninety percent of children diagnosed with ADHD or ADD have some dyslexic-related symptoms and inner-ear–related balance and coordination signs similar to those previously described.

If 90 percent of both dyslexic and ADHD- (or ADD-) diagnosed children share overlapping symptoms and over 96 percent have diagnostic inner-ear signs, are not both named disorders reflections of one and the same inner-ear dysfunction? Obviously! But to date, this commonsense observation has not been officially recognized.

Additionally, the combined use of anti–motion sickness antihistamines *and* stimulants offers those patients the best chance of improvement.

- The anti–motion sickness antihistamines improve the "typical" dyslexic aspects of the inner-ear syndrome more than the ADD or ADHD aspects, and
- The anti–motion sickness stimulants or antidepressants improve the ADD or ADHD aspects of the inner-ear syndrome more than the dyslexic part.

For this very reason, combining these medications where possible triggers the widest and highest degree of improvement while allowing stimulant doses to be minimized.

Also, the fact that the anti–motion sickness stimulants were shown to be as effective as the antihistamines in controlling or preventing motion sickness—and thus enhancing inner-ear functioning—further supports my hypothesis that the inner ear is responsible for both dyslexia and ADHDor ADD.*

Phobias and Related Mental and Behavioral Disorders

Having studied the dyslexic case material presented thus far, it should be obvious to the reader that dyslexics may have difficulty processing motion input and are thus more often prone to motion-related phobias: fears of moving elevators, escalators, cars, planes, trains, buses, carnival rides, crowds, etc. Inasmuch as the scanning mechanisms of dyslexics periodically become fixed or stuck to sensory impressions, thoughts, and motor events, dyslexics are prone to obsessive-compulsive or perseverated symptoms.

Hyperactivity and overactivity states predispose individuals to temper outbursts, drifting and wandering natures, and rapid

*For more detailed information, see my book *Total Concentration* (1990).

boredom and the inability to stick with tasks; especially when the hyperenergetic states are combined with concentration difficulties. Hypoactivity and low energy levels frequently leave individuals feeling tired, drained, depressed, even introverted. By contrast, racing energy levels predispose or force individuals to exhibit extroverted behavior—requiring distinction from bipolar conditions.

This topic will be developed further in Chapter XI, inasmuch as the content is too important and lengthy to remain a mere subgrouping.

Balance and Coordination

As stated, the inner ear regulates all balance and coordination mechanisms; therefore, an inner-ear dysfunction will frequently result in some delay or disturbance in balance and coordination mechanisms. As a result of impaired balance and coordination functioning, some dyslexics appear "klutzy" or clumsy, while others—both children and adults—are accident-prone and may bruise easily and thus appear to be abused. It is interesting that some dyslexics, like Bruce Jenner, through compensation or because they are gifted, become athletes despite poor eye-tracking coordination and impaired writing coordination. I have repeatedly observed athletes who are gifted in one or two sports and yet poor in others, and some are even klutzy and accident-prone. In other words, the balance and coordination circuits in dyslexics are very specific and often function independently of one another. We are not dealing with an all-or-none phenomenon that either impairs or spares *all* inner-ear–related mechanisms.

The *majority* of dyslexics are neither extremely "klutzy" nor athletically gifted. Almost all exhibit some dysfunction of balance and coordination, however slight. Even bed-wetting and soiling may result from poorly coordinated motor (involuntary sphincter) control. The so-called antidepressant medication traditionally used to treat these symptoms was discovered to improve a wide variety of other dyslexic symptoms, especially concentration and activity levels. And in some, the antidepressants also result in significant improvements in typical dyslexic symptoms, further suggesting that dyslexia and ADD are both reflections of a common denominator. And since the antidepressants have been shown to be potent anti–motion sickness medications, it seems likely that this common denominator is inner-ear related.

Last but not least, improperly balanced muscle tone aggravated by the tugging of opposing muscles may intensify or trigger such symptoms as flat feet; toeing-in or -out; knees turning in or out; "loose" ligaments, muscles, and joints, as well as "double-jointed" states; buckling muscles, and sudden falling; improperly aligned eyes (strabismus); and even scoliosis.

Dyslexics have as much difficulty coordinating multiple motor tasks as they have coordinating multiple visual and/or auditory inputs. For example, upon testing, many dyslexics cannot simultaneously talk and perform a repetitive motor task. They are able to do one or the other, but not both. Some dyslexics have difficulty driving a car while listening to the radio or conversation; they cannot concentrate on both tasks at the same time.

And some cannot maintain eye/facial contact and process speech at the same time. Thus, this avoidance of eye contact is compensatory and does not represent the presence of emotional malfunctioning.

Psychosomatics

Headaches, dizziness or light-headedness, nausea, vomiting tendencies, as well as stomachaches and other gastrointestinal symptoms are often triggered by motion sensitivity due to an inner-ear/cerebellar dysfunction. When the latter dysfunction affects the visual system, then the following symptoms may occur: blurring, double imaging, object or word movement, and size changes, as well as other related illusions, light sensitivity (photophobia), head tilting, poor eye-muscle alignment, etc. Hand tremors and muscle tone variations, including "jelly legs," toeing-in and -out, a tendency toward slouching, scoliosis, enhancement of strabismus, and a host of other "previously misunderstood" symptoms can often also be traced to an inner-ear dysfunction. Ear ringing or tinnitus, as well as noise buildups or recruitment result when the inner ear is directly impaired, occasionally triggering social anxiety or avoidance of crowds (noise).

A disregulation of the primitive autonomic or reflex nervous system by an impaired inner-ear/cerebellar dysfunctioning may also result in:

- Smooth muscle reflex–based symptoms: bed-wetting, soiling, etc.
- Vascular (blood vessel) and related autonomic or reflex symptoms: excessive sweating, cold hands and feet, flushing or blanching, dizziness upon suddenly sitting up, standing up, or bending, etc.
- Reflex disturbances involving swallowing (i.e., choking); breathing (fast, slow, dysrhythmic, etc.—sometimes triggering fears of suffocating and even panic); heart rhythms (unexplained skipped or fast beats, etc.—also triggering

anxiety); impaired sucking, nose blowing, blinking, and grasp reflexes, etc., in younger children—often compensated for over delayed time spans; speech impediments (i.e., stuttering, stammering, etc.).

- Eating reflexes may also be impaired, perhaps explaining predispositions to anorexia, bulimia, as well as sensitivity to food-related textures, smells, appearances, etc; related body image distortions (i.e., illusions of being too fat, ugly, etc.) are also often found to be coexisting anorexic determinants.

Self-Esteem and Body Image

In my clinical experience, the most important symptoms characterizing dyslexic syndrome are those impairing self-esteem and body image, and thus they are the most crucial to effectively treat and eliminate. Self-esteem is significantly impaired when dysfunctioning inner-ear/cerebellar mechanisms result in even mildly decreased sensory-motor and related memory-speech-cognitive functioning—triggering feelings of stupidity, ugliness, and variations thereof. Most important, favorable responses to inner-ear-enhancing medications and nutrients rapidly lead to improved esteem, irregardless of age or how long these feelings were previously present, suggesting a strong physiological linkage. Also reinforcing this cerebellar-esteem linkage is the frequent and even normal response to a motor accident or faux pas: reflexively calling oneself "stupid," "dumb," "idiot," and even referring to the accident or dyscoordinated event as "ugly."

My studies and those of prior scientists (i.e., Lord Sherrington) recognized that cerebellar integration of [all] sensory [and motor] mechanisms, especially proprioception, or the sensors telling us where all our body parts and boundaries are in space, is crucial for determining the physiologically based sense of body image. Accordingly, an impaired integration may result in feeling ugly, as well as related illusions/delusions of having deformed facial and/or body characteristics, including feeling too fat, too short, having a long or poor nose structure, etc. And as previously indicated, it is quite possible that eating disorders (anorexia, bulimia, etc.) are triggered by impaired eating reflexes as well as distorted body image mechanisms, often responding to conditioning and other therapies that may alleviate primary as well as codetermining mechanisms.

Summary

Fifteen major categories of dyslexic functioning as well as their respective symptoms and mechanisms have been described. The reader has been provided with both the quality and a qualitative analysis of the wide-ranging symptoms characterizing the dyslexic disorder. Similar symptoms may result from nondyslexic, non–inner-ear mechanisms and causes. Invariably, however, the symptoms' qualities will be distinctly different. Thus, dyslexic disorders may be distinguished (by a doctor) from nondyslexic disorders.

Frequently, psychological and physiologically based stress, fatigue, concussion states, and so forth, may trigger the appearance of typical dyslexic symptoms. One usually finds that either a dyslexic or inner-ear disorder already existed and that the apparent trigger merely exaggerated the problem, or that an inner-ear disturbance was newly created and therefore the symptoms were newly acquired.

Additional Insights

Before concluding this chapter, I would like to leave the reader with something new to think about.

As mentioned earlier, dyslexics sometimes experience greater difficulty spelling shorter words than longer words, mirroring the greater difficulty some have in reading smaller as opposed to larger words. Upon observing the relative ease with which an occasional dyslexic learns to read, write, and spell despite the continued presence of dyslexic reading, writing, and spelling errors—even for simple words—I realized that an important explanatory mechanism was still eluding my grasp. Analysis of the spelling errors characterizing adult dyslexic professionals was needed before the above mechanisms became clear: Dyslexic doctors, dentists, lawyers, and others frequently display more difficulties with smaller words than with the infinitely more complex technical words they learned in graduate school.

One common denominator was found linking these observations: The more difficult words that were found to be easier to recognize, write, and spell were invariably learned when older. I suddenly found an explanation linking all of these seemingly atypical and paradoxical facts:

- In spite of the increasing difficulty needed to process those tasks required for each succeeding grade, with age some dyslexics compensate and thereby find it easier to read, write, and spell.

- If the initial dyslexic misperceptions and conflicting perceptions of the relatively simple reading, writing, and spelling forms are not erased from an individual's memory but instead remain active, imprinted alongside new, correct, compensated learning experiences, then simple letter and word configurations will be remembered incorrectly.

- Newly learned words—more complicated forms—perceived after compensation has occurred do not conflict with previously mislearned forms and are thus more accurately remembered for reading, writing, and spelling.

This seemingly impossible-to-explain or paradoxical dyslexic learning style, whereby simple words are harder to remember than more complicated words, has led to further investigation and an explanation that has far-reaching importance:

- One cannot glibly tell parents that their children will never learn new languages because of persistent reading, writing, and spelling difficulties with the original "learned" language. Although that prediction is true for the dyslexic majority, there are exceptions, and these exceptions must be dealt with.

To date, I have treated dyslexics who were linguistically gifted, as well as those whose self-compensation or favorable response to treatment resulted in gifted writers, editors, and professionals in all of life's endeavors. As a result of the amazing capacity for dyslexics to compensate, it is all but impossible for experts to accurately predict outcomes on the basis of early diagnostic evaluations.

- The earlier one treats dyslexics, the less *mislearning* there is, the less time these dyslexic impressions are superimposed upon one another, and the less retained they are.
- At times this eidetic style of functioning is a compensa-

tory one for dyslexics. Thus, for example, many dyslexics recognize the meaning of seen words only when actually hearing them while reading.

- The same reasoning holds true for the dyslexic mechanisms: The longer they are in force, the more likely they are to remain imprinted forever—perseverated—and consequently, the more difficult they are to compensate for academically, medically (even with medications), and psychologically, resulting in irreversible emotional scarring.

The difficulty in erasing early mechanisms and styles of perceptions and/or motor responses is consistent with, and can explain a series of, known psychological observations:

- The vivid perceptions of children most frequently dampen with age—a phenomenon similar to what happens with dyslexic symptoms. However, occasionally, vivid perception and memory will persist with age, accounting for eidetic or "gifted" visual, auditory, and/or photographic memory functioning in older individuals.
- At times this eidetic style of functioning is a compensatory one for dyslexics, and allows them to compensate for their underlying impairments.
- Childhood neuroses and even psychoses are frequently caused by the retention of early vivid memory or fantasy impressions, which remain unconsciously present and active for life, conflicting with newer or more accurately learned impressions. Accordingly, the aim of psychotherapy and psychoanalysis is to revive and retrieve these "hidden" false but active impressions and erase them

from an individual's memory banks. Conditioning therapies, on the other hand, attempt to bury these perseverated memories still deeper by strengthening newer, more realistic and adaptive memories and mechanisms.

Stated another way, recognition that *early learning* and *early mislearning* may *stick* or *perseverate* as a result of a physiological mechanism affecting memory functioning may help explain:

- The predisposition of some children to neurosis, psychosis, behavior disorders, and so on.
- The increased benefits from child psychotherapy versus adult therapy, and early learning versus belated learning.

Although perseverated functioning was initially viewed as an unusual and atypical physiological maladaptive mechanism, there exists another completely different explanation:

- If perseverated memory results in the oversticking of memory impressions and difficulty in erasing, might not the absence of normal memory functioning in dyslexics result from rapid erasures and therefore the absence of normal degrees of perseveration?
- Might there not be degrees of perseveration? And might we not have missed this in viewing only extreme rather than normal variations of this sticking mechanism?
- Might not brainwashing or bias be viewed in terms of exaggerated or perseverated memory mechanisms resistant to normal and appropriate erasure?
- Do not bias or perseverated memory patterns coexist with realistic memory patterns, mirroring the manner in

which dyslexics simultaneously reverse and misidentify small words more readily than complicated ones? In other words, originally ingrained memory and thought functions may persist, resisting correction or erasure, despite the *coexisting* pressure of *normal,* contradictory memory and thought patterns acquired later.

- Might not acute stress factors, such as that experienced during extreme periods of emotional and physical trauma, trigger perseverationlike memory mechanisms that render forgetting difficult and at times even impossible, resulting in what is psychiatrically referred to variously as traumatic neurosis, war neurosis, or other similar terms?

XI

Phobias and the Inner Ear

Who could have predicted that my dyslexic research would lead me to recognize that the physical basis of a large variety of phobias and related so-called mental disorders was similar to that of dyslexia and its variable symptomatic fallout? Certainly not I!

My psychiatric practice and my studies of dyslexia eventually forced me to draw two unexpected conclusions:

I

The vast variety of phobias seen by psychiatrists did not fit into the traditionally accepted psychoanalytical theories, just as the dyslexic symptoms did not fit into the century-old thinking-brain or linguistic theories. As a result, the understanding, explanation, and response of phobias to psychotherapy and psychoanalysis appeared to be as incomplete as the similar explanations and treatment of dyslexia.

Improvements in phobias via psychotheraphy were

noted. Cures were seldom if ever seen. To say the least, crucial scientific explanations and determinants were missing. The traditionally proposed psychological theories that attempted to explain phobias were most incapable of realistically accounting for their shapes, forms, variable intensities, onset, and disappearance, as well as the various combinations of phobias often appearing in any one person.

In other words, given the personality profile and background of any individual, psychiatric theory was completely unable to predict or explain the specific phobias, or combinations of phobias, to which he or she might be heir—without stretching theory to ridiculous limits. In fact, there was no way to predict which patients would develop phobias and which would not. Thus, traditional theories could not satisfactorily explain why one patient was afraid of cars, another of buses, another of trains, another of planes, another of heights or bridges, another of walking across wide-open areas, another of various combinations of the above; or why still others feared crowds, social events, department stores, food markets, losing control, tunnels, swimming underwater (especially with eyes closed) or just plain swimming. . . .

Even the generalized mechanisms assumed responsible for the *universally* occurring phobias (such as fears of insects, snakes, mice, and so on) escaped comprehensive, meaningful interpretations.

Reluctantly I was forced to admit that the traditionally accepted and espoused theories of phobias just did not fit or explain the clinical facts of phobic life. Crucial insights were missing. Indeed, there existed a scientific void.

II

Dyslexic children and adults periodically complained of phobias identical to those I attempted to treat and understand in my psychiatric practice. Moreover, many dyslexic patients who were medically treated spontaneously reported significant improvements in their phobias and self-esteem, as well as in their more typical dyslexic symptoms. As the title of this book indicates, the vast majority of my dyslexic patients felt stupid, dumb, and ugly—the very same feelings expressed by my phobic patients in psychiatric treatment.

Was it possible that many phobias were part of the dyslexic disorder? And if so, what were their determining inner-ear mechanisms? Was it possible that phobic patients in my psychiatric practice were also dyslexic without my knowing it? Could their hidden inner-ear dysfunctioning or dyslexia account for their feeling stupid, dumb, and ugly? Might dyslexic or inner-ear mechanisms better account for the shapes, forms, and combinations of phobias than did the traditionally accepted but significantly incomplete psychiatric explanations?

Various conditioning therapies and antidepressant medications (or concentration stimulants) as well as antipanic drugs (such as Xanax and Valium) appeared to help a significant number of phobic patients. Was it possible that conditioning therapy helped phobics just as eye conditioning and occupational-therapy conditioning helped dyslexics—by improving the functioning of the underlying inner-ear circuitry via "practice-makes-perfect" mechanisms or via compensatory feedback loops?

Do the so-called antidepressants help phobics as they do dyslexics—by improving the strength and force of compensating concentration and related mechanisms in dyslexia while perhaps simultaneously fine-tuning the mechanisms regulating and controlling anxiety? And do the anti–motion sickness medications improve the phobias among dyslexics as a result of their improving the underlying inner-ear mechanisms that I now suspected were crucial in determining phobic symptoms in general?

Only years later, after I repeatedly asked these questions, did scientific publications acknowledge that all antidepressants used to help concentration, activity, and anxiety disorders, as well as most of the antipanic medications, were all anti–motion sickness or antivertigo agents.

Motion-Related Phobias

These questions triggered answers. And, as the answers seemed to correlate with all the known facts concerning phobias and dyslexia, I became increasingly excited and enthusiastic. Unexpectedly and suddenly, the boundaries of dyslexic research expanded beyond belief. I was once again off to a new beginning.

I suddenly knew what elevators, escalators, buses, trains, cars, planes, and walking across wide-open spaces had to do with one another. They were all motion-related!

I knew that the inner ear processes the total motion input. And I also knew that the inner ear processes each type and quality of motion via a specific and distinct independent circuit, thus accounting for the various forms of motion sickness. For example, one can be carsick and bus-sick without being plane-sick. One can be elevator- and escalator-sick and not be carsick. One can even be prone to circular motion sickness, as on carnival rides, while feeling fine riding in a straight line or moving up and down. In other words, motion sickness is most frequently direction-specific. In some individuals motion sickness and/or dizziness, nausea, and vomiting are triggered by non–motion-related stimuli: visual, auditory, or olfactory signals, or even crowds.

From these insights I suddenly knew why phobic individuals are prone to varying patterns and qualities of motion and crowd phobias. Simply stated, the patterns and forms of motion phobias are related to and determined by corresponding patterns of underlying and dysfunctioning inner-ear circuits, which process these motion activities. Moreover, the name of the phobia was found to be relatively irrelevant, merely signifying the surface *trigger* that provokes or intensifies dysfunctioning inner-ear mechanisms, thus resulting in anxiety, motion sickness, dizziness, and avoidance phenomena, or phobias. Once a specific motion-related situation or circumstance triggers panic, anxiety, dizziness, motion sickness, imbalance, or fear of losing control, this very same situation will be anticipated and avoided in the future.

Since one of the functions of the inner-ear system is to control and regulate motion-related mechanisms, any inner-ear dysfunction and resulting anxiety may predispose some dyslexics to rapid and long-lasting anxiety buildups and anxiety states. Inasmuch as intense, overwhelming, emotionally traumatic anxiety or panic states result in vivid memories and reminders of danger situations, it is only natural that these danger situations will be avoided until the trauma can be emotionally overcome and the memory erased. If, via perseveration, this memory is not readily erased, and if this persisting vivid memory triggers anxiety responses that rapidly escalate, then the memory of the resulting anxiety and panic serves as a second trigger, with both mechanisms and the resulting triggers predisposing an individual to a corresponding phobia.

Non–Motion-Related Phobias

Although the motion-related phobias and one's predisposition to them may now be explained in terms of inner-ear–related mechanisms, the reader may justifiably wonder: Are non–motion-related phobias also triggered via inner-ear mechanisms?

The answer is *yes!* Once I recognized the relationship between the inner ear and motion phobias, it seemed only reasonable to see just how far I could go in analyzing the remaining phobias for possible inner-ear–related determinants and mechanisms.

Compass-Related Phobias

I had already guessed that dyslexic children who fear getting lost—and dyslexic adults who fear new places and thus avoid traveling—have an underlying compass-related orientation and directional disturbance. Obviously, if one's sense of direction and memory for direction are significantly impaired, it is reasonable to avoid straying into new or disorienting situations. Does not the inner ear process compass-related directional, orientational, and memory functions?

School Phobias

Upon analysis, most school-phobic children examined by me turned out to be dyslexic. Their school phobia represented either a conscious or unconscious attempt to avoid the emotionally devastating and humiliating feelings of stupidity triggered by their academic frustration.

According to traditional psychiatric theory, school phobics are overpampered, overloved, spoiled, "homesick" children and thus are fearful of leaving their parents. Although this theory may hold for a few cases, it is hardly true for the vast majority of school phobics. In the majority of cases the parental concern for their children, and perhaps even overconcern, is secondary to their loving attempts to help their troubled children overcome a frightening and misunderstood "emotional" disorder. In other words, psychoanalysts mistakenly viewed concerned parents' attempts to help their children as the cause of the problem. Once again, cause and effect were scientifically found to be reversed.

Ignored by psychiatrists was the obvious fact that most school phobias occur with increasing grade levels, when the pressure and complexity of schoolwork become increasingly difficult. If fear of separating from parents were primarily responsible for this phobia, then it would arise right from the start, when children begin school, and would diminish with each succeeding school year by virtue of the improvement to be expected from conditioning and adaptation.

Frequently, a school phobia may appear to arise when a child is emotionally traumatized by an unfeeling teacher or peer. Thus, there may be an obvious or visible emotional situation that triggers the onset of the phobic disorder. However, upon deeper examination, one invariably finds evidence of a predisposing dyslexic factor, a factor subconsciously "inviting" teachers and peers to act out unthinking, unfeeling, even sadistic statements and actions. Occasionally, guilt-ridden dyslexic children and even adults will unconsciously provoke others to abuse or insult them, thereby attempting to satisfy their underlying guilt feelings and a resulting need for punishment. They feel stupid and dumb and think they are disappointments to their parents and teachers; they may see themselves as worthless.

Those dyslexics who cannot vent their academic and social frustration and anger turn it upon themselves in the form of self-abuse, and many become depressed. Not infrequently, school phobias are triggered by the compass confusion or disorientation experienced by children in schools in which they feel lost. Also, in some individuals fluorescent lighting may trigger anxiety, disorientation, vertigo, and hyperactivity/distractibility. Those who are thus affected develop a need to avoid these stimuli.

Fears of Heights, Bridges, Walking: Imbalance Phobias

What causes fears of heights and bridges, and even irrational-seeming thoughts of jumping out of windows, off train platforms, etc.? In retrospect the answer appears simple: imbalance mechanisms resulting from a dysfunctioning inner-ear system!

One does not have to be "klutzy" to avoid phobically "dangerous" situations that provoke inner feelings of imbalance and fear of falling. Dyslexic athletes may experience imbalance and vertigo and fear heights, whereas clumsy dyslexics may not be affected by heights. Although an inner sense of imbalance is crucial to fears of heights and bridges, it is not an absolute determining factor. The specific reaction to this imbalance determines whether one will be fearful, remain fearful, or deny the fear altogether in an attempt to overcompensate by skydiving, mountain climbing, or pursuing some other height-related activity.

Imbalance mechanisms sometimes reveal themselves in anxiety dreams: nightmares about flying, falling, being pushed off a building or bridge or out of a window, and so forth. In a similar fashion, imbalance mechanisms may trigger these very same fears and thoughts during one's waking hours. Some patients even experience an irresistible, magnetic-like gravitational pull toward the ground they're looking at from a height. All too often, these very same patients instinctively feel like jumping just to get rid of the unpleasant sensation. They are not suicidal! Just the opposite! They are panicky lest they be "forced" to jump. Others feel pulled to the side and even upward—the latter effect no doubt triggering floating sensations and even flying dreams.

Agoraphobia

Agoraphobia—a fear of leaving home and walking in wide-open spaces—is clearly related to a dysfunctioning inner-ear system. Invariably, agoraphobics fear fainting, passing out, losing control, dizziness, and imbalance symptoms. Accordingly, an agoraphobic will leave the house and walk across the street only if escorted by a trusted companion, someone to hold on to should something happen.

Analysis of agoraphobics clearly reveals that most feel dizzy when crossing a wide-open space: Open spaces trigger in them feelings of dizziness and imbalance, as well as fears of passing out. They require an escort because of an inner-ear dysfunction, not because they are immature and dependent, as has been commonly thought. Moreover, the dizziness quickly triggers anxiety mechanisms, which rapidly escalate. The escalation of anxiety in many phobic patients clearly suggests that the fine-tuning or inhibition of this danger signal—anxiety—is malfunctioning, and that this malfunction may be inner-ear–related as well. This impaired inhibiting or "breaking" mechanism might readily explain escalating anxiety or panic attacks with and without agoraphobia.

Agoraphobics feel most comfortable when walking next to a building, a railing, a bench, or a trusted companion—anything or anyone to hold on to should they suddenly become dizzy, feel off balance and faint, or lose control. Open spaces, especially intersections, offer no visible evidence of support, and accordingly trigger several anxiety-ridden concerns: What would happen to me if I suddenly lost my balance and fell or passed out while cars were zooming by me? Who would take care of me in that situation if I were all alone? Intersections, with their crisscrossing of cars in opposite directions, require decisions about stopping and going; they require that one distinguish the meaning of red and green lights; and they present the danger of losing one's balance or tripping. This set of demands results in visual overloading and causes distraction and memory uncertainty and thus triggers warning signals, such as anxiety, panic, and avoidance.

Despite the differing clinical terms, individuals who fear open spaces and individuals who fear heights and bridges share one and the same basic anxiety: a fear of falling. And underlying this anxiety is a common dysfunction: an unstable balancing mechanism. Also, open spaces trigger disorientation in some individuals since they lack concrete orienting/familiar markers telling them where they are in space and time.

Perceptual and Crowd Phobias

Perhaps you are now curious about the relationship between crowd phobias and dyslexia. I was, too!

Dyslexics have reported experiencing sensations of dizziness, imbalance, almost a loss of consciousness, while looking at certain wallpaper patterns or designs, book patterns in libraries, can configurations in food stores, clothing patterns in department stores, or "moving-people patterns" along New York City's crowded streets. Upon testing a wide range of these dyslexics with my 3-D Optical Scanner, I inadvertently provoked these very same responses. It became apparent that *visual* patterns or *visual crowds* may trigger motion sickness and anxiety reactions in a fashion similar to the motion triggers—buses, cars, planes, elevators, escalators, and carnival rides. Moreover, these visually triggered symptoms frequently responded very favorably to medications, and the phobia either lessened or disappeared.

Noise patterns or crowds, even smells, may serve to discombobulate some dyslexics. They will avoid parties and restaurants and hence suffer from social phobias, restaurant phobias, etc.

Water phobias exist as well. Many dyslexics report motion-sickness responses while watching the ocean rolling to the shore. Overly sensitive individuals feel the same way about ripples on a pond. These patterns serve as visual triggers. Interestingly, those individuals fearing thunder and other noises hear them significantly louder than do normal subjects. Yet, paradoxically, they do not hear their own voices as loud, whereas others do.

Some dyscoordinated dyslexics justifiably fear drowning, for they simply cannot learn the movement patterns necessary for swimming and survival. Others feel lost and thus panicky when their feet cannot touch bottom and/or when their eyes cannot fixate and see the water's floor.

Speech Phobias; Public Speaking Phobias

The recognition that auditory discrimination and speech mechanisms of an inner-ear origin are often subtly impaired in dyslexics, and that the resulting symptoms and associated anxiety improve significantly on inner-ear–enhancing medications, led to a simple insight: that speech and social phobics may have an inner-ear dysfunction and thus dyslexic-related symptoms. Indeed, a series of research efforts over many years has proven this insight to be scientifically valid.

Sensory-Deprivation Phobias

Many dyslexics are afraid of diving or swimming underwater, especially with their eyes closed. One dyslexic patient reported complete disorientation while scuba diving—he could not distinguish up from down. In fact, he almost drowned because he swam downward while thinking he was swimming upward. Only the pressure buildup in his ears made him realize his error and saved his life.

Swimming underwater is a problem for some dyslexics only when their eyes are closed. In the dark they become completely confused, disoriented, and frightened. Although some refuse to swim underwater under any circumstances, others merely refuse to close their eyes. Seeing provides an orienting input and thus avoids anxiety.

A dyslexic child may become fearful of the dark and even of falling asleep, thus "preferring" insomnia or falling asleep with his eyes open while watching television or reading a book. Dyslexics have reported experiencing severe dizziness upon closing their eyes, especially prior to falling asleep. Others have reported severe dizzy spells only during sleep. As mentioned, some dyslexics report nightmares concerning falling, floating, and spinning. Still others experience sleepwalking and all sorts of nightmares and night terrors—many of which unexpectedly responded favorably to the anti–motion sickness medications.

You are no doubt wondering why and how these symptoms arise. Psychologists were equally curious, which accounts for the wide range of psychological theories to explain these phenomena. However, I frequently found physical mechanisms to be responsible for these symptoms.

As explained in Chapter X, concentration and eye-fixation *mechanisms* tend to minimize or eliminate dizziness, imbalance, and other inner-ear symptoms. These compensatory visual-targeting inner-ear mechanisms are sharply reduced when swimming underwater with one's eyes closed, when closing one's eyes before falling asleep, and when actually sleeping.

Some individuals are even fearful of being tired; hence, they are compulsively driven to get enough sleep; some resort to coffee and drug "regulation." Concentration is significantly reduced with fatigue and may result in significant intensification of dyslexic symptoms as well as fears of losing control, passing out, and disorientation.

Why should dyslexics be frightened of tunnels or experience claustrophobia? This question was the most difficult to answer.

Many dyslexics have reported a dread of being trapped in a room without a window or door for escape. For this reason, many such individuals will not go to a movie unless they can sit close to an exit (movie phobias); they need a way out in case something should happen to them or in the event that they feel threatened by a loss of control. They fear fainting, passing out, losing consciousness, and experiencing escalating degrees of anxiety. They need a visible means of escaping these dreadful feelings should they arise: They need to know that they can escape to the outside.

In other words, claustrophobics feel trapped by inescapable inner, "deadly" feelings; they feel better when there is a visible, external way out. When there is no visible way out, it is as if their inner sense of feeling overwhelmed is confirmed externally; their anxiety escalates even further, and they feel even more trapped. Stated another way, their feeling free to escape from their external environment really reflects the need to escape from their inner environment, which often consists of escalating or improperly controlled anxiety or dread. Visible signs of escape are reassuring, whereas the absence of such is devastating.

What do tunnels, moving and stationary elevators, closed-off rooms, and underwater situations have in common, except for the fact that they trigger claustrophobia? As suggested earlier, they are all encircling environments that may be difficult to escape from and thus intensify feelings of being trapped and losing control of one's feelings and anxieties. But why should these environments trigger anxiety in the first place?

One additional thought occurred to me. All of the above

situations are *shielding* environments—environments that en-
circle individuals and completely shut them off from their
"normal" surroundings. They appear to be "sensory depriva-
tion" environments. Is it possible that shielding environments
may impair the inner ear's ability to receive and utilize vital
electromagnetic and related visual signals needed to maintain
and even regain orientation and contact with one's surroundings, especially if the inner ear is already somewhat impaired in
these functions?

Dyslexics already have impaired "antennae" secondary to
their inner-ear dysfunction. Accordingly, dyslexics receive incoming signals in a partially blurred fashion, but are able to
compensate for it. If they pass through a shielding environment, then the signals coming in are further impaired and
their "radio" functioning and reception become similar to that
of one's car radio when riding through a tunnel. In a "tunnel,"
dyslexics' inability to function properly or maintain contact
with the outside world may result in severe anxiety and appropriate avoidance mechanisms or phobias.

Movement-Inhibiting Phobias

A new patient of mine recently explained, "I feel dizzy every
time I go into a closed-off situation—not anxious." And others claim, "I can't stand in a line and wait. . . . It makes me
dizzy. . . . I feel well only when I can move." Upon analyzing
these and similar data, it appeared reasonable to assume that
some inner-ear–dysfunctioning patients *need motion* to function better. They are *motion-seeking*, the opposite of those
prone to motion sickness.

As a result, *movement-inhibiting or -restrictive environments* and/or the perception of enclosed spaces may trigger vertigo and/or claustrophobic anxiety warning signals, similar to the adaptive motion-sickness responses that attempt to get predisposed subjects out of physiologically "dangerous" or unpleasant motion-overloading situations.

External Versus Internal Triggers

Before continuing with an explanation of the universal phobias (common phobias that exist, and have always existed, in every society), I must clarify what I mean by external and internal triggers and their corresponding response mechanisms, that is, phobias.

Thus far the inner-ear–related phobias or phobic mechanisms described were *released* or *triggered* by specific external stimuli, or *external triggers:* cars, buses, planes, trains, elevators, escalators, bridges, heights, and crowds; visual, auditory, and olfactory configurations. Psychoanalysts have viewed these triggers as sexual symbols, indicating that cars, buses, planes, etc., represent aspects of the sexual anatomy and/or intercourse. Perhaps, but not necessarily so.

My research indicates that these triggers may be symbolic only of specific motion stimuli to which an impaired inner-ear system is sensitive and to which it therefore reacts abnormally. In fact, there is significant evidence to suggest that the cerebellum, the computer for the inner-ear system, modulates and regulates anxiety—as well as sexual and aggressive drives and emotions—as it does the other sensory and motor mechanisms. Hence, improper fine-tuning of all these instincts and reflexes may predispose individuals to a corresponding series of sexual and aggressive symptoms. In other words, sexual and aggressive instincts may indeed contribute to the presence of phobias and related mental disorders. However, these instincts, as well as the anxiety mechanisms they trigger, may be impaired primarily by an underlying physiologically based regulating dysfunction previously overlooked in psychiatric research.

Internal triggers may also provoke abnormal phobic and other responses. Thus, for example, dysfunctioning inner-ear mechanisms may be released by such internal triggers as abnormal chemical states, diabetes, thyroid disease, shifting hormone levels during menses and menopause, tumors, and any other disorder that impairs the function of the cells that are essential to the inner-ear system.

The significance of both external and especially internal triggers in provoking phobias and related mental disorders has been significantly overlooked both by psychiatrists and other medical researchers. The presence of phobias in the absence of any clear-cut physical or neurological disorder has led to the assumption that the released mental symptom is of primary psychological or mental origin, i.e., caused by conflicting emotions. Overlooked was Freud's ingenious insight that underlying all mental and emotional disorders exists a physical component, or "somatic compliance."

Now, to return to the universal phobias . . .

Universal Phobias

Such universal phobias as fears of insects, snakes, knives, and so on, have always been known, regardless of how primitive or complex the society. As might have been expected, these phobias were viewed by psychoanalysts as sexually or aggressively determined, and the corresponding trigger was viewed as having a sexual or aggressive symbolic significance.

The universal phobias I am talking about deliberately exclude realistic or *traumatic phobias*—phobias that result from a real trauma, such as being attacked by an animal, bitten by an insect, attacked by a knife or weapon, or sexually or aggressively molested and abused. I eventually came to view universal phobias as release symptoms—the release of old, buried fears dating back to our original animal origins and heritage; fears reflecting the instincts and reflexes inherited by animal species for survival over millions and millions of years.

Few of us are fully aware of how inherited reflex patterns are crucial to our survival, and how dependent these reflexes are on triggers. For example, the newborn infant has a sucking reflex once his cheek is touched, a crying reflex when spanked, a breathing reflex that responds to changing oxygen levels in the air and blood, and an eye-tracking reflex provoked by moving visual triggers. All of these reflex motor patterns are inherited. They were imprinted in our genes during an evolutionary process or survival of the fittest.

Animal species are known to have inherited sexual, aggressive, and flight patterns of response to certain external stimuli: colors, scents, noise patterns, and visual configurations, such as the shapes of insects and other animal forms. Humans no longer need many of these inherited response patterns; the response patterns have been neutralized or buried by strong inhibitory mechanisms or counterforces that hold them in check. These antiquated reflex patterns are controlled or regulated by our central nervous systems unless there is some impairment within the inhibitory forces. In the presence of such an impairment, old, buried fears and anxieties are released from inhibitory control and surface as symptoms of phobias. In other words, currently unnecessary patterns of response may be released from inhibition by triggers that, under normal circumstances, would have no triggering potency. I have frequently observed dyslexics experiencing difficulty with certain motor reflexes—difficulty holding a pen, spoon, or knife and fork properly—utilizing animal-like grasping mechanisms. Some dyslexics have difficulty with reflexes needed to process sound inputs and speech outputs rapidly. Others have difficulty "learning" to blow their noses or swallow pills, that is, difficulty with coordinated reflex responses. Also, many dyslexics are given to releasing anxiety and motion-sickness responses when triggered by stimuli that do not affect nondyslexic individuals. Thus, many dyslexics display fears of snakes and other animals by which they have never been threatened.

Keeping all of these observations in mind, I reasoned as follows:

- If the inner ear and cerebellum are responsible for coordinating, inhibiting, and/or releasing normal reflexes, and
- If some reflexes are poorly inhibited and coordinated among dyslexics, and
- If some anxiety and motion-sickness release mechanisms are "abnormally" triggered in dyslexics, and
- If the cerebellum or inner-ear system is an "organ" whose prime function, according to Nobel Prize winner Sir John Eccles, is inhibition,
- Then might not a dysfunctioning inner-ear or cerebellar system with failure in inhibitory power result in the re-

lease of old, primitive instincts and reflexes, i.e., universal phobic responses?

This reasoning can explain how universal phobias may occur without any external trauma or trigger. It also accounts for the universality of these fears and their complete independence of specific patterns of child-rearing and personality profiles. Needless to say, external triggers may, under traumatic circumstances, also precipitate the release of corresponding universal phobias. Thus, for example, an attacking dog or a bee sting or a hissing snake may resonate with and trigger the release of a corresponding phobia in predisposed individuals. Would this concept not also explain why and how reflex and conditioning therapies that attempt to inhibit or suppress primitive responses can be helpful?

Incomplete Psychiatric Assumptions

Most clinicians, psychiatric and otherwise, assume that a disorder is psychologically or emotionally determined if obvious physical or physiological factors cannot be found. In the absence of a clearly defined physical basis for a disorder or symptom, psychoanalysts and psychiatrists quite naturally propose the presence of unconscious, unseen, intangible emotional or mental mechanisms. Unfortunately, errors have been and still are being made.

The absence of detectable physical findings may be due either to faulty clinical examinations or to physicians' inability to detect and recognize the presence of existing physical and physiological dysfunctioning. The entire dyslexic riddle was a consequence of faulty medical assumptions, circular reasoning patterns, incomplete neurological examinations, denial of the presence of inner-ear–related signs and symptoms, and even the imaginary belief in the presence of cerebral signs where none existed. The so-called absence of concrete physical factors in dyslexia initially led to the assumption and conviction that this disorder and its various symptoms were psychologically determined. Two factors were found to result in this error:

- The stated absence of tangible, physical signs does not necessarily mean that these signs are really absent, and that they cannot be detected by another clinician, or by newer, more advanced diagnostic medical instruments.
- The assumption and, especially, the conviction that a symptom or disorder is psychologically determined must be based on more than the absence of physical findings; it must be based on the presence of positive, tangible psychological factors and explanatory mechanisms.

Anyone can postulate that psychological mechanisms are responsible for a disorder—even cancer—for which there is no currently established physical cause. However, the mere assumption of a psychological cause or trigger does not warrant conviction or psychological treatment until positive supporting evidence is found. My research into phobias and a host of related, so-called emotionally caused disorders led me to recognize that accepted scientific "fact" was often, in reality, mere fantasy. In addition, the widespread acceptance of the Prozac-related group of selective serotonin reuptake inhibitors (SSRI) for use in anxiety disorders clearly highlights the physiological versus psychological cause and treatment of these disorders.

The study of dyslexia and the inner-ear mechanisms responsible for dyslexic symptoms led me to the unexpected but clearly demonstrated physical basis of phobias. Moreover this physical basis was experimentally proven. The fact that phobic symptoms respond favorably to medications administered specifically to improve inner-ear functioning further added to my conviction that the primary cause and basis of phobias is a dysfunctioning inner ear.

Although psychological mechanisms and triggers may provoke phobias that are related to the inner ear, and although some phobias are entirely due to psychological factors, my research has clearly demonstrated that a majority of the phobias examined to date are clearly not of a primary psychological origin. Psychological mechanisms may, and do, cause nondyslexic academic symptoms. However, these psychologically determined academic symptoms are different in quality, shape, and form from their dyslexic counterparts, and therefore must be treated differently. And as repeatedly stated, emotional stress and conflict may trigger and/or intensify inner-ear–related symptoms, dyslexic and/or phobic.

Although there still exists a medical bias against psychological medicine, nonpsychiatric physicians are all too eager to attribute psychological causes and motives to patients' symptoms in the frustrating absence of feasible physical findings. Unfortunately psychiatrists and psychologists are similarly inclined to accept these psychological diagnoses without medically double-checking the patients and without clear-cut positive evidence to support a psychological diagnosis.

I have never quite forgotten an episode that occurred during my psychiatric residency at Kings County Hospital in Brooklyn, New York. While I was working in the psychiatric admitting room, a confused, disoriented young man was transferred to me from the medical emergency room. Although I was inexperienced in psychiatry during my first year of residency, I sensed the man's confusion was not of psychological origin. Despite his having been cleared medically, I reexamined him neurologically and found him to have suspiciously abnormal signs suggesting a brain dysfunction.

As a result of my examination, I called the medical emergency room, told the referring medical residents what I thought, and refused to accept the patient for admission to a psychiatric ward despite his loud verbal ramblings and disturbing behavior. A conflict inevitably resulted between the residents in the emergency room and me. The patient was transferred back to the medical emergency room. My superior was contacted and a telephone argument resulted that lasted for hours, with time out on both sides to examine new patients. By morning the patient settled the argument: He developed a temperature of 104 degrees, became increasingly incoherent, and developed clear-cut, irrefutable signs of an infection of his nervous system. Despite antibiotics and rigorous treatment efforts, he died of a rare infectious disease of the nervous system.

Although my diagnostic abilities are far from perfect, and I have had my share of unfortunate errors, my reasoning remains sound: Assumptions are only assumptions, regardless of the individuals making them, and traditionally accepted convictions without logic and without proof are still only assumptions.

Earlier in my career, some of the psychoanalytic literature on phobias and related mental functioning just never sat well with me despite my repeated attempts to read and reread the content for better understanding and conviction. However, when in doubt, especially when inexperienced, it is often best to suspend judgment until increasing clinical experience allows for realistic and more sound reappraisals.

Following my realization that a majority of phobias are physically based and shaped by inner-ear mechanisms, I once again reread *The Psychoanalytic Theory of Neurosis,* by one of the most outstanding analysts in the history of the psychoanalytic movement, Otto Fenichel. Lo and behold, there was a written correlation between phobias, hysteria, and dizziness and a tendency toward motion sickness. There was just one rub: Fenichel believed that the inner-ear symptoms in phobias were a *result* of early childhood conflicts surrounding pleasurable or sexual inner-ear sensations and/or stimulation.* I had demonstrated the opposite to be true. The inner-ear symptoms of dizziness, equilibrium sensations, and motion sickness correlate with phobias solely because all four symptoms are directly related to and caused by an inner-ear dysfunction.

No doubt, a physiologically determined sensitive inner ear may predispose children and adults to intense sensations. And these sensations may serve as a nucleus for coexisting emotional conflicts. However, in my experience, these conflicts are not necessary for phobic formation. And medications that improve inner-ear function very often relieve the phobia, despite the continued assumed presence of an unconscious emotional conflict.

According to classic psychoanalytical theory, if a student or patient can't *see, feel,* and meaningfully *accept* stated analytical facts, then these students or patients must be defensively re-

---

*See Fenichel's argument in Appendix C.

sisting this acceptance because of unconscious emotional factors and conflicts. But this is not necessarily so.

To test my own inner-ear theory of phobias, I examined all my phobic patients with the 3-D Optical Scanner for inner-ear dysfunction. All phobics tested were found to have abnormally low blurring speeds, indicative of a dysfunctioning inner ear. Moreover, all such patients were questioned about past evidence of dyslexic symptoms. All patients revealed clear signs and symptoms of dyslexia.

In addition, a significant number of treated dyslexics revealed improvement in phobic symptoms—a finding highly consistent with my inner-ear theory and inconsistent with traditional analytical theory. I then began treating phobic patients with the same medications I successfully used to treat dyslexia. Many of these phobics suddenly and dramatically showed signs of improvement—improvement that did not occur when treated by me psychiatrically.

In summary, over a period of many years I recognized the relationship between phobias and the inner ear from two seemingly independent lines of research:

1. The vast majority of phobias psychiatrically examined and psychotherapeutically treated could neither be successfully explained nor helped by utilizing traditional analytical theories. Something crucial was missing.
2. Dyslexic children and adults were frequently noted to display a series of motion-related, compass-related, academic-related, and balance-and-coordination–related phobias identical to those seen in a typical psychiatric practice. These dyslexia-related phobias could be physiologically and psychologically explained and better

treated utilizing anti–motion sickness medications. And *all* medications and therapies currently utilized to treat anxiety disorders can be explained by enhancement of known inner-ear mechanisms.

To highlight the correlation between dyslexia, inner-ear dysfunction, and phobias, a series of phobic cases will be presented. Analyze their content and judge for yourself.

XII

Phobias—Case Histories

In writing this chapter, I have tried to present the clinical content in a manner and sequence similar to the way I experienced it. However, for the sake of clarity, I was forced to group and organize the clinical data so that its meaning and significance would be more readily apparent.

Although puzzles and riddles are fascinating to solve, who would have published this book if the data were presented as they first appeared to me: random and seemingly disconnected, scrambled, and "dyslexic"? In the preceding chapter, "Phobias and the Inner Ear," I presented the theories that I found useful in explaining and better organizing a confusing array of phobic symptoms that appeared completely independent of and separated from one another, except by name. In retrospect, these seemingly disconnected clinical phobic and learning syndromes no longer appear scrambled, blurry, and confusing. In fact, the vast variety of phobic and learning symptoms have now been readily united under a common theoretical cause: the inner ear and cerebellum.

Phobias have always cropped up in dyslexic case histories. However, no one seemed to pay these symptoms any attention. In other words they were blocked out of scientific view by bias—scientifically denied.

The reverse was true as well. Dyslexic symptoms have invariably characterized phobic cases in psychiatric treatment. Unfortunately, these dyslexic symptoms were completely overlooked. Once again scientific bias was found to be responsible for this amazing oversight.

As a result of my research, the presence of phobias in dyslexia, and the frequency of dyslexia among phobics, can no longer be denied or scientifically "blurred out." Phobias are part and parcel of the dyslexic disorder and are caused by the same dysfunction—but are triggered by different mechanisms.

One aim of this chapter is to introduce you to some of my phobic patients. After reading, hearing, and feeling their thoughts and experiences, try to dissect the separate but interwoven psychological and physiological factors that determine and shape their various symptoms. Form your own theories.

Initially, I had no idea that the phobic patients in my psychiatric practice were dyslexic, despite their being under my psychotherapeutic care for many years. I was merely interested in psychologically treating their symptoms by listening to their free associations and then explaining and resolving their *assumed* emotional conflicts. My phobic patients *never* hinted at dyslexic symptoms until specifically questioned for them, despite years of careful psychiatric observations. This experience clearly suggested to me that all psychiatric patients must be actively questioned and examined for inner-ear–related symptoms. Waiting for psychiatric patients to verbalize their problems spontaneously and freely may result in wasted years and misdiagnoses.

Slowly and unexpectedly I came to realize that the phobias displayed by psychiatric patients were similar, then identical, to those revealed to me by dyslexic children and adults. Slowly I came to recognize that these phobias improved and even disappeared when dyslexic patients were treated with anti–motion sickness medications. (Remember: No one should treat oneself, even with over-the-counter medications.)

This chapter will carry these insights a giant step forward and show you a validated new method of understanding, diagnosing, and treating phobias of inner-ear origin. Furthermore, the cases to be presented will allow you to test my theories as well as any you may have formulated on your own.

Phobics—Case Histories

Margarita Magaro

Margarita, an attractive thirty-seven-year-old flight attendant, was examined by me for phobias and other symptoms that had been plaguing her for some time. These phobias were

- Fear of crossing streets
- Fear of being alone in a strange city
- Fear of skiing, a sport she had once loved and in which she had excelled
- Fear of making decisions

Margarita also suffered from:

- Dizziness, particularly when turning to the right
- Fatigue

- Blurred and fuzzy vision most of the time
- Poor handwriting ability
- Memory instability for names, dates, and numbers
- Reading and concentration difficulties since childhood
- Chronic confusion about where she was

In spite of these difficulties or because of them, she chose to be a flight attendant.

When I asked Margarita to tell me about her symptoms, she replied:

> I am dreadfully afraid to make mistakes when I am asked to read something, particularly in the presence of others. I cross my eyes and say I am unable to see, deliberately making myself "blind" to justify my statement.
>
> I cannot make a decision. I think first one way and then another, and finally I make up my mind at the last possible moment.
>
> . . . It is the same when I have chores to do. I wait until I can no longer procrastinate. It's terrible.
>
> And . . . permeating these actions, there is an all-pervasive sense of anxiety and fear that has become worse and worse.

Examination revealed that Margarita's phobias and related symptoms were due to a dysfunctioning inner-ear system. Accordingly, she was placed on medication. Shortly afterward she wrote to me excitedly:

Everything looks and feels so crisp and fresh! I am calmer, more in control of myself, able to make judgments and arrive at decisions. *No more procrastinating!*

I'm feeling no more anxiety or fear—it is all easier. I can drive a car with assurance, play tennis, and I have vacationed alone for the first time in twelve years!

Also, I'm unbelievably better organized! One week after being on medication, I returned home and was shocked to see the disorganized, messy state of my house. I went through the house and garage, cleaning, discarding, and reorganizing like mad. Just as my chaotic, messy house reflected the old me, it now reflects the new me. It is uncluttered, purposeful, fresh, and bright.

Margarita is euphoric about her newfound freedom. Although she wrote the following words, I can imagine her saying them with her intriguing, charming Italian accent: "I hope that my ability to cope will give me more energy and time to devote to others. . . . Thank you."

Anne Massie

Very often parents seek help for their children and inadvertently find help for themselves. This was the case with Anne Massie.

Anne had brought her son Tom for treatment, and he had responded extremely well. Anne then sought help for herself: She was suffering from incapacitating phobias that were destroying her way of life, as well as deeply upsetting her loved ones. Anne's phobias were

- Fear of talking to people, because the words might come out backward or might not come out at all
- Fear of speaking on the telephone
- Fear of driving on the freeway
- Fear of the water
- Fear of heights

Initially, Anne denied or "forgot" having had academic problems in grammar school. She was not able to read, and she recalled fooling her mother and teachers by memorizing the words on the page. She could not properly recognize the words she tried to read. As she became older, she learned to read despite the persistence of letter and word reversals and a resulting memory instability for what she read. Right/left directional difficulties persisted into adulthood.

Although not a very good student, Anne managed to pass her courses. She related the following seemingly paradoxical pattern of good versus poor coordination skills:

On two separate occasions I climbed a tree and then had to be rescued because I was afraid of falling. I never went climbing again.

Although I was a poor dancer, I was an excellent horseback rider. I loved horses and riding.*

I was very artistic and earned my living as a painter. Yet, my writing was never really neat.

Anne continued:

---

*Dancing requires greater degrees and different types of leg and body balance and co-ordination than does horseback riding.

I married and had two beautiful children. The marriage, however, did not work out and we got divorced. I supported my children and myself with my portrait painting.

My ex-husband then took our children to South America.

I almost went out of my mind, I was devastated.

I was unable to get my children back. I was unable to paint. . . . I went into analysis, which did help. Then I met a wonderful man whose love and understanding attracted me. We married and had a son, who has filled our lives with joy. Both of my other children were never far from my thoughts. I can only hope that when they are ready, they will seek me out.

The overwhelming stress resulting from Anne's extreme disappointment over losing her children, over not being able to establish personal contact with them, and over the realization that she could do nothing more until they were ready to see her triggered a series of phobias that increased in severity and number over a period of years.

I had become afraid to talk to people. I feared the words would come out backward or not come out at all. And I feared sounding and appearing stupid. I reached the point where I avoided speaking on the telephone. My mind would blank out . . . I could not get the words out. Eventually the ringing of the telephone was enough for panic to set in. It was terrible.

I had always driven on the freeway without any difficulty. Suddenly I was frightened to do so. My fears extended to include heights. I was an excellent swimmer and

enjoyed the water. But [then] I became mortally afraid of
the water.

I developed headaches that became more and more frequent and intense, increasing my sense of confusion, anxiety, and inadequacy. I had become so depressed and isolated
that I was almost unable to function.

It was our son, Tom, whose need gave me the strength to
come to Dr. Levinson's office and ultimately to receive help
for us both.

Anne was examined, diagnosed as dyslexic with associated
phobias, and placed on medication.

Tom's and Anne's progress reports indicated a turnaround
for both. On a visit a year later, Dr. Massie, Anne's husband,
commented on their son's improvement:

Undeniable and unreal! We note progress in his speech,
concentration, memory, reading, and writing—better
spacing between letters, and coordination. Before our
visit Tom would have never entertained the thought of
tennis lessons. Recently he not only took tennis lessons,
but they have revealed an aptitude for the game! He is
playing with experienced players and handling himself
very creditably. You can't imagine what this has done for
his confidence.

Tom now has many newfound relationships with others
of his own age. We are so pleased at his progress.

In no way can we attribute this improvement to coinci-
dence or any other factor but your correct diagnosis and
treatment. We are grateful.

I thanked Dr. Massie and then questioned Anne about the changes she had noticed in herself this past year.

I am painting again after fifteen years! And I have sold several paintings already. This is a marvelously heady feeling for me!

I have friends that I enjoy talking to, both in person and *on the telephone*! No longer does the ring of the phone and the possibility of answering the phone strike terror in me.

I drive on the freeway once again; it is no longer a fearful vortex, sucking me into its center and oblivion. . . .

This summer I have gone *swimming*—can you believe it? Once again I am able to enjoy the sport and the water.

My whole world has changed. The shadows are gone and the colors are bold and bright. I have more energy, fewer headaches. I can concentrate and organize my thoughts and activities without going into a tailspin. I feel more self-confident and better about myself as a person.

My memory still leaves something to be desired: I forget names and regress somewhat under stress, but these are slight drawbacks.

I feel an improvement in almost every area, especially inside. There is an inner calm and stability; I feel almost reborn.

Anne's improved self-concept and general feeling of well-being spring from her achievements and joy, not only in her progress, but in her son's as well. Her case clearly indicates how emotional stress and conflict may trigger a disruption within a preexisting compensated but impaired inner-ear system, and thus the emergence or reemergence of dyslexic and phobic symptoms.

It must be emphasized that although emotional stress and conflict were triggers, they did not cause, create, or shape the *forms* of the resulting phobic symptoms. The forms of the phobic symptoms were determined by the pattern of impaired inner-ear mechanisms. Accordingly, the resulting phobic symptoms improved when the underlying mechanisms responded favorably to medications improving inner-ear functions and mechanisms. What's more, the fact that Anne was a poor dancer and a superb rider highlights two major physiological factors:

- Each motor and sensory function is controlled or processed by its own corresponding channel; thus, athletes may be gifted for one motor task and klutzy for another.
- Interest and concentration are potent compensatory factors that are often crucial in leading to improved inner-ear functioning.

Susan Smith

Seeing Susan's perpetual smile, one would never guess that she was the victim of severe, paralyzing phobias and assorted dyslexic symptoms.

For many years Susan suffered from:

- Fear of crossing streets
- Fear of becoming lost
- Fear of riding escalators
- Fear of going on elevators alone
- Fear of driving and of being in cars
- Fear of being in the city alone

- Fear of heights, which resulted in avoidance of bridges, cable cars, tunnels, etc.
- Fear of water and of drowning

Other symptoms were

- Poor sense of time
- Poor sense of direction, and right/left difficulty
- Clumsiness

Susan's many problems clearly illustrated the interwoven nature of phobias and related dyslexic symptoms. The following is an excerpt from our discussion. By listening carefully to her content you will be rewarded with unique insights into the inner-ear mechanisms responsible for phobias, dyslexia, and the associated balance/coordination/rhythmic difficulties. This is not merely the best way to understand these mechanisms—it is the only way!

"As a child, I had a lot of trouble staying upright. I was falling constantly. I tried roller skating and ended up on my backside most of the time. I was falling, tripping, and bumping into things and people; it was terribly humiliating.

"I was extremely afraid of crossing streets. My mother was still picking me up at school, helping me cross the street, etc., even when I was quite old. When I crossed on my own, I was afraid of being struck by a car because I had no idea where the cars were coming from. I was confused: I didn't know whether to cross the street when the light was red, as my mother told me to do, or to cross when the light was green, as my teacher advised. What I ended up doing was running across the street and praying a lot.

"In retrospect I think my mother was confused, too. I recall that she had trouble crossing the streets. We'd start crossing, a car would come, she would go back, the car would start, she would go forward, the car would stop—it was like a dance. Whenever a car approached, she would just stop. I did the same thing, I guess, and a couple of times I was almost killed.

"When I walked, I always crossed the street at the narrowest place. If it was a quiet street or a narrow one, it was okay, but if it was a busy or very wide street, I had a problem. I would simply wait until there were no cars. After I had my baby daughter, I virtually stopped crossing streets. I felt responsible for her, so I didn't go anywhere. I walked around the block or went to the park, where I could sit.

"I was always very apprehensive about escalators and elevators. With my husband or friends I would go up the escalator but never down. I was terrified of falling. Actually, I feared that my foot might become caught on the step; I would panic, become light-headed. For years my therapist worked with me through behavior therapy and desensitization. I was finally able to go down escalators, but with great difficulty and fear. It created a problem when my husband and I went out: We always had to find an elevator or staircase.

"I was afraid of riding in an elevator unless someone was with me; I was afraid the door would crush me. Actually it's always been like that: If I'm with somebody, my husband or a friend, I give them the responsibility of taking care of me and protecting me.

"My therapist showed me how to hold the door of the elevator open so that it wouldn't close. I became better as long as I could hold the door open. I felt it couldn't crush me and I would be okay. If for some reason I can't control the door and keep it open until I step in safely, I start to panic and scream; I can't help it. I am also afraid of riding the subway or a train for the same reason: I am afraid of the door closing on me and crushing me.

"I was always afraid of becoming lost. When I began college, I generally got lost. Inadvertently, I would take the wrong buses and would have to ask people for directions; it was a nightmare. That's one of the reasons I dropped out of school. I was phobic, particularly about Manhattan: I was and still am afraid of getting lost there.

"Early in our marriage my husband tried to teach me how to drive and I just couldn't learn. Whenever I was in a car, I believed the other cars would crash headlong into us. I wasn't able to judge how far away the cars were; it's slightly better now, but I do close my eyes and fall asleep. Perhaps it's a way of escaping.

"I was also terrified of bridges and looking down. I was afraid of cable cars, too. I wouldn't look down; I didn't want to know that I was that high up and that I might fall off.

"As a child, it was difficult for me in other ways, too. I was terrified of my father. He was a very bright man, although not educated. He valued education and brightness. My sister was very, very bright: Her IQ was around genius level, and she didn't have the problems that I had. My father kept telling me that she was smart but that I was kind of dopey. So his whole life was really invested in my sister's being bright, and he kind of gave up on me.

"From the beginning I was a disappointment to him; he had wanted a boy—he made that very clear. He would send me to get things for him, but I never seemed to get what he wanted. Particularly, I dreaded his sending me to his car to get his business books. He would go into great detail describing which books he wanted and their location in the trunk of his car, but

I had no idea what he was saying. I couldn't open the trunk, or I would mix the keys up. I would stand there in the street, sweating, because I was so afraid of him. He had a violent temper. If by chance I got the trunk opened, I couldn't tell which side was right and which was left. It was horrible.

"My father insisted I take piano lessons, and he would make me practice in front of him every night. I faked it. I read the music for the right hand pretty well, but not the music for the left hand. It was a disaster. The last piano teacher I had told him he was wasting his money. I knew I was a big disappointment to him.

"I've always had a problem with time. I'm always late because I'm very slow, partly because I drop things constantly. I never seem to allow enough time; my judgment is off. If I have company, I invite them at a certain time, but I'm never ready. I don't mean to be late. I just have no conception of time: I don't know if it's months or years since a particular event; I can't remember. I just have very little time sense.

"The same thing with being clumsy. I've always been klutzy and people have always laughed at me. I learned to make fun of myself. That way I developed a good sense of humor and had lots of friends.

"Due to all my fears, I became very overprotective of my daughter. I wouldn't allow her to ride a bicycle or roller skate because I was afraid she would hurt herself. It was hard for both of us. As a result, I saw a psychiatric social worker about this problem. Later, I began to see the psychiatrist in behavior modification therapy. After years of my being in therapy, he began to think I might have a learning disability. He had been teaching me to cross the streets, and he came to realize that I had no idea from which direction cars were coming—they could have come from the sky as far as I was concerned.

"Then I heard you speak on TV, Dr. Levinson. I thought, Oh, my god, he really knows. I read your book and knew I had to see you."

Susan left my offices with a definite diagnosis of dyslexia and a program of treatment to follow. After years of thinking of herself as klutzy and not too smart and having to battle her different phobias daily, Susan now feels tremendous relief, knowing that she has a physical problem with a prescribed treatment. She is not crazy or stupid.

Rita Drown

Rita, age twenty-six, suddenly experienced weird sensations while visiting a museum and looking at the paintings on exhibit. The ground beneath her suddenly seemed to shift, and the strange feeling intensified while walking, making her feel uneasy and unsteady—off balance. Moving her head downward or sideways triggered feelings of disorientation and intensified her imbalance and dizziness. Complete concentration was needed to prevent swaying, falling, or tripping. Needless to say, she became frightened and upset about these symptoms.

Rita visited one of the most prominent neurologists. His examination revealed "absent signs of disease of the nervous system—no signs of vestibular or proprioceptive dysfunction."*

---

*Despite these alleged or reported "absent" neurological findings, when I examined Rita, she showed definite evidence of cerebellar-vestibular (inner-ear) dysfunction. Also, as will be noted, her symptom indicating that the ground beneath her feet felt "soft" and "mushy" was indicative of an inner-ear–determined proprioceptive impairment. It represented an external displacement of inadequate proprioceptive (joint, muscle, and tendon) sensations within her to the floor beneath her feet.

Although Rita denied feelings of anxiety and tension or personal marital or emotional conflict, the doctor nevertheless diagnosed her as suffering from "neurotic trends."

New symptoms continued to develop. In her mind, objects appeared to turn or spin, whereas external situations remained stationary or merely tilted or angled. Feelings of nausea occurred and began to intensify. Dizziness and light-headedness resulted while walking significant distances. The ground beneath her felt "soft" and "mushy," as though she were walking on a mattress. She suddenly began to fear walking across wide-open spaces (agoraphobia).

As a result of increased symptoms, Rita consulted a noted and well-respected ear, nose, and throat specialist. After a complete physical examination, including an ENG, the specialist concluded that Rita's symptoms were probably of an emotional nature, due to anxiety and tension states.

Rita's symptoms tended to oscillate with time, remitting and intensifying unexplainably. New symptoms developed. Her vision periodically became blurry. She began to fear choking when she ate. Her agoraphobia intensified. She consulted another gifted neurologist. In his report, he stated she was suffering from a subtle disturbance of the integration of eye movements, body balancing, and the stabilization of the visual fields. He said this was presumably due to a disturbance of the brain stem—visual cortex circuits. He found there was no history of a disease process . . . no multiple sclerosis. He further reported that Rita had gone through a period of great difficulty with reading. However, he noted, a recent alteration in her glasses seemed to improve that problem. Although this doctor correctly determined the site and physiology of Rita's disturbance, the relationship of these symptoms to her preexisting but hidden dyslexic disorder was not recognized.

Rita's symptoms persisted. She could not accept or understand the contradictory explanations given her. There was no meaningful help. Psychiatric treatment was frequently recommended. She continued to seek help from an endless series of psychiatric and nonpsychiatric physicians.

Following examination, a prominent group of specialists at a famous clinic concluded that Rita's disorder was emotionally based. She was advised to vacation and rest. Upon returning from a rest vacation in Florida, her symptoms suddenly returned in full force. She stopped eating because she was afraid that she would choke while swallowing her food. She lost fifteen pounds. She became increasingly fearful of venturing from home unless accompanied by a trusted companion.

Having read of my research with academic and phobic disturbances, Rita sought my help. Questioning revealed a series of additional symptoms: She had difficulty concentrating and remembering the sequence of the words she wished to say, as if her brain were slowing down. Objects were seen as tilted, and people moving were noted to bob up and down and vibrate from side to side unless she restricted her eye movements. She could not maintain eye contact while talking to someone without becoming severely dizzy. If she looked to the side, it was easier for her to understand what was said, and at the same time this prevented blurred and oscillating vision.

In addition, she spontaneously revealed having had severe math and directional difficulties when younger.

Neurological and physiological eye tracking and ENG testing clearly revealed evidence of an obvious and severe inner-ear dysfunction, supporting the second neurologist's findings.

Unfortunately, Rita's confusing and frustrating experience with clinicians and their resulting diagnostic conflicts is typical. Physicians frequently overlook or deny obvious inner-ear signs and symptoms and are all too ready to diagnose misunderstood but typical inner-ear symptoms as "neurotic."

Beware! Pay heed to three basic facts of medical-psychiatric life:

- The absence of medical findings by no means warrants the conclusion and conviction that these undetected findings are not there!
- The absence of medical findings does not justify the conviction that the patient's symptoms are neurotic.
- The diagnosis of neurosis by physicians is merely an *assumption* unless one can clearly demonstrate and prove a psychologically determined cause-and-effect relationship between hidden, unconscious conflicts and resulting symptoms. Moreover, the assumed neurotic cause must be able to explain completely the shape and form of the symptoms as well as their onset, remission, and variations.

No doubt some readers are wondering: Did Rita favorably respond to medical treatment? The answer is no: She did not benefit from two trials of prescribed antihistamines and gave up. However, the understanding provided by my diagnosis and explanations facilitated her gaining a measure of control that she did not have before. She could compensate better and avoid provoking physiological and even psychological triggers.

Rita might have benefited from an exploratory trial of psychotherapy. This trial would have aimed at uncovering possible hidden conflicts and relieving them, thus minimizing or eliminating the emotional triggering of her inner-ear dysfunction. However, she was not interested in this exploratory procedure.

Summary

A wide-ranging series of phobias has been presented so that the reader may experience and "see" the clinical content needed to comprehend fully the complex but fascinating relationship between phobias and the inner ear.

There have been many chapters and books written on phobias. Most often the reader is *told,* rather than shown, the cause-and-effect relationships determining phobic symptoms. My phobic theories are derived entirely from the insights provided by my many patients. I thought it only fair to share these patients and their insights with you.

Although all inner-ear–related phobias share an underlying common denominator, each case has its own characteristics and thus requires a correspondingly unique understanding if appropriate diagnosis and treatment are to be effective. In many ways the clinical variations seen among phobics mirror those seen among dyslexics.

These variations were found to be caused by a complex equilibrium consisting of dysfunctioning versus compensatory forces utilizing very specific combinations of physiological circuits. Thus, children with poor reading ability may become compulsive readers, and children and adults fearful of heights may eventually become skydivers. Just as dyslexic symptoms may be intensified or reinforced by the development of emotional scarring, the same is true for inner-ear–determined phobic symptoms. Thus, any attempt to treat these "mixed" physiological-emotional disorders only with medicines, or only with psychoanalysis, or only with conditioning, is simplistic.

One needs a *holistic* diagnostic-therapeutic approach to phobias that is identical to that needed for dyslexics. I truly hope that the theoretical and clinical insights provided in chapters XI and XII will catalyze a new beginning in understanding and treating phobias and related "emotional" disorders physiologically *and* psychologically—that is to say, holistically.

Predictably, the new insights derived from my study of phobias and the inner ear have added incredibly exciting dimensions to my earlier concepts of both dyslexia and phobias:

- The symptomatic horizons of dyslexia have been dramatically expanded, encompassing a wide range of phobias and related emotional symptoms never before conceived of as part of the dyslexic syndrome.
- The physiological basis for phobias and related mental disorders—Freud's ingeniously conceived "somatic compliance"—suddenly materialized into scientific consciousness.
- For the very first time, the physical basis of the above-described "mental disorders" could be seen, explored, diagnosed, and understood.
- For the very first time, devastating phobic disorders could be holistically conceptualized and treated utilizing a combined medical-psychological approach.
- For the very first time, patients could be told the real physical meaning and significance underlying and determining their phobic and related mental symptoms,

thereby minimizing their self-accusations and feelings of hopelessness, stupidity, and ugliness.

- For the very first time, psychiatry, psychology, and psychoanalysis were united with their physically determined neurological origins.

Perhaps you would like to pause here for a moment and reflect. There is certainly a wealth of exciting new content to be properly assimilated and digested. The insights and clinical content thus far presented represent a new scientific beginning. Feel your way around. And for those who desire further insight into this topic, read my book *Phobia Free* (1986).

I hope that the remaining chapters will spark and catalyze your curiosity, for I will now present a series of success stories, each highlighting new and undreamed-of accomplishments by people with the complex disorder often called *dyslexia*. No doubt you will now fully understand the naïveté in defining this multidimensional syndrome as if it were merely a severe reading disorder.

XIII

Successful Despite Dyslexia

The names of such famous dyslexics as Edison, Einstein, Nelson A. Rockefeller, George S. Patton, and Charles Schwab have been frequently mentioned in books and magazines, as well as on television and radio. However, little is really known about their inner feelings and dyslexic symptoms.

In this chapter I will portray the lives of successful dyslexics and their dyslexic family members, as well as describe their responses to treatment. I have examined dyslexic physicians, scientists, writers, artists, teachers, engineers, architects, and businesspeople. All had become successful despite their dyslexic disorder.

With proper determination, intelligence, and guidance, many dyslexics have succeeded long before I ever treated them. In fact, many dyslexics would never have succeeded were it not for their need to prove to others—and themselves—that they were not stupid, worthless, and incompetent. In other words, their dyslexia served as a motivation to succeed.

It is anticipated that the following case histories and favorable responses to treatment will bring new hope to, and trigger a realistic optimism in, all dyslexics and all parents, teachers, and clinicians trying to guide dyslexics to success and even fame.

One Family—Three Generations

Dr. Walker

Age: Eighty years
Problems: Stuttering, balance/coordination

Mrs. Linda Thompson

Age: Thirty-one years
Problems: Word insertions, focusing difficulties, apprehension/phobias

Stacy Thompson

Age: Thirteen years
Problems: School-related

It is not often that one has the opportunity to examine and treat three generations of the same family. However, this did occur when Mrs. Thompson and her daughter, Stacy, visited my offices. Shortly afterward Dr. Walker, Mrs. Thompson's father, also came to my Medical Dyslexic Treatment Center.

Mrs. Thompson is a successful businesswoman. Her father was a successful dentist when examined at eighty years of age.

When I questioned Mrs. Thompson about her symptoms, she responded that from the time she was a child, she had always felt different from others, but she never understood the nature of her differences. However, when her daughter, Stacy, exhibited similar difficulties, Mrs. Thompson was very concerned and anxious to help her: "I was viewing TV and saw you, Dr. Levinson. To my amazement you were describing the precise symptoms that I had lived with all my life—symptoms and feelings that I had never confided to a living soul. These symptoms were:

- *Word insertions:* adding words that have nothing to do with what I was stating or writing. The questioning glances of others when these incidents occurred made me embarrassed. What was worse, I didn't know why I said what I did. Therefore, when I was around others or in a group of strangers, I was very quiet. If I were to speak to someone face-to-face, I felt extremely uncomfortable and unconsciously held myself rigidly.
- *Apprehension:* associated with heights, bridges, and escalators. Despite a love of skiing, I have felt anxious and apprehensive whenever I looked down a slope or mountain.
- *Angulation and drifting of words/letters off a page:* when writing, even though the page was lined
- *Difficulty in writing down an idea or a thought:* By the time I would get started, the idea would be gone. It was infuriating!
- *Focusing problem:* When driving, particularly at night or when I was tired, I found that I would turn my head to one side in order to see properly.

"I seemed to have all the symptoms you described. . . . I quickly called my husband into the room to listen to your discussion. I was shocked to learn that these symptoms were part of the disorder known as dyslexia. I had never even heard of it before, let alone known I had it. I realized that my daughter, Stacy, so like me, probably had the same disorder.

"Stacy was experiencing failures and problems in school. Although a bright, outgoing child, she thought of herself as stupid because she had academic difficulties associated with reading, writing, math, etc. Not even her friendliness, athletic agility, and eager-to-please mannerisms softened the blow of being different from her friends. Her need to study longer in order to learn, only to forget quickly what she had learned, her poor performance on tests—all reinforced her feelings of inadequacy and stupidity.

"Stacy and I sometimes spoke for hours about her problems and feelings. To help ease her pain, I revealed the difficulties that I had experienced in school and when I took tests. I told her that I had wanted so badly to be liked by my peers that I would often do favors, even the laundry, for my friends when I attended college.

"However, once I put aside my books and no longer needed to take tests, everything became easier. My innate abilities and strong desire to succeed took over, and I forged ahead. 'Your father and I have built a successful oceanography business. I succeeded because of, or in spite of, my difficulties. This will happen to you, too, Stacy,' I said.

"I wanted so much to infuse her with self-confidence and an appreciation of the things she could do. What I told her helped—only temporarily, however. With your appearance and discussion on the show, I thought, Perhaps now I can do something of more permanent value for Stacy.

"My husband and I picked her up at camp, and excitedly I

told her about our scheduled appointments at your Medical Dyslexic Treatment Center. She listened attentively and hopefully."

Therapeutic Responses: Stacy, Mrs. Thompson, and Dr. Walker

Stacy and her mother were examined. Both were found to be dyslexic. An individualized regime of medication was prescribed for each. The Thompsons felt improvement. They urged Dr. Walker, Mrs. Thompson's father, to seek consultation, too, for the problem of stuttering, which he had had most of his life. Additionally, he had recently developed a difficulty with coordination. He came and was also diagnosed as having inner-ear–related symptoms. Treatment was prescribed.

Two years later the Thompsons came from Canada for a revisit. The thirteen-year-old young lady who sat across from me was happy and excited to tell me about all the wonderful new changes in her life.

"Before I saw you, Dr. Levinson, and was put on medication, I was either failing my courses or just about passing them," Stacy said. "Now I am getting A's and B's—it's incredible! I just can't believe it! I used to feel different, dumb, afraid no one would like me.

"I wanted so much to be liked by the girls that I would buy them things or do favors for them. I was never sure if it was me they really liked or the things I did for them. Now I'm myself, and if someone doesn't like me, I can deal with it. It's no longer as important as it once was.

"I always loved to draw. But I draw better now than ever before. I also find that I ski, race, and play tennis much, much better than I ever did. My coordination and balance are better and I feel wonderful!"

Extremely pleased with Stacy's progress, I turned my attention to Mrs. Thompson. She, too, looked happier and less tense and anxious than during our last visit.

"My difficulties with expressing myself—those word insertions—are a thing of the past," Mrs. Thompson stated. "Also, I feel more comfortable conversing with others; I'm still not the chattiest person at a gathering, but I'm no longer the most quiet either. I even communicate more with my husband. I've said more to him these past two years than I did in all the years we have been married up until then. He's amazed at the change.

"I always used a Dictaphone in business because I wanted to be sure all my ideas and thoughts were recorded. I also preferred using the telephone so that I would not have to speak face to face with a customer. However, I am now able to converse face to face without discomfort. Also, I can synchronize my thoughts and my writing: No longer must I use the Dictaphone to be sure I don't lose an idea.

"Driving is also much easier. I can focus better, and no longer do I turn my head sideways to see better.

"Skiing, a sport the entire family enjoys, is a lot more fun these days, too. I do not feel apprehensive when I am at the top of a slope or mountain. I just take off without a twinge of anxiety!

"Last year, my husband and I went to Scotland. Although we had been there before, I marveled at the countryside. The flowers and foliage were gorgeous; the purples, whites, and blues were breathtaking. I did not remember them as having the sharpness, vividness, and clarity that I saw now. Even my husband was surprised by my reactions. I felt as though scales had been removed from my eyes.

"The anxiety that I previously experienced whenever I was

on a bridge or escalator or in any situation where heights are involved is no longer present. All in all, we have come a long way, Stacy and I.

"My father, too, has experienced good results. Can you believe it? At age eighty-two he no longer stutters—after a lifetime of stuttering!

"His balance is also much improved. He no longer trips or stumbles at the least provocation. Every day he walks one to two miles—without his cane.

"Recently, he had a cataract operation. As a result of the operation and the medication, his vision is 20/20. He says that he can see more clearly and better than he ever did in his whole life. He says, 'Too bad that I have this old chassis. I feel so good inside!'

"This past year I visited my parents at their home in Indiana. It was the first time that I had seen my father since he started taking medication for his dyslexic symptoms. We spent a wonderful afternoon together, conversing in a manner that we had never before enjoyed. Previously, if we talked, it was only for a few moments: He would be off to do one thing or another. I learned little things about my dad that afternoon that I never knew. He never used to sit long enough for us to share much of ourselves. What a shame, but I shall always be grateful for those precious moments we spent together that day."

Both Dr. Walker and Mrs. Thompson are examples of adults who have achieved success despite having dyslexia.

Dr. Walker ran away from home at the tender age of thirteen at the time of his mother's death. He worked at odd jobs to support himself. When he was twenty years old he married a registered nurse. No doubt her influence and his desire to make something of himself motivated him to return to school. He worked and attended high school, college, and then dental school. Despite the Depression, a family to support, and his dyslexia, he succeeded in becoming a successful dentist. His wife was always very supportive and helped him in every way.

Dr. Walker was a very successful man, truly young in heart and spirit. He did free orthodontic work for those children whose parents were unable to afford these services. And he derived tremendous gratification from helping youngsters in need.

Susan Stafford

Age: Twenty-four years
Problems: Reading, spelling, coordination, and concentration

"The large number of children who experience school phobias and academic difficulties motivated me to enter the field of special education. Everything I read in the field convinced me the experts were missing something crucial. Accepted theories about learning disabilities and dyslexia did not sufficiently explain the scope and complexity of the disorder.

"I could not subscribe to the view that the cerebral cortex was the site of the problem. These theories did not make any sense to me. . . .

"The reason I felt so strongly about this is that I am dyslexic. Although I have reading and spelling problems, I score high on differential aptitude tests for abstract and mechanical reasoning. Obviously, someone with brain damage could not have a high score in abstract reasoning and math.

"Since I felt the data on learning disabilities was insufficient and certainly not helping dyslexic children to deal with school-

related and other problems, I decided to enter the field of research in special education and put my firsthand experience
and learning to good use."

These are the sentiments of vivacious, bright Sue Stafford, a
graduate student in special education. My first impulse was to
compliment her for her honest, open, and straightforward
thinking. Young learning-disability teachers with firsthand
dyslexic experience, armed with the latest scientific knowledge,
could significantly make a difference where it counts—in the
classroom. The driving force behind my years of research has
been to help dyslexic children medically and to promote understanding and proper guidance among teachers, parents, and
clinicians. Between medical treatment and an emotionally supportive environment in the classroom, children can be spared
the humiliating and debilitating effects of dyslexia.

Concerned and knowledgeable teachers and educators are
vitally needed. Medication is only half the solution; the other
half is the implementation of psychoeducational techniques to
minimize, compensate for, or totally eradicate many of the
symptoms of dyslexia. This should be our first priority, and it
certainly was Sue's.

I needed to find out what Sue's problems were. So I proceeded to question her about her first awareness of her difficulties.

Sue continued:

"I was in the first grade when I experienced that dreaded
disease 'school phobia.' I was unable to master the skills or the
phonetics required to read. It wasn't until the sixth grade that
I finally learned to read—to satisfy school requirements, not
for pleasure!

"I recall I was always a poor speller and would become upset and embarrassed if I had to spell aloud. The other activity I absolutely disliked was gym because I was so uncoordinated. I remember falling off the balance beam once and feeling so humiliated. I was always the last one selected as a partner in my gym classes. Actually, whenever I played any sports or tried to perform in gym, I became physically ill and dizzy.

"I also had what I thought was an unusual auditory impairment as a young child, which compounded my many other problems." (She had difficulty processing what she heard—resulting in delayed and even scrambled understanding.)

Sue was frequently upset as a child and did not understand why she felt angry. To justify her feelings, she would pick fights with her brother. Eventually, Sue realized that her frustration was due to her reading difficulty. And her frustration intensified when she had more and more material to read.

"I could never understand why the school could not label my problem and help me.

"Fortunately, my difficulties did not interfere with me socially. I wanted very much to be a part of the group and pushed myself to participate and become involved with my friends, to convince myself and them that I wasn't different. As a result, I did not have the peer problems I sometimes encounter in my students.

"Another important factor is the support I always received from my parents. They were satisfied, and so was I, with my grades even though I was a C student."

Sue continued to find certain academic courses, such as literature and history, difficult because of the quantity of material to be read. She said she relied mainly on lectures because she was never able to complete all the readings for each college course. She even failed an art history course because the quantity of material was overwhelming. She experienced blurring of letters and words and focusing difficulties when she read, which resulted in headaches and eye fatigue.

"Sometimes, I felt as though I were in a fog, especially in the mornings. I would find myself shaking my head, as though to clear it. The problem of concentration and being 'out of it' was more pronounced if I had a respiratory infection or an allergy attack.

"Two summers ago my reading problem was very severe. I consulted an optometrist, who prescribed glasses for my problem (poor focusing) and vision therapy. The glasses did not help much; in fact, they made me feel dizzy. But the exercises did help. Unfortunately, they did not get at the heart of the problem, and I found when I was tired that the exercises did not help at all.

"My last year in college was easier because I had learned to organize my work better. I was also taking more education courses, which I found very interesting. When I read *A Solution to the Riddle Dyslexia,* I thought, This really makes sense! I knew I had to see Dr. Levinson."

Testing and consultation disclosed what Sue already knew: that she had dyslexia. She was given an appropriate program of treatment, and I asked her to record any reactions she noted and send them to me. Sue called and excitedly relayed her results.

"After only two days on medication, I was fairly sure my reading and balance were better; however, I wasn't 100 percent sure. Within six days I was positive! Not only was my head clearer, but also letters and words were more distinct. I was reading faster with good comprehension and no fatigue and frustration.

"My balance was better. I could close my eyes and stand on one foot. I could never do that before!

"I am so excited about my reactions that I have changed the subject of my thesis; it will now deal with new theories of learning disabilities, and your hypothesis on dyslexia will head the list."

Several months later, I received a letter from Sue, in which she stated: "Everything is going well. My greatly increased ability to concentrate, read, and comprehend are still with me. I finished all the required reading for all my courses this past semester—for the first time! I was even able to begin outside readings for my thesis, and I am elated. . . . For the first time I find all the reading I am doing very exciting and pleasurable.

"I no longer have a focusing problem: The vision training has become beneficial, along with the medication. During my last vision training session, to my great surprise, I was able to walk the balance beam backward! The month before I saw you, I worked on balance activities quite a lot and never got very far with them. As I told you, I never could get very far with them as a child, either.

"I was discussing with a friend, also in special education, my newfound ability to stand on one foot. I told him that now I feel that I have one focal point of gravity, at my heel, as opposed to many. In other words, previously I had the feeling that I was being pulled from all directions. He replied, 'What you are saying is that you feel your vertical axis in relationship to your body, something we are aware that children with learning problems lack.' I found this most interesting and thought you would, too.

"I have also noticed that emotionally I feel as though I am freer. I am not constantly on guard for fear that I may reveal my disabilities. I also feel more focused. My thoughts and actions are not as scattered as they once were. It is somewhat analogous to the sensation I feel with my balance, as previously mentioned—of having one focal point when I stand on one foot. [A relationship between physical balance and focus and mental balance and focus was confirmed by the brilliant research of Leiner, Leiner, and Dow (1991), indicating that the cerebellum contributes to the learning not only of motor skills, but also of some cognitive, language, and emotional skills.]

"My spelling, grammar, and sentence structure are also greatly improved. My mother, who has always proofread my school papers, tells me I now make very few errors in those areas. She was particularly excited after reading some pages of my thesis.

"My report would not be complete without the inclusion of my responses to an interruption of medication. Within one day after I stop taking the medication, I feel a big difference:

- The first night I have dreams of falling and of not being able to stay balanced.
- The next morning I feel 'out of it' and tend to keep feeling that way until I resume the medication three days later.
- There is no desire to read, and when I try, I have trouble tracking, even when reading just a few lines. My eyes feel as though they are pulling at each other and causing me to see double.
- I feel more unsteady.
- My old habit of head shaking to clear the fog is back.

"When I resume my medication, the positive results return: I feel great again; reading becomes easier and letters darker and sharper."

Sue's responses are to be expected. I tell my patients that eventually the positive improvements will be sustained, even when off medication.* The precise time this occurs is different for each individual, but generally it is between one and four years.

Sue concluded her remarks: "I am tremendously excited, not only about my improvements via your treatment, but also about the wonderful possibilities for help that now exist for the millions of children and adults afflicted with dyslexia and related learning disabilities."

Just prior to the first publication of this book, I received the following letter from Susan, in which she enthusiastically describes her most recent improvements and how they are changing her life. I can think of no better way to summarize the phenomenon of success among dyslexics:

"I am writing this letter by hand to illustrate to you the changes in my handwriting that have taken place in the last few months. There is a smoothness, evenness, and fluidity that I never had before; it is as though the writing literally flows out of my hand, although I am still holding the paper at a ninety-degree angle to my body, and am therefore writing away from myself.

---

*After the first eight weeks on medication, patients were initially advised to stop medication on weekends and holidays to minimize development of an immunity to the drug. With increasing insight, this procedure was changed. A more detailed explanation is found in the section dealing with treatment.

"This is my last year at Bank Street School; I will be graduating in June. My last two classes are very demanding, but I am most proud to say that I am *ahead* in all the readings. As I have written before, I used to do as little reading as possible. I can't begin to describe the enjoyment I am now experiencing by participating in the class discussions of these readings.

"After a long day of teaching and as a student, I don't feel tired or overloaded. Even though my schedule is as busy as, if not busier than, it was, I seem to require less sleep—six to eight hours of sleep as opposed to the ten to twelve hours I used to need. I have also noticed a change in my dream patterns and content. Previously my dreams were hectic, debilitating, and at times bizarre and fragmented. Now they are peaceful and relaxed. I think this has a lot to do with my requirement for less sleep.

"I have also noticed an interesting change with regard to my spelling. I still forget and confuse the spelling of words that were learned prior to taking my medication, but new words I have read in the literature, particularly in the last two months, I am able to correctly picture in my mind. When I became aware of this interesting phenomenon, I thought it was a fascinating concept, dealing with developmental sequences in cognitive thinking.*

"I have been applying to colleges and universities for possible acceptance into a Ph.D. program in educational psychology/special education research! I never before enter-

---

*Successfully treated dyslexic professionals and those who spontaneously improved on their own often experience no problems with spelling newly learned words, regardless of complexity. Yet they frequently retain their prior difficulties in spelling simpler words. In retrospect, it appears that they have a problem forgetting or erasing improperly learned spelling word patterns—however simple they may be.

tained the possibility of such a venture, but now I realize that it is a possibility for me—and I am on an all-time high contemplating it.

"My excitement and enthusiasm for your theory of dyslexia has motivated me to discuss it with many people from the local school systems in my area. In fact, I will be presenting information during a few staff meetings in several districts. I have found that I receive very little criticism because I present myself as a case in point of the success of your medication treatment. I will also be discussing your theory of the inner-ear or cerebellar-vestibular system at Bank Street College during a presentation on the use of medications in special education, along with the role of the teacher.

"Additionally, I have noticed that I have developed an ability to calculate large numbers in my mind. I have always been a good math student, but I did need to work out the solution to problems on paper because I had trouble retaining the numbers and processes in my mind. However, while teaching a computer course, I became aware that I was able to calculate the solutions to problems in my mind.

"There have been so many changes in the last six months that I am truly amazed. I never considered myself impulsive, but I realize now that I was. I would be upset if I did not make quick decisions about everything, from buying a dress to deciding whether or not to take a job. I would jump into a situation or volunteer my time to a project, and then find that I did not have time in my schedule to fulfill my promise. Recently, though, I have discovered that I actually enjoy thinking about arriving at a decision—I realize that I don't have to make a split-second decision. I also don't feel overwhelmed when I do decide on a course of action. Finally, I feel good about my decision and don't perseverate . . . about an impulsive choice.

"Along with this loss of impulsive behavior has come the feeling of calmness, of being able to sit back and absorb what is going on without being the one always talking and monopolizing the conversation to prove that I know something. In fact, I don't think I talk as fast as I used to because I am not afraid any longer that I will forget what it is that I wish to say.

"One day, for no apparent reason, it occurred to me that I read better lying on my stomach. I mentioned this one day in class, and several people have since told me that they have had some of their students try this position with interesting success. Children who display dyslexialike symptoms tend to find this position very comfortable when reading. It seems logical that lying on one's stomach may have a harmonizing effect on the inner-ear system; it probably has something to do with the law of gravity.

"My balance and posture have improved so much that I can hardly believe it! I had always had the tendency to slouch, but I now feel as if I internally stand straight. I no longer get backaches between my shoulder blades. Also, I can walk in high-heel shoes without falling forward and looking like a klutz!

"Every day I notice something else that has changed for the better in my behavior, personality, or perception about the world. All these changes together have contributed to the wonderful feeling that I have about myself, especially these last months.

"Once again, I deeply thank you for everything."

Susan Stafford gives ample proof that one can be successful despite being dyslexic. If anything, her dyslexia has been a strong motivation in determining her goals and aspirations.

Sue had succeeded in college prior to treatment. As a result of treatment, she was completing her master's degree with greater energy, enthusiasm, and ease than she ever thought possible. Moreover, she was looking forward to her Ph.D., a degree she never before dreamed of attaining.

I hope that millions of dyslexics will benefit from Sue's current and future insights, and that all dyslexics will eventually respond successfully to medical treatment as did Sue.

Gary England

Gary England became my patient after his charming daughter, Molly, responded favorably to my recommended treatment. Gary's wife's introduction, and Gary's own description of his symptoms and responses to medication, cannot be improved upon. Here is their original content, only very slightly edited:

> After reading Gary's letter and report to you, I felt I should add some additional information. He is very modest about his accomplishments, which have been many, including "Outstanding Young Man in America." He has written two books on weather, is considered the number-one weather authority in Oklahoma, and has a higher recognition factor than the governor of Oklahoma. (Each of his books sold over 40,000 copies. . . .)
>
> In regard to the medication he is taking, the results are amazing. He also assures me that he feels better than he has in years and is so thankful to you for your research in this area. . . .

> Thanks,
> (signed)
> Mary England

Gary's report follows:

"I have no recollection of specific problems in my elementary school years except that I never did well, mainly receiving C's and D's.

"During my mid-school years it was about the same. School was very difficult for me. I can recall quite vividly the frustrations of trying to do well in high school, but the results were generally still in the C and D range. I kept making the same grades as the kids who were thought to be dumb. I gave up trying to read books for book reports and reverted to using Classic Comic Books because my reading was very slow and I always had to reread each sentence to make sense. The authors' logic and word sequences always seemed jumbled to me.

"I also recall during that period a teacher saying in class that he would rather have someone who was of average intelligence who tried rather than 'Gary England, who is smart and will not try.' I believe it is very possible that my inability to make accomplishments in school is in some degree the reason that my mother said, 'Well, Gary *was* the most active of my boys. I became rather 'wild and wooly,' as they say in western Oklahoma.

"Shortly after high school I joined the Navy. I remember that when I took a sonar test, the instructor told me I could not tell the difference between a whale and a battleship. I tried very hard to do well on the test, but it was impossible for me to determine the difference in the sonar returns from the various targets. It was overwhelmingly confusing and frustrating. Everyone around me at least scored something, but my score was a flat zero.

"My college years were a time of high hopes. However, it was a major struggle. I couldn't read well. The sentences didn't make sense. I probably studied more than most people. I seemed to have it down and then would panic during the tests and get through only the first few problems or questions. I flunked algebra and made B's in higher math. I took an oral Spanish class, never understood a word, and made an F. However, I made an A in atmospheric geophysics. In the higher-level math and science courses, it seemed I could more clearly visualize what an equation or theory was all about.

"In the lower-level courses, I could never remember all the little details. During tests in those areas, it was like there was not just a short circuit in my brain, but a total blackout.

"At one point I was taking an art-appreciation class and we were used in a research project in rote-memory learning. There was this little cylindrical tube that rotated and it had fifteen short words on it. You could only see one word at a time. As I recall, we were tested to see how long it took each student to remember all fifteen words in sequence. There were three hundred students in that class. I was the last to finish. In fact, I never really finished, as I couldn't memorize the fifteen words after two hours. Talk about frustration and feeling dumb . . . that was a low point. I finally received a Bachelor of Science degree in mathematics and meteorology in 1965.

"During the years since 1965, my wife and I have accomplished a great deal and have become what is considered quite successful. All this time I went through life feeling frustrated and fearing I was a little on the dumb side but still managing to put myself in the top one-percent income bracket in the United States. I was not aware I had a problem other than a lack of brains.

"When someone told me a joke, I nearly always didn't understand it at the time. Later, I guess after my subconscious put the words in the proper sequence, it would pop into my conscious mind and I then would understand it.* In fact, I was never very good in initial face-to-face business discussions. Much of what people said to me or plans that were laid out just did not register. The logic wasn't mine and the sequence didn't fit my sequence. However, after thinking by myself, I could sort it out until it meant something to me. Only then could I act on it and discuss it.

"I can recall, many times in recent years, reading a newspaper and discovering that a certain sentence made absolutely no sense. Some of the words were missing. I would call my wife in and, in a state of total frustration, point out to her the crazy sentence. Then, when explaining it or reading it to her, I would see all the words. This word-missing situation happened frequently when television advertisements appeared on the screen in printed form. I watched one TV station ID for several weeks before I saw the missing words. Sometimes I found that the words were there but were in the wrong place in the sequence. Brother, that is startling! I know my left and right directions. However, when driving I become lost more often than not unless I know the area exactly. Turns off of highways bring panic, and the result is that I normally take the wrong turn. To make the proper turns I have to visualize very intently the entire sequence of where I'm coming from and where I must go and integrate that with the road signs in order that the

---

*Remarks such as these indicate that dyslexics frequently evidence delayed auditory processing and discrimination. Similar time lags were noted during their reading, writing, and speech mechanisms, until it became clear that this lag was a general inner-ear–related phenomenon in dyslexia. Because dyslexics frequently report scrambling of words read and heard, it appeared reasonable to assume that their time lags reflected attempts at compensating for their signal-scrambling dysfunction.

proper decision can be made. But at 55 mph, it seems there is never enough time.

"In 1975 my daughter Molly was tested and found to have symptoms of dyslexia. During a conversation with the doctor, I told him of my experiences. When I walked out of his office that day, it was like a great cloud had been lifted. I wasn't dumb, but had some of the same problems as Molly. Our conversation allowed me to realize and identify my various problem situations more rapidly. It helped a great deal to know what was going on, but it was still very frustrating to read poorly, miss words, scramble sequences, not understand what people were saying to me. I still had a poor memory, became lost while driving, and all of those other things.

"Every day I was becoming more aware of when I was having a malfunction, so to speak. When Molly came back from the visit to your office, I was almost desperate for help.

"When you prescribed medication, I waited for instant improvement. It wasn't instant, but it began. I can really read for the first time in my life, and I have read several books. My memory—I'm telling you, it's exciting to have one now! In the past, if I attempted to remember a name from years ago or sometimes from the day before, I drew a blank. Now names pop into my mind from ten years ago.

"My memory seems to be improving daily. When I read the newspaper, the editorials make sense. When I watch television and the printed words come up, they are normally all there. I don't become lost as often while driving. Now I can sit in a business meeting, understand what is going on, and enter into active discussion. (However, my wife still says I don't hear a word she says!)

"My improvement has been significant and I really feel

good about it. There are times when I still experience various dysfunctions and I find myself lost, sentences seem to be messed up, I am unable to recall the name of a good friend, [etc.]. It is good to report, though, that such situations seem to be fewer and fewer as time goes by."

Gary became Chief Meteorologist for Oklahoma City's KWTV—a public figure who indeed is very successful despite dyslexia.

Sula Kaufman, Ph.D.

Dr. Sula Kaufman, formerly a pianist and music instructor at the Juilliard School, contacted me when she was sixty years of age and very young, working as a researcher and writer. She had suffered from dyslexia throughout her life. Upon examining her, I was impressed with her intelligence, perceptiveness, and charm. I asked her to record her symptoms and medication responses. Since there was no way that I could improve upon Dr. Kaufman's sincerely expressed report, I decided to present her statement just as she wrote it, with only slight modification.

"Hiding from prying eyes was the one skill I practiced to perfection during my growing years. . . . With time, it became second nature to pretend that all my difficulties were nonexistent. Perhaps it was a skill I acquired to survive, for as a child I had to cope with a condition I could not comprehend. This pretense helped me to erect a fairly positive self-image, although there is little doubt in my mind that the dysfunction must have had a dominant role in shaping my character, and was unquestionably a factor in shaping my life. . . . My childhood was filled with apprehension and terror. I knew that in certain situations I could undergo a complete change in behavior, a total metamorphosis in the way I felt. It always happened at the most unexpected and awkward moments, and I used to dread it in advance. When caught and exposed, I would stand there shaking and trembling. I also had an overwhelming fear of water and an extreme intolerance of heights.

"Being afraid of water, of course, made me afraid of swimming. I fought hard to overcome this terror: I took swimming lessons and made myself float. At times I even managed a few swimming strokes with a kind of desperate determination to overcome my absolute terror. I never could even attempt to overcome my extreme fear of heights. It used to be the only situation in which I would become nauseous and light-headed. Then, too, I always had a persistent problem with spelling, an inability to memorize the multiplication table or a simple short poem. My handwriting is often illegible even to myself—the lines are never straight and the size as well as the spacing between the letters changes twice or even three times on one page. On the other hand, I always had a very good memory for content. Although I could not memorize the multiplication table, I could always remember dates and telephone numbers, and as a student I had a good head for mathematics and languages. The contradictions did not stop there, for while I lacked the necessary balance to ride a bicycle, I was a good and agile dancer.*

*As previously noted, in inner-ear–determined dyslexic's balance and coordination impairments are circuit-specific rather than all-or-none. Thus, it should be perfectly consistent that some coordination functions are adequate, while others are impaired, and still others might be gifted.

"My inability to memorize the multiplication table and my poor spelling seemed to me mere trifles. These were more than adequately compensated for, as I was an excellent student and an avid and voracious reader. On the one hand, there was in me always an awareness that something was radically wrong with the way I functioned; on the other hand, I knew myself to be a highly capable and competent person. I always felt totally secure in some areas, while in others I was, and still am, plagued by constant devastating doubts. . . .

"I began to feel intense and persistent light-headedness combined with severe disorientation some eight years ago, after being in a car accident. Because this barrage of discomfort started soon after the accident, I did not think at the time that a connection existed between the condition responsible for my phobias, spelling, etc., and the total mess I found myself in so suddenly. The frequent X rays that were taken failed to explain or support my description of the symptoms I had. It was indicated to me more than once that my condition was largely psychological, postmenopausal, and not atypical of hysterical and hypochondriacal women. Had it not been for the tests given to me in your office, I probably would have never made the connection and would have never guessed that the accident had aggravated an existing condition.

"The sensations artificially brought on by the tests were identical in kind and severity to the disorientation and light-headedness I lived with for the longest time after the accident. They affected my capacity to think as my mental process became enveloped as if by haze or fog; to top it off, I also became markedly aphasic, and the slightest turn of my head used to bring on severe dizziness. I fell repeatedly for no apparent reason. At night my bed became a heaving, slanting surface; the sensation of sliding down to the floor was so strong that I used to hold on to prevent it.

"During that period I was also subject to fainting spells. Driving was a problem; going in reverse was particularly impossible. But most difficult of all was the abrupt change in lifestyle from a very active one I found myself steadily gliding into a deteriorating one.

"Eventually, however, my condition did stabilize to the point that I could function selectively.

"I must hasten to tell you that only one drug you prescribed for me gave me tremendous relief; with another there was an immediate excessive weakness, including chest pains and continuous cold sweat. A third drug had neither a positive nor a negative effect on this aspect of my functioning. The effective drug also had a fantastic effect on me in other ways. Never in my life did I feel as well as I did when taking it: I had boundless energy, but what pleased me most was that it was not euphoric; rather, anything and everything I did was done effortlessly and with gusto. Most of all, I enjoyed a feeling of being enormously alive. The only negative effect it had was that I started driving much too fast and had to slow down a bit. Another thing was that all through that time, I got up in the morning feeling rested, wide awake, and ready for action. What a contrast it was with my lifelong feeling of morning fatigue. The fly in the ointment was that I started 'ballooning'—the weight gain in those few short weeks was considerable.

"Perhaps I should tell you about how well I felt for the duration of the medication therapy. Indeed, I do retain the memory of how good it feels to be functioning fully. There was a kind of quiet uninterrupted flow of energy I had always hoped to have. In my former 'normal' state of being, in order to accomplish anything, I must exercise determination, self-discipline, and willpower, and in addition I must impose upon myself an external regimen carefully monitored by a rigid schedule. In this state there is always a sensation of a real physical barrier between volition and completion of a task, whereas the effect of the medicine allowed the two parts [to flow together]."

Dr. Kaufman described her feelings further in a telephone conversation:

"I am no longer afraid to admit I lacked something, but I first needed to overcome an emotional resistance. My spelling, always poor, never really bothered me. My physical disabilities, such as lack of balance, were terrible. I could not walk a narrow path; it was not a question of fear—I simply could not walk. The whole world turned upside down for me. I felt ill and I would begin to tremble. I lost my sense of dignity.

"I never did feel stupid though. I felt different. I never encountered any one person who acted or felt the way I did, or had a selective inability to function in certain areas.

"There were numerous men who told me I was beautiful. I think I flirted and courted those compliments because it was the only way to confirm to myself that I was beautiful and not ugly. I felt as though my hands did not go with my body. It was terrible. Only when I was dancing did I feel total and beautiful.* I even used to nag my husband to tell me I was beautiful. Not that he did not say it voluntarily; it was just that I had a need, a craving, to confirm my existence.

"You cannot imagine how excessive my need was to do well

*Here again, we find clinical indications that some inner-ear–dysfunctioning patients require movement and motion to feel well, further explaining the mechanisms triggering *motion-deprived phobias.*

academically. It was more than a simple need to achieve: It was a vital necessity to counteract my disability.

"I have not played the piano lately because my disability has worsened in recent years. It used to be that on a bad day I would lose the feeling in my left hand. I could not concentrate on both hands. When you play the piano, you use both hands but you look at the middle of the keyboard; you are aware of the periphery. But I could not see the periphery—I could not even look for the periphery. I would lose my place and it shook me up terribly. I did not know what I was doing. [Inner-ear–dysfunctioning patients frequently complain of tunnel vision. This is in marked contrast, statistically, to a study by Geiger and Lettvin (1987), indicating that the peripheral vision of dyslexics is enhanced. Although some dyslexic patients have sensitized peripheral vision—they see and are distracted by more stimuli than they should be—the majority do not. Favorable responses to medications tend to correct both the typical and atypical peripheral-visual dysfunctioning in dyslexics. For more details, refer to my paper, "Abnormal Optokinetic and Perceptual Span Parameters in Cerebellar-Vestibular Dysfunction and Learning Disabilities or Dyslexia" (1989)].

"Another strange phenomenon would occur: I would be playing quite fluently, and suddenly I wouldn't be able to move my hands; the motion would be gone and my fingers would become quite stiff. I had been told I had arthritis in my hands and that that was the reason for the loss of motion and stiffness. But that was not so. It was as though my hands and my mind were two separate beings without direct communication.

"The medication you prescribed was amazing. Previously my playing would fluctuate, especially in the last few years. . . . After taking the medication the first time, I selected a complicated piece and began to play. I was astounded at how well I did. I was functioning in a fluid style. I acted automatically. I did not have to think: 'I must do this now and next I must do that, etc.' I felt my hands were truly mine, acting in unison with my wishes, doing what I wanted them to do.*

"The only functions that seem to be unaffected by the medication are my writing and spelling. When I write anything, I must check every other word with the dictionary. I can look up a word, write it, and then come across it on the next page, but again I must look it up.

"Dr. Levinson, I am sharing my experiences and feelings with you and your countless other patients so that they will not feel stupid anymore."

I referred Dr. Kaufman to an endocrinologist on the suspicion that she had a hidden hypothyroid disorder. Laboratory findings verified this suspicion, and she responded favorably to treatment.

Once again, it is crucial to note that dyslexia may coexist with other medical disorders and that the resulting symptoms may be codetermined. Thus, Dr. Kaufman's fatigue and difficulties were due to two factors requiring two different but concurrent approaches. As you may remember, my daughter Joy also was diagnosed as having dyslexia complicated by hypothyroidism.

---

*In the presence of inner-ear dysfunctioning, the reflex-coordinated and integrated motor (and even cognitive) patterns break down or *decompose* into their individual steps. Successful treatment reintegrates or *recomposes* these steps into a smooth, reflex-comprehensive whole.

"The Princess and the Pea"

Randy Martin, a dynamic female executive in her forties, was to all outward appearances extremely self-confident, bright, articulate, in total command of herself and her world. Inwardly, however, she was filled with anxieties, phobias, and doubts with regard to her physical and mental well-being.

As an infant, Randy suffered a severe ear infection with high temperatures.

As a young girl, she was a slow reader and experienced difficulty with spelling, math, memory-related activities, and grammar. Randy was seized by a fear of falling whenever she had to climb down stairs; she would remove her shoes in order to be sure she would not fall. Her health was complicated by a thyroid condition, and she was extremely sensitive physically—even to touch sensations. Her mother would jokingly refer to her as "the princess and the pea" because of this extreme physical sensitivity. Remarks like these, particularly from her mother, always stung.

Throughout her adult life, Randy had been motivated by a strong desire to excel and prove her worth and ability. She knew she had to work harder than others to achieve.

Randy was extremely active in a number of organizations in a variety of fields—business, the women's movements, and civic matters, such as pollution. She felt better about herself if she was very active and involved. Thus, her schedule was very full and demanding. No sooner had one challenge been successfully met than she sought another. She needed to be constantly busy, forever proving to herself and others that she wasn't really dumb.

Admired and respected by colleagues and friends, Randy

nevertheless could not rid herself of the feeling that she was really stupid. Even her many successes did not totally convince her. Her constant round of activities kept others from getting too close to her. She was afraid that they would find out that she had "fooled" them into thinking she was very bright and exceptionally competent.

The many physical and psychological demands placed upon Randy's time and energy produced a lifestyle that became more and more stressful and filled with a great deal of discomfort. Once she attended an international conference and, when she returned home, experienced "burnout"—anxietylike symptoms. She had sweaty palms, shortness of breath, feelings of faintness and of being off balance, difficulty swallowing, and the sensation of being "out of it." Although she had always loved the excitement and bustle of the city, she suddenly felt that she couldn't stand it anymore:

> I could not tolerate the city. It had become unbearably stressful for me. I couldn't breathe; there was too much movement, too much activity.
>
> I became afraid to drive and afraid to fly. I had always been an excellent driver, but now I was even more frightened to be a passenger in a car. I felt the car would fly away and crash!

Randy was scheduled to fly to San Francisco to attend an important seminar, and she was in a state of panic. She visited her physician and described her neurophysiological symptoms and phobias, explaining that she had to attend the seminar and needed help to do so. The physician had been a flight surgeon at one time, and he stated that he thought her motion phobias were suggestive of an inner-ear problem. He prescribed an antihistamine that he thought might help. She took the medication.

Randy flew to San Francisco and rented a car while she was there. While attending the conference, she read a great deal of material and participated very actively with an intellectually stimulating group. She felt fine—entirely free of symptoms.

While in San Francisco, Randy saw me on a TV program. She listened keenly to my explanation of the relationship between the inner ear and learning.

> Something clicked inside me. When I returned home, I again saw a TV rerun of the *Donahue Show* in which several of your patients described their symptoms. With a burst of shock I thought, These are my symptoms these people are describing!
>
> Then and there I made an appointment to be examined.

Tests verified that Randy did indeed have inner-ear dysfunctioning and associated dyslexia. In fact, special inner-ear testing (ENG) produced a precise replica of the anxiety attacks she had been experiencing on and off for many years.

When she was told the diagnosis, Randy's initial reaction was one of relief that there was something definitely wrong of a physiological nature. Therefore, she was not crazy. That was an immensely profound experience for her:

> I feverently wished I could tell my mother, See, I'm not stupid. I am smart. All my life, while my mother was alive, I could never please her, never be as smart or as correct as she wanted me to be. I wanted to shout from the highest

rooftop, See, I was right! Something was wrong and it wasn't my fault!

In the light of her diagnosis, Randy's fears of driving, flying, and any fast movement became understandable. For Randy everything moved five times faster than for a "normal" person. Thus, a car moving forty miles per hour appeared to be moving two hundred miles per hour.* Her other neurological symptoms and difficulties also became comprehensible, including her supersensitivity. No longer did she feel in the wrong because of this body sensitivity.

Randy's second reaction to her new knowledge was anger—anger that no one had been able to diagnose her problem before. She was particularly furious with her psychoanalyst. She visited his offices:

I yelled two thousand dollars' worth. I was livid with anger. I had been afraid to fall down the stairs because my balance and coordination was off, not because I was afraid of success. My inability to walk from one block to another at times was due to this problem of coordination and not of the mind. My fears and phobias were also related to my inner-ear disorder and not to my mind.

Randy recalled that during 1975 her life had been particularly stressful because she had been involved in very difficult and important business negotiations. She had been required to travel between Cleveland and Detroit frequently. She was working and pushing very hard. She experienced what she

*Difficulties with speed or time perception are characteristic of inner-ear–dysfunctioning dyslexics.

called mini-seizures: faintness, difficulty in breathing and swallowing, a feeling of being off balance, panic attacks, etc.

I visited a renowned neurologist and complained about these symptoms. After exhaustive tests and examinations he concluded that there was nothing wrong with me from a neuromedical viewpoint.

I am furious with these so-called experts who make you feel stupid and crazy. Now I am free; I know that I am not stupid, nor am I allowing my imagination to take over.

I felt a sense of great relief; over and over, the thought that I was free kept returning to me. I did not have to look for hidden, psychological meanings in my actions or feelings. I now knew that they were physiologically based, not psychologically based, as my doctors thought and I feared.

Randy was placed on medication to help compensate for her inner-ear dysfunctioning. She felt much better almost immediately. She is no longer taking medication on a regular basis. A virus or a toothache will trigger the dizziness, lack of coordination, or other symptoms of dyslexia. At these times she takes the medication, and the symptoms are alleviated.

Randy stated that the single most important result of her visit to my offices was the realization that her lifelong difficulties and problems were of a neuromedical nature and not of her doing. She understood for the first time why her life had been such a struggle. She had achieved her goals, but with a much greater expenditure of time, energy, and effort than was required of others. With this understanding came self-acceptance.

Randy no longer feels driven to move from one activity to

another, no matter how worthwhile. She is still very involved in business, civic, philanthropic, and entrepreneurial affairs, but her involvement is motivated by genuine desire, not the need to prove her intelligence. She has learned to acknowledge her brightness and no longer requires outside approval to feel successful and smart.

In all areas of her life—personal, business, and social—Randy has truly become her own person. Her pain has been lessened. She still seeks new challenges, not to prove herself but to fulfill herself. She has learned to acknowledge her talents and to accept the fact that when difficulties occur, they have a physical basis and can be dealt with accordingly.

As a result of all she has endured, Randy has become adamant about the need for revision in our dealings with the learning-disabled. She has reiterated that her values and attitudes about herself and important others would have been different, and the course of her life altered, if her condition had been diagnosed when she was a child. Randy has been urging that neurophysiological, psychological, and educational forces combine as a single unit to deal with learning disabilities in order to help children develop self-esteem in the learning environment and to find school a positive, fulfilling experience instead of a psychologically debilitating one leading to failure and negation. She has suggested the formation of support groups to reinforce new ideas and concepts. She believes that strengthening one's ego or self can best be achieved when people with similar disabilities assist one another to cope, to move ahead past the disabilities to reasonable success.

I agree with her! Ideas such as Randy's are valid and realistically possible if individuals who share these views work through their local communities and schools to implement them. Without implementation, such concepts are valueless.

One such support group had already been created by a large group of my Sacramento patients. They met on a regular basis for the purpose of sharing information and experiences as well as helping one another to better understand and deal with their or their children's dyslexic symptoms. They provided assistance and guidance in dealing with teachers, school systems, and interpersonal relations. The group published a newsletter from time to time, and members explained and discussed the assistance they had received at my Medical Dyslexic Treatment Center.

Randy was successful even before she knew she was dyslexic. But she became even more successful.

XIV

Asperger Syndrome Versus Social Dyslexia

As readers will by now have clearly recognized, my patients—not experts—conveyed to me the vast majority of crucial insights described within this work. And the remaining clarity regarding the complex scope and depth of the dyslexic syndrome was "accidentally stumbled upon" during my scientific attempt to understand and reconcile the typical and, especially, the atypical symptoms characterizing dyslexics with inner-ear/cerebellar mechanisms.

Among the thousands and thousands of dyslexics I examined, a very small number—perhaps only a handful or two—demonstrated significant difficulties in normally reading the facial and body expressions of others. Similarly, they appeared to have obvious problems in reading and/or expressing their own feelings nonverbally and even verbally—the latter lacking the expected depth and richness often characterizing those with high intellects.

These unique dyslexic children were frequently described by their parents as socially inept, socially awkward and dyscoordinated, and even naive or "socially dumb." Accordingly, I wondered: Is it possible for social/emotional (internal and external) processing to require normal primary inner-ear/cerebellar functioning? Or might the above-described "social language disorder" be mixed in with typical dyslexics—and thus have an entirely unique non-inner-ear/cerebellar origin?

In any event, I termed these socially impaired LD cases "social dyslexics" since they experienced varying problems in reading their own feelings and expressions as well as those of others. And I treated them medically in a manner identical to the more typical dyslexics.

Having recently stumbled over the term *Asperger syndrome* and its symptoms, I was forced to wonder: Is Asperger syndrome a form of what I termed "social dyslexia"? And if so, is the social core of Asperger syndrome, as well as its overlapping typical dyslexic, ADD, balance/coordination, and even anxiety symptoms, treatable with inner-ear/cerebellar–enhancing medications?

As luck would have it, a bright, gifted, Englishman in his sixties with previously diagnosed Asperger syndrome "accidentally" read about my dyslexia research recently and wondered to himself: Is my Asperger syndrome part of my dyslexia? And might I be helped with medications that help dyslexics?

And the logical basis of his reasoning was simple. After taking an antihistamine, Benylin, for sleep, he retrospectively wondered to himself: "Is it possible for a simple antihistamine to result in dramatic improvements in my severe phobic and typical dyslexic symptoms as well as a gradual disappearance of the symptoms comprising my Asperger syndrome?" Adding to his conviction was the fact that all his symptoms gradually returned upon stopping the Benylin. And upon restarting his Benylin and other inner-ear/cerebellar–enhancing medications and nutrients following consultation with me, his resulting improvements were even better than those he accidentally obtained alone. The results included the gradual ability to read and express verbal and nonverbal body language, and a reduction in social putdowns experienced.

Although my other "social dyslexics" had shown significantly greater improvements in their typical dyslexic symptoms versus atypical social symptoms, the above-proven Asperger case with inner-ear/cerebellar dysfunction suggested:

1. A linkage or relationship between "social dyslexia," Asperger syndrome, and inner-ear/cerebellar dysfunction
2. A positive improvement in social processing utilizing inner-ear–enhancing medications, and
3. A clear distinction between Asperger syndrome and autism, a difference as great as that between alexia and dyslexia, and between aphasia and dysphasia or minor verbalization difficulties

I hope the investigation of additional cases will result in the insights needed to clearly understand and medically treat children and adults diagnosed with Asperger syndrome. Before concluding here, however, I would like to emphasize that my patient, John Bailey, had independently arrived at all the above insights himself before I even saw him. I anticipate that his discovery and recovery will follow in later works.

Perhaps my discussion will be more thoroughly understood

if John Bailey describes his thoughts and responses in his own words:

> I'd like to explain the train of thought leading me to the conviction that Asperger Syndrome was Dyslexia or that Asperger Syndrome was a subset of symptoms within the Dyslexia spectrum. As is well known, these two separately named disorders are distinctly defined: Dyslexia is thought to be a reading disorder whereas Asperger Syndrome is an impairment with properly understanding and expressing body language.
>
> As you know, Professor Sacks is a well-known UK expert on Asperger Syndrome and my prior physician and therapist. He told me that Asperger Syndrome was considered by the medical establishment to fall within the autistic spectrum since the early 40's and that there was no cure. Like all other authorities, he believed my dyslexic problems with reading, writing, concentration, short-term memory and speech were completely unrelated to Asperger Syndrome and thus were of no consequence. In other words, Asperger Syndrome and Dyslexia had nothing to do with one another, despite this amazing overlap of symptoms. My logic told me otherwise. And the more I read, the more convinced I became that Professor Sacks and others were incorrect.
>
> Then I attended the Paul Shattock lecture, which clearly showed that the peak in his specially developed urine test was different for Asperger Syndrome patients vs. normal individuals and those with Autism. Then he added: "Oh, I don't know why—but the peak for dyslexic patients falls in the same place as those with Asperger Syndrome."

Why didn't he know why? Or at least explore this fascinating correlation? Is it that traditionally minded scientists are trained "not to rock the boat?" I then asked him: "Do your results not suggest that Asperger Syndrome and Dyslexia may reflect one and the same disorder—especially since they have overlapping symptoms?" Professor Shattock responded: "It's not possible that Asperger Syndrome and Dyslexia are similar disorders since Asperger Syndrome was in the Autistic Spectrum." But I asked, "Why do Asperger Syndrome and Autistic people have different peaks in your test?" Professor Shattock just ignored my question and went on with his discussion.

His "non-response" to a simple question made me more determined than ever to explore the relationship between Asperger Syndrome and Dyslexia.

Then, by chance, I took Benylin for sleep. And I was amazed to find that both dyslexic and Asperger Syndrome problems had significantly lessened. So it seemed evident to me that these different-appearing Asperger Syndrome and Dyslexic symptoms reflected one and the same thing. It is interesting that my so-called Asperger Syndrome symptoms and phobias occurred and disappeared with treatment in an interrelated way with my many and varied dyslexic symptoms, including the physical ones: Thus, for example, I have experienced dramatic improvements in seeing detail, experiencing time, enhanced facial expressions, vocalization (deeper and less childish), verbal expression and thinking, and obtaining and using information from my brain.

That's when I read about your use of antihistamines to treat dyslexia and related phobia and ADD symptoms. By the way, all my phobic or anxiety symptoms had also disappeared on the Benylin. With my improvement, all my prior insights fell into place—thank God. However, Professor Sacks still does not believe me. But then I'm just a patient— and he's an expert and thus is not expected to change his prior beliefs!!

Regards,
John

There is another problem that I believe should be emphasized: The complete list of Asperger syndrome versus dyslexia symptoms has not been properly thought out, and cannot while these lists remain in different spectrums.

When the two lists are compared, they are the same except for the fact that Asperger syndrome has two or three extra symptoms. So why not just get rid of the term Asperger syndrome and have just one slightly enlarged dyslexia list?!

When I talk to dyslexics in your office and at work, I realize they also have some Asperger syndrome traits—but don't know it. For example, severe dyslexics have the same difficulties looking at you and talking. So I believe it's important to question dyslexics more thoroughly about Asperger syndrome traits. It seems to me that severe dyslexic symptoms may sometimes snowball and create associated social and related inhibitions—which are then called Asperger syndrome.

XV

Variations of Dyslexia—
With Case Histories

A clear understanding of the symptoms and mechanisms defining dyslexia inevitably led to the discovery that:

- Dyslexia need not occur in "pure" form.
- Dyslexia need not be of a hereditary or congenital origin.

In other words, two more assumptions and convictions about this disorder were proven to be incomplete and thus tragically misleading to millions and millions of patients:

Dyslexia *may* be inherited and *may* occur in "pure" form—but needn't.

By recognizing the *quality* of the symptoms and mechanisms characterizing dyslexia, it became apparent that many patients suffering from whiplash injuries, concussions, etc., had dyslexialike symptoms. They complained of such "psycho-somatic" symptoms as blurred vision; difficulty reading because of poor tracking; concentration and memory difficulties; slurring of speech and word-finding memory uncertainty; impaired writing and spelling; poor balance and coordination; dizziness; and motion sickness.

Moreover, young children with severe or repeated ear infections were occasionally noted to stop talking or walking properly; some actually became hyperactive and distractible. Early-reading children suddenly began to stumble, fumble, trip, and fall, demonstrating reading reversals and typically dyslexic tracking, memory, and concentration difficulties.*

As a result of these observations, I came to the realization that these children *acquired* dyslexia in their early grades. They were not born dyslexic! Additional observations and research led me to discover that many children with mental retardation, cerebral palsy, and deafness had dyslexialike symptoms. Thus, I began to wonder:

- Is it possible that the mentally retarded, cerebral-palsied, and deaf might also be dyslexic?
- Would this assumption not account for their dyslexialike symptoms?

---

*Not only was dyslexia *acquired* after birth by a variety of conditions, but a series of puzzling observations reported to me by parents and patients alike indicated that dyslexialike symptoms frequently lessened or disappeared altogether during infections, allergic episodes, periods of asthma, etc. Only in retrospect did these parents realize, after reading *Smart but Feeling Dumb*, that the improvements were due to the use of antihistamines during the illness.

Prior to my research, traditional theory maintained that:

- You were either dyslexic or retarded.
- You were either dyslexic or cerebral-palsied.
- You were either dyslexic or deaf.

But this is not so! Over a period of many years I clearly proved that:

- Dyslexia may be *acquired* as a result of whiplash and concussion states as well as ear infections, mononucleosis, or any disorder affecting inner-ear functioning.
- Dyslexia may remain hidden and *mixed in* with other coexisting disease states, such as mental retardation, cerebral palsy, and nerve deafness.

In fact, dyslexics may even appear retarded and may therefore be misdiagnosed as such. I have called these cases "pseudoretarded."

These insights led me to treat the above and related *variations* of dyslexia medically. As a result of treatment:

- *Acquired* dyslexics may suddenly be able to function more normally, return to work or school, and once again resume enjoyable, "successful" living.
- *Mixed* dyslexics suddenly blossom in their overall functioning regardless of whether or not they still have mental retardation, cerebral palsy, or nerve deafness.*
- *Pseudoretarded* children suddenly appear *obviously* normal or only dyslexic.

*Over the years, I came to realize that children frequently diagnosed with Pervasive Development Disorder (PDD), autism, and similar conditions may also have inner-ear dysfunctioning and thus might benefit from treatment.

To highlight and illustrate these observations, I will now present you with a series of successfully diagnosed and treated cases—never before recognized to be dyslexic, never before believed to be treatable.

Acquired Dyslexia: Postconcussion Syndrome

Mary Ann Adams

Diagnosis: Acquired Dyslexia/Postconcussion Syndrome

Mary Ann Adams, thirty-nine, sustained a severe head injury in an automobile accident in July. During the accident she struck her head on the windshield and consequently suffered a severe *organic brain syndrome.* She was referred to me by her neurologist for diagnosis and treatment.*

Mary Ann was found to have exceptionally severe, magnified dyslexialike symptoms. Her speech was marked by a severe word-finding and articulation impairment as well as significant slurring and stuttering. She became unable to read: The print appeared blurry and in motion. Her writing drifted aimlessly from one side of the page to the other. Her spelling became severely impaired. Simple computations became a major burden. Her concentration and memory functions regressed, almost coming to a halt. Her balance and coordination were totally off. She could not stand alone or walk unless someone held her arm to compensate for her poor balance and weak muscle tone.

---

*Her neurologist, Dr. Augusta Alba, who was deputy director at Goldwater Memorial Hospital, New York University Medical Center, was very familiar with my research. We shared quite a number of patients and favorable responses.

She became fatigued easily and suffered headaches, vertigo, and motion sickness.

She developed a multitude of phobias: She feared walking, talking, elevators, escalators, crowds, and cars. She became easily confused and panicked, blanking out, freezing, becoming what appeared to be catatonic.

Mary Ann was diagnosed to have a very severe impairment of her inner-ear and cerebellar system and was treated with a combination of medications. Within a relatively short period of time she dramatically improved. As of this date, her reading, writing, spelling, math, memory, speech, concentration, directionality, balance, and coordination are almost within normal limits. Her phobias are gone.

Mary Ann was advised to return to work six months after treatment began. However, her employer, a telephone company, refused to take her back at the time. They couldn't believe she would ever be able to function again.

Often accident cases are thought to be malingerers, who can work but do not wish to. In this case Mary Ann *demanded* to go back to work. They refused to take her back. It took a multitude of physical examinations before she was allowed to return to her job, but once she returned she worked exceptionally well.

Acquired Dyslexia: Ear Infections

Troy Dudas

Diagnosis: Pseudoretardation

I first examined Troy when he was six years old. He appeared to be in a fog, unable to communicate his thoughts verbally and demonstrating a significant lag in understanding my questions. He seemed retarded.

Troy had suffered from ear infections from eight months of age to four years. As a result of a severe speech articulation problem and generalized memory difficulties, Troy was tested by a psychologist in his school district. Testing revealed Troy's IQ to be normal despite low to normal scores in vocabulary, listening ability, and understanding of instructions. Many testers would have been misled by these low scores and would have misjudged him as being borderline mentally retarded or having a low-normal IQ.

Three months after medical treatment Troy was psychologically reevaluated. In the doctor's report it was noted that while his growth pattern was uneven and although more complete testing was needed, there was evidence of changes in Troy's ability to attend and to concentrate. The doctor concluded that maturation alone could not account for Troy's growth in attention, concentration, auditory memory, and visual-motor integration. The doctor felt that my medication had apparently given Troy an increased awareness of his surroundings and a better ability to reflect and interact. The change was dramatic to him, since he had observed Troy's progress for over a year. In addition Troy's teacher remarked on his increased participation in class. The report concluded "that readiness for learning language activities had been enhanced."

FIGURE A

Patients are asked to draw Figure A when they visit me for the first examination. Mary's first drawing is Figure B. After two months on medication she drew Figure C. Almost a year after her first visit, her writing and drawing were much improved (Figure D).

FIGURE B

FIGURE C *(Two months on medications.)*

FIGURE D *(Twelve months on medications.)*

According to Troy's mother, "After only two or three weeks of treatment he began to question everything. Over the past year he has demonstrated a significant improvement in speech, awareness, memory, and behavior. . . ."

Upon reexamination, I found Troy to be a very different boy from the one I had met a year earlier. Not all of his difficulties have been alleviated, but he is significantly better and happier.

I feel Troy would have benefited significantly from an early tonsilectomy, adenoidectomy, and insertion of draining tubes in his ears. These procedures would have offered him a 95-percent chance of avoiding repeated ear infections and the severe dyslexic speech and related symptoms he demonstrated.

Troy was fortunate. His parents were interested and determined. His school system was cooperative. The psychologist testing him was alert and gifted. And he responded favorably to my medical treatment. Had any one of these essential ingredients been missing, the ending could have been significantly different.

John Cahill

Diagnosis: Pseudoretardation

John is a sixteen-year-old southerner who was brought to me by his grandfather for diagnostic evaluation. Prior psychological tests revealed low IQ's (Verbal IQ [VIQ] = 72; Performance IQ [PIQ] = 78). Thus, he was diagnosed mentally retarded by several prominent psychologists. As a result of this diagnosis, no learning-disabilities school would take him, despite a willingness by his guardian and grandfather (a billionaire) to contribute significantly to the school, and indications from his guardian and clinical exams that this youngster was not re-tarded.

Six weeks after medications, John was retested locally. His IQ jumped to 125. Did his IQ really jump, or did the medications facilitate its real but hidden appearance on tests? Prior to treatment, John's auditory discrimination capabilities had been so impaired that he could not significantly comprehend the questions asked of him, certainly not on timed IQ and related tests. His greatest improvement in tests and clinical trials was in auditory discrimination and processing. Following successful treatment and private tutoring, John no longer needed special schools and classes.

John's case highlights a reliable rule of thumb: Clinical impressions of IQ are far more reliable in dyslexics than formal IQ scores.

Mixed Dyslexia: Dyslexia and Decreased IQ

Joe Gust

Diagnosis: Mixed Dyslexia

Joe Gust, a sixteen-year-old student, attends an occupational high school in Michigan, a special school for the learning-disabled. Joe is neurologically impaired and has a low IQ.

Joe's parents brought him to my offices to have him tested and evaluated. Testing revealed that Joe was a mixed dyslexic. He had an impairment within his thinking brain, affecting his IQ, mixed with dyslexia of inner-ear origin. Joe was placed on a regimen of medication to help him compensate for his dyslexic symptoms and their effect on his decreased thinking or IQ functions.

A year later Joe returned to my Medical Dyslexic Treatment Center for reevaluation. One look at Mrs. Gust's face told me that it had been a good year for Joe. Clinical examination revealed he had improved in his coordination/balance and speech.

I asked Mrs. Gust to tell me what changes she had discerned in the past year. She began: "We feel Joe's progress since he has been on medication to be very good. Joe always had a problem with coordination, and this was the first area of improvement. I noticed Joe was moving better—jumping up and down and feeling good about it.

"The next thing I noticed was that Joe was picking up books, looking through them, and even reading. This, without any urging from me. I used to ask him to read a book, but he would say, 'No, I don't wanna.' Or he would back away from me.

"I gradually became aware that Joe's memory was better. I would tell him to complete three chores before I returned home from work that evening. But he would only remember to do one. Now he remembers to do all three. Sometimes I don't even have to tell him; he does them on his own.

"Regardless of his problems, Joe has always been persistent; he's not a quitter. For example, he failed driver education, but he took it over and earned a driver's permit. When we return home, he will have his license. We are real proud of him."

I asked Mrs. Gust if Joe noticed any differences in himself.

"Well, he has told me that he feels a whole lot better about himself. Whenever we go to the store, he says, 'Let me drive, Mom, I can do it.'

"He says that he knows now that he is not dumb. He seems to have a better understanding of his problems. His outlook, in general, is good.

"Another accomplishment for Joe is that he has a paper route with seventy-five customers. Occasionally he has a little trouble with the numbers on the houses, but he is able to figure them out for himself. The first few times he did his collecting of money, my husband went with him to help. When they returned home he said that Joe did not really need his help—he had managed just fine.

"Before your treatment Joe could tell the difference between a nickel, a dime, and a quarter; but if the money was mixed together, he had to sit down and figure out which denomination was which. That is no longer necessary. He can now calculate mentally.

"At school he works in the cafeteria, taking inventory, doing the ordering, and waiting on students and faculty—and doing a good job, too!"

I asked Mrs. Gust what other changes she or the teachers at Joe's school had noticed during the year.

"Joe's speech is definitely better—no stuttering or hesitation. He is calmer when he speaks and does not speak as loudly as he did. His vocabulary is better, and he appears to think before he speaks. When we discuss something, he waits to speak, as though he is thinking, and then he says what he wants to say calmly and quietly. He is more inquisitive about everything, too, wanting to know the whys and wherefores of things.

"Joe is able to express himself better. Previously, if anyone on the block teased him or called him names, he would not answer. He would keep his feelings inside. I would tell him that he did not have to accept that kind of behavior from anyone. Now he expresses his anger and even explodes from time to time when he is teased.

"In school Joe is more coordinated in sports, especially basketball. Last year it was hard for him to pass the basketball to another person without passing it to the wrong person first. This year he is able to do it correctly the first time. He also received B's in volleyball, Frisbee, football, and indoor soccer.

"Joe's writing is better: His letters are even and he writes in a straight line, not all over the page. His spelling and math have also improved: He can add and subtract pretty well. Last year he just could not grasp these concepts. Now he is working on multiplication. You know, he's just blossoming daily.

"His concentration is better. There are times when he is doing something and someone will walk into the room; he'll look up just for a second and then go right back to what he was doing before, without a break in his concentration.

"The teachers are amazed at his progress. They are very pleased because he is grasping more than they had ever expected him to.

"When we returned home from New York last year, I insisted that he be placed in reading and math classes. In the reading class he jumped from second-grade level to fourth-grade level in just one year.

"You would not believe the number of people who call me from Joe's school, wanting to know your name and inquiring how we received information from you.

"His reading teacher wrote that Joe's word recognition of newly learned words was good, as was his comprehension. His left-to-right discrimination has been consistent, and he has not exhibited any reversal problems during oral reading sessions.

"Joe's attitude toward his reading lessons has been good. He seems comfortable with himself and what he is doing in reading. Joe is becoming less dependent upon continuous teacher supervision during reading instruction."

I asked Joe if he noticed any differences or changes in himself. He responded that he felt better about himself, about the things he could do now. When I asked him if he felt smarter now, he replied, "No, not yet, but I'm getting there."

Mrs. Gust continued: "Joe's improvement has been a gradual change, but I see it more and more every day, and so does everyone else. It has been the answer to our prayers and we are very, very happy. Thank you."

Joe is more in control of himself and he has a more positive self-image and attitude. Obviously, he is able to perform within his limitations—to drive a car, have a paper route, follow instructions, and complete chores at home. As a result, he has a new sense of accomplishment and purpose. Although Joe is still retarded, his overall level of functioning has significantly improved.

Lisa Green

Diagnosis: Mixed Dyslexia (Mental Retardation and Dyslexia)

Lisa Green is a shy, gentle, somewhat withdrawn sixteen-year-old with a history of severe neurological impairment. Her IQ is 40. In addition to her cerebral impairment, she suffers from a coexisting inner-ear dysfunctioning and a resulting dyslexia.

Lisa experienced the following symptoms:

- Reading—inverted letters; read on preprimer level
- Math—needed objects, such as balls, in order to add or subtract
- Spatial relations—lack of comprehension/awareness

- Sense of time/memory—unable to recall days of week, months of year; little recall for numbers
- Direction—right/left confusion
- Speech—difficulty with speaking in sentences, rarely spoke spontaneously
- Coordination/balance—very poor; unable to tie shoelaces
- Behavior—very shy, somewhat introverted; phobic about strangers; experienced highs and lows in moods

At the time of her consultation, Lisa was diagnosed as a mixed-dyslexic and was placed on medication to help compensate for her inner-ear/cerebellar–determined dyslexic symptoms. Upon examination one year later, Lisa revealed significant improvements in concentration and memory, reading interest, verbalization, and perception and understanding of relationships between objects and events, as well as enhanced recognition of highway signs, and the ability to copy them. Before treatment, these very same signs were confusing and impossible for her to understand.

A third visit indicated additional improvements. This update is based on my own examinations and Mrs. Green's observations:

- Reading—continues to show interest in books and reading and to improve her recognition of words
- Writing—interest in cursive writing but concentrating on printing, which has improved with respect to spacing of letters, straightness of letters/words, awareness of margins, and speed of writing
- Spelling—written recall of words much better; oral recall still not mastered

- Behavior—frustration/anxiety levels have improved, but she needs to learn to cope with situations over which she has no control; more stable moods—less highs and lows; a little more confident
- Math—ability to do simple calculations mentally, e.g., $3 + 1 = 4$; awareness that she has five fingers on each hand
- Coordination—ability to tie her shoelaces
- Speech—more spontaneous; speaks more
- Sense of time/memory—much better: knowledge of days of the week and months of the year; order of items

Lisa's mother reported: "On the whole I am very pleased with the improvements Lisa has made and am eager to work to help her do even better. However, she still needs to develop more interest in her physical appearance."

Mixed Dyslexia: Cerebral Palsy

Howard Stevens

Diagnosis: Cerebral Palsy and Dyslexia

Twenty-six-year-old Howard Stevens has cerebral palsy. His parents brought him for consultation because he suffered from dyslexialike symptoms over and above the motor-speech-coordination problems of cerebral palsy. His dyslexic symptoms were highlighted by reading difficulties, distractibility, a poor sense of balance, and an equally impaired spatial sense.

The Stevenses tried to help Howard as much as possible with his dyslexia-related symptoms at home and thus enrolled him in a private school. Unfortunately, the school ignored their observations suggesting greater than apparent intellectual abilities and so concentrated primarily on improving his motor difficulties. School personnel repeatedly stated that they were experts and knew best how to understand and deal with Howard.

His parents were very frustrated. Educators assumed that Howard was retarded, but his parents knew that he was "brilliant": At a young age, he made up his own sign language for words he couldn't say. Thus, if he wanted to say "apple sauce," he would pull his shirtsleeve—apple (pull) sauce. As he grew older, his sign language became even more developed and ingenious. Because Mr. and Mrs. Stevens have a great sense of humor, they would often discuss something funny and find him laughing in the next room. Howard understood their humor, and sometimes he would laugh even before a story had been completely told. He understood and even anticipated the ending.

With only minimal testing, his school labeled him mildly retarded. One doctor spent thirty minutes with him and said his IQ was 65 or thereabouts. The Stevenses knew Howard was of at least average intelligence.

Although initially Howard had a teacher who worked with him as his parents did, Howard's total experience with the school was bad. This one good teacher just did not have the necessary time for Howard, because there were other needy children in the class, too. The following year Howard was placed with retarded children. He knew they were retarded, and cried for a week. Despite his parent's protests, he remained in this class for almost two years.

Then Howard was placed in a class for physically and otherwise handicapped children. Again it was a misplacement, because most of the children were younger. One day his parents visited the school. Instead of finding him at a typewriter learn-ing spelling or reading, they found him behind a screen. He was practicing putting on his clothes, although he dressed himself at home. And the school knew this. Unfortunately, he remained in this class for several years.

When Howard entered junior high he was again misplaced with a professional supposedly qualified for teaching the hear-ing- and physically-impaired. "But she was a *regular teacher,* a cold, cold person who screamed at the children and lacked un-derstanding. The first day of school Howard stopped to touch her, a habit of his. Because he held her more tightly than he should have (one of his symptoms), she yelled at him loudly and coldly, "Let go of me immediately!" There was no gentle admonishment and especially no, "Welcome to school."

Mrs. Stevens complained to the administration about the teacher repeatedly yelling at the children and their negative and even regressive responses. However, the school supported rather than reprimanded the teacher. That winter was difficult. Howard was subject to tremendous frustration and developed anxiety attacks.

At one point Mr. and Mrs. Stevens were told that Howard was doing beautifully and were encouraged to take a vacation. Upon returning ten days later, they received an urgent call from the school. The teacher claimed that Howard had done terrible things and consequently received "mild" punishment. Howard allegedly had thrown temper tantrums and broken a typewriter. What his parents did not know until years later (from a hearing-impaired girl who had been present) was that the teacher had shaken Howard by the hair and then pushed him into the typewriter table, knocking the typewriter over. They were also not told that Howard had been locked in a room for a period of time. He had screamed and yelled to be released. These were the tantrums the teacher had referred to.

In fact, the day after their return from vacation, Howard refused to go to school—even with his parents.

The school told his parents half-truths about Howard's behavior and finally suggested that he enroll in a place for the mentally impaired.

The Stevenses met with the people at the new place and felt that they were kind. The staff loved Howard because he was the only child that communicated with them. Initially, he was happy with all this interest and attention. But two weeks later, when his parents visited him, the light had gone out of his eyes. Suddenly, intuitively, they knew. "Howard, you pretended to be retarded to get into this place, didn't you?" "Yes, I did," he answered. They brought him home.

Mr. and Mrs. Stevens heard me on TV several times, and discussed my book with Howard's teacher and several doctors. They felt my success with many dyslexics would enable me to go beyond Howard's cerebral palsy symptoms—would allow me to see beyond the obvious and help to correct his balance and spatial difficulties. They wanted to help their son. They hoped I could help.

And so the Stevenses and Howard left my office with a program of treatment and increased hope for the future. They finally understood what was wrong with their son, and prayed that treatment would be helpful. But at the very least, they were on the right track.

Stella Peters

Diagnosis: Mixed Dyslexia—Cerebral Palsy, Dyslexia, and Phobias

Stella, twenty-five, attractive, with a childhood history of cerebral palsy, came for medical diagnosis and treatment because of phobias and a history of dyslexialike symptoms.

In addition to her typical cerebral palsy symptoms, Stella had experienced reading, writing, and spelling difficulties as a child. She continued to stutter and suffer motion sickness when riding in a car.

Within two months of treatment, Stella experienced a series of remarkable changes. She elatedly reported that her speech was so much better that she was able to speak on the telephone for the very first time in her life. Her friends are astonished at this improvement. She felt that if only she had had this medication as a child, her whole life would have been completely different.

Stella feels able to communicate with the outside world without the fear of stuttering, without the anticipation of acute embarrassment. Her extreme fear of falling or being knocked over has been greatly reduced as a result of an improved sense of balance and coordination. In fact, Stella no longer feels unsteady when walking around her home; she is more in control of her movements and thus feels more confident.

She is no longer phobic about speaking and walking. As an unexpected bonus, her reading, concentration, and memory have improved as well.

Larry Mann

Diagnosis: Mixed Dyslexia

Larry is a twenty-five-year-old with mixed dyslexia: He has cerebral palsy and dyslexia—two separate but overlapping neurological conditions.

He had always been slower than his peers in reading, writing, and speech. But his family and teachers attributed all of Larry's symptoms to the cerebral palsy. However, he also had an inner-ear/cerebellar impairment resulting in dyslexia, a fact not known until he was examined in my office.

Because of his chemical sensitivity, it took Larry longer than usual to reach therapeutic dose levels of medications. However, once he was on full dosage, his improvements became apparent:

- Larry's writing became better.
- His speech became distinct and clearer, and he became better able to express himself. His thinking process showed improvement once his signal scrambling improved.
- His fear of heights diminished: Larry could climb a ladder, something he had never done before.
- His reading comprehension and speed improved, with fewer reversals.

His mother noted that Larry will now go up the escalator. However, he is still afraid to go down but wants to try. His panic is gone, but his anxiety remains.

Larry's attitude is significantly better because he is encouraged by his improvements to date. He works for a large department store. And they have promised him a permanent full-time job if he increases his writing and speaking skills.

In summary, the promise of a job, the improvements brought about by the medication, and tutorial reading and speech help are all potent motivational factors in helping Larry realize his maximum potential.

Down's Syndrome

As most readers know, children born with Down's syndrome have deficient IQ's and flaccid muscle tones. Because of this muscle tone and poor coordination, it appeared that in addition to a cerebral impairment, there coexisted a hidden inner-ear/cerebellar dysfunction in Down's syndrome individuals. This assumption was recently supported by studies indicating a smaller than normal cerebellum and the presence of abnormal plaques.

As a result, parents sought consultation to determine if Down's children might have a treatable inner-ear/cerebellar dysfunction. With a "nothing to lose and something possibly to gain" philosophy clearly in mind, I have over the years treated a small number of Down's children demonstrating clear-cut evidence of an inner-ear/cerebellar deficit.

Alyssa's favorable responses are typical of those treated. This case once again highlights the commonsense dictum that any improvement is dramatically better than none, while clearly illustrating the benefit of investigating a variety of major disorders for hidden evidence of "mixed dyslexia."

Alyssa

Alyssa was a very pretty and delightful fourteen-year-old when initially examined by me. Her mother's descriptions highlight both the reason Alyssa was brought for consultation and her response to treatment.

Reasons for coming:

"Alyssa projects many dyslexic symptoms, despite having Down's syndrome. She was very late to walk, taking her first steps at thirty months. . . . Her visual-motor integration was very poor. . . . Teachers noted that she was very distractible and hyperactive. . . .

"Following an occupational therapy program for the next seven years resulted in many exciting improvements; i.e., her gait improved dramatically, no longer did her left eye turn in, and she was able to run and swing, catch a ball, and start to read and write.

"She now reads on a fourth-grade level but tends to skip words and lines, requiring a very slow reading speed and a finger or pointer. . . . Oral reading is significantly easier than that silently done, no doubt due to her known auditory strength.

"Her letter formations are still very poor, and she can't perform cursive writing. Size and spacing are erratic. Addition and subtraction facts are impossible to remember. And she can't follow more than two-step commands.

"The most distressing inadequacy is her speech. She finds it very difficult to articulate, organize, and sequence her thoughts so as to express herself in sentences. And she often forgets her thoughts in midsentence.

"Alyssa cannot tie her shoelaces and is slow in buttoning.

Her balance is poor and she cannot ride a two-wheel bike. Despite all our efforts, she could not rollerskate on her own.

"Historically, Alyssa has always tested significantly poorer in the motor versus cognitive part of her IQ tests."

Response to medications:

"In school, her teacher reports her functioning more independently and appearing self-confident, often raising her hand to respond to questions and defending herself against more aggressive classmates. Her penmanship has improved—better letter formation, sizing, and spacing. She can now better recall addition and subtraction math facts. And multiplication seems more successful.

"Her speech is improving. It is slower, better articulated, and more complex. She still searches for words—but this occurs less often than before.

"Spelling memory is better—she can easily recall her ten weekly spelling words for testing. And she can successfully participate in games such as What's in Grandma's Basket?

"Alyssa reads well, but comprehension is still weak, as is following directions. Although improved, she still occasionally skips lines and reverses or omits letters when copying."

Primary Cerebellar Disorders—Cerebellar Ataxia

Independent research has recently demonstrated that children and adults with proven cerebellar structural disorders manifest a wide range of speech, cognitive, concentration, and memory symptoms, as well as more obvious balance/coordination/rhythmic symptoms. These observations have not only validated my prior inner-ear/cerebellar concepts of dyslexia, but opened up the possibility that some individuals with proven cerebellar damage may respond favorably albeit mildly to the medical treatment I developed for dyslexics.

Since dyslexics do not exhibit obvious structural damage to the cerebellum and may only suffer from a "reversible" neurotransmitter dysfunction, judging from their rapid and often dramatic responses to treatment, I would anticipate that those with severe cerebellar difficulties will demonstrate mild to moderate therapeutic improvements. However, any favorable response is infinitely better than none. And with increasing experience, I have little doubt that the discovery of new and more effective medications will result in more significant improvement.

To highlight the above insights, I will now present the responses of children born with cerebellar ataxia. This is a congenital neurological disorder in which children manifest severe imbalance and dyscoordination and thus cannot stand or walk unassisted.

I began to treat individuals with this severe cerebellar disorder many years ago. Thus, the following responses are typical and might be expected to occur for others with similar diagnoses.

Tom Fried

Tom is an eight-year-old born with a cerebellar disorder preventing him from standing and walking unassisted. Typically, he also manifests a host of severe speech and hand coordination difficulties as well as many other sensory-motor problems considered significantly less important than the inability to navigate.

Over the years I've helped a number of similar cases—with

the clear recognition by parents that there was absolutely nothing to lose and perhaps something beneficial to gain.

Tom's parents reported the following responses to medication:

"Tom can now stand for ten to fifteen minutes unassisted versus one minute a few weeks ago. He can now take ten small but well-balanced steps alone, whereas he could only crawl in a highly unbalanced manner before. His muscle tone is stiffer and not so flabby. This enables him to be steadier rather than rapidly falling.

"In addition, we've seen a lot of unexpected and thus unhoped-for improvements. For example, his eyes are straighter and not so turned in. Now he started reading; previously it was painful for him to even look at a page. And his headaches are gone. He can now recognize, remember, and track words with my finger as a marker. None of this was possible before. His eyes just seem better coordinated and thus work better together.

"Writing and drawing are now possible since his fine motor coordination has improved. It just didn't exist before.

"Although general memory was always good, it's now even better since his concentration is markedly improved, and his severe distractibility is hardly a problem at this time.

"There are obvious changes in speech, too. He can pronounce words better and even complete them. Tom also appears to have more facial expression than before—perhaps due to his overall improvement in muscle tone. And drooling has stopped.

"Overall he seems more together—and more focused. Thus, he can play for hours by himself—something not possible before treatment.

"Although we clearly recognize these improvements are far from the cure we would ultimately like, these 'minor' improvements in Tom are like miracles to us. Thanks!"

Mixed Dyslexia: Nerve Deafness: Pervasive Developmental Disorder or Global Developmental Delay

Erin O'Sullivan

Diagnosis: Pseudodeafness, Pseudoretardation

Five-year-old Erin O'Sullivan had frequent ear infections as an infant. He thus spent a lot of his time at the pediatrician's office—and was on antibiotics continuously.

At eight months he was still not sleeping through the night and was exhibiting signs of insomnia due to hyperactivity. At one and a half, it was obvious to his parents that he was slower than his peers in speaking and walking. However, his parents were reassured that there was no cause for alarm. "Our pediatrician told us that if Erin was not walking by nineteen months, then he would check matters further."

Although walking by two and a half years of age, Erin did not speak at all. He even lost the few words he knew when he was one and a half. His ear infections continued and his speech appeared to get worse, suggesting a correlation between the two.

Erin's parents became increasingly concerned and consulted his pediatrician once again. This time even he became alarmed. He suddenly wanted Erin tested for hearing and speech, and suggested the possibility that draining tubes be placed in Erin's ears in order to lessen the frequency of ear infections. A complete neurological examination was also advised. The O'Sullivans were suddenly overwhelmed.

A speech and hearing evaluation found Erin to have a severe receptive and expressive language delay.

When five months pregnant with Erin's sister, Mrs. O'Sullivan was told by one of the examining doctors: "I'm sorry, but your son is deaf and should be enrolled in a special school that can deal with deafness and resulting speech disorders." He further added: "I cannot guarantee that your new baby will not be born with the same deficiencies." Moreover, he advised against further testing and the insertion of the draining ear tubes, conveying an attitude of hopelessness.

Mrs. O'Sullivan dissolved into tears. She sank into despair, both for her little boy and her yet-to-be-born baby. Fortunately, her maternal instincts rebelled against the doctor's advice and its unfeeling quality. She took her son to another medical center, whereupon he was diagnosed as having a hearing loss, but not a total one, and "a global developmental delay with maximum deficits in the area of language."

Despite mounting medical costs and debts, the O'Sullivans moved to another area of the state, where their son could receive special speech and language therapy. At the same time, draining tubes were surgically implanted in his ears, and his adenoids were removed.

They continued to search for additional answers and help. Erin was retested. His parents were told that children with the same degree of hearing loss as Erin's generally acquire speech. The fact that Erin had not done so indicated that something else was wrong, possibly an "auditory processing problem."

Following this examination, the O'Sullivans attempted to

enroll Erin in a language-delayed children's program within the public school system. However, prior to admission, Erin had to take an IQ test. A test performed by a student psychologist who worked with him indicated that his IQ was 70—within the retarded range.

Mrs. O'Sullivan blew her top. She insisted that a more realistic evaluation be given by someone more experienced in dealing with deaf children. The retesting resulted in an IQ of 100. Erin was then permitted to enroll in a language-delayed children's program for four-year-olds. He was also fitted with a hearing aid to help compensate for his poor auditory acuity.

Erin's parents still sought additional help. Upon reading my medical text *A Solution to the Riddle Dyslexia*, they realized that Erin's auditory discrimination difficulties might respond to my treatment. Also, they believed the disorder was caused by ear infections that impaired his inner-ear functioning. The same doctor who had advised his parents against the trip to New York now expresses great delight over the results of that visit.

When I initially examined Erin, he was extremely hyperactive and distractible, and he verbalized very little. As a result, I did not know whether Erin was mentally retarded. He was certainly dyslexic and suffered from a severe difficulty in processing auditory input. Only a successful trial on medication would determine whether he was retarded.

In retrospect, it is obvious why Erin was thought to be deaf. He definitely had an auditory acuity problem. In addition, however, he had a severe auditory discrimination problem that compounded his inability to listen and understand speech.

According to the O'Sullivans and Erin's doctor, the boy has progressed verbally two and a half years in the past year. He has begun printing, reading, participating in sports, socializing with his peers, fighting with his sister, and so on. His attention span has increased but is still short. He still becomes easily frustrated and distracted. He is much, much better than before.

Upon retesting, Erin's auditory discrimination was found to be a year below his chronological age—an amazing change. There was also improvement noted in his auditory sequential memory, his knowledge of functional use of objects, and his verbal ability.

In conclusion Mrs. O'Sullivan added: "Lots of things have happened to Erin in the last year: He is in school, he has a sister at home to play with and talk with, and he is a year older and wiser . . . but I know the medication has been the answer to our prayers."

Erin has not been cured. He is being helped. He was not retarded; he just appeared to be. His specific type of dyslexia and hearing loss were caused by a series of ear infections that did not respond appropriately to antibiotics.

Erin's story illustrates why you should always seek a second or even third opinion if you are not satisfied with your first doctor's evaluation. (As you may recall, the doctor treating my daughter Joy gave me incorrect advice at first, too.)

Pseudoretardation

David Kim

Diagnosis: Pseudoretardation

Mrs. Kim was both laughing and crying when she related to me her six-year-old son's improvement:

"I am so proud of him now. . . . David is still a little bit slow, *but he is learning* and that's what is important. He can

pick up a book and read it. He can write. He knows his mathematics. It is so different . . . so different. He can even listen
and speak normally now."

Her eyes brimming with tears and her voice choked with
emotion, David's mother happily related the progress he had
made in a year and a half.

David's case is particularly significant in that he was labeled
retarded by his school system. David, six years old, appeared
retarded but was really dyslexic. In a sense, he suffered from
the same auditory discrimination difficulties as Consuelo
Brody (Chapter VIII). His auditory or sound input drifted, so
he experienced speech as "blurry" and thus poorly understood
it. He found it difficult or impossible to answer questions in a
meaningful and appropriate fashion.

When he was first brought to me for examination and treatment, David's symptoms were:

- Severe memory instability for seen and heard letters and
  words, despite the fact that his mother worked with him
  three hours a day
- Angled and discombobulated writing and drawing
- Poor memory retention for numbers, and poor number
  concepts
- Memory uncertainty for sequences, such as days of the
  week, months of the year, and so on
- Poor coordination and balance and a resulting accident-
  proneness
- Significantly delayed and impaired speech development
  with a severely limited vocabulary. (David began speaking
  words when he was three and a half years of age, and sentences when four and a half.)

- Delayed or scrambled auditory input with resulting speech comprehension difficulties. For example, it was necessary to repeat words and sentences several times before David understood what was said. At times one even had to point to objects before he could connect the sound with the meaning.
- Motion-related fears, such as fear of escalators and of heights.

As an infant of five months, David developed a severe ear infection and a temperature of 105 degrees, and suffered a resulting seizure. From that time on, his development was noted to be significantly slower than normal. He had difficulty walking, with toilet training, and with learning to identify objects.

School was a disaster; he had to repeat kindergarten. He seemed unable to learn.

According to Mrs. Kim:

His speech was very poor. He wanted to speak but he couldn't get the words out. David would want to relate a particular occurrence in school, but he was unable to make himself understood. He would break it up into pieces and we would receive the information mixed up, i.e., the end of the story first, the first part of the story in the middle, etc. We could not make sense out of what he said, and he would become very frustrated with us because we could not understand him. He wanted so badly to express himself but could not.*

---

*The differences between inner-ear–determined speech symptoms and those of aphasia secondary to cerebral impairment must be clearly distinguished if children such as David are to be properly diagnosed and successfully treated.

David was reexamined by me six months after treatment began. His mother noted that there were definitely significant and dramatic changes present:

Before I could work with David for a week straight about a particular subject. He would have a day or two off from school, and when we returned to the point where we had left off, he would have no recollection of what we had studied together. There was nothing. It was as if his brain had lost everything. It was terrible, but I kept on trying. I had to.

Now David comes home from school, sits on the living-room floor, and begins to do his homework—without any prodding from me. Or he sits down and opens a book to read for a school assignment. Without any problems!

Reevaluation one year later revealed a continuation of David's marked improvement. His speech is now spontaneous, fluent, and in appropriate sequence. He no longer demon-strates significant memory instability for word recall. His pre-viously severe lags in auditory input, speech, and motor output are hardly evident. His mother is delighted that he can con-verse with her about school and social situations in a manner that she never dreamed possible:

His questions reflect a normal, healthy curiosity, but they floor me because they are sensible and intelligent. Previ-ously he was unable to organize his thoughts logically and in sequence. Now he has no problems in relating events; he speaks coherently, logically, and comprehensively—no small miracle!

David's balance and coordination have also significantly improved. He is able to ride a twenty-six-inch bike. He can jump—not too high, but he can jump—something he could not do before. His emotions are steadier and his ability to tolerate stress has improved. His advance has continued despite the separation and divorce of his parents.

What would David's outcome have been had his mother not stood by him and worked with him in a determined and intelligent manner? What would have happened had his mother accepted the school's misdiagnosis that he was retarded, and not sought better understanding and medical help? What happens to millions of dyslexics who are similarly misdiagnosed and go medically untreated and emotionally uncared for?

Autism

Not infrequently, parents of autistic children have requested that I examine them for possible inner-ear dysfunctioning and attempt to treat related dyslexialike symptoms. Although many researchers have reported (inner-ear) cerebellar abnormalities in autistic children, my research, as reported in *A Solution to the Riddle Dyslexia,* clearly differentiates autistic speech and related symptoms from those I've correlated with inner-ear dysfunctioning. Indeed, it seems strange that whereas most traditional experts were reluctant to accept the relatively minor speech and academic symptoms in dyslexia to be of inner-ear origin, these very same researchers did not hesitate to blame the severe aphasic-like speech and related autistic symptoms on a cerebellar basis.

Having studied many thousands of dyslexic children, I

came to see clearly that the symptoms defining the core dyslexic and autistic syndromes are as qualitatively different as night and day. However, since (inner-ear) cerebellar dysfunctioning may, and sometimes does, characterize autism, it seemed reasonable to assume that autism might be viewed as a *mixed* cerebral (CNS) and cerebellar dysfunctioning. Accordingly, I attempted to treat mixed-autistic children with inner-ear–enhancing medications. To date, the numbers treated have been small, and thus the results uncertain.

There have been several cases where the speech, concentration, memory, balance, and coordination functioning mildly improved, but the children always remained clearly autistic. That never changed. Should these results be confirmed in larger studies, they would suggest:

- That autism is clearly not of a primary cerebellar origin, although cerebellar mechanisms may be involved; and
- That a trial of inner-ear–enhancing medications is worth trying in order to relieve some, even if not the major, autistic symptoms.

Pseudo-Autism—a Variation of Pervasive Developmental Delay (PDD) and/or Severe Language Delays

Although PDD is now traditionally considered to fall within the autistic spectrum, my clinical/therapeutic experience suggests otherwise:

- With time, development and both medical and nonmedical therapy, children with PDD having autistic-like communication impairments frequently improve, often to the point where they are then diagnosed as having dyslexia, ADD, OCD, etc.

- By contrast, truly autistic children appear to retain their basic autistic-noncommunication characteristics and diagnosis, regardless of the improvement occurring over time and with most known therapies, recent exceptions possibly aside.

Because of these clinically based observations, I suggest creating a diagnostic category called *pseudo-autism.* These are children who, when younger, appear to have some autistic-like features, yet demonstrate higher cognitive and related communication functioning and manifest a favorable prognosis— often improving with age so that all the autistic-like functioning disappears.

Wayne

Wayne is a nine-year-old referred to me with a diagnosis of autism. During his initial visit, I could not for certain distinguish the presence of true autism versus severe language delay with PDD. However, the presented history, as well as his remarkable language improvement related to medical treatment, suggested he must have been PDD with autistic-like features—a disorder best called *pseudo-autism.*

His mother relates the following background:

Wayne's motor development was on time or early. By 18 months he had not started talking and was hyperactive. . . . He was recognized to have fluid in his ears and draining tubes did initiate mild language development, although his hyperactivity intensified.

By 3½, he was still largely unable to communicate, although my sister's 3 children with similar delays "pulled out of it." On sensory integration therapy, he was found to have vestibular (inner-ear) and tactile deficits—but this only slightly calmed him down.

By 5, he was still severely language impaired but beginning to count and identify the alphabet. After a severe flu with vomiting at age five, we accidentally noted significant improvement in his hyperactivity and some verbal enhancement. This eventually led me to recognize his negative reactions to food allergies. He had also made significant improvements on Benadryl—but our doctor frightened us into stopping it. Significant loss of "developmental improvements" followed.

By 3rd grade, Wayne still had difficulty processing language. However, he was reading on a 3rd grade level with decent comprehension, despite needing his finger to avoid skipping words and sentences. Somehow, he remembers the multiplication facts better than addition and subtraction. And spelling seemed to be a strength. Writing is poor unless he draws his letters.

He is very sensitive to noise; especially affected is his right ear. Concentration is poor, and distractibility is significant. Although he loves sports, his coordination is poor.

Favorable Response to Treatment:

Wayne has made wonderful progress after just 3 months of medical treatment. His language (receptive and expressive) processing has more than doubled in quality and quantity. His speech is clearer, and he uses more words and longer sentences to express himself. And he more rapidly understands what he hears. Concentration is greatly improved and distractibility is all but gone. And his impulsivity is no longer a problem. It used to propel him to do "weird" looking things. Now he no longer acts strange. He can now watch TV for an hour, play complicated games, and no longer seems spacey and out-of-it as before. He can focus his eyes better while listening—something impossible for him before. In other words, he can look, listen, and understand—all at the same time. His coordination is so improved that he can participate in slow-pitch softball: much greater ability to catch, throw, hit, and run. He can shoot baskets and began skateboarding.

In summary, I have successfully treated many cases like Wayne's—and they often rapidly and dramatically improve. However, the treatment responses to true autism resemble those seen in Down's syndrome—where the basic disorder is still clearly recognizable despite diverse and subtle improvements in perception as well as in balance/coordination/concentration, etc.

XVI

A New Beginning

In *Smart but Feeling Dumb,* I have tried to portray the true depth and scope of dyslexia, an inner-ear disorder affecting approximately 20 percent of the world's population according to my research. This book was designed to capture and describe the essence, quality, and meaning of the many and varied symptoms and feelings characterizing and defining this previously misunderstood and oversimplified disorder. I hope it has provided both the layperson and the clinician with the scientific insights needed to better understand, diagnose, and treat dyslexia through a holistic medical/educational/physiological approach.

This book's content and design were inspired by the emotions and energies characterizing the struggle and determination of thousands upon thousands of my dyslexic patients. Their energies have fueled the forces needed for the successful completion and subsequent updating of *Smart but Feeling Dumb,* despite my writing inexperience.

For the sake of millions of suffering dyslexics, I truly hope that I have properly transformed the trust, efforts, and case histories of my patients into a book they can be proud of—a book and effort they well deserve.

Although *Smart but Feeling Dumb* must end, the diagnostic/therapeutic insights derived from this work continue to escalate endlessly.

To highlight—to symbolize—this point, I would like to present the interested reader with "A New Beginning," as experienced and described by two very recently understood and treated adults. It is anticipated that their rapid and dramatic medically based improvements will catalyze a new beginning for millions and millions of dyslexics young and old, who are desperately searching for meaningful understanding and the help needed to attain goals and ambitions not otherwise possible.

Christopher Wayland

Introduction

When Chris initially consulted me, he was noted to be an extremely bright twenty-nine-year-old clerk at the Chicago Stock Exchange—extremely frustrated at "going nowhere." Although he complained primarily of severe difficulties with reading/spelling and concentration/distractibility, he evidenced a majority of the dyslexia-related symptoms described within the Self-Test, page xx.

His rapid and dramatic improvements with medical treatment transformed this gifted and skeptical individual into a successful, happy, and admired stock trader. These "amazing changes" facilitated his rise to occupational/economic success and enabled him to contemplate a major career change that would never before have been possible.

Chris agreed to write and publish this summary of his life before and after medical treatment in order to help others as he was helped. However, for the sake of readers primarily interested in help, I decided to reverse his written sequence—placing "Favorable Responses to Treatment" before his "Background of Special Education Failures." And since it is best to end with a positive note, I decided to footnote this latter negative but important contrasting content so that interested readers might more readily appreciate the depth and degree of frustrations characterizing even gifted dyslexics prior to medical treatment.

In many ways this sharp contrast between Chris's new beginning and his past failures, despite extensive traditionally based tutoring, serves to highlight the vital need for *Smart But Feeling Dumb* and the research that will eventually cure and prevent dyslexia.

Favorable Responses to Medication

"Despite initially feeling a complex mixture of hope and cynicism, the medications and nutrients prescribed for me by Dr. Levinson triggered responses within me that were surprisingly rapid, dramatic and amazing. Until the day I die, I will always regard my visit to Dr. Levinson as one of the biggest milestones in my life: like marriage or seeing your first child born. After initially starting treatment, my life changed incredibly for the better. Although I hoped for even a mild improvement, it was as if I went through a renaissance. I didn't realize what a blur of a life I was living in until after I got better. Very soon after starting medication, I was reading books, admiring architecture I had never before noticed, speaking with friends and family with a new and unanticipated clarity and understanding, while developing a completely new-found self-confidence in all areas of my life.

"At work, I soon became able to think and make decisions at lightning speed—qualities essential for a stock trader. As a result, I rapidly advanced to the highest levels in my field—entering an upper echelon marquee group of traders. For the first time in my life people began to regard my work and actions with a respect and "awe" that embarrassed me.

"When I spoke, the words were formulated and shot out of my mouth instantly and accurately. Suddenly my sentences were describing exactly what I was thinking—a first for me. This resulted in an even greater sense of confidence. I had completely lost the previously embarrassing and humiliating hesitations and word finding pauses (e.g., uuuummm, aaahhh) that usually filled the void between my sentence fragments. My mind and memory became razor sharp—at least compared to the way I functioned before. I can remember being on line at a Wendy's restaurant very soon after starting treatment. And while looking over at a large picture of Dave Thomas, which had The Wendy's Pledge on it, I spontaneously read it from top to bottom without losing my place or having to stop once. This sounds trivial now, but this was the first time in my life reading was so easy and effortless. Before medication, I would have avoided reading Dr. Seuss to a 5-year-old because of my embarrassing reading style—or difficulty. Needless to say, my life feels more complete and I'm so much happier than ever before. Now the floor next to my bed is littered with books of all kinds: Fiction and Nonfiction.

"Within 3 months of medication, I began speed-reading through pages of books I used to get completely bogged down in before. One afternoon at Barnes & Noble, for example, I read an entire book while standing in front of the shelf where I had pulled it from. It just happened! And I wasn't trying to save some cash. It was truly amazing. At night, instead of zoning out watching bad sitcoms, I read for hours on end. I feel a need to catch up for all the many past years I avoided reading. Previously I used to read only a page or two and be forced to put the book down. Hard to believe, but I got through college without ever completing a book—and maybe even a chapter. Now I haven't even felt the need to buy a TV—since I'm busy reading all the time.

"My peripheral vision has also greatly improved. About a month ago I walked into the lobby of a building where I have worked during the past 5 years. And I surprisingly said to myself: 'Wow, what a humongous lobby.' I just never saw its true dimension before—I saw just a 'tunnel.'

"There's also another very important fact to comment on, perhaps the most interesting of all. I've just taken about 10 strokes off my golf game. That was impossible to do before treatment, and completely unexpected. And best of all, I am now making plans to attend graduate school. That's something I would have deemed impossible just three months before I started treatment, although I had always harbored this impossible dream!

"Because of my many improvements and enhanced confidence, I have recently retired from trading and look forward to the next chapter in my life: A life that I feel is wide open to me now, Grad-School, starting my own business . . . ? I feel like I can accomplish whatever I set out to do—no longer fearing failure. Without sounding corny or disingenuous, I feel deeply indebted to Dr. Levinson for the new life I am living today and the new career I will soon begin."

A one-year follow-up—just before publication:

The following additional content was added in order to highlight how medication-based improvements continue to occur over time—even in adults.

Spanish in El Salvador

"About a year ago I went on a trip to El Salvador. I was one of ten people representing my church. I wasn't too familiar with my fellow travelers. Only two of us had a good command of the Spanish language: myself and another woman who has been to Latin America several times. I thought, 'Boy, do I have my work cut out for me.' Although I was a Spanish major in college, it had been nearly 10 years since I had spoken Spanish on a daily basis.

"Upon arriving in El Salvador, we were greeted by members of our sister parish. Suddenly it was as if someone threw a switch: I was speaking almost perfect Spanish. Though some of my verb conjugations were off, my speech and comprehension was better and faster than it had ever been at its best. And my best was at college over 10 years ago.

"During college I had spent roughly 6 months studying in Mexico. At the time I felt I had gained a fairly good command of the language. However, even at that time I was not speaking half as well as the Spanish I was now speaking and comprehending in El Salvador.

"Once again, the only thing I can attribute this incredible change to is my treatment with Dr. Levinson. There is no other explanation I have as to why I would be able to speak and understand Spanish with far greater skill after a 10-year hiatus."

Snowboarding in Colorado

"When I retired from my stock trading career, I didn't want to merely jump into the next phase of my life. I decided to take a few months off to think over the next phase of my life. So I moved to Colorado.

"There isn't much to do in Colorado in winter if you are not skiing or snowboarding. So I decided to take up snowboarding. I was initially very apprehensive since I had tried skiing as a child and failed miserably. As a result, I gave it up at the time after a few lessons.

"However my current experiences with snowboarding in Colorado were as astounding to me as was my recent Spanish speaking abilities in El Salvador. Although I did come down hard on my backside a couple times the first day, by the second day I had the hang of it. My instructor told me I was well ahead of the bell curve for a beginner. Now I have been at snowboarding for a month and I'm 'catching air' (jumping). These are feats I don't think would have been possible prior to treatment."

Ice Skating in New York

"I actually enjoy visiting Dr. Levinson because it gives me a wonderful excuse to see New York—one of the most exciting cities in the world. During this most recent visit, I was encouraged (forced) to go ice-skating with a friend. Once again, as a child I remember falling and thus sitting on the ice most of the time I was supposed to be skating. So I was more than a bit nervous before my Central Park debut. After all, the park was loaded with people; and the 'observation deck' was packed too. Let's face it, what's more fun than watching people 'bite the dust' on a public rink? After my first loop around, which was a bit shaky, I rapidly gained confidence and I blended into the crowd as far as my skating ability was concerned. To be honest, I was no Eric Heiden. However, after my friend and I were done, I realized that I did not fall once. Not once!"

Vocabulary

"In the past year, I have also noticed that my vocabulary has spontaneously increased. Although I may have developed an understanding for more descriptive and intricate words prior to treatment, I never before felt natural and comfortable in my speech patterns. Previously, it was a major chore attempting to express my basic thoughts while concentrating as hard as I could to avoid embarrassing misstatements. As a result, the idea of actually enhancing my speech so that it might sound attractive or eloquent was a foreign concept to me.

"Now, talking is easier—amazingly so. Not only can I express my thoughts infinitely better than before, but I can actually introduce a rhythm or iambic pentameter or initiate strategically placed pauses like some of the amazing speeches given by JFK or MLK."

Summary

How I Got to Dr. Levinson

"I knew I was just as intelligent, if not more so, than others I saw getting ahead in life. Although none of the many experts I saw had ever officially diagnosed me with a learning disability despite numerous tests, I felt otherwise. As a result, I recently began to educate myself on the subject—out of desperation.

"Many books I scanned stated the obvious: People with LD don't do as well in school as others. Wow, what a revelation! Then one day, as if by divine intervention, I came across *Smart But Feeling Dumb* by Dr. Harold Levinson. My hand just sort of reached out and reflexly grabbed this title off the shelf without the cooperation of my head or other hand. This book and its content was like finding a diamond in the rough. Instead of just telling you about the one or two standard learning symptoms, it listed approximately 45 related to ADD/dyslexia; and it claimed that ADD and dyslexia were merely two sides to the same coin.

"Despite my severe difficulties with reading, I devoured this book—especially since the title described the way I inwardly felt. Of the 45 or dyslexia-related symptoms stated, I self-diagnosed myself to have perhaps 40 of them—symptoms I or the many other experts who saw me never even considered part of a learning disability, like anxiety about crossing a street. In the past, I attributed this strange fear to my growing up in the Boston area. As you might know, Boston has the worst drivers outside of the third world or Italy.

"I knew I had to see Dr. Levinson as soon as I finished his book. Not only did his ideas seem logical, he appeared to be the only expert who claimed that medical treatment could reverse the many symptoms of my disorder.

"Before going, every single person I asked told me I was a fool, and that I would soon find out that Dr. Levinson was a snake-oil salesman—a term one of his quoted critics called him. Though my apprehension was great, I flew to New York. (What can I say, I'm a risk taker.) While sitting in Dr. Levinson's parking lot 20 minutes early, I felt nervous as hell and wondered: If this guy turns out to be some sort of motivational salesman or castor-oil practitioner using smoke and charms to release my poison energy, I'll just walk out and cut my losses. I'll just go back to Chicago and suffer the ridicule and 'I told you so' from all my friends and family.

"When I entered the waiting room, it looked no more exciting or typical than that of your average dentist or GP. The staff seemed friendly and levelheaded. And the other patients and families waiting, especially those having been treated, seemed very happy and open about the improvements that had taken place since their first visit. As a result, my fears lessened and I began relaxing a little.

"After hours of testing and a final consultation, I was told by Dr. Levinson that all my primary symptoms were inner-ear/cerebellar determined and that the usual diagnosis was Dyslexia and ADD; and that the prescribed medication and nutrients offered me a 75–85 percent chance of being helped.

"Although elated on the inside, I remained extremely calm. I had to control my relief as well as the dread that I had a 15–25 percent chance of not responding to treatment. Fortunately, 'God's bookies' were right for me!"

A Background of Tutorial Failures

"I remember constantly being told throughout my childhood how bright I was. Not just by my mother and father, but also from their friends and my teachers. However, my scholastic career was anything but stellar. I rarely cracked the C level on report cards throughout grade and middle school.

"Teachers would tell my parents how I didn't apply myself. I took so many Special Tests that I even began to remember the answers from the years before. This would of course skew the Experts' data, further compounding their frustration as well as mine. The result of years of testing proved inconclusive.

"Eventually outside experts were called in since the Andover Public School system washed their hands of me. These new guys reeked of intelligence. They were in the big time Ivy Leagues. They were the most highly trained, highly touted and highly paid experts of them all. Their walls were adorned with so many diplomas and honors you couldn't see what color the walls were. Surely they would have answers to my problems.

"For days these men of great scholarship and their trusty assistants fussed over me with test after test. However, I began to realize their special tests seemed as silly as the previous ones given me by the school experts. After days of trial and error, these outside experts had a eureka moment and an amazing recommendation: I needed remedial classes. Their special custom-made tests wouldn't lie. We were told that once the remedial classes began, all my past problems would be resolved.

"As a result, my parents, being of some means, enrolled me in a private boarding school where special classes would be provided liberally. These classes were taught by special teachers. Just like a big corporation promotes inadequate people in order to keep them away from the machinery of the operation, I believe these special teachers were promoted in order to keep them away from the real students—those expected to go on to greatness at Harvard or Yale. However, these experiences weren't a complete failure. Though the special classes were about as useful to me as a ukulele is to a house cat, the school did provide me with small regular classes and a lot of tutoring.

"Although I never really learned the 3 R's and spelling, I began to master the tricks that would get me through the next 10 years of my school life. The key trick was memorization. I began to teach myself ways to keep large amounts of information in my head and how to regurgitate it onto test answer sheets. As a result, my grades improved, my parents felt vindicated, and my life moved on.

"While attending a small liberal arts college in the Midwest, my powers of memorizing lectures I attended rose to a new level—enabling me to maintain a "B" average throughout my 4 years of higher education. I swear that I never completed more than 1 or 2 reading assignments the entire time.

"Following college I moved to Chicago. After a few jobs in sales, which I failed at entirely, I began to work as a runner for one of the big stock exchanges. Eventually I was hired by a small trading company as a clerk (assistant to the traders): the pace was very fast; I was severely overworked and underpaid. Although superiors felt I was competent, they were not willing to give me a shot at the big intensity high stakes trading. I toiled in this stalemate for years. This was when I was forced to find out for myself what was wrong with me and how to get medical help for my learning disorder."

Joan Sparks*

Flutist Joan Sparks, forty, has enjoyed a career of musical variety which includes solo, chamber music, and orchestra performances throughout the mid-Atlantic region. As an orchestral flutist and piccolo player, Joan has appeared with the Philadelphia Orchestra, Concerto Soloists of Philadelphia, the Delaware Symphony, and the Bethlehem Bach Festival Orchestra. A member of the award-winning flute and harp duo A Deux, she and partner Anne Chaffin tour, record, and present their own series at the Grand Opera House in Wilmington, Delaware. Chamber music credits include concerts with the Grand Chamber Players, the Wilmington Music Festival, and the Mid-Atlantic Chamber Music Society. A solo recitalist, Joan has performed in venues throughout the region. She holds a bachelor's degree in music performance from the University of Delaware and a master of music degree from Temple University. Her doctoral degree from Temple is currently on hold. Major teachers are Murray W. Panitz, who held with distinction the position of principal flute of the Philadelphia Orchestra for twenty-four years before his death in 1989, and Trudy Kane, the principal flutist of the Metropolitan Orchestra in New York City. Joan currently is a faculty member at Immaculata College and maintains a private studio as well. She makes her home in Wilmington, Delaware, where she lives with her husband and two children.

Joan wrote a log of her diagnosis and treatment of dyslexia. Here is her story in her own words:

"Two months ago, I was diagnosed by Dr. Levinson as

---

*Taken from a presentation in *A Scientific Watergate—Dyslexia*.

dyslexic, and I began the program of medications and vitamins that he prescribed. The change has been and continues to be profound. I have kept a record of each medicine and its effect as they were added to my daily routine. Each addition or increase in medication had a specific effect, and thus continue in combination to have a cumulative positive improvement. The following is a summary of my experience as a patient of Dr. Levinson."

July 1, 1992 Appointment with Dr. Levinson. Took part in a blind study in which I was given a pill and was told that it was either a placebo or an antihistamine. About 20 minutes later, I went into the Ladies' Room and noticed that the floor tiles were not in motion as they had been earlier in the day. As I later learned, I had been given the antihistamine.

July 2 Began first medication, an antiemetic, antihistamine. I began, as with all medications prescribed by Dr. Levinson, with one quarter of a tablet. I noticed the next morning as I did my usual three-mile walk/run, that the objects around me did not bounce around as much with every step. I felt as if I were in a movie, since all of the things around me (trees, houses, the roadway, etc.) now moved smoothly and in a controlled manner. As I increased the dosage, the effect continued to increase, until I had a still horizon at all times. Until this point (as in the case with all the other medications) I had no idea that this was part of being dyslexic. The other benefit of this first medication is that I am no longer dizzy after exercising (I run and swim).

July 12 Began the vitamins. No significant improvement

noticed at first. After two months, I find that my hair, skin, and nails are healthier.

July 30 Began the antidepressant. Immediately my peripheral vision was more in focus. I could see in stereo; objects had depth. I could look at a tree in the distance and see definition in the leaf and branch formations. I could also see depth in the leaves and branches. In general, all objects as well as my depth perception began to take on more clarity. I began to write more neatly without trying, and I wrote in a straighter line. Perhaps the most surprising event was the first time I went to the grocery store. I again experienced the phenomenon that the objects around me moved when I did, and in an orderly manner; I felt as if I was gliding down the aisles (I had previously hated to grocery shop and only went in desperation). The objects I wanted were where I expected them to be. I left the grocery store and realized that I was not dizzy and confused as I had always been before. Later that day as I was balancing the check book I again realized that I was not tense, dizzy, and confused as I always had been in the past when working with numbers.

As time went on, I noticed an improvement in my night vision. The lettering on directional signs was no longer blurred out, but was clear and crisp. Street lights and the headlights of oncoming cars no longer had halos around them. I found that I would work at the PC longer, without tension, and the words were much more quiet on the screen. In general any information that was acquired through reading, whether words or music, was more available, my eyes were tracking better than before: better than when I had worn Irlen lenses, or after the two courses of vision therapy I had taken in previous years.

August 7 Driving to Maine. My personal panorama became larger and more well-defined. As I read road signs, I could feel my left eye begin to cross over, and then snap back into place. The left eye always crossed when I concentrated on an object. (It also was nearsighted, and I have noticed that it is much less nearsighted, with the improvement dating from the addition of the antidepressant.) The guardrail supports did not blur out as they had before. I realized that I had always avoided looking at them because the blurring out would make me uncomfortable. The same was true with the lane dividing lines, when they were on new, black pavement, and were newly painted. I began to not have to squint any more to focus on the road, signs, or anything else I needed to read. Words were clear, and it took much less effort to take them in.

One day, while on vacation, I forgot to take my afternoon dosage of medicine and vitamins. The next morning I got up early to go and buy donuts as a special treat for the kids. This meant a drive of six miles. As I drove, I realized that I was gripping the steering wheel tightly, and was feeling anxious about where I was going. I have been vacationing at the same spot once a year for eighteen years now. The trip to Congdon's Donut Shop was a ritual. As I drove into the lane back to the house (with the requisite dozen donuts of various flavors) after nearly turning down the wrong lane (there are two close together off of the county road), I realized that I had not taken my medicine the previous afternoon. This was how I had felt all the time prior to July 2. I took the morning dosage, and within a half an hour, I again felt the improvements I had come to enjoy.

August 11 Began the next vitamin. No noticeable change.

August 21 Took my seven-year-old son Christopher to see Dr. Levinson. I had long suspected that Christopher and I shared similar perceptual problems. After my diagnosis, I realized that the best thing to do for Christopher was to have his problems diagnosed early. This is his first grade year, the year he learns to read, and especially important. As it turned out, my instinct was correct. Christopher is beginning the same medication regimen as I. One incident at the appointment was particularly poignant. Christopher and I were in the nurse's office, waiting to be briefed on the routine. We were given release forms to sign, giving consent to make data available to Dr. Levinson from Christopher's appointment. As I pointed to the three lines for his signature, Christopher said, "Mom, you'll have to show me each one, one at a time. The letters and lines are bouncing around so much I can't tell where you said to put my name." I replied, "You know, I was just remembering the first time I was here. The lines and letters were bouncing around for me then, too. But today, since I've been taking the medicine Dr. Levinson told me to take, the letters are still." He said, "*That's* why I'm here!"

August 22 Began the final addition to my regimen, which is another antiemetic and antihistamine. To my astonishment, I see even more clearly. Now the letters on any page are entirely still. I had feared that even with Dr. Levinson's prescription, words would never be entirely still on the page. They are now. In fact, information is now not only more available, it is aggressive. It is with amazement that I now see words pop out at me, with ease and clarity. My peripheral panorama is greater than ever before. The periphery of my vision is organized, no longer chaotic. I find I can

look with comfort at things I had always avoided, such as
the computer screen; plaid, houndstooth check, or striped
patterns on clothing and furniture; Oriental rugs; certain
floor tile patterns; escalator steps; and most important to
me, music.

I have not mentioned other sensory improvements, because in some ways these improvements are more subtle.
The improvement in my hearing is most important to me as
a professional musician. I have always had a good ear: My
sense of pitch is often called "perfect pitch," and even
though it could be capricious, it still could hold me in good
stead, especially when sight-reading (which for obvious reasons had always been the area of most concern for me). Since
I have been taking the program prescribed by Dr. Levinson,
I have noticed a far greater acuity in my hearing. I can now
hear three- and four-part counterpoint as all four voices
moving at once. Before, I had always been forced to segre-
gate one voice and follow it. In fact, I had to make a firm
rule for myself at the time of the final medication addition:
I could not listen to classical music on the car stereo, because
it was so beautiful and so clear, and too distracting. I have
been enjoying a tremendous improvement in reading music
in general. My eyes track the notes clearly at fast tempi. The
notes no longer blur out. My sense of rhythm is better.
Complicated rhythmic patterns come more quickly. I no
longer need to constantly check patterns of musical notes, or
even repeated notes, because they stay put. They are where I
remember them to be. The same sense of depth and stereo I
have visually is improved aurally as well. I hear, with greater
distinction, fast technical passages when I or others play
them. I can hear the quality of chords, and identify them.

There are improvements in terms of tactile facility. Certain musical technical passages and trills which were always particularly difficult for me are easier to learn and retain.

In general, I seem not to have to make the extra effort it always took to do any of the tasks that involve analytical use of my senses. As mentioned earlier, information is now not only more available, it is aggressive. As a consequence, I no longer feel mentally numb at the end of the day, or even at mid-day. I can read for longer periods of time, and retain more of what I read. I skip lines much less when I read, and can find my place readily when I look away from the page. My memory is better. I have noticed improvement in such things as remembering a phone number after seeing it only once, or remembering people's names. I spell better. Background noise is not as distracting. I don't have to take time to process what I have heard in order to respond, so that now I can come up with witty repartee, and fast answers in meetings and discussions. I enjoy conversation with groups of people much more. I can process others' words and respond with a speed that was previously unknown to me. Finally, I am writing this at my PC, typing without looking down at the keyboard. This is a first for me.

There are some considerations that need to be mentioned, not necessarily as negative, but in terms of cautions. I have learned to eat a much larger breakfast, and have had to incorporate a 3:00 snack into my schedule. I did gain about five pounds at first, but now that I have adjusted to a new (and healthier) pattern of eating, I have lost it. I cannot drink alcohol with the same abandon as before. One glass of wine is about it at social occasions. One glass has the effect of three. I also notice fatigue, in terms of not enough sleep, and have had to be more careful to approach an eight-hour sleep schedule. I cannot let myself become too hungry. The one symptom that prevails when I am not cautious of the above-mentioned items is that I feel groggy, and have the sense that I am indeed taking medications. Otherwise, I have no sensation that I am taking anything other than vitamins.

Yesterday, I took an audition for the first time since starting Dr. Levinson's program. I took the audition for the sole purpose of determining how well my visual acuity would stand up under pressure. I purposely chose one of the most difficult concertos in the repertoire and prepared the orchestral excerpts at a faster tempo than is required. In the morning, as I drove west on the Pennsylvania Turnpike, and as the adrenaline started to kick in, I noticed that the landscape was clear and sharply defined. Before the medication, my peripheral vision would become even more chaotic with nerves. This time the periphery was clearer than earlier in the day, and more available. The highway divider supports were absolutely distinct and not blurred out, and I read words on highway signs clearly. As I warmed up before the audition, I could, clearly and with control, track the music, without experiencing the blurring out that had always happened when I was nervous. I went into the audition, and during the playing of the concerto, realized that I was more nervous than I needed to be. I saw everything. It was there on the page. All I had to do was play. As the audition progressed, I was able to let go of the nervousness, and achieve a greater degree of control than I ever had before, allowing me to finesse such things as speed and amplitude of vibrato, the tonguing patterns I was using, and the loudness of my breathing. I "nailed" each one of the treacherous orchestral excerpts, for the first time, using an assertiveness I had never attained before.

In conclusion, the most important and least understood aspect of dyslexia is its subtlety, and myriad effects. I had considered my collection of symptoms little more than charming (and not-so-charming) idiosyncracies. The range and depth of the improvement has indicated to me that dyslexia is a disorder that impacts the dyslexic to a greater degree than even the dyslexic can comprehend. I am grateful that my son, with all his talent and intelligence, will be able to assume his role in society (and he will be a person who will make a contribution) without the struggle to simply keep up. He will be able to realize his full potential, which is his, and every child's, right.

Appendix A

Medications and Related Chemicals in the Treatment of Dyslexia

This section about the medications used for the successful treatment of dyslexia and related inner-ear–determined disorders has been purposely separated from the patient responses and text to emphasize a major point that cannot be sufficiently stressed: *No one should treat him- or herself, regardless of whether medications are judged harmless and regardless of whether medications can be bought without a physician's prescription!*

Therefore, *for those physicians* who may be consulted by patients who have completed this book, I will list the various chemical structures that I used in clinically determined doses and combinations during the past thirty-five years in treating dyslexics, phobics, and various other behavioral, emotional, and "psychosomatic" disorders of inner-ear or cerebellar-vestibular origin.

Helpful Medications for Dyslexia and/or Related Inner-Ear–Determined Disorders

Chemical Name	Brand Name
Meclizine hydrochloride	Antivert
Cyclizine hydrochloride or lactate	Marezine
Dimenhydrinate	Dramamine
Diphenhydramine hydrochloride	Benadryl
Promethazine	Phenergan
Scopolomine	Transderm-Scop
Hydroxyzine hydrochloride	Ataraz
Methylphenidate hydrochloride	Ritalin
Dextroamphetamine sulfate	Dexedrine
Pemoline	Cylert
Pseudoephedrine hydrochloride	Sudafed
Imipramine hydrochloride	Tofranil
Amitriptyline hydrochloride	Elavil
Brompheniramine maleate Phenylephrine hydrochloride Phenylpropanolamine hydrochloride }	Dimetapp
Chlorpheniramine maleate	Chlor-Trimeton
Ergoloid mesylate	Hydergine
Deanol acetamidobenzoate	Deaner

Vitamin B complex
Ginger root
Niacin
B_6
B_{12}
Lecithin or choline

Additional Helpful Drugs

Over the past fifteen years, I have become increasingly aware of a great many other inner-ear–enhancing drugs—antihistamines, antidepressants, antianxiety or antipanic agents, including B-blockers and Dilantin, an anticonvulsant—which have had beneficial effects on inner-ear problems. Some are most useful for anxiety disorders, others for ADD or ADHD, others for mood or depressive disorders, others for vertigo, and so on. And some should only be used on adults. But all have triggered improvements in overlapping syndromes!

Accordingly, I will list them by general category—including *Piracetam,* a European drug shown helpful in minimizing the reading, speech, and memory functions in dyslexia. Interestingly, upon researching this drug, I found it to be an antivertigo agent as well.

Piracetam—Nootrophil

B-blockers:

Tenormin	atenolol
Inderal	propanolol

Antipanic and Antianxiety Agents:

Ativan	lorazepam
Valium	diazepam
Librium	chlordiazepoxide
Xanax	alprazolam HCl
Miltown	meprobamate

...depressants and Related Antianxiety Drugs:

Norpramin	desipramine HCl
Pamelor	nortriptyline HCl
Prozac	fluoxetine HCl
Sinequan	doxepin HCl
Wellbutrin	bupropion HCl

Stimulants:

Caffeine	——
Desoxyn	methamphetamine HCl

Anticonvulsants:

Dilantin	phenytoin sodium
Clonidine	——

Antihistamines:

Seldane	terfenadine
Tavist	clemastine fumarate

It is important to note that favorable medication responses are chemically specific. And although the medications listed above are those triggering the greatest frequency of positive responses, I have personally observed (or have been told about) improvements from just about every medication known to characterize each of the major drug groups: antihistamines, stimulants, antidepressants, antianxiety agents—including the antipanics, B-blocker drugs, and so on.

Physicians and interested clinicians may further benefit from the chapters on medication in my scientific text *A Solution to the Riddle Dyslexia* and from a recently completed study, "Dramatic Favorable Responses of Children with Learning Disabilities or Dyslexia and Attention Deficit Disorder to Antimotion Sickness Medications: Four Case Reports" (1991).

Some of these medications were initially used because of theoretical considerations. However, clinical experience with thousands of patients over many years led me to the use of some additional substances I initially overlooked. Existing theory is often insufficient to predict a totally holistic chemical treatment plan.

Thus, for example, patient A or her parent noted learning difficulties beginning only when allergy treatment with medication X was stopped. In retrospect, it became clear that antihistamine X had unexpectedly enabled patient A to compensate for her dyslexic disorder until allergy treatment stopped (the patient had been on antihistamines for a severe allergic disorder from age two to eight). This case clearly highlights the fact that the early use of medications may be helpful in preventing the dyslexic symptomatic fallout.

I eventually came to realize that although antihistamine X was sold by a drug company as an antihistamine, the same medication might also have anti–motion sickness potency and thus could be effective for treating inner-ear disturbances. I then began testing similar antihistamines on cases not responding to the typical anti–motion sickness medications with which I initially became familiar.

Patient B or his parent spontaneously noted that certain vitamins recommended by his pediatrician seemed to increase concentration and even improve hyperactivity. I became familiar with this effect and began to use it to my patients' advantage.

Another patient, C, researched various chemical substances tending to increase memory, concentration, and hyperactivity. Thus, I became familiar with those chemicals, such as Hydergine.

A colleague reported to me that one of his depressed patients on antidepressants suddenly noted an improvement in his reading ability. As a result, I concluded that certain antidepressants may work in a fashion similar to the stimulants used by psychiatrists to treat activity and concentration disorders, ADD, and ADHD. I also realized that many of the typical antidepressants had been reported to help with phobias, behavioral disorders, and bed-wetting. And fairly recently, a wide variety of stimulants and antidepressants were shown to have anti–motion sickness potential, and thus might be considered to be inner-ear enhancers (Kohl, Calkins, and Mendell, 1986).

Inasmuch as many individuals suffering from phobias, bed-wetting, behavioral disorders, and depression also suffer from dyslexia, it became reasonable to use antidepressants and antianxiety or antipanic drugs for dyslexic or inner-ear–determined symptoms and evaluate their responses, especially when patients did not respond favorably to my more "traditional" pharmaceutical agents and since Valium was reported to help vertigo.

Parents frequently reported that sugars and dyes produced hyperactivity and distractibility in their children. As a result, I advised parents to use a specific variation of the Feingold diet and avoid *only* those dyes having an adverse effect. Any substance triggering regression was to be avoided.

I hope that the above examples will enable the reader to better understand how the list of medications and chemical substances evolved and how my treatment results increased from 50 percent effective to 75 to 80 percent effective. The crucial factor in developing a successful treatment method for dyslexics has been my ability to listen seriously to what parents and patients tell me. Unfortunately, clinicians often sidestep the remarks of parents and patients, judging them as biased and failing to recognize their own biases and the resulting devastating consequences.

Appendix B

Responses to Medication

Reading Activity

Increased spontaneous reading activity

Diminished dysmetric tracking and finger pointing

Improved fixation ability

Improved foreground-background differentiation (i.e., decreased blurring and increase in degree of letter blackness)

Decreased or eliminated reading reversals

Increased reading speed and accuracy

Increased interest in reading

Writing Activity

Increased spontaneous writing activity

Smoother rhythm and increased legibility

Improved spacing between letters and words

Increased horizontality in writing

Increased use of cursive writing (printing usually easier)

Decreased writing reversals

Increased use of grammatical details (such as periods, commas, etc.)

Increased writing speed

Increased word content

Decreased number of spelling errors

Spelling

Increased spelling recall and decreased letter reversals (insertion and omissions)

Arithmetic

Increased mechanical alignment

Increased memory for calculations

Directionality, Spatial Organization, and Planning

Increased right-left differentiation

Decreased rotations

Increased detail in drawing

Improvements in figure drawings

Improved spacing in writing

Improved relationships to spatial coordination tasks (such as ball playing, catching, throwing, batting, etc.)

Increased ability to tie shoelaces, etc.

Balance and Coordination

Increased ability to ride a bike, dribble a basketball, etc.

Decreased clumsiness (such as tripping, falling, and various pastpointing and prepointing activities)

Increased feeling of internal steadiness

Foreground-Background Activity (Sensory)

Increased foreground clarity

Improved background suppression of irrelevant and distracting events (such as visual, acoustic, etc.)
Decreased acoustical blurring and scrambling

Speech

Increased spontaneity of speech
Decreased slurring, where present
Increased rate and improved rhythm of speech
Increased verbal content
Decreased stuttering, stammering, and hesitations

Sequence Activity and Memory

Increase in sequence memory (such as days of the week, months of the year, spelling, multiplication, etc.)

Time Sense

Increased sense of time and time sequences

Concentration and State of Consciousness

Improved and increased clarity of consciousness and associated improvement in memory

Mood

Improved and increased stability of mood

Self-Image

Decreased feelings of inferiority and stupidity
Decreased defensive attitude
Increased self-assertiveness
Increased positive attitude

Body Image

Improved, as reflected in *Goodenough* figure drawings, and generalized sensorimotor activity

Improved visual, acoustic, tactile, temperature, olfactory, and proprioceptive modulation

Frustration Tolerance
Increased frustration tolerance
Increased concentration and attention span

Anxiety Tolerance
Increased anxiety tolerance

Socialization
Increased and improved socialization, especially with peers

Acceptance of Symptoms
Decreased denial
Increased ability to tackle, understand, and accept symptoms
Increased ability to ask questions spontaneously

Dysmetric Dyslexic and Dyspraxic Phobias, Inhibitions, Counterphobias, Characterological Development
Improved

Appendix C

Otto Fenichel on Phobias

Compare my reasoning and proposed mechanisms to account for phobias with the following ones described by Otto Fenichel:

Fear of high places later may be replaced by the conversion symptom of getting dizzy spells when looking down from high places. This symptom is physical expression of a mental anticipation of actual falling. . . .

Fears of falling, of heights, car and railway phobias, show at first glance that they are developed in an attempt to fight pleasurable sensations connected with equilibrium stimulation. . . .

Phobias of vehicles, rooted in the warding off of erogenous sensations of equilibrium and space, have definite relations to the somatic disease of seasickness. The vegetative excitements aroused by equilibrium sensations in a purely physical way have a distinct similarity to sensations of anxiety, and these excitements may have become associatively connected with "too much sexual excitation" in childhood. Neurosis and seasickness, then, may influence each other. Persons with claustrophobia and similar neuroses probably tend more toward the development of seasickness; and an occasional seasickness in a hitherto nonneurotic person may mobilize infantile anxieties and have the effect of a trauma reactivating the memory of a primal scene. There are also conversion hysterias which are an elaboration of vehicle phobias in the sense that vomiting or dizziness, as a physical anticipation of feared equilibrium sensations, may have supplanted the anxiety.*

*Otto Fenichel, *The Psychoanalytic Theory of Neurosis,* New York: W. W. Norton, 1945, pp. 197, 202–203.

Appendix D

Criticism and Its Analysis

General Considerations

Positive responses to my research abound. Critics, however, have argued that my concepts are too simple to be true, too complicated to be understood, unproven by independent observers, and incompatible with the cortical theories of dyslexia. . . . My clinical research designs in evaluating the effects of medication on dyslexics have also been criticized for lacking "double-blind" controls.

Although I feel that any reader who has completed *A Solution to the Riddle Dyslexia* and *Smart but Feeling Dumb* is sufficiently educated to answer these critics and even analyze their motives, these critics deserve a more personal response.

My concepts are neither too simplistic nor too complicated. They are merely realistic. All of my concepts were derived from and are consistent with the analyses of more than 35,000 dyslexic cases. All of my concepts are in harmony with:

- The known and updated physiology of neurological and mental science
- The instincts, feelings, and symptoms of *all* dyslexics
- The experience of *all* educators and clinicians who have taken the time and effort to speak meaningfully to and examine dyslexic patients
- The data of all scientists who have attempted to duplicate my results—and many have
- The observations of all scientists, clinicians, educators, and patients who have come to my Medical Dyslexic Treatment Center or followed and tested my successfully treated patients.

General Neurophysiologic or Diagnostic Considerations

In fact, *all* of my neurological and physiological inner-ear clinical findings were *independently* confirmed by renowned neurological and ear, nose, and throat physicians and scientists in a "blind" and thus thoroughly unbiased fashion. It is interesting to note that the very same neurologists who examined my dyslexic patients found and reported inner-ear–related signs and symptoms 96 percent of the time. Their findings are of special significance, because these neurologists were, and probably still are, of the belief that dyslexia is of cortical origin—despite the *complete statistical absence* of cortical findings in their case reports and the rather high (96 percent) incidence of inner-ear–system signs and symptoms. (Refer to Chapter XV.)

In personal correspondence, Drs. Christine G. Kuipers and Cornelis Weggelaar, Bureau Dijkveld, The Hague, The Netherlands, state, "We wish to thank you for your most interesting book on dyslexia. We did some experiments with an improvised form of your blurring-speed device. The results seem to confirm yours, so we intend to perfect our apparatus. . . ."

Also, George Pavlidis, in a paper entitled "Do Eye Movements Hold the Key to Dyslexia?"* states:

> Dyslexics have been found to exhibit during reading erratic eye movement (EM) patterns and characteristics, which are different from those of all other readers. The present study shows the dyslexics' erratic EMs are present not only in reading but also in the simple sequential task of trying to follow light sources, each of which is illuminated sequentially. These results could manifest a central malfunction in dyslexics, namely sequential disability and/or oculomotor malfunction.

Similar eye-movement disturbances were reported earlier by Zangwill and Blakemore.**

Additionally, Fawcett and Nicolson (1992) confirmed a balance impairment in dyslexics and proposed an "automatization deficit" identical to my inner-ear theory. Leiner, Leiner, and Dow (1991) presented an array of *independent* data clearly and definitively indicating that the cerebellum plays a key role not only in the acquisition of motor skills as traditionally known, but also in the development of computing, cognitive, and language skills.

---

*George T. Pavlidis, "Do Eye Movements Hold the Key to Dyslexia?" *Neuropsychologia* 19 (1981), pp. 57–64.
**O. L. Zangwill and C. Blakemore, "Dyslexia: Reversal of Eye Movements During Reading," *Neuropsychologia* 10 (1972), pp. 371–73.

Rodolfo Llinas, following a personal and scientific review (1989) of my concepts indicating a cerebellar-vestibular–determined spatial-temporal sensorimotor dysfunction in dyslexia, gave a lecture before the Rodin Remediation Academy and the New York Academy of Sciences (1992) entitled "Cerebellar Involvement in Temporal Sensory-Motor Processing: Relevance for Speech, Reading, and Writing."

Professor Kohen-Raz and I have jointly confirmed, via his ataxiometry (balance) methods, that there exists a clear cerebellar-vestibular (CV)–determined balance impairment in dyslexics versus controls, that this balance impairment correlates significantly with diagnostic CV neurological signs, and that compensatory ocular fixation and tracking mechanisms may be triggered.

A cerebellar-determined ocular fixation instability was confirmed in dyslexia by Raymond, Fagan, and Kaplan (1986) after Fagan visited the Medical Dyslexic Treatment Center and modeled his testing after parameters used in the 3-D Optical Scanner.

Fagan and associates showed improved ocular fixation and balance on meclizine in "The Failure of Antimotion Sickness Medication to Improve Reading in Developmental Dyslexia: Results of a Randomized Trial" (1988). But they paradoxically concluded that this medication did not help reading scores or other related dyslexic symptoms. In other words, these authors equated the disorder called dyslexia with its severe reading score symptom, also called "dyslexia." And so the medication was shown to help dyslexics but not their "dyslexia."

Unfortunately, this study was not only double blind, it was *triple blind*. In other words, Fagan and fellow researchers completely failed to properly read and understand the pitfalls characterizing (1) the traditional concepts of dyslexia, and (2) poorly designed and implemented pharmacological studies. For details, refer to my research paper, "Dramatic Favorable Responses of Children with Learning Disabilities or Dyslexia and Attention Deficit Disorder to Antimotion Sickness Medications: Four Case Reports" and the following section.

General Medical—Therapeutic Considerations

Do not these findings lend support to my method of diagnosis?

I did not publish "double-blind" studies—sugar versus "real" pills—in my medication studies. As stated earlier in this text, the dyslexic patients' responses to medications were so dramatic and so unexpectedly diverse, it seemed senseless to waste patients' time and suffering on sugar pills.

If only one of approximately five or six medications helped any one dyslexic patient, and if the symptoms returned when the medications were stopped or given in too low or too high doses, and if the therapeutic effect was found to be independent of the pill's color, shape, or size or the expectations of patient, parent, and clinician, then it seemed reasonable to correlate my 75- to 80-percent improvement rate with a *real* medication effect despite my not using double-blind studies. Moreover, sugar pills or placebos do not result in such dramatic long-lasting improvements 75 to 80 percent of the time.

Most frequently, the pattern of responses obtained from patients was:

- Unanticipated by patient, parent, or researcher: Improvements occurred in areas not previously known or thought of as symptoms to patients. Thus, for example, patients frequently stated: "The print is so much sharper now. I never realized my vision was blurry. My headaches and light-headedness [or fogginess] are gone. I thought that was the way everyone felt."

- Contrary to expectation: Individuals desiring academic improvement were disappointed to find only positive balance, coordination, and related physical changes, and the reverse.

Every physician must at some point decide whether or not a specific medication is working on a given patient. Most often this decision is based on two crucial facts:

- What the patient says, how the patient feels, and the observations of friends and family members
- One's own clinical assessment, especially where laboratory data are not available for decision-making purposes.

How do physicians know if the medication they are using on any given patient is *really* working or not? Can they really distinguish "real" from "fake" or imaginary improvements? Do physicians perform double-blind studies—using sugar versus "real" pills—on each patient before making vital decisions about medication selection, dose changes, and/or medication changes when either *no* effects or side effects occur?

The answer to all of these questions is obvious: no!

Even if the medications used by physicians were initially subjected to double-blind studies, how does one really know if a "real" or "sugar" effect is currently working on any given patient?

One doesn't!

In the final analysis a physician's clinical judgment and assessment of all available data is what counts in his therapeutic decision making. This judgment is either *sound* or *not sound* and is independent of whether blind studies were performed years before the drug was marketed.

The majority of drugs I use are known to improve inner-ear–related symptoms: vertigo, dizziness, imbalance, motion sickness, concentration, and so on. In fact, double-blind studies proved most of these drugs effective in helping these inner-ear–related symptoms long before I and many of my colleagues began using them.

Should I have begun my medication research by reinventing the wheel? Should I therefore have begun giving my inner-ear–dysfunctioning dyslexic patients sugar pills as well as "real" pills, waited three months to retest them, tried another double-blind trial if the first one did not work, and then waited another three months to retest them all over again—even before I knew clinically whether the medications helped such inner-ear–related dyslexic symptoms as reading, writing, and spelling?

Once I knew the medications helped dyslexics, and witnessed responses similar to those you have read, should I have conducted "real" versus sugar medication trials, or should I have attempted to treat as many patients as possible, as rapidly and effectively as possible? Should I have wasted three to twelve months of a dyslexic child's life merely to "prove" what I already knew—merely to avoid criticism?

I leave it to the reader to decide.

More and more clinically minded researchers share my point of view: Often, but not always, clinical medication trials are easier and thus more rapidly and efficiently conducted. And most important, one can zero in on positive and negative medication effects; crucial insights are thus more readily seen and heard. Double-blind studies are often most helpful when the data obtained from clinical trials are uncertain.

For double-blind studies to be performed accurately, scientifically, one really must know:

- How to measure the anticipated clinical responses
- The doses and their variations needed to obtain a clinical response, if one is to happen
- That patients will respond to only one of approximately five to ten medications, suggesting that the study use sequentially but "blindly" chosen chemical groupings where responses are initially negative
- That school grades do not invariably reflect improvement, that is, many improved individuals obtain the same grades with significantly less effort
- That any one or group of the fifteen categories of functioning may improve on any given medication; therefore, *all* these variables should be measured, not just reading or writing variables

For me to have jumped into double-blind studies initially would have been a significant mistake. And I believe the same is true for all researchers who "blindly" perform traditional procedures like robots rather than like scientists.

Summary

Inasmuch as my research efforts have been:

- The first to portray truly the scope and panorama of the various symptoms and signs characterizing dyslexia
- The first leading to a successful *medical* means of accurate diagnosis, prediction, treatment, and even prevention for a disorder that completely eluded all prior traditional medical approaches
- The first to recognize that phobias and related emotional, behavioral, "psychosomatic," social, and Asperger symptoms may be due to the same inner-ear dysfunction creating the dyslexic symptomatic fallout
- The first to recognize the concepts of *acquired* and *mixed* dyslexia, and thus enable the mentally retarded, cerebral-palsied, deaf, and other disabled individuals to be successfully treated for their dyslexic disorders
- The first to lead to a medically based understanding of successful educational techniques, and the first to create such techniques
- The first to explain holistically and encompass *all* other theories and methods of successful treatment

it seems reasonable to ask my critics a few questions:

- If indeed my research efforts have succeeded, whereas so-called traditionally accepted techniques have led *only* to scientific confusion and failure, is it not possible that there may be something wrong with "traditional" methods and techniques as they have been—and are yet being—practiced?

- Have not traditional assumptions and techniques created a dyslexic riddle in which "parallels intersect and straight lines form loops"?

I challenge my critics:

- Find me another text, scientific or popular, that can match or exceed the insights and therapeutic responses provided by my patients in *Smart but Feeling Dumb* or in my medical textbook, *A Solution to the Riddle Dyslexia*!
- Reassess the motivation for your criticism!
- For the sake of *all* dyslexics, carefully read and observe my research and duplicate it!
- Suspend judgment until you have spoken to, analyzed, diagnosed, and similarly treated thousands of dyslexics or as many dyslexics as it takes to form a sound, realistic conclusion!

Denial of Cerebellar Data

As stated in my "A 2003 Dyslexia Update" (see page 1) and detailed in *A Solution to the Riddle Dyslexia,* Chapter XIII, Drs. Sidney Carter and Arnold Gold, professors of neurology and pediatrics at Columbia Presbyterian Hospital, The Neurological Institute, New York City, eventually examined twenty-two dyslexic cases sent them in 1968–73 "blindly"—that is, without any knowledge that they were participating in a study that was eventually published by Dr. Jan Frank (1973) and me.

And an analysis of their "blindly" reported neurological findings confirmed:

- That 96 percent, or twenty of twenty-two, dyslexics had signs and symptoms diagnostic of, or consistent with, a cerebellar-vestibular (inner-ear) dysfunction or deficit
- That *none* had hard and fast neurological signs of a cerebral deficit; and
- That nearly 90 percent (fourteen of sixteen) of the dyslexics examined by Dr. Gold were stated by him specifically to have "cerebellar deficits"

Accordingly, these and other data "blindly" reported by special electronystagmography (ENG) clearly, definitively, and independently confirmed that dyslexia was related to, and most probably due to, a cerebellar deficit.*

The Denial

There was only one problem: Drs. Carter and Gold later denied having found these signs—both publicly and privately—to other "critics" espousing century-old theoretical views: . . . Dr. Carter told *Infectious Diseases,* "Both Dr. Gold and I doubt that we interpret our findings as being consistent with cerebellar deficit." He went on to say, "the concept of cerebellar-vestibular dysfunction in dyslexic children is foreign to us, and we do not understand the Frank-Levinson hypothesis" (*Infec-*

*This chapter is dedicated to two outstanding *New York Times* reporters, William Broad and Nicholas Wade. Their brilliant book *Betrayers of the Truth: Fraud and Deceit in the Halls of Science* is a must for all those really dedicated to helping mankind—rather than themselves.

tious Diseases, vol. 4, no. 7, July 1974, p. 15). Drs. Gold and Carter refused to explain their "denial" when contacted by phone or in writing. Why? Perhaps my answer is too simple: to preserve the status quo, and protect their own research "territory."

Analysis of the Cerebellar Signs: Qualitative and Quantitative

Before continuing with the "cerebellar denials," the reader deserves a clear and factual presentation of these hotly disputed cerebellar data so that he or she might objectively judge this presentation.

In fourteen of sixteen patients he examined, Dr. Gold reported findings similar to the following report on a particular patient (from a letter):

> There was a deficient cerebellar deficit that was manifested by a mild finger-nose-finger dysmetria and a moderate impairment of rapid alternating movement. Catching, throwing, and kicking were poorly performed.

And despite the presence of only cerebellar neurological findings, Dr. Gold characteristically diagnosed "minimal cerebral dysfunction" without any hard and fast neurological evidence of cerebral dysfunction.

I provide a detailed quantitative analysis of my findings and the findings of Drs. Carter and Gold in my book *A Solution to the Riddle Dyslexia.* An in-depth presentation of the controversy surrounding my research, and my critics' attacks on my work, is found in my book *A Scientific Watergate—Dyslexia.*

The Orton Dyslexia Society finally sponsored a meeting to resolve and "objectively" review all the data used to postulate that dyslexia was of cerebellar-vestibular (inner-ear) origin and to resolve any possible confusion created by conflicting reports of Drs. Gold and Carter. There were, however, a number of serious problems with the setup, discussed in Chapter XIII of *A Solution to the Riddle Dyslexia.*

The denial by the traditionalists of both recent and past neurophysiological advances in cerebellar functioning has not prevented some advances in research.

In their landmark research paper entitled, "The Human Cerebro-Cerebellar System: Its Computing, Cognitive, and Language Skills" (1991), neuroscientists Leiner, Leiner, and Dow summarize a vast array of evidence leading them to conclude (emphasis added):

> The role of the cerebellum in these [cognitive and language] human functions has tended to be obscured by the *traditional preoccupation* with the motor functions of the cerebellum which have been widely observed in other vertebrates as well . . . Anatomical evidence and behavioral evidence combine to suggest that *this enlarged cerebellum (in the human brain) contributes not only to motor function but also to some sensory, cognitive, linguistic, and emotional aspects of behavior.*

And although my critics find *A Solution to the Riddle Dyslexia* "dangerous" and claim it presents no supporting research, it does contain much *referenced and quoted* material concerning cerebellar functioning, including an excerpt from Ray Snider's

1958 *Scientific American* article, "The Cerebellum." Part of that passage follows:

> [In addition] to the management of the body's equilibrium and muscular activity, . . . in 1942 Averill Stowell and I . . . established that the cerebellum is equally involved in the co-ordination of the sensations of touch, hearing and sight.

Criticism, Bias, and Slander

Much of the criticism aimed at my work is significantly biased and perhaps even slanderous. Since this response begged for an analysis, I decided to do just that within my book called *A Scientific Watergate—Dyslexia*.

After reading my analysis of, and response to, the criticism I've received, I'm sure readers of my books will better understand why the traditionalists have not medically solved any of the diagnostic/therapeutic riddles characterizing dyslexia, despite extensive research efforts over the past hundred years. Might they have been too busy creating and defending their riddles from any and all "controversial" solutions?

Although I have repeatedly stated that 75 percent of dyslexic patients *improve* on medications (25 percent mildly, 25 percent moderately, 25 percent dramatically, and 25 percent do not), I have been continually attacked by defensive and offensive critics for claiming to cure 100 percent of patients. I challenge anyone to find any statement of mine claiming to cure anyone! Perhaps these critics who repeatedly use the word "cure" fear that this medical treatment will eventually put them out of "business"—financially, scientifically, or egoistically.

Following my appearance on *The Donahue Show* in 1981, together with Olympic star and dyslexic Bruce Jenner, a tremendous interest in dyslexia as well as in my research was triggered. Unfortunately, some of the interest was of a "sour grapes" nature, like the following letter from Gerald Ente, M.D., to the Nassau-ACLD *Newsletter* (December 1982–January 1983) following a *Donahue* rerun.

. . . Some of you have asked me about a doctor from Fresh Meadows, Queens, who claims almost 100% cure for dyslexia. He has gotten some recent TV and newspaper publicity and has recently authored a book on the subject, relating it to inner ear problems. I am not saying that his method doesn't work, but I question that only "he or his associate" can perform this amazing cure, that the fee is $500, that this fee is totally payable before the cure is produced, that there is 5–6 month waiting time, and that he cures "almost 100%" of his cases. This is all too "pat" for me. With a problem so complex, with causation so diversified (see next paragraph), and with such variable manifestations, this sort of advertising gimmickry reminds me of the "Tell you what I'm going to do," garter-sleeved, wax-mustached, early days huxter selling Lydia Pinckum's Vegetable Compound, the elixir of youth, or those guys who had us all believing that we must make our poor readers crawl on their bellies for a few years. How many desperate people will clutch at this straw, spend big bucks, and be disappointed . . .

Dr. Ente's criticism no doubt came after he read—*or completely misread*—the following content sent by my office to those interested in my diagnostic/therapeutic methods:

My Correspondence (1981)

Dear Correspondent:

As a result of the influx of individuals interested and inquiring about Dr. Levinson's methods of diagnosing and treating dyslexic individuals, this form letter was expediently drafted.

The diagnostic procedure takes approximately 2.5 hours and is completed in one visit. It includes all neurological, ocular, "inner-ear" and psychoeducational testing to make an adequate diagnosis. This diagnosis can be made and explained in almost 100% of the cases seen.

In addition, a treatment plan is determined on the basis of the test findings. Thus far, 75% of individuals will have a favorable therapeutic response to various combinations of medications and 25% will not. The favorable responses will vary from mild to dramatic, and is thus far not predictable.

The total fee for this diagnostic-treatment evaluation, including follow-up telephone consultations, is $500. This fee *must* be paid at the time of the examination.

Appendix E

Letters to the Editor

Enclosed are a series of comments I sent to editors on a number of new dyslexia-related research publications. I believe their review will enable the reader to better understand this research, especially from the vantage point of *Smart but Feeling Dumb*.

This review was written to the Editor, *New England Journal of Medicine,* in February 1992. It is a critique of a recent research paper by Shaywitz and colleagues entitled "Evidence That Dyslexia May Represent the Lower Tail of a Normal Distribution of Reading Ability."

Fallacious Assumptions and Convictions in Dyslexia Research?

To the Editor: In a recent study,[1] Shaywitz et al. challenged the "commonly held belief that dyslexia is a discrete diagnostic en-

[1] S. E. Shaywitz et al. "Evidence that Dyslexia May Represent the Lower Tail of a Normal Distribution of Reading Ability," *New England Journal of Medicine,* (January 16), 1992, vol. 326, pp. 145–50.

tity."[2] Upon analysis, a wide range of questions were raised concerning some basic assumptions and convictions characterizing this and prior research.

Might a mistaken analogy with cerebral alexia have led these (and other) authors to unwittingly *equate* and *conceptually confuse* the total syndrome of overdetermined and variable (reading, writing, spelling, math, memory, speech, etc.) symptoms called dyslexia with *only* its reading-score impairment, also termed dyslexia?[3] How else can one explain the study's title or conclusion's wording: "reading ability follows a normal (rather than bimodal) distribution, with dyslexia at the lower end of the spectrum" and "dyslexia occurs along a continuum that blends imperceptibly with normal reading ability."[4]

Could biased conceptions and reading cutoffs as well as highly selective sampling have misled researchers into *denying* the clinical presence of reading-score–"cured" and –overcompensated dyslexics as well as their co-existing reading symptoms (ocular fixation, tracking, perseveration and orientation errors, blurring, diploplia, oscillopsia, photophobia, etc.) and

---

[2]M. Critchley. *The Dyslexic Child.* Springfield, Ill.: Charles C. Thomas, 1970.

H. N. Levinson. *A Solution to the Riddle Dyslexia.* New York: Springer-Verlag, 1980.

H. N. Levinson. *Smart but Feeling Dumb.* New York: Warner Books, 1984.

[3]Frank and H. N. Levinson. "Dysmetric Dyslexia and Dyspraxia: synopsis of a continuing research project," *Acad Ther Publ,* 1975–76, vol. 11, pp. 133–43.

J. Frank and H. N. Levinson. "Compensatory Mechanisms in Cerebellar-Vestibular Dysfunction, Dysmetric Dyslexia and Dyspraxia," *Acad Ther Publ,* 1976, vol. 12, pp. 5–27.

H. N. Levinson. "The Cerebellar-Vestibular Basis of Learning Disabilities in Children, Adolescents and Adults: hypothesis and study," *Perceptual and Motor Skills,* 1988, vol. 67, pp. 983–1006.

J. Frank and H. N. Levinson. "Dysmetric Dyslexia and Dyspraxia: hypothesis and study," *Journal of the American Academy of Child Psychiatry,* 1973, vol. 12, pp. 690–701.

[4]Shaywitz et al.

underlying neurophysiological determinants?[5] Accordingly, might reading scores in dyslexia *not* be limited to "the lower end of the spectrum" measuring reading ability?[6]

Have these authors also misassumed that the presence of normal (or above) reading scores in previously diagnosed ("dyslexic") dyslexics implied the complete absence of the above-mentioned reading and related (writing, spelling, math, etc.) symptoms and "soft" neurological signs—and thus the absence of the syndrome they clinically define?[7] Without further testing, how else could one have (erroneously) concluded that the dyslexic disorder does not exist as a "discrete diagnostic entity"?[8] Have similar oversights led to the artificial fragmentation of reading-score–compensated dyslexic populations into diverse groups of related nosologic entities, depending on the intensity or focus of leading symptoms, e.g. dysgraphia, dyscalculia, dysnomia or dysphasia, dyspraxia, learning disabilities, ADD, etc.?[9]

Should not the traditional static and fallacious reading-score–dependent tunnel view of dyslexia be reconceptualized as dynamic resultants of specifically overdetermined neurophysiological and neuropsychological dysfunctioning vs. compensatory mechanisms?[10] Might not these interacting vectors readily explain the drift and fluctuations of reading (and other

---

[5]H. N. Levinson, "Abnormal Optokinetic and Perceptual Span Parameters in Cerebellar-Vestibular Dysfunction and Learning Disabilities or Dyslexia," *Perceptual and Motor Skills,* 1989, vol. 68, pp. 35–54; and Critchley, 1970; Frank and Levinson, 1976; and Frank and Levinson, 1973.

[6]Shaywitz et al.

[7]Levinson, 1980 and Frank and Levinson, 1976.

[8]Critchley and Frank and Levinson, 1975–76.

[9]Levinson, 1980; and Levinson, 1988.

[10]Shaywitz et al.; and Levinson, 1980; and Frank and Levinson, 1976.

related) scores in dyslexia from abnormal to normal or above, and the reverse? Are these vectors not triggered favorably by maturation, drugs, and other helpful therapies and negatively by regressive mechanisms, overloading or the unmet demand for increased processing speed and capacity with increasing age, grade, and task-complexity?[11]

Might not answers to these and related questions result in a solution to the riddle—dyslexia?[12]

Harold N. Levinson, M.D.

The Inner-Ear or Sensory-Motor Basis of Dyslexia

As a medical clinician and researcher having examined and treated over 20,000 dyslexics during the last 25 years, I found Sandra Blakeslee's September 15, 1991, *New York Times* article titled, "Study Ties Dyslexia to Brain Flaw Affecting Vision and Other Senses," welcome news—despite a few gaps and errors requiring elaboration. In short, the apparent efficacy of colored lenses in improving reading symptoms and Dr. Livingstone's recognition of an abnormality in the rapid visual processing of dyslexics, challenged anew the traditionally held language theory of dyslexia. And comments by Dr. Paula Tallal of Rutgers correctly indicated that dyslexics also manifested similar impairments in rapid auditory, tactile, speech, and coordination processing.

[11]C. R. Wilshire et al., "Piracetam and Dyslexia: effects on reading tests," *Journal of Clinical Psychopharmacology,* 1987, vol. 7, pp. 230–35.
H. N. Levinson, "Dramatic Favorable Responses of Children with Learning Disabilities or Dyslexia and Attention Deficit Disorder to Antimotion Sickness Medications: four case reports," *Perceptual and Motor Skills,* 1991, vol. 73, pp. 723–38.
[12]Levinson, 1980.

Since dyslexia is a syndrome affecting all sensory-motor and coordination systems, including speech, are we to postulate a separate theory for each? Or is there a hidden common denominator and general theory sufficient to explain all? Yes!

As a result of my studies dating back to 1973, this researcher demonstrated that the visually related reading symptoms and photophobia or light sensitivity in dyslexia (and anxiety disorders) were due to a cerebellarvestibular (CV) or "inner ear" disorder that impaired rapid visual fixation, tracking and processing. A similar dysfunction in rapid auditory and tactile processing was recognized and diagnosed by specifically designed Rapid Auditory and Tactile Scanners. Additionally the inner-ear and related circuits were found responsible for processing *all* sensory-motor signals to the brain; and that a dysfunction resulted in signal drifting and scrambling to all vital interrelated brain systems linked by feedback circuits, akin to drifting, blurred and scrambled TV channels. And inner-ear stabilizing antimotion sickness antihistamines and stimulants—similar to those used by the astronauts to prevent space sickness and "space dyslexia"—were capable of compensating for *all* known dyslexic symptoms in 75 percent of treated cases, thus further corroborating their CV origin. All these CV conceptualizations have been independently validated by such world renowned neurophysiologists as Henrietta and Alan Leiner and Robert Dow in a pre-print from Behavioral Brain Research. And Sir John Eccles, Nobel Laureate in cerebellar research, reaffirmed my view before the Rodin Dyslexia Foundation (1986) that dyslexia and its visual disorder were of a primary cerebellar origin.

Since Dr. Livingstone's visual findings and theory of dyslexia are the *latest* rather than the *first* presented on this subject, it appeared strange to read Dr. Drake Duane quoted by Blakeslee as stating: "This is the first observation that the visual system may be involved in dyslexia, and it is extremely important." As *the* leading medical spokesman for the Orton Dyslexia Society and its pure language doctrine, Dr. Duane was as critical of my visual findings and concepts before millions on *The Donahue Show,* as his organization was initially in 1974. Perhaps he *just* saw the visual light and his conversion from the pure Orton-Language theory is *new?*

Harold N. Levinson, M.D.

Appendix F

From Scientific Denial to
Revisionism or "Plagiarism"

Denial of the Cerebellar-Vestibular (CV)
Role in Dyslexia & Related Disorders

As readers of this and my other scientific works well know, for the past one hundred years the traditionalist-trained dyslexia experts denied a CV role in dyslexia, despite all supporting evidence provided by my research and thousands of my patients. This self-serving denial was well documented in my book *A Scientific Watergate—Dyslexia* (1994), as was the referenced and quoted criticism of my CV research. Needless to say, this denial delayed or prevented millions of dyslexics from benefiting from the groundbreaking insights summarized within this updated work.

Denial of Originality—Via Improper Referencing

Based on the CV-Dyslexia and related research initially delineated and later published by my colleague Dr. Jan Frank and me in 1973, a wide range of "new- era" independent validating cerebellar studies has appeared. But then another interesting denial occurred: Concomitant with the acceptance of my CV-Dyslexia concepts, there appeared clear evidence of the "denial of originality" by some of these validators—a phenomenon often referred to as scientific revisionism. Interestingly, I had previously described this "plagiaristic-like" phenomenon, as "Acceptance Without Proper Reference" in *A Scientific Watergate—Dyslexia*. Thus, for example:

Lancetgate

My research content concerning the presence of CV-determined balance/coordination/rhymic symptoms in dyslexia, as well as the use of antimotion sickness medications in dyslexia, and the term "CV-Stabilizers," is quoted in a distinguished medical journal, *The Lancet,* by Rae and coauthors. Yet Rae's colleagues and/or others are mistakenly referenced—clearly but erroneously suggesting that originality was theirs.* Although inadvertent errors frequently occur, the failure to correct this error when pointed out to *The Lancet* and the author is clearly unscientific at best.

---

*Taken from Rae et al's study in *The Lancet* entitled, "Metabolic Abnormalities in Developmental Dyslexia Detected by 1H Magnetic Resonance Spectroscopy," June 20, 1998:

> Dyslexic people are often uncoordinated with poor balance and delayed motor milestones such as crawling, walking, and learning to ride a bicycle (10,22). Anti–motion sickness medications, which may be considered "cerebellar vestibular stabilizers," have been shown to improve reading performance in dyslexia (23).

Sheffieldgate

Two psychologists, Nicolson & Fawcett, from the University of Sheffield, in UK, were first introduced to my cerebellar ideas by a Journal referee, Professor Kohen-Raz, in 1992. Their paper, entitled "Automatism Deficits in Balance for Dyslexic Children" (*Perceptual and Motor Skills,* 1992, 75, 507–529) was accepted upon their acknowledgment of the cerebellar role I discovered responsible for dyslexia (and which explained completely their presented "automatism" theory). At the time, these researchers complied with the journal's request and familiarized themselves with my CV concepts.

Based upon my CV research, Nicolson and others have since published other validating articles on the cerebellum and dyslexia. Although utilizing my content, they tended to reference my original papers and books less and less as time went on. And suddenly a clear-cut explanation was shown me. Nicolson, now editor for the journal of the British Dyslexia Association, called *Dyslexia,* actively discouraged researchers who sought publication in this journal from referencing me. As a result, his editorial decisions advanced what I termed "originality by denial," or "scientific revisionism."

The Big Rationalization

In a personal meeting and conversation with Professor Nicolson, I attempted to clarify and resolve what I considered to be his paradoxical referencing attitudes. So I asked him several questions:

- If my patient-based scientific methodology is wrong and thus not worthy of referencing, how is it that this clinically based investigatory tool was the only one that solved most all of the prior riddles of dyslexia, whereas your methods and those of your colleagues led absolutely nowhere for over a century?
- If my research is not worth referencing, as you've told others, why did you reference my CV publications initially, when it was to your advantage? And why have you used and still use my clinically derived concepts as if they were obtained by your research and those of your colleagues who previously denied a CV role in dyslexia for years and years?

I am still waiting for a reply. His silent response still rings loud and clear!

Summary: The Role of Self-Serving Denial in Research

Why was this appendix added? readers may be wondering. The reason is simple! For science and research to progress more rapidly, it is crucial:

- To present new concepts, regardless of criticism
- To expose the self-serving needs of some "politically minded" researchers often preventing, delaying, and/or claiming originality for ideas not their own. And most often, their pseudoscientific justifications are nothing more than nonsensical *rationalizations*.

Supporting Data—A Letter from Professor Kohen-Raz

For the sake of brevity, I will merely include here a letter written to me by Professor Kohen-Raz concerning the above. Its content says it all:

The Hebrew University of Jerusalem
School of Education

Sept. 1, 1998

Dear Dr. Levinson,

Thank you very much for sending me the recently published paper in the *Lancet* by Rae and collegues documenting the neurophysiological correlates of cerebellar dysfunction in learning disabled populations. It is a great satisfaction to see that the pioneer work you started forty years ago is now supported by hard evidence gathered by virtue of contemporary computerized technology. However, I was perplexed to realize that your research and clinical reports are neither mentioned nor cited in the paper, whilst there is extended reference to the paper of Nicolson et al. published in *Perceptual and Motor Skills*. As you will remember, as a referee to Nicolson's publication, I urged the authors to familiarize themselves with your work, which they did. They subsequently included your results in their paper, citing your research. I very much hope that a due amendment will be published in the *Lancet*.

With best regards
yours

Reuven Kohen-Raz, Ph.D.
Emeritus
Professor and Head, Dep. Spec. Education

Bibliography

Ackermann, H., D. Wildgruber, I. Daum, and W. Grodd. "Does the Cerebellum Contribute to Cognitive Aspects of Speech Production? A Functional Magnetic Resonance Imaging (fMRI) Study in Humans." *Neuroscience Letters* 247[2–3] (May 15, 1998): 187–90.

Adler-Grinberg, D., and L. Stark. "Eye Movements, Scanpaths, and Dyslexia." *American Journal of Optometry and Physiological Optics* 55 (1978): 557–70.

Adrian, E. D. "Afferent Areas in the Cerebellum Connected with the Limbs." *Brain* 66 (1943): 289–315.

Agras, S., D. Sylvester, and D. Oliveau. "The Epidemioloy of Common Fears and Phobias." *Comprehensive Psychiatry* 10 (1969): 151–56.

Allen, G., R. B. Buxton, E. C. Wong, and E. Courchesne. "Attentional Activation of the Cerebellum Independent of Motor Involvement." *Science* 275 (March 1997): 1940–43.

Allington, R. "Dyslexia Has Little to Do with Reading: A Riddler's Solution." *The Review of Education* 7[2] (1981): 153–58.

American Psychiatric Association. *Diagnostic and Statistical Manual of Mental Disorders.* Washington, D.C.: Author, 1987.

Asmundson, G. J., D. K. Larsen, and M. B. Stein. "Panic Disorder and Vestibular Disturbance: An Overview of Empirical Findings and Clinical Implications." *Journal of Psychosomatic Research* 44[1]: (Jan. 1998) 1: 107–20.

Ayres, A. J. *Sensory Integration and Learning Disorders.* Los Angeles, Calif.: Western Psychological Services, 1972.

———. "Learning Disabilities and the Vestibular System." *Journal of Learning Disabilities* 11[1] (1978): 30–41.

Baloh, R. W., V. Honrubia, and A. Sills. "Eye Tracking and Optokinetic Nystagmus." *Annals of Otology, Rhinology and Laryngology* 86 (1977): 108–14.

Baren, M. "Hyperactivity and Attention Disorders in Children." *The Health Information Network* 1012 (1994): 27.

Bastecky, 1., Z. Boleloucky, and O. Skovronsky. "Psychotropic Drugs in Acoustic and Vestibular Disorders." *Activitas Nervosa Superior (Prague)* 23 (1981): 187–88.

Baumann, M. L. "Neuroanatomic Observations of the Brain in Autism." In *The Neurobiology of Autism,* edited by M. L. Baumann and T. L. Kemper. Baltimore, MD: Johns Hopkins University Press, 1994.

Bender, L. *A Visual-Motor Gestalt Test and Its Clinical Use.* New York: American Orthopsychiatric Association Research, 1938. (Monograph no. 3).

Benedikt, M. "Uber Platzchwindel." *Allgemeine Wiener Medizinische Zeitung* 15 (1870): 488.

Berquin, P. C., J. N. Giedd, L. K. Jacobsen, S. D. Hamberger, A. L. Krain, J. L. Rapoport and F. X. Castellanos. "Cerebellum in Attention-Deficit Hyperactivity Disorder: A Morphometric MRI Study." *Neurology* 50[4]: (April 1998) 1087–93.

Black, J. L. et al. "Smooth Pursuit Eye Movements in Normal and Dyslexic Children." *Perceptual and Motor Skills* 59 (1984): 91–100.

Blakeslee, S. "Study Ties Dyslexia to Brain Flaw Affecting Vision and Other Senses." *New York Times,* September 15, 1991, pp. 1, 30.

Blau, H. Personal correspondence, April 12, 1982.

Blythe, P., and D. McGlown. *An Organic Basis for Neuroses and Educational Difficulties.* Chester, UK: Insight, 1979, 93–94.

Boniver, R. "Influence du Piracetam sur le fonctionnement du système vestibulaire." *Acta Oto-Rhino-Laryngologica Belgica* 28 (1974): 293–99.

Brain, R. *Diseases of the Nervous System.* London: Oxford University Press, 1955.

Briggs, G. G., and R. D. Nebes. "Patterns of Hand Preference in a Student Population." *Cortex* 11 (1975): 230–38.

Broad, W., and N. Wade. *Betrayers of the Truth: Fraud and Deceit in the Halls of Science.* New York: Simon & Schuster, 1982.

Brody, J. "Two Doctors Offer Dyslexia Theory: Faulty Link Is Suspected Between Brain and Ear." *New York Times* (April 29, 1974) p. 20.

Brookler, K. "Simultaneous Bilateral Bithermal Caloric Stimulation in Electronystagmography." *Laryngoscope* 4 (1971): 101–09.

Brookler, K., and J. Pulec. "Computer Analysis of Electronystagmography Records." *Transamerican Academy of Ophthalmology and Otolaryngology* 74 (1970): 563–75.

Brown, B. et al. "Predictive Eye Movements Do Not Discriminate Between Dyslexic and Control Children." *Neuropsychologia* 21(1983): 121–28.

Burde, R. M. et al. "Ocular Motor Dysfunction in Total and Hemicerebellectomized Monkeys." *British Journal of Ophthalmology* 59 (1975): 560–65.

Carlton, R. M., G. Ente, L. Blum, N. Heyman, W. Davis, and S. Ambrosino. "Rational Dosages of Nutrients Have a Prolonged Effect on Learning Disabilities." *Alternative Therapeutic Health Medicine.* 6[3]: (May 2000) 95–91.

Carr, D. B., and D. V. Sheehan. "Evidence That Panic Disorder Has a Metabolic Cause." In *Biology of Agoraphobia,* edited by J. C. Ballenger, 100–111. Washington, D.C.: American Psychiatric Press, 1984.

Carter, S., and A. Gold. "The Syndrome of Minimal Cerebral Dysfunction." In *Pediatrics,* edited by M. H. Barnet and A. Einhorn. New York: Appleton-Century-Crofts, 1972.

Cheek, C. W. "Electronystagmography in Children with Specific Learning Disabilities." Unpublished doctoral dissertation, Wichita State University, 1969.

Coffin, J. M. "Cerebellar Deficiency Model of Dyslexia Upheld." *Clinical Psychiatry News* (January 2000).

Committee on Early Childhood, Adoption and Dependent Care,

American Academy of Pediatrics. "Middle-Ear Disease and Language Development." *News and Comment* 35 (1984): 5.

Conners, C. K., and J. S. Werry. "Pharmacotherapy." In *Psychopathological Disorders of Childhood,* edited by H. C. Quay and J. S. Werry, 336–86 NewYork: Wiley, 1979.

Cooper, P. M., and R. T. Pivik. "Abnormal Visual-Vestibular Interaction and Smooth Pursuit Tracking in Psychosis: Implications for Cerebellar Involvement." *Journal of Psychiatry and Neuroscience* 16[1] (March 1991) 30–40.

Critchley, M. *The Dyslexic Child.* Springfield, Ill.: Charles C. Thomas, 1969.

Crowe, R. et al. "Panic Disorder and Mitral Valve Prolapse." In *Anxiety: New Research and Changing Concepts,* edited by D. F. Klein and J. G. Rabkin, 103–16. New York: Raven Press, 1981.

Courchesne, E. et al. "Hypoplasia of Cerebellar Vermal Loboles VI & VII in Autism." *New England Journal of Medicine* 318 (1988): 1349–54.

Courchesne, E., J. Townsend, and O. Saitoh. "The Brain in Infantile Autism: Posterior Fossa Structures Are Abnormal." *Neurology* 44 (1994): 214–23.

Courchesne, E. "New Evidence of Cerebellar and Brainstem Hypoplasia in Autistic Infants, Children, and Adolescents: The MRI Imaging Study by Hashimoto and Colleagues." *Journal of Autism and Developmental Disorders* 25 (1995): 19–22.

Courchesne, E., J. Townsend, N. A. Akshoomoff, O. Saitoh, R. Yeung-Courchesne, A. J. Lincoln, H. E. James, R. H. Haas, L. Schreibman, and L. Lau. "Impairment in Shifting Attention in Autistic and Cerebellar Patients." *Behavioral Neuroscience* 108 (1994): 848–65.

Delacato, C. H. *Treatment and Prevention of Reading Problems: (Neuro-Psychological Approach).* Springfield, IL.: Thomas, 1959.

Denckla, M. B. "Brain Behavior insights through imaging." Paper presented at the Learning Disabilities Association National Conference, Chicago, IL, February 25, 1991.

———. "A neurologist's Overview of Dyslexia." Presented at The New York Academy of Sciences and The Rodin Remediation Academy, The XX Rodin Remediation Conference: Temporal Information Processing in the Nervous System: Special Reference to Dyslexia and Dysphasia. New York: September 12–15, 1992.

De Quiros, J. B. "Vestibular-Proprioceptive Integration: Its Influence on Learning and Speech in Children." Proceedings of the Tenth Interamerican Congress of Psychology, Lima, Peru, 1966. Mexico City: Editorial Trillas, 1967.

De Quiros, J. B., and O. L. Schrager. "Diagnosis of Vestibular Disorders in the Learning Disabled." Journal of Learning Disabilities 9 (1976): 39–58.

———. Neuropsychological Fundamentals in Learning Disabilities. Novato, Calif.: Academic Therapy, 1979.

Dichgans, J. "The Influence of Peripheral Vision on Ambient Ego Orientation." Research Program Bulletin 15 (1977): 376–85.

Dow, R. S., and R. Anderson. "Cerebellar Action Potentials in Response to Stimulation of Proprioceptors and Extroceptors in the Rat." Journal of Neurophysiology 5 (1942): 363–71.

Dow, R. S., and G. Moruzzi. The Physiology and Pathology of the Cerebellum. Minneapolis, Minn.: University of Minnesota Press, 1958.

Duffy, F. H. et al. "Dyslexia: Regional Differences in Brain Electrical Activity by Topographic Mapping." Annals of Neurology 7 (1980): 412–20.

"The Dyslexia Dilemma." Harper's Bazaar (November 1988) pp. 212, 243.

"Dyslexia: Does This Unusual Childhood Syndrome Begin as an Ear Infection?" Infectious Diseases 4 (July 1974): 15.

Eccles, J. C. "The Cerebellum as a Computer: Patterns in Space and Time." Journal of Physiology 229 (1973): 1–32.

———. "Learning in the Motor System." Progress in Brain Research 64(1986): 3–17.

———. Personal correspondence, 1976, 1987. And a letter to the Rodin Remediation Academy, 1989.

Eccles, J. C., M. Ito, and J. Szentagothai. The Cerebellum as a Neuronal Machine. New York: Springer-Verlag, 1967.

Elterman, R. D. et al. "Eye Movement Patterns in Dyslexic Children." Journal of Learning Disabilities 13 (1980): 16–21.

Ente, Gerald, M.D. "Ask the Doctor," Nassau County, New York,

Chapter of the Association for Children with Learning Disabilities *Newsletter* 1:1 (Dec. 1982–Jan. 1983): 4.

Fagan, J., B. Kaplan, and E. S. Edington. "Failure of Antimotion Sickness Medication to Improve Reading in Developmental Dyslexia: Results of a Randomized Trial." *Journal of Developmental and Behavioral Pediatrics* 96 (1988): 359–66.

Fawcett, A. J., and R. I. Nicolson. "Automatisation Deficits in Balance for Dyslexic Children." *Perceptual and Motor Skills* 75 (1992): 507–29.

The FCLD Guide for Parents of Children with Learning Disabilities. Created and published for The Foundation for Children with Learning Disabilities (FCLD), New York, by Educational Systems, Inc., 1984. (ISBN 0-931112-01-X)

Feingold, Helene, and Ben Feingold. *The Feingold Cookbook for Hyperactive Children and Others with Problems Associated with Food Additives and Salicylates.* New York: Random House, 1979.

Fenichel, O. *The Psychoanalytic Theory of Neurosis.* New York: W. W. Norton, 1945.

Ferenczi, S. "Disease or Pathoneurosis." In *Further Contributions to the Theory and Technique of Psychoanalysis,* edited by J. Richman. New York: Basic Books, 1954.

Fernandes, C. M., and J. Samuel. "The Use of Piracetam in Vertigo." *South African Medical Journal* 68 (1985): 806–808.

Flax, N., R. Mozlin, and H. Solar. "Learning Disability, Dyslexia, and Vision." *American Academy of Optometry* 55 (1984): 399–403.

Frank, J., and H. N. Levinson. "Dysmetric Dyslexia and Dyspraxia: Hypothesis and Study." *Journal of the American Academy of Child Psychiatry* 12 (1973): 690–701.

————. "Dysmetric Dyslexia and Dyspraxia: Synopsis of a Continuing Research Project." *Academic Therapy* 11 (1975–76): 133–43.

————. "Compensatory Mechanisms in Cerebellar-Vestibular Dysfunction, Dysmetric Dyslexia and Dyspraxia." *Academic Therapy* 12 (1976): 5–27.

————. "Seasickness Mechanisms and Medications in Dysmetric Dyslexia and Dyspraxia." *Academic Therapy* 12 (1976–77): 133–49.

———. "Anti-Motion Sickness Medications in Dysmetric Dyslexia and Dyspraxia." *Academic Therapy* 12 (1977): 411–25.

Frank, L. M., and E. L. Hartwig (editors). *Perspectives on Dyslexia— Special Issue,* The Orton Dyslexia Society—Research Division, Maryland: The Orton Dyslexia Society, June 1983.

Fox, S. "Audiologists Take On Autism with Auditory Training." *AD-VANCE for Speech-Language Pathologists and Audiologists* (April 6, 1992): 10–11.

Freud, S. "Case History of Schreber, Papers on Technique and Other Works." In *The Standard Edition of the Complete Psychological Works of S. Freud, 1911–1913,* edited by J. Strachey. Vol. 12. London: Hogarth, 1958.

Furman, J. "The Speech Thing." *The New Republic* (August 17–24, 1992): 14–15.

Galaburda, A. M. "Neuropathological Evidence for Elective Afflic-tion of the Magnocellular Visial Subsystem." Presented at The New York Academy of Sciences and The Rodin Remediation Academy, The XX Rodin Remediation Conference: Temporal In-formation Processing in the Nervous System: Special Reference to Dyslexia and Dysphasia, New York: September 12–15, 1992.

Galaburda, Albert, and Thomas Kemper. "Cytoarchitectonic Abnor-malities in Developmental Dyslexia: A Case Study." *Annals of Neurology* 6 (1979): 94–100.

Galaburda, Albert et al. "Developmental Dyslexia: Four Consecutive Patients with Cortical Anomalies." *Annals of Neurology* 18 (1985): 222–23.

Gao, J. H., L. M. Parsons, J. M. Bower, J. Xiong, J. Li, and P. T. Fox. "Cerebellum Implicated in Sensory Acquisition and Discrimina-tion Rather Than Motor Control." *Science* 272[5261] (April 26, 1996): 545–7.

Geiger, G., and J. Y. Lettvin. "Peripheral Vision in Persons with Dyslexia." *New England Journal of Medicine* 316 (1987): 1238–43.

Gelb, Harold. *Clinical Management of Head, Neck, and TMJ Pain and Dysfunction.* Philadelphia: W. B. Saunders, 1977.

Geschwind, N. "Why Orton Was Right." *Annals of Dyslexia* 32 (1982): 13–30.

————. "Dyslexia, Cerebral Dominance, Autoimmunity, and Sex Hormones." In *Dyslexia: Its Neuropsychology and Treatment,* edited by G. Pavlidis and D. Fisher. New York: Wiley, 1986.

Geschwind, N., and P. Behan. "Left-Handedness: Association with Immune Disease, Migraine, and Developmental Learning Disorder." *Proceedings of the National Academy of Sciences of the United States of America* (1982): 5097–5100.

Gilbert, L. C. "Functional Motor Efficiency of the Eyes and Its Relation to Reading." *University of California Publications in Education* 11 (1953): 159–231.

Goddard, S., and P. Blythe. "Dyslexia-Dyspraxia and Other Specific Learning Difficulties."

Goldrick, S. G., and H. Sedgwick. "An Objective Comparison of Oculomotor Functioning in Reading Disabled and Normal Children." *American Journal of Optometry and Physiological Optics* 59 (1982): 82.

Goodenough, F. L. *Draw-a-Man Test: The Measurement of Intelligence by Drawings.* Yonkers-on-Hudson, N.Y.: World Book, 1926.

Griffin, D. C., H. N. Walton, and V. Ives. "Saccades As Relates to Reading Disorders." *Journal of Learning Disabilities* 7 (1974): 310–16.

Guedry, F. E., J. M. Lentz, and R. M. Jell. "Visual-Vestibular Interactions: Influence of Peripheral Vision on Suppression of the Vestibulo-Ocular Reflex and Visual Acuity." *Aviation Space and Environmental Medicine* 50 (1979): 205–11.

Guye, A. "On Agoraphobia in Relation to Ear Disease." *Laryngoscope* 6 (1899): 219–21.

Halliwell, J. W., and H. A. Sloan. "The Effects of a Supplemental Perceptual Training Program on Reading Achievement." *Exceptional Children* 38 (1972): 613–19.

Hartwig, E. L., ed. *Perspectives on Dyslexia—Medical Research Update,* The Orton Dyslexia Society—Research Division, Maryland: The Orton Dyslexia Society, August 1984.

Hashimoto, H., M. Tayama, K. Murakawa, T. Yoshimoto, M. Miyazaki, M. Harada, and Y. Kuroda. "Development of the Brainstem and Cerebellum in Autistic Patients." *Journal of Autism and Developmental Disorders* 25 (1995): 1–18.

Helfgott, E., R. G. Rudel, and R. Kairam. "The Effect of Piracetam on Short- and Long-Term Verbal Retrieval in Dyslexic Boys." *International Journal of Psychophysiology* 4 (1986): 53–61.

Hildreth, G. *Learning the 3 R's.* Minneapolis, Minn.: Minneapolis Educational Publishers, 1936.

Hunt, R. D., R. B. Minderaa, and D. J. Cohen. "Clonidine Benefits Children with Attention Deficit Disorder and Hyperactivity: Report of a Double-Blind Placebo-Crossover Therapeutic Trial." *Journal of the American Academy of Child Psychiatry* 24, 5 (1985): 617–29.

Huston, A. M. *Common Sense About Dyslexia.* Lanham, Md.: Madison Books, 1987.

Ito, M. *The Cerebellum and Neural Control.* New York: Raven Press, 1984.

Ivry, R. "Cortical and Cerebellar Involvement in Processing Temporal Information." Presented to The New York Academy of Sciences and The Rodin Remediation Academy, The XX Rodin Remediation Conference: Temporal Information Processing in the Nervous System: Special Reference to Dyslexia and Dysphasia, New York, N.Y., September 12–15, 1992.

Jacob, R. C. et al. "Otoneurological Examination in Panic Disorder and Agoraphobia with Panic Attacks: A Pilot Study." *American Journal of Psychiatry* 142 (1985): 715–19.

Jongkees, L. B. W., J. P. M. Maas, and A. J. Philipszoon. "Clinical Nystagmography." *Practical Otorhinolaryngology* 24 (1962): 65–93.

Jordan, D. R. *Attention Deficit Disorder: ADHD and ADD Syndromes.* 2nd ed. Austin, TX: Pro-Ed, 1992. p. 5.

Kaga, K., R. R. March, and Y. Tanaka. "Influence of Labyrinthine Hypoactivity on Gross Motor Development of Infants." In *International Meeting of the Barany Society,* edited by B. Cohen, 374, 412–20. *Annals of the New York Academy of Sciences,* 1981.

Kane, J. M. et al. "Panic and Phobic Disorder in Patients with Mitral Valve Prolapse." In *Anxiety: New Research and Changing Concepts,* edited by D. F. Klein and J. G. Rabkin, 327–40. New York: Raven Press, 1981.

Kerr, J. "School Hygiene in Its Mental, Moral, and Physical Aspects." *Journal of the Royal Statistical Society* 60 (1897): 613–80.

Klein, D. F. "Anxiety Reconceptualized." In *Anxiety: New Research and Changing Concepts,* edited by D. F. Klein and J. G. Rabkin, 235–63. New York: Raven Press, 1981.

Koestler, A. *The Ghost in the Machine.* New York: Macmillan, 1968, p. 164.

Kohen-Raz, R. "Developmental Patterns of Static Balance Ability and Their Relation to Cognitive School Readiness." *Pediatrics* 46 (August 1970): 276–84.

———. *Learning Disabilities and Postural Control.* London: Freund, 1986.

Kohl, R. L., D. S. Calkins, and A. J. Mandell. "Arousal and Stability: The Effects of Five New Sympathomimetic Drugs Suggest a New Principle For the Prevention of Space Motion Sickness." *Aviation, Space, and Environmental Medicine* 57 (1986): 137–43.

Kolata, G. "Studies Dispute View of Dyslexia, Finding Girls As Afflicted As Boys." *New York Times,* August 22, 1990, pp. A1, B6.

———. "Study Reports Dyslexia is Not Unalterable, As Experts Have Been Assuming." *New York Times,* January 16. 1992, p. A18.

Korner, A. F., and E. B. Thoman. "Visual Alertness in Neonates As Evoked by Maternal Care." *Journal of Experimental Child Psychology* 10 (1970): 67–78.

———. "The Relative Efficacy of Contact and Vestibular Stimulation on Soothing Neonates." *Child Development* 43 (1972): 443–53.

Lambert, N., and J. Sandoval. "The Prevalence of Learning Disabilities in a Sample of Children Considered Hyperactive." *Journal of Abnormal Child Psychology* 8 (1980): 33–51.

Langner. T. S., and S. T. Michael. *Life, Stress and Mental Health.* New York: Macmillan, 1963.

Lannois, M., and C. Tournier. "Les lésions auriculaires sont une cause déterminante fréquente de l'agoraphobie." *Annales des maladies de l'oreille, du larynx, du nez et du pharynx* 14 (1899): 286–301.

Lauter, J. L., O. Lynch, S. B. Wood, and L. Schoeffler. "Physiological and Behavioral Effects of an Antivertigo Antihistimine in Adults." *Perceptual and Motor Skills* 88 (1999): 707–32.

Leiner, H., and A. Leiner. Personal correspondence, June 3, 1991.

Leiner, H. C., A. Leiner, and R. S. Dow. "Does the Cerebellum Contribute to Mental Skills?" *Behavioral Neuroscience* 100 (1986): 443–54.

————. "The Human Cerebro-Cerebellar System: Its Computing, Cognitive, and Language Skills." *Behavioral Brain Research* 44, 2 (1991): 113–28.

Lentz, J. M., and W. E. Collins. "Motion Sickness Susceptibility and Related Behavioral Characteristics in Men and Women." *Aviation Space and Environmental Medicine* 48 (1977): 316–27.

Lenzi, P., and I. Milanesi. "Etude clinique d'un nouvel antivertigineux: la 2-pyrrolidone acetamide." *Clinica Otorinolaringologa dell' Universita de Milano* 24 (1969): 513–21.

Lerer, R. J., M. P. Lerer, and J. Arner. "The Effects of Methylphenidate on the Handwriting of Children with Minimal Brain Dysfunction." *Journal of Pediatrics* 91(1977): 127–32.

Lesevre, N. "L'Organisation du regard chez les enfants d'age scolaire lecteurs normaux et dyslexiques (étude électroculographique)." *Revue de Neuropsychiatrie Infantile et d'Hygiene Mentaie de L'Enfance* 16 (1968): 323–49.

Levin, A. P. et al. "Lactate Induction of Panic: Hypothesized Mechanisms and Recent Findings." In *Biology of Agoraphobia,* edited by J. C. Ballenger, 82–97. Washington, D.C.: American Psychiatric Association, 1987.

Levinson, H. N. *A Solution to the Riddle Dyslexia.* New York: Springer-Verlag, 1980.

————. "The Cerebellar-Vestibular Basis of Learning Disabilities in Children, Adolescents and Adults: Hypothesis and Study." *Perceptual and Motor Skills* 67 (1988): 983–1006.

————. "Abnormal Optokinetic and Perceptual Span Parameters in Cerebellar-Vestibular Dysfunction and Learning Disabilities or Dyslexia." *Perceptual and Motor Skills* 68 (1989): 35–54.

————. "Abnormal Optokinetic and Perceptual Span Parameters in Cerebellar-Vestibular Dysfunction and Related Anxiety Disorders." *Perceptual and Motor Skills* 68 (1989): 471–84.

————. "A Cerebellar-Vestibular Explanation for Fears/Phobias." *Perceptual and Motor Skills* 68 (1989): 67–84.

————. "The Cerebellar-Vestibular Predisposition to Anxiety Disorders." *Perceptual and Motor Skills* 68 (1989): 323–38.

————. Comment on Richar Allington's review of *A Solution to the Riddle Dyslexia (The Review of Education)* 7[2] 153–58, *The Review of Education*, 7[2] 235–44.

————. "The Diagnostic Value of Cerebellar-Vestibular Tests in Detecting Learning Disabilities, Dyslexia, and Attention Deficit Disorder." *Perceptual and Motor Skills* 71(1990): 67–82.

————. *Total Concentration*. New York: Evans, 1990.

————. "Dramatic Favorable Responses of Children with Learning Disabilities or Dyslexia and Attention Deficit Disorder to Antimotion Sickness Medications: Four Case Reports." *Perceptual and Motor Skills* 73 (1991): 723–38.

————. "The Use and Efficacy of the Antimotion Sickness Medications in the Treatment of Learning Disabilities or Dyslexia." Submitted for publication.

————. *Phobia Free*. with Steven Carter. New York: Evans, 1986.

————. *Smart But Feeling Dumb*. New York: Warner, 1984.

————. *Smart But Feeling Dumb*. New York: Warner, 1994.

————. *The Upside-Down Kids*. with Addie Sanders. New York: Evans, 1991.

————. *Turning Around—The Upside-Down Kids*. with Addie Sanders. New York: Evans, 1992.

————. *A Scientific Watergate-Dyslexia Research*. Great Neck, N.Y.: Stonebridge Publishing, Ltd., 1994.

Linden, M., T. Habib, and V. Radojevic. "A Controlled Study of EEG Biofeedback Effects on Cognitive and Behavioral Measures with Attention Deficit Disorder and Learning Disabled Children." *Biofeedback and Self-Regulation*. In press.

Lindsay, H. "Cerebellar Deficiency Model of Dyslexia Upheld." *Clinical Psychiatry News* (January 2000).

Livingstone, M. S. et al. "Physiological and Anatomical Evidence for a Magnocellular Defect in Developmental Dyslexia." *Proceedings of the National Academy of Sciences of the USA* 88 (1991): 7943–47.

Livingstone, M. "Parallel Processing of Form, Color, Motion, and Depth: Anatomy, Physiology, Art and Illusion." Presented at The New York Academy of Sciences and The Rodin Remediation Academy, The XX Rodin Remediation Conference: Temporal Information Processing in the Nervous System: Special Reference to Dyslexia and Dysphasia, New York: September 12–15, 1992.

Llinas, R. R. "The Cortex of the Cerebellum." *Scientific American* 232 (1975): 56–71.

Llinas, R. "Cerebellar Involvement in Temporal Sensory Motor Processing Relevant to Speech and Writing." Presented to The New York Academy of Sciences and The Rodin Remediation Academy, The XX Rodin Remediation Conference: Temporal Information Processing in the Nervous System: Special Reference to Dyslexia and Dysphasia, New York, N.Y., September 12–15, 1992.

Lorenz, K. "Companionship in Bird Life." In *Instinctive Behavior,* edited by C. H. Schiller 83–111. New York: International Universities Press, 1957.

———. "Comparative Study of Behavior." In *Instinctive Behavior,* edited by C. H. Schiller, 239–49. New York: International Universities Press, 1957.

Lovegrove, W. J., M. Heddle, and W. Slaghus. "Reading Disability: Spatial Frequency Deficits in Visual Information Store." *Neuropsychologia* 18 (1980): 111–15.

Lubar, J. F. "Discourse on the Development of EEG Diagnostics and Biofeedback for Attention-Deficit/hyperactivity Disorders." *Biofeedback and Self-Regulation* 16 (1991): 202–25.

Mann, D. M. A., and T. Iwatsubo. "Diffuse Plaques in the Cerebellum and Corpus Striatum in Down's Syndrome Contain Amyloid 7 Protein (A7) Only in the Form of A742." *Neurodegeneration* 5 (1996): 115–20.

Marks, I., and P. Bebbington. "Space Phobia: Syndrome or Agoraphobic Variant?" *British Medical Journal* 2 (1976): 345–47.

Martin, N., and W. J. Oosterveld. "The Vestibular Effects of Meclizine Hydrochloride-Niacin Combination (Antivert)." *Acta Otolanyng* 70 (1970): 6–9.

Masland, R. L. A review of *Smart but Feeling Dumb,* reprinted from the New York Branch of the Orton Dyslexia Society Newsletter, Vol. VIII, No. 3, February 1985.

Masland, R. L., and C. Upsrich. A review of *A Solution to the Riddle Dyslexia. Bulletin of the Orton Society,* pp. 256–61.

Mazza, D. L. et al. "Prevalence of Anxiety Disorders in Patients with Mitral Valve Prolapse." *American Journal of Psychiatry* 143 (1986): 349–52.

McClure, J. A., P. Lycett, and J. C. Baskerville. "Diazepam as an Antimotion-Sickness Drug." *Journal of Otolaryngology* 11(1982): 253–59.

McMahon, A. Personal correspondence, 1975.

Money, J. "Dyslexia: A Post-Conference View." In *Reading Disability: Progress and Research Needs in Dyslexia,* edited by J. Money. Baltimore: Johns Hopkins University Press, 1962.

Morgan, W. P. "A Case of Congenital Word Blindness." *British Medical Journal* 2 (1896): 1378.

Mosse, H. L., and C. R. Daniels. "Linear Dyslexia: A New Form of Reading Disorder." *American Journal of Psychotherapy* 13 (1959): 826–41.

Murphy, J. M. Review of *A Solution to the Riddle Dyslexia,* "Understanding Dyslexia: a Story of Scientific Detection." *International Schools Journal* 1 (1981): 83–91.

Nicholson, R. I., A. J. Fawcett, E. L. Berry, I. H. Jenkins, P. Dean, and D. J. Brooks. "Association of Abnormal Cerebellar Activation with Motor Learning Difficulties in Dyslexic Adults." *The Lancet* 353[153] (1999): p. 1662.

Nicolson, R. I., and A. J. Fawcett. "Developmental Dyslexia: The Role of the Cerebellum." Submitted to *Dyslexia: International Journal of Research and Practice* April 1999.

Nicolson, R. I., A. J. Fawcett, and P. Dean. "Time Estimation Deficits in Developmental Dyslexia: Evidence of Cerebellar Involvement." *Proc. R. Soc. Lond. B. Biol. Sci.* 259 (1996): 43–47.

North, A. F. "Screening in Child Health Care: Where Are We Now and Where Are We Going?" *Pediatrics* 54 (1974): 631–40.

Oldfield, R. C. "The Assessment and Analysis of Handedness: The Edinburgh Inventory." *Neuropsychologia* 9 (1971): 97–113.

Oosterveld, W. J. "The Efficacy of Piracetam in Vertigo." *Arzneimedizinische- Forschung* 30 (1980): 1947–49.

Orton, S. P. *Reading, Writing and Speech Problems in Children.* New York: W. W. Norton, 1937.

———. "Discussion of a Paper by Dr. J. G. Lynn." *Archives of Neurology and Psychiatry* 47 (1942): 1064.

Othmer, S., S. F. Othmer, and C. S. Marks. "EEG Biofeedback Training for Attention Deficit Disorder, Specific Learning Disabilities, and Associated Conduct Problems." 1991. Available from EEG Spectrum, Inc., 16100 Ventura Blvd., Suite 10, Encino, CA 91436.

Page, N. G. R., and M. A. Gresty. "Motorist's Vestibular Disorientation Syndrome." *Journal of Neurology, Neurosurgery, and Psychiatry* 48 (1985): 729–35.

Paradiso, S., N. C. Andreasen, D. S. O'Leary, S. Arndt, and R. G. Robinson. "Cerebellar Size and Cognition: Correlations with IQ, Verbal Memory and Motor Dexterity." *Neuropsychiatry, Neuropsychology, and Behavioral Neurology* 10[1] (January 1997): 1–8.

Pavlidis, George T. "Do Eye Movements Hold the Key to Dyslexia?" *Neuropsychologia* 19 (1981): 57–64.

———. "Erratic Eye Movements and Dyslexia: Factors Determining Their Relationship." *Perceptual and Motor Skills* 60 (1985): 319–22.

Pellionisz, A., and R. Llinas. "Space-Time Representation in the Brain: The Cerebellum As a Predictive Space-Time Metric Sensor." *Neuroscience* 7 (1982): 2949–70.

Perold, R. P. Personal correspondence, March 26, 1993.

Pierce, J. R. "Optometric Development Vision Therapy and Academic Achievement." *Review of Optometry* 114 (1977): 48–63.

Pitts, F. N., and J. N. McClure. "Lactate Metabolism in Anxiety Neurosis." *New England Journal of Medicine* 277 (1967): 1329–36.

Polatajko, H. J. "A Critical Look at Vestibular Dysfunction in Learning-Disabled Children." *Developmental Medicine & Child Neurology* 27 (1985): 283–92.

Powers, W. H. "Metabolic and Allergic Aspects of Inner-Ear Dysfunction." In *Clinical Ecology*, edited by L. D. Dickey, 637–44. Springfield, Ill.: Charles C. Thomas, 1976.

Prechtl, H. F., and J. C. Stemmer. "The Choreiform Syndrome in Children." *Developmental Medicine and Child Neurology* 4 (1962): 119–27.

Previc, F. H. "A General Theory Concerning the Prenatal Origins of Cerebral Lateralization in Humans." *Psychological Review* 98 (1991): 299–334.

Rae, C., M. A. Lee, R. M. Dixon, A. M. Blamire, C. H. Thompson, P. Styles, J. Talcott, A. J. Richardson, and J. F. Stein. "Metabolic Abnormalities in Developmental Dyslexia Detected by H Magnetic Resonance Spectroscopy." *The Lancet* 351[119] (1998): 1893–1952.

Rapoport, M., R. van Reekum, and H. Mayberg. "The Role of the Cerebellum in Cognition and Behavior: A Selective Review." *Journal of Neuropsychiatry and Clinical Neuroscience* 12[2] (2000): 193–98.

Raymond, J. E. et al. "Fixational Instability and Saccadic Eye Movements." *American Journal of Optometry and Physiological Optics* 65 (1988): 174–81.

Redmond, D. E., Jr. "Alterations in the Function of the Nucleus Locus Coeruleus: A Possible Model for Studies of Anxiety." In *Animal Models in Psychiatry and Neurology*, edited by I. Hanin and E. Usdin, 293–304. New York: Pergamon, 1977.

Redmond, D. E., and Y. H. Huang. "New Evidence For a Locus Coeruleus—Norepinephrine Connection with Anxiety." *Life Sciences* 25 (1979): 2149–62.

Robinson, D. A. "Adaptive Gain Control of Vestibulo-Ocular Reflex by the Cerebellum." *Journal of Neurophysiology* 39 (1976): 954–69.

Rooney, T. G. A letter to from District Principal, New Hyde Park-Garden City Park Union Free School District, April 21, 1975.

Rubin, Nancy. "Wen Smart Kids Cant Lern." *Ladies' Home Journal* 101, 2 (February 1984): 66.

Safer, D. J., and R. P. Allen. *Hyperactive Children: Diagnosis and Management*. Baltimore, Md.: University Park Press, 1976.

Sarnoff, C. A. "Normal and Pathological Psychological Development

During the Latency Age Period." In *Child Development in Normality and Psychopathology,* edited by J. R. Bemporad, 146–73. New York: Brunner/Mazel, 1980.

Schmahmann, J. D., and J. C. Sherman. "The Cerebellar Cognitive Affective Syndrome." *Brain* 121 (1998): 561–79.

Sekitani, T., B. F. McCabe, and J. H. Ryu. "Drug Effects on the Medial Vestibular Nucleus." *Archives of Otolaryngology* 93 (1971): 581–89.

Sharp, V. "Adolescence." In *Child Development in Normality and Psychopathology,* edited by J. R. Bemporad, 174–218. New York: Brunner/Mazel, 1980.

Shaywitz, S. E. et al. "Prevalence of Reading Ability in Boys and Girls: Results of the Connecticut Longitudinal Study." *Journal of the American Medical Association* 264 (1990): 998–1002.

Shaywitz, S. E. et al. "Evidence that Dyslexia May Represent the Lower Tail of a Normal Distribution of Reading Ability." *The New England Journal of Medicine* 326, 3 (January 16, 1992): 145–50.

Shaywitz, S. E., B. A. Shaywitz, K. R. Pugh, R. K. Fulbright, R. T. Constable, W. E. Menci, D. P. Shankweiler, A. M. Liberman, P. Skudlarski, J. M. Fletcher, L. Katz, K. E. Marchione, C. Lacadie, C. Gatenby, and J. C. Gore. "Functional Disruption in the Organization of the Brain for Reading in Dyslexia." *Neurobiology* 95 (1998): 2636–41.

Sheehan, C. *The Anxiety Disease.* New York: Scribner, 1983.

Silva, P. et al. "Some Developmental and Behavioral Problems Associated with Bilateral Otitis Media with Effusion." *Journal of Learning Disabilities* 15 (1982): 417–21.

Silver, L. B. *The Misunderstood Child: A Guide for Parents of Learning Disabled Children.* 2nd ed. New York: Tab Books, 1991.

Silver, L. B. "The 'Magic Cure': A Review of the Current Controversial Approaches for Treating Learning Disabilities." *Journal of Learning Disabilities,* Vol. 20, No. 8 (October 1987): 498–505.

Simpson, E. *Reversals.* Boston: Houghton-Mifflin, 1979.

Sleator, E. K., and W. E. Pelham. *Dialogues in Pediatric Management: Attention Deficit Disorder.* East Norwalk: Appleton-Century-Crofts/Prentice-Hall, 1986.

Snider, R. S., and A. Stowel. "Evidence of a Projection of the Optic System to the Cerebellum." *Anat. Rec.* 82 (1942): 448–49.

———. "Evidence of a Representation of Tactile Sensibility in the Cerebellum of the Cat." *Federation Proc.* 1 (1942b): p. 82.

Snider, R. "Cerebro-Cerebellar Relationships in the Monkey." *Journal of Neurophysiology* 15 (1952): 27–40.

———. "The Cerebellum." *Scientific American* 174 (1958): 84–90.

Snider, R. S. "Receiving Areas of the Tactile, Auditory and Visual Systems in the Cerebellum." *Journal of Neurophysiology* 7 (1944): 331–57.

———. "Recent Contributions to the Anatomy and Physiology of the Cerebellum." *Archives of Neurology and Psychiatry* 64 (1950): 196–219.

Snider, R. S. "A Fifth Cranial Nerve Projection to the Cerebellum." *Federation Proc.* 2 (1943): p. 46.

Spitz, R. A. "Hospitalism: An Inquiry Into the Genesis of Psychiatric Conditions in Early Childhood." In *The Psychoanalytic Study of the Child.* Vol. 1, 53–74. New York: International Universities Press, 1945.

Stanley, G., G. A. Smith, and E. A. Howell. "Eye Movements and Sequential Tracking in Dyslexic and Control Children." *British Journal of Psychology* 74 (1983): 181–87.

Stehli, Annabel. *The Sound of a Miracle.* New York: Avon, 1992.

Stein, J. F., and M. Glickstein. "Role of the Cerebellum in Visual Guidance of Movement." *Physiological Reviews* 4 (October 1992).

Stevens, L. J., S. S. Zentall, M. L. Abate, B. A. Watkins, S. R. Lipp, and J. R. Burgess. "Essential Fatty Acid Metabolism in Boys with Attention-Deficit Hyperactivity Disorder." *American Journal of Clinical Nutrition* 62 (1995): 761–68.

Stevens, L. J., S. S. Zentall, M. L. Abate, T. Kuczek, and J. R. Burgess. "Omega-3 Fatty Acids in Boys with Behavior, Learning, and Health Problems." *Physiology and Behavior* 39[4/3] (1996): 915–20.

Stockwell, C. W., E. S. Sherard, and J. V. Schuler. "Electronystagmographic Findings in Dyslexic Children." *American Academy of Ophthalmology and Otolaryngology (Transactions)* 82 (1976): 239–43.

Stroud, M. H., and E. Rauchbach. "Caloric and Optokinetic Nystagmus in Cerebellar Patients." *Annals of Otology, Rhinology and Laryngology* 85 (1976): 136–38.

Tallal, P. "Neural Basis of Temporal Perceptual Motor Processing: Implications for Speech and Reading." Presented at The New York Academy of Sciences and The Rodin Remediation Academy, The XX Rodin Remediation Conference: Temporal Information Processing in the Nervous System: Special Reference to Dyslexia and Dysphasia, New York: September 12–15, 1992.

Townsend, J., E. Courchesne, and B. Egaas. "Slowed Orienting of Covert Visual-Spatial Attention in Autism: Specific Deficits Associated with Cerebellar and Parietal Abnormality." *Development and Psychopathology* 8 (1996): 563–84.

U.S. Congress. *Public Law 94-142. Education For All Handicapped Children Act.* U.S. Congress, November 29, 1975.

U.S. Office of Education. *Education of Handicapped Children: Implementation of Part B of the Education of Handicapped Act.* Federal Register 1, Part 2., U.S. Washington, D.C.: Department of Health, Education and Welfare, August 23, 1977.

Vail, P. Review of *A Solution to the Riddle Dyslexia.* In *Independent School.* February 19, 1982.

Vurpillot, E. *The Visual World of the Child.* London: Allen & Unwin, 1976.

Weissman, N. J. et al. "Contrasting Patterns of Autonomic Dysfunction in Patients With Mitral Valve Prolapse and Panic Attacks." *American Journal of Medicine* 82 (1987): 880–88.

Wender, P. H. *Minimum Brain Dysfunction in Children.* New York: Wiley, 1971.

———. *The Hyperactive Child, Adolescent, and Adult: Attention Deficit Disorder Through the Lifespan.* New York: Oxford University Press, 1987.

———. "Minimal Brain Dysfunction: An Overview." In *Psychopharmacology: A Generation of Progress,* edited by M. A. Lipton, A. DiMascio, and D. F. Kilan. New York: Raven, 1978.

Wilsher, C. R., D. Bennett, C. Chase, K. Connors, M. DiIanni, L. Feagans, L. J. Hanvik, E. Helfgott, H. Koplewica, P. Overby, M. J. Reader, R. G. Rudel, and P. Tallal. "Piracetam and Dyslexia:

Effects on Reading Tests." *Journal of Clinical Psychopharmachology* 7 (1987): 230–35.

Wilson, V. J., M. Maeda, and J. I. Franck. "Inhibitory Interaction Between Labyrinthine, Visual and Neck Inputs to the Cat Flocculus." *Brain Research* 96 (1975): 357–60.

Wiser, A. K., N. C. Andreasen, D. S. O'Leary, G. L. Watkins, L. L. Boles Ponto, and R. D. Hichwa. "Dysfunctional Cortico-Cerebellar Circuits Cause 'Cognitive Dysmetria' in Schizophrenia." *Neuroreport,* 9(8) (June 1, 1998): 1895–9.

Wiss, T. "Vestibular Dysfunction in Learning Disabilities: Differences in Definitions Lead to Different Conclusions." *Journal of Learning Disabilities* 22 [2] (February 1989): 100–101.

Witty, P. A., and D. Koepel. "Sinistral and Mixed Manual Ocular Behavior in Reading Disability." *Journal of Educational Psychology* 27 (1936): 119–34.

Wolff, P. "Impaired Motor Timing Control in Developmental Dyslexia." Presented to The New York Academy of Sciences and The Rodin Remediation Academy, The XX Rodin Remediation Conference: Temporal Information Processing in the Nervous System: Special Reference to Dyslexia and Dysphasia, New York, N.Y., September 12 15, 1992.

Wood, C. D., B. Cramer, and A. Graybiel. "Anti-Motion Sickness Drug Efficacy." *Otolaryngology, Head and Neck Surgery* 89 (1988): 1041–44.

Wood, C. D., and A. Graybiel. "A Theory of Motion Sickness Based on Pharmacological Reactions." *Clinical Pharmacology and Therapeutics* 11(1970): 621–24.

Zangwill, O. L., and C. Blakemore. "Dyslexia: Reversal of Eye Movements During Reading." *Neuropsychologia* 10 (1972): 371–73.

Zinkus, P., M. I. Gottlieb, and M. Shapiro. "Developmental and Psychoeducational Sequelae of Chronic Otitis Media." *American Journal of the Disabled Child* 132 (1978): 1100–04.

Index